W9-BKZ-608

CZECH REPUBLIC

Regensburg

Straubing

Upper Bavaria (East)
Pages 198–209

Lower Bavaria
Pages 178–197

LOWER BAVARIA

Landshut

Passau

UPPER BAVARIA (EAST)

Rosenheim

Salzburg

The University District
Pages 102–113

Around the Isar
Pages 90–101

The Museums District
Pages 114–131

Old Town (South)
Pages 58–73

Munich

THE UNIVERSITY DISTRICT

THE MUSEUMS DISTRICT

OLD TOWN (NORTH)

AROUND THE ISAR

OLD TOWN (SOUTH)

Munich
& The Bavarian Alps

DK EYEWITNESS TRAVEL

Munich
& The Bavarian Alps

Main Contributors
Izabella Galicka, Katarzyna Michalska

Penguin
Random
House

Produced By Wydawnictwo Wiedza i Życie
S.A., Warsaw

Contributors Izabella Galicka, Katarzyna Michalska

Consultant Sergiusz Michalski

Illustrators Lena Maminajszwili, Bohdan Wróblewski, Piotr Zubrzycki

Photographers Dorota And Mariusz Jarymowiczowie

Cartographers Magdalena Polak, Dariusz Romanowski, Kartographie Huber (Munich)

Jacket Design & Graphics Paweł Kamiński

Graphic Designer Paweł Pasternak

Editors Robert G. Pasieczny, Dorota Szatańska

Technical Editor Anna Kożurno-Królikowska

Designers Ewa Roguska, Piotr Kiedrowski

Dorling Kindersley Limited

Editor Lucilla Watson

Translator Mark Cole (Linguists for Business)

Dtp Designers Jason Little, Conrad Van Dyk

Production Sarah Dodd

Printed and Bound in China
First American Edition 2002

18 19 20 21 10 9 8 7 6 5 4 3 2 1

Published in the United States by
DK Publishing, 345 Hudson Street,
New York, New York 10014

**Reprinted with revisions 2006, 2008,
2010, 2012, 2014, 2016, 2018**
Copyright © 2002, 2018 Dorling
Kindersley Limited, London
A Penguin Random House Company

A catalog record of this book is available
from the Library of Congress.

ISSN 1542-1554

ISBN 978-1-4654-6823-9

Floors are referred to throughout in
accordance with European usage; i.e. the
"first floor" is the floor above ground level.

MIX
Paper from
responsible sources
FSC
www.fsc.org   FSC® C018179

Introducing Munich and the Bavarian Alps

Munich Area by Area

The snow-clad Alps forming a backdrop to a lakeside wildflower meadow

**The information in this
DK Eyewitness Travel Guide is checked regularly.**
Every effort has been made to ensure that this book is as up-to-date as possible
at the time of going to press. Some details, however, such as telephone numbers,
opening hours, prices, gallery hanging arrangements and travel information are
liable to change. The publishers cannot accept responsibility for any consequences
arising from the use of this book, nor for any material on third party websites, and
cannot guarantee that any website address in this book will be a suitable source of
travel information. We value the views and suggestions of our readers very highly.
Please write to: Publisher, DK Eyewitness Travel Guides, Dorling Kindersley,
80 Strand, London, WC2R 0RL, UK, or email: travelguides@dk.com.

◀ **Title page** The Antiquarium, the great hall of Munich's Residenz **Front cover image** Neuschwanstein Castle in Autumn, Bavaria
Back cover image The rooftops and spires of Munich Old Town

Contents

Horse head roundel at Munich's Marstall building, formerly a stables

The distinctive twin-towered Frauenkirche, one of Munich's most prominent landmarks

Burg Trausnitz castle in Landshut, Lower Bavaria

HOW TO USE THIS GUIDE

This guide will help you to get the most out of your stay in Munich and the Bavarian Alps. The first section, *Introducing Munich and the Bavarian Alps*, locates the city and the region geographically and gives an outline of its history and culture. The subsequent sections, *Munich Area by Area* and *The Bavarian Alps Area by Area*, describe the main sights and attractions. Feature spreads, with maps, illustrations and drawings, focus on important sights. Information about accommodation and restaurants is given in *Travellers' Needs*, while the *Survival Guide* provides useful tips on everything you need to know, from money to getting around.

Munich

In this guide, Munich has been divided into five central areas and a Further Afield section. Each of the five areas opens with an introduction to the part of Munich it covers, describing its history and character. This is followed by a Street-by-Street illustration of the heart of the area. The most important sights and attractions are covered in detail on two or more full pages and are also shown on the area map. Finding your way around each chapter is made simple by the numbering system used throughout.

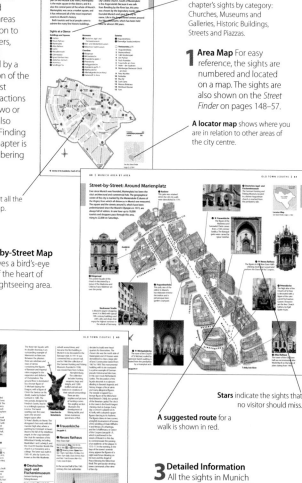

Sights at a Glance lists the chapter's sights by category: Churches, Museums and Galleries, Historic Buildings, Streets and Piazzas.

1 Area Map For easy reference, the sights are numbered and located on a map. The sights are also shown on the *Street Finder* on pages 148–57.

A locator map shows where you are in relation to other areas of the city centre.

Numbered circles pinpoint all the listed sights on the area map.

2 Street-by-Street Map This gives a bird's-eye view of the heart of each sightseeing area.

Stars indicate the sights that no visitor should miss.

A suggested route for a walk is shown in red.

3 Detailed Information All the sights in Munich are described individually. Addresses and practical information are provided. The key to the symbols used in the information block is shown on the back flap.

1 Introduction

The landscape, history and character of each region is described here, showing how the area has developed over the centuries and what it offers to the visitor today.

The Bavarian Alps

Each map in this section concentrates on a specific theme: *Museums and Galleries, Churches, Squares, Parks and Gardens, Remarkable Bavarians.* The top sights are shown on the map; other sights are described on the following two pages.

Colour coding makes each area in the guidebook easy to find.

2 Regional Map This
shows the main road network and gives an overview of the whole region. All entries are numbered and there are also useful tips on getting around the region by car and train.

3 Detailed Information on each Sight

All the important towns and other places to visit are described individually. They are listed in order, following the numbering on the regional map. Each entry contains detailed information on opening times and how to get there.

Story boxes explore specific subjects further.

For all the top sights, a Visitors' Checklist box provides the practical information you need to plan your visit.

4 Major Sights At least one
page is dedicated to each major sight. Historic palaces and parks are shown in detail. Dissected views of buildings and floorplans of museums and galleries and buildings are colour-coded to show you the best ways to enjoy the exhibits.

INTRODUCING MUNICH & THE BAVARIAN ALPS

DISCOVERING MUNICH AND THE BAVARIAN ALPS

The following tours have been designed to take in as many of Munich's highlights as possible and to discover the natural beauty and cultural heritage of its surrounding region. First comes a 2-day tour of the city, followed by a 7-day tour for those who want to spend more time exploring Munich's attractions. The latter comprises seven single day trips that can be taken individually or combined. The same is true for the 7-day tour covering Munich and Bavaria. Finally, two themed itineraries have been designed for anyone looking to tailor their trip according to a specific interest. For each of these itineraries, extra suggestions are provided for those who want to extend their stay. Pick, combine and follow your favourite tours, or simply dip in and out and be inspired.

A Tour of Bavarian Baroque

- Marvel at the grand Baroque buildings of **Asamkirche**, **Theatinerkirche** and the **Schleißheim Palace** in Munich.

- Follow a "Baroque trail" to Lower Bavaria via **Scheyern**, **Metten**, **Osterhofen**, **Aldersbach** and **Passau**.

- Admire *Lüftlmalerei* paintings, Baroque splendour and traditional Bavarian architecture in **Bad Tölz**, **Benediktbeuern**, **Kochel am See** and **Mittenwald**.

- Travel via picturesque **Murnau**, **Ettal** and **Oberammergau** to the UNESCO World Heritage Site, **Wieskirche**.

Key

— A Tour of Bavarian Baroque

— A Tour of Bavarian Mountains, Castles and Monasteries

— A Week in Bavaria

Eichstätt
Nördlingen
Harburg
Ingolstadt
Donauwörth
Neuburg an der Donau
Danube
Lech
Paar
Augsburg
Friedberg
Wertach
Landsberg am Lech
Andechs
Feldafin
Memmingen
Ottobeuren
Wessobrunn
Starnberger See
Schongau
Hohenpeißenber
Kempten
Steingaden
Wieskirche
Murnau
Wasserburg
Ober-ammergau
Lindau
Füssen
Ettal
Lake Constance
Bad Hindelang
Schwangau
Linderhof
Garmisch-Partenkirchen
Eibsee
Oberstdorf
Zugspitze
Mittenwald

Wieskirche, Upper Bavaria (South)
Constructed in 1754 at the spot where a farmer's wife had seen tears flow from the eyes of an abandoned statue of Christ, this church is regarded as a masterpiece of 18th-century southern German architecture.

◄ Viktualienmarkt (The Victuals or Food Market) in Munich, by Domenico Quaglio

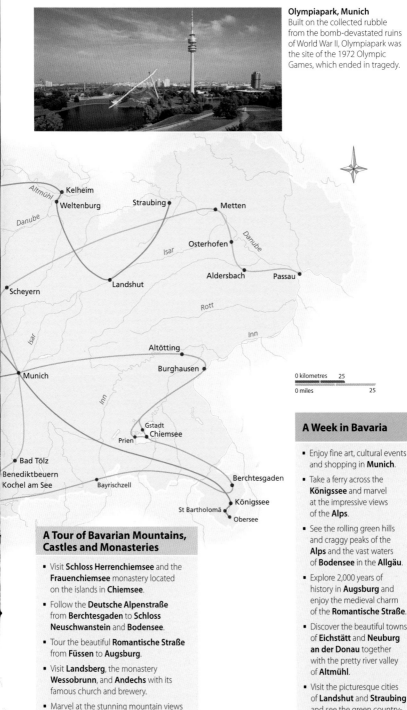

Olympiapark, Munich
Built on the collected rubble from the bomb-devastated ruins of World War II, Olympiapark was the site of the 1972 Olympic Games, which ended in tragedy.

Kelheim

Altmühl

Weltenburg

Straubing

Metten

Danube

Osterhofen

Isar

Danube

Aldersbach

Passau

Scheyern

Landshut

Rott

Isar

Inn

Altötting

Munich

Burghausen

Inn

0 kilometres 25

0 miles 25

Gstadt
Chiemsee

Prien

Bad Tölz

Benediktbeuern

Kochel am See

Bayrischzell

Berchtesgaden

Königssee

St Bartholomä

Obersee

A Week in Bavaria

- Enjoy fine art, cultural events and shopping in **Munich**.

- Take a ferry across the **Königssee** and marvel at the impressive views of the **Alps**.

- See the rolling green hills and craggy peaks of the **Alps** and the vast waters of **Bodensee** in the **Allgäu**.

- Explore 2,000 years of history in **Augsburg** and enjoy the medieval charm of the **Romantische Straße**.

- Discover the beautiful towns of **Eichstätt** and **Neuburg an der Donau** together with the pretty river valley of **Altmühl**.

- Visit the picturesque cities of **Landshut** and **Straubing** and see the green countryside of Lower Bavaria.

A Tour of Bavarian Mountains, Castles and Monasteries

- Visit **Schloss Herrenchiemsee** and the **Frauenchiemsee** monastery located on the islands in **Chiemsee**.

- Follow the **Deutsche Alpenstraße** from **Berchtesgaden** to **Schloss Neuschwanstein** and **Bodensee**.

- Tour the beautiful **Romantische Straße** from **Füssen** to **Augsburg**.

- Visit **Landsberg**, the monastery **Wessobrunn**, and **Andechs** with its famous church and brewery.

- Marvel at the stunning mountain views around **Starnberger See**.

Two Days in Munich

Spend two days in Munich to get a first impression of Bavaria's vibrant capital. Explore the sights in the historical city centre and the buzzing University District.

- **Arriving** Munich Airport is located about 28 km (17 miles) northeast of the city. S-Bahn trains S1 and S8 and the Airport–Bus take 45 minutes to the city's main railway station.

- **Transport** Munich has an excellent public transport system; visitors can take advantage of buses, trams, the U-Bahn and S-Bahn.

Day 1

Morning Start the day at Munich's landmark, **Frauenkirche** *(pp64–5)*. Admire the views from the twin pepperpot towers and see the mysterious black footprint beneath them, which is believed to have been left by the Devil. At **Marienplatz** *(p66)* watch the figures dance to the clock chimes of the **Neues Rathaus** (New Town Hall) *(p63)*. Next, climb the tower of **Peterskirche** *(p66)* for a stunning view. Explore the quaint market **Viktualienmarkt** *(p68)* before heading to the **Jüdisches Zentrum** (Jewish Centre) at Jakobsplatz *(p69)*. Don't miss the interesting **Münchner Stadtmuseum** *(p69)*, a complex of six buildings, which houses the town museum.

Afternoon After lunch, stroll through the medieval lanes around the city's former private residences, **Münzhof** *(p87)* and **Alter Hof** *(p87)*. Stop for a drink in the famous tavern **Hofbräuhaus** *(p88)* before browsing the shops in luxurious **Maximilianstraße** *(p88)* and Theatinerstraße. Marvel at the Baroque splendour of **Theatinerkirche** *(p83)* and be awed by the dazzling interiors of the two churches on Neuhauser Straße; **Bürgersaal** *(p62)* and **Michaelskirche** *(p62)*. End the day by spending the evening around **Gärtnerplatz** *(p68)*.

Day 2

Morning Head to the bustling Prinzregentenstraße to visit the **Bayerisches Nationalmuseum** *(pp112–13)*, which houses an eclectic collection of artworks. Continue on to the **Haus der Kunst** *(p111)*, which showcases exhibitions of contemporary artists. Afterwards, enjoy a stroll in the **Englischer Garten** *(p110)*.

Evening Devote the evening to shopping in the trendy stores and stopping to admire the Art Nouveau architecture in the lively district of **Schwabing** *(p109)*. Follow the elegant **Ludwigstraße** *(p106)*, pass the university, **Ludwig-Maximilians-Universität** *(p107)* and St Ludwig's church, **Ludwigskirche** *(p107)* to **Odeonsplatz** *(p109)*, where the **Feldherrnhalle** *(p82)* marks the beginning of the historical city centre.

> **To extend your trip…**
>
> Make a day trip to **Dießen** *(p216)* to see the artwork in the early Rococo Marienmünster and enjoy the beautiful scenery around Ammersee.

A Week in Munich

Take time out to see the memorable sights of Bavaria's capital, including interesting museums, iconic churches and historical buildings.

- **Arriving** Arrive and depart from Munich Airport.

- **Transport** A good public transport system helps to easily get around the city. Buses, trams, the U-Bahn and S-Bahn are quick and reliable.

Days 1 and 2

See the city itinerary above.

Day 3

Explore beautiful courtyards, rich museums and the Renaissance Antiquarium in the **Residenz** *(pp78–81)*. Next, relax in the formal greenery of the **Hofgarten** *(p89)*. After a stroll along the Isar river,

Golden sculpture of St Mary with the Church of Our Lady in the background, Marienplatz

visit the fascinating **Deutsches Museum** *(pp98–101)*.

Days 4

Spend the day immersed in fine arts in the **Museums District** *(pp114–31)*, where visitors will be spoilt for choice. Choose between seeing ancient art in the **Staatliche Antikensammlungen** *(p118)* or the **Glyptothek** *(p119)*, admiring exquisite 14th- to 18th-century paintings in the **Alte Pinakothek** *(pp122–5)*, 19th century masters in the **Neue Pinakothek** *(pp126–9)* and modern art and design in the **Pinakothek der Moderne** *(pp120–21)*, or head to the striking **Museum Brandhorst** *(p130)*.

Day 5

Get ready to see great architecture and the wonders of modern technology in this part of Munich. Explore the superbly landscaped **Olympiapark** *(pp138–9)* and look out for the elegant sweeping roofs of the Olympic sports facilities. Take the lift up to the Olympiaturm and enjoy the lovely views of the city and the Alps. Head to the other side of the street to the **BMW Museum** *(pp138–9)*, which is a real treasure chamber full of vintage and futuristic vehicles.

Days 6

Be impressed by the beauty and ducal splendour of the stately **Schloss Nymphenburg** *(pp136–7)*. Look out for the portraits of the city's beautiful women in the Schönheitsgalerie. See the incredibly ornate carriages of the Bavarian kings in the palace's Marstallmuseum and the enchanting pavilions in the spacious park. Next, take a stroll through the adjacent **Botanischer Garten** (p138). Don't miss the impressive greenhouses.

Day 7

Start the day close to the Isar river at the monumental **Annakirche** (p94) in the pretty district of Lehel. Cross the river to the impressive Bavarian parliament building, **Maximilianeum** (p95) on the right bank. At Max-Weber-Platz board the tram for a long, but worth-while trip to **Bavaria-Filmstadt** (p142), one of Europe's major film studios, located outside the city. Take time out to visit the well-to-do suburb of **Grünwald** (p142). Continue via tram to medieval **Burg Grünwald** (p142), which has an interesting Roman collection.

To extend your trip...
Spend a day in **Freising** (p169) and another exploring **Wasserburg am Inn** (p208) and **Dachau** (p175).

A Week in Bavaria

- **Duration** 7 days – extends to a 10-day tour with the extra suggestions.

- **Airports** Arrive and depart from Munich Airport.

- **Transport** Towns and cities around Munich can be reached by trains and buses. To explore the countryside, a rental car is recommended.

Days 1 and 2: Munich
See the city itinerary on p12.

Day 3: Königssee
Head southeast from Munich in the direction of the snow-capped Alps. Arrive at crystal-clear **Königssee** (p204), which has a lovely fjord-like setting between sheer mountain ridges. Take the electric-powered tour boat to St Bartholomä and listen to the famous echo along the way. Next, admire the impressive escarpment of the legendary Watzmann massif and take a pleasant walk to enchanting Obersee. Return to Munich to spend the night.

Cruising the Danube near Kelheim, Lower Bavaria

To extend your trip...
The stunning scenery and thrilling landscapes are unmissable in this part of Bavaria. Take time out to go hiking in the mountains here.

Day 4: The Allgäu
Take a day trip to the **Allgäu** (pp226–41) and admire the gently rolling green hills, the vast Bodensee (Lake Constance) and the lovely village of **Wasserburg** (p237). Explore the historical city centre of **Lindau** (pp238–9), located on an island in the lake. Marvel at the beauty of the peaks of the Alps en route to the health resorts of **Oberstdorf** (p236) and **Bad Hindelang** (p236). Nearby, the Breitach river gorge and Sturmannshöhle cave are major attractions. Spend the evening back in the city of Munich.

To extend your trip...
Spend a day hiking, sunbathing or sailing at **Lake Constance** (p237).

Day 5: Augsburg and the Romantische Straße
Founded by the Emperor Augustus, **Augsburg** (pp252–7) has an impressive Mannerist town hall and fine art work in the Gothic Dom St Maria. From the former Roman city, follow the **Romantische Straße** (p250) north. Along the route, look out for pretty gabled houses in **Donauwörth** (p250), the fantastically preserved castle in **Harburg** (p249) and the romantic historic town centre of **Nördlingen** (pp246–7) in its unusual setting in the Ries basin, the impact crater of an enormous meteorite.

Day 6: Neuburg to Weltenburg
Take a detour and go via **Ingolstadt** (pp170–71) to visit **Neuburg an der Donau** (pp172–3). This former ducal residence offers a strikingly beautiful historic town centre. From here, continue on to **Eichstätt** (pp166–7), one of most delightful towns in Bavaria, located in the **Altmühl Valley** (p187). Follow the river to Kelheim and go along the Danube to **Weltenburg** (p186). Stop to explore its age-old monastery located on the river bank.

To extend your trip...
Spend the day kayaking on the rivers and go on a "fossil hunt" (p168) in the quarries of the Altmühl river valley.

Day 7: Lower Bavaria
Make an early start for a day trip to **Landshut** (pp182–4), one of the most impressive destinations in Lower Bavaria. Don't miss the Gothic **Martinskirche** (p184) and the ancient castle, **Burg Trausnitz** (p185). In **Straubing**, (pp188–9) explore the charming town centre and admire the famous Roman treasure in the **Gäubodenmuseum** (p188).

Königssee and the pilgrimage church of St Bartholomä

A Tour of Bavarian Baroque

- **Duration** 7 days – extends to a 10-day tour with the extra suggestions.
- **Airports** Arrive and depart from Munich Airport.
- **Transport** The public transport system is best for exploring Munich and its surrounding areas. For countryside destinations a rental car is recommended.

Starting from Munich, this tour highlights outstanding Baroque architecture in the city and its immediate hinterland as well as in different regions of Bavaria. For more on Bavaria's traditional architecture, see pp26–27.

Day 1 and 2: Munich
Devote two days to discovering superb Baroque buildings in the city. Munich's quintessential Baroque church is the **Asamkirche** (pp70–71) close to the medieval **Sendlinger Tor** (p72). The adjacent **Asam Haus** (p72) was the home of Egid Quirin Asam. A short walk through the historical lanes in the city centre leads to the **Damenstift St Anna** (p73). In the northern part of the Old Town, don't miss the **Preysing-Palais** (p82), the **Theatinerkirche** (p83) and the **Cuvilliés-Theater** (p81) of the **Residenz** (pp78–81). Spend the next day visiting **Schleißheim Palace** (pp176–7) known for its gallery of Baroque painting. Be sure to check out its unique Baroque park.

Day 3 and 4: Baroque Trail from Munich to Lower Bavaria
Follow a "Baroque trail" from Munich to Lower Bavaria. Visit the Benedictine monastery in **Scheyern** (p169) before seeing the opulently decorated Michaelskirche and library of the local Benedictine abbey in **Metten** (p186). Next, check out Osterhofen's stupendous **Asambasilika** (p197) and the church of Mariä Himmelfahrt in **Aldersbach** (p196). Spend an entire day in the Baroque city

of **Passau** (pp192–5) and listen to the daily concert in the impressive **Dom St Stephan** (p192), which boasts one of the biggest organs in the world. Return to Munich for the night.

> **To extend your trip…**
> Explore the hilly region of the **Bavarian Forest** (p197) and the primeval forest in **Nationalpark Bayerischer Wald** (p191).

Day 5: Bad Tölz, Kochel am See and Mittenwald
Discover *trompe l'oeil* paintings, called *Lüftlmalerei* (p216), Baroque splendour and traditional Bavarian architecture, south of Munich, in **Bad Tölz** (p224). A must visit is the former Benedictine monastery and its late Baroque church in **Benediktbeuern** (p223). In **Kochel am See** (p223), see the Michaelskirche and explore the traditional Alpine buildings in **Freilichtmuseum Glentleiten** (p223). Finally, head to **Mittenwald** (p222) and admire its fantastic mountain views and explore an interesting museum of violin-making here.

> **To extend your trip…**
> See the pretty architecture of the monastery at **Tegernsee** (p224) and visit its popular brewery. Relax and enjoy the wonderful mountain views from the lake.

Late Gothic town hall featuring the coat of arms in Kempten

Day 6: Murnau to Oberammergau
South of Munich is home to pretty **Murnau** (p219), which offers wonderful mountain views, Enrico Zucalli's Nikolauskirche and the small Baroque Mariahilf-Kirche. Admire the modern art of the famous **Blaue Reiter group** (p219) in the Art Nouveau Münter-Haus. Another Baroque masterpiece is the Benedictine abbey found in picturesque **Ettal** (p220). Nearby, is **Oberammergau** (p220) with its lavishly painted houses. Continue on to the UNESCO World Heritage Site, **Wieskirche** (pp218–19), a Rococo jewel and an impressive highlight of this tour.

Day 7: Kempten, Memmingen and Ottobeuren
Discover Baroque splendour and Rococo opulence in romantic **Kempten's** (pp240–41) Residenz and St-Lorenz-Basilika. **Memmingen** (pp230–31) boasts beautiful Gothic half-timbered houses, but also a great town hall with Rococo stuccowork and the Kreuzherrenkirche with Baroque interior decoration. Baroque grandeur is also the signature feature of **Ottobeuren** (p233) – the "Swabian Escorial" is one of the biggest monastic complexes in Europe.

> **To extend your trip…**
> Enjoy wellness in accordance with the principles of Sebastian Kneipp in nearby **Bad Wörishofen** (p233).

Opulent interiors of the famous Cuvilliés-Theater, Munich

A Tour of Bavarian Mountains, Castles and Monasteries

- **Duration** 7 days – extends to a 10–day tour with the extra suggestions.
- **Airports** Arrive and depart from Munich Airport.
- **Transport** A rental car is highly recommended.

This tour takes in famous castles and beautiful Alpine landscapes. For more on Bavaria's castles see pp50–51.

Day 1: Burghausen and Altötting

Head east to **Burghausen** *(p202)* at the Austrian border and explore Europe's longest castle – which will take up some time. In nearby, **Altötting** *(p202)* the Heilige Kapelle, which houses the famous Black Madonna is one of Germany's oldest Marian shrines and is worth a visit.

> **To extend your trip…**
> Follow the Inn river valley to **Wasserburg** *(p208)*, **Rott** and **Neubeuern** *(p209)* and go on a scenic drive from **Aschau** *(p206)* via **Geigelstein** to **Reit im Winkel** *(p205)*.

Day 2: Chiemsee

Head for the vast **Chiemsee** *(p207)* southeast of Munich. Start early in the morning to catch a boat either from Gstadt or Prien's waterfront area, Stock to Herreninsel, the largest island on the lake. **Schloss Herrenchiemsee** *(p206)*, built by Ludwig II, is located here. The palace was never finished, but is nonetheless incredibly luxurious considering it's still incomplete. From Herreninsel, take another boat to Fraueninsel, where the Benedictine monastery Frauenchiemsee is a sight to see.

Day 3 and 4: Upper Bavaria and the Allgäu

Discover some of the most beautiful parts of the Bavarian Alps on the **Deutsche**

Alpenstraße *(pp224–5)*. Begin in **Berchtesgaden** *(p204)*, and be sure to visit the Salzbergwerk (salt works). Take time out to spend a day in quaint **Bayrischzell** *(p225)* and go hiking in the Wendelstein mountains. In **Garmisch-Partenkirchen** *(p221)* take the train to **Eibsee** *(p221)* and then the cable car up Germany's highest peak, Zugspitze. Watch out for breathtaking views of the Alps. In **Linderhof** *(p220)*, see another of Ludwig's fairytale castles. Next, continue on to Schwangau to see **Schloss Hohenschwangau** *(p234)*, which is open for visitors. Don't forget to visit **Schloss Neuschwanstein** *(p234)*, Bavaria's most famous castle.

> **To extend your trip…**
> Take a wonderful drive and enjoy panoramic views of the Alps and the Allgäu en route to **Lindau** *(pp238–9)*, located on Bodensee.

Day 5: The Allgäu to Northern Swabia

Enjoy the beautiful scenery along the southern part of the Romantische Straße. Start in **Füssen** *(p234)* at the foothills of the Alps. Its medieval castle houses a wonderful art gallery. From the village of Schwangau, it is not far to **Steingaden** *(p218)* and **Wieskirche** *(p218)*. **Schongau** *(p218)* has its medieval city centre and its castle from the 15th century intact, when

the town was the second ducal residence. Close to **Augsburg** *(pp252–7)*, **Friedberg** *(pp250–59)* is still protected by centuries old defensive walls.

> **To extend your trip…**
> Follow the Romantische Straße north up to Würzburg in Franconia.

Day 6: Landsberg am Lech, Hoher Peißenberg and Andechs Monastery

Visit the historic city of **Landsberg am Lech** *(pp214–15)*. Explore its lovely alleys and squares, see its striking architecture and walk through the famous Bayertor and along the medieval town walls. Close by is the imposing monastery at **Wessobrunn** *(p216)*. Soak up the great views of mountains and lakes on Hoher Peißenberg east of **Hohenpeißenberg** *(p218)*. Afterwards, make a pilgrimage to the **Andechs Monastery** *(p216)* known for its famous church and brewery.

Day 7: Starnberger See

Spend a relaxing day at **Starnberger See** *(p217)*, enjoying the stunning mountain views. Next, follow the trail of Bavaria's famous King Ludwig II. Ludwig was a frequent visitor to Possenhofen's palace, where Austria's empress, Elisabeth, spent her childhood. A historic small ferry takes visitors from Feldafing to pretty Roseninsel with its romantic park and villa.

King Ludwig II's magical Schloss Neuschwanstein in the Allgäu

Putting Munich and the Bavarian Alps on the Map

Southern Bavaria, the southernmost part of Germany, consists of three administrative regions: Upper Bavaria (Oberbayern), Swabia (Schwaben) and Lower Bavaria (Niederbayern). The region borders the Czech Republic, Austria and, across Lake Constance, Switzerland. To the north it is bounded by the Danube, and the south by the Alps. Munich, on the River Isar, is the capital, with almost 1.5 million inhabitants.

Key

— Motorway
— Major road
— Secondary road
— Railway
— National border
— Ferry route

0 kilometres   100

0 miles   100

For keys to symbols *see back flap*

Central Munich

Central Munich boasts a variety of architectural styles, and each of the five areas has its own unique atmosphere. Marienplatz, and the Old Town around it, abounds in old-world architecture, and is the main tourist area. Along the River Isar, green areas are flanked by grand 19th-century urban thoroughfares. The great thoroughfare of Ludwigstraße/Leopoldstraße sets the tone for the northern quarter, which includes the picturesque Schwabing and Englischer Garten districts. The suburb of Maxvorstadt to the northwest has a wealth of museums and art galleries.

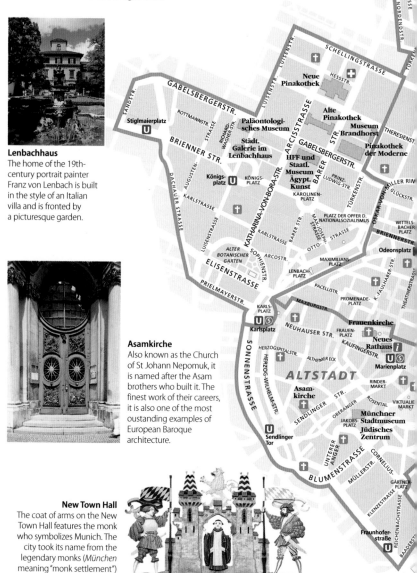

Lenbachhaus
The home of the 19th-century portrait painter Franz von Lenbach is built in the style of an Italian villa and is fronted by a picturesque garden.

Asamkirche
Also known as the Church of St Johann Nepomuk, it is named after the Asam brothers who built it. The finest work of their careers, it is also one of the most oustanding examples of European Baroque architecture.

New Town Hall
The coat of arms on the New Town Hall features the monk who symbolizes Munich. The city took its name from the legendary monks (*München* meaning "monk settlement") who settled there.

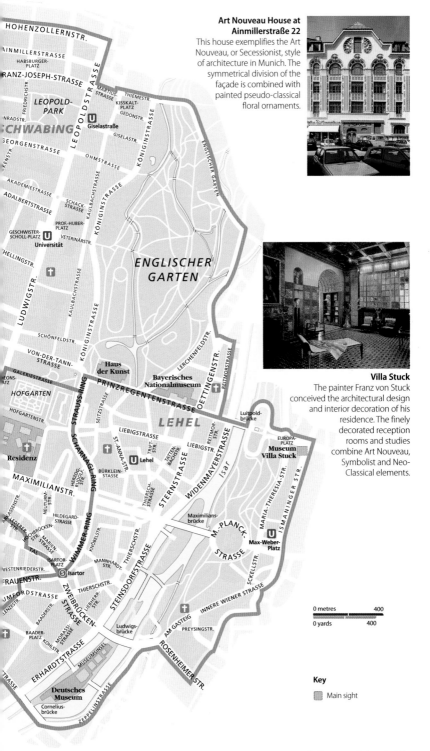

Art Nouveau House at Ainmillerstraße 22

This house exemplifies the Art Nouveau, or Secessionist, style of architecture in Munich. The symmetrical division of the façade is combined with painted pseudo-classical floral ornaments.

Villa Stuck

The painter Franz von Stuck conceived the architectural design and interior decoration of his residence. The finely decorated reception rooms and studies combine Art Nouveau, Symbolist and Neo-Classical elements.

0 metres 400
0 yards 400

Key

Main sight

For keys to symbols *see back flap*

A PORTRAIT OF THE BAVARIAN ALPS

Three out of every four Germans say they would like to live in Bavaria, especially southern Bavaria, and it's not hard to see why. It is one of the most picturesque and also one of the most prosperous parts of Europe. For many foreigners, Bavaria is quintessentially German; this is not, however, strictly true, as Bavaria has always nurtured its own distinct political framework and culture.

Southern Bavaria is inhabited by three main groups of people: a branch of the Swabian tribes of Württemberg, in the western region, who are the descendants of the legendary Baiuvarii; the Upper Bavarians, in the central region, and the Lower Bavarians, centred in the eastern region.

To this day, there are still distinct regional differences in the Bavarians' dialect, folklore and cuisine and, arguably, in their mentality as well. The shared characteristics that they have are a love of tradition, a certain conservatism and a strong sense of loyalty to the Free State of Bavaria (Freistaat Bayern). Bavarian culture and customs were developed as much in court circles as by the peasantry. This development on two social levels has left its mark on the character of the people and their traditions. The latter include an affinity with the soil, and a tendency to a certain stubbornness and defiance coupled with warm hospitality and friendliness. These qualities are combined with tolerance and at times a fondness for absolute rulers and politicians ranging from men such as Maximilian I, Maximilian I Josef and Franz Josef Strauß to eccentrics and dreamers such as Ludwig II.

Summer in the old quarter of Lindau

◀ Marching band on the streets of Augsburg in northern Swabia

Peaceful sub-Alpine landscape

The Landscape of the Bavarian Alps

When they look up at the sky, Bavarians see the colours of their national flag – white and sky-blue. On clear days the sky takes on a Mediterranean translucence; this may be because Bavaria is the bridge between northern Europe and the Mediterranean region. Munich is in fact much closer to Venice than it is to Berlin.

Bavaria's mild climate and varied scenery combine to create an idyllic landscape. Lush green meadows populated with grey and brown Alpine cattle alternate with thick woodland, countless brooks and streams, rocky outcrops, lakes and rolling hills, against which rise majestic Alpine peaks. When the famous

Bay window of a house in Garmisch-Partenkirchen

Föhn (warm Alpine wind) blows, the Alps can be clearly seen from as far as 100 km (60 miles) away. The local architecture complements the scenery perfectly. Picture-postcard towns and villages, large monasteries, castles and palaces, and village churches with their onion domes fit together in perfect harmony. A typical feature of the region is the way in which high art is combined with kitsch. Exquisite Baroque churches and monasteries with ephemeral frescoes stand side by side with simple peasant art, while the splendid Neo-Classical architecture of the Wittelsbachs contrasts with the enchanting fairy-tale castles of Ludwig II.

Nativity scene painted on the façade of a house in Hindelang

Religion, Tradition and Culture

Bavaria is a land of defiant, ritualised Catholicism, which once effectively blocked the march of Protestant Germany to Rome. It is no surprise then to find that Bavaria has its own conservative ruling party, the CSU, and that in place of the ubiquitous "Guten Tag", the people here greet each other with "Grüß Gott" ("Greetings to

God"). The Bavarian national anthem, which (before the advent of 24-hour broadcasting) was once played every day when the local television station closed for the night, begins with the words: "God be with you, land of Bavaria."

Catholic ritual is omnipresent – during the celebration of Sunday Mass, at church fairs, and during processions and pilgrimages. However, piety expresses an affirmation of life rather than prudishness. Many stereotypes are attached to the Bavarians: among the best known are green hats with feathers in them, short *Lederhosen* and knee-socks, beer-mugs joyfully held on high.

Folk traditions have survived too: perhaps nowhere else in the world is there such a proliferation of folk festivals and music groups. Almost everywhere you can see the characteristic but regionally differentiated men's *Trachten*, which includes a short jacket with bone buttons, and the women's *Dirndl*, with their wide, low-cut dresses and a narrow waist-coat. Simplified versions of these costumes are also worn as everyday clothing, even by Bavarian politicians. More refined and lavish versions are worn when attending official functions or going to the opera.

Futuristic style museum (foreground) and administrative building of the BMW works in Munich

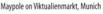

Maypole on Viktualienmarkt, Munich

Beer-drinking is another integral part of South Bavarian folk tradition. Some 620 breweries work to quench beer-lovers' thirst. Bavaria has some of the oldest breweries in the world (including the Weihenstephan brewery), and it was the first place where a ducal decree (1516) banned the use of any other ingredients than barley, hops and water in beer-making. The best way to drink beer is from a large, litre mug, known as a Maß, or "measure", preferably in a beer garden beneath a chestnut tree, in the cellars of a monastic brewery, or in a marquee to the strains of folk music, as during the famed Oktoberfest.

The Sources of Bavaria's Wealth

For centuries, farming and trade have been the main sources of Bavaria's wealth. It is the biggest supplier of farm produce in Germany. It also has the largest hop harvest in the world. After World War II Bavaria's economy expanded enormously, with some of Germany's largest companies based here, such as Audi, BMW and Siemens. Bavaria also has chemicals, aircraft, printing, electronics and tourism industries.

The Maß – the best way to drink beer

Landscape of the Bavarian Alps

Southern Bavaria is one of Germany's most picturesque and scenically varied regions. To the south it is bordered by the Alps, with their breathtaking limestone peaks and verdant slopes. To the north it is bounded by the Danube, with its marshy flood plains. The region's landscape consists of undulating hills and many mountain streams and lakes, which were formed by glaciers during the Ice Age. Much of the terrain takes the form of pasture and fields, or is covered in forests, while industrialization has remained unobtrusive.

Alpine meadows are covered in lush grass which produces high-quality hay and provides rich grazing for cattle.

Mountain peaks with breathtaking escarpments are a common sight.

A hop plantation in Hallertau, which is the largest hop-producing region in Bavaria. Wooden poles overgrown with hops are a characteristic sight.

Mountain streams have over millennia cut their way through the Alpine rocks, creating scenic gorges. The picturesque Wimbachklamm is accessible to hikers.

Local buildings harmonize with the surrounding landscape.

Southern Bavarian Lakes

Huge glaciers that melted centuries ago left many lakes in southern Bavaria. Their limpid waters attract water-sports enthusiasts and swimmers. This breathtakingly beautiful environment is ideal for walking and many other outdoor activities.

This marina on Chiemsee, also known as the Bavarian Sea, is one of the finest spots in southern Bavaria for amateur yachting.

The Zugspitze, rising to a height of 2,962 m (9,718 ft), is the highest German peak.

Forests are thick and extensive, covering a major portion of the mountainous terrain.

Plants and Animals of the Bavarian Alps

Southern Bavaria's varied natural scenery has remained largely unspoiled thanks to careful protection and clean air. Animals and plants occur in several bands of vegetation. While in the higher parts of the Alps only mosses and lichens grow, at altitudes of under 1,500 m (4,900 ft) there is an abundance of flora and fauna. The forests contain a wealth of plants, animals and birds, while the extensive meadows and marshes are covered in various grasses, and the clear waters of the rivers and lakes are home to many species of fish. The parks and nature reserves help to preserve endangered species.

The grey-brown Alpine cow is especially common in the Allgäu, a region known for its dairy products.

Chamois can negotiate rough terrain and steep slopes and are a common sight on mountain hikes.

Marmots peep out from mountain screes and crevasses, emitting their characteristic whistling call.

Ravens appear in large flocks over ploughed fields, searching for worms and leftover grains of corn.

Butterflies share the flowery Alpine meadows with bees, gadflies and grass-hoppers. The most colourful of the butterflies is the peacock butterfly.

Trout is the most common species of fish to be found in Bavaria's mountain streams. They thrive in the clear, unpolluted waters.

Edelweiß is an increasingly rare sight in the Alps. This protected Alpine flower is a favourite decorative motif in the Bavarian national costume.

The gentian is the "national" flower of Bavaria. It is honoured in song and is used in making the famous gentian schnapps.

Architecture of the Bavarian Alps

The architectural landscape of southern Bavaria features a large number of churches and monasteries. These noble buildings, in perfect harmony with the surrounding landscape, are topped by onion-domed towers. Although each architectural era created a legacy of fine buildings, it was during the Baroque period (the late 16th to the early 18th century) that the region flourished architecturally. New churches were built, and existing ones endowed with stunning ornamentation. In southern Bavaria architectural splendours were built in the 19th century, including the fairy-tale residences of Ludwig II.

Altenstadt basilica is one of the many Romanesque buildings in Bavaria.

Gothic

The Gothic style of architecture is widely represented in Bavaria, although its impact in Europe went far beyond this region. As well as in surviving town houses, the Gothic style in Bavaria is seen in fortified residences and religious buildings. A specific regional characteristic is the wide nave of Gothic churches. The oldest Gothic church was built in Laufen. The largest is the Frauenkirche in Munich, and the most resplendent is the St Martin and Kastulus in Landshut. The use of pointed arches and ribbed vaulting made it possible to create much higher, light-filled spaces. Gothic architecture reached its apogee in the mid-15th century.

The Chapel of St Sigismund in Blutenburg Castle is a typical example of late Gothic religious architecture.

Entrance to the St Ulrich and St Afra church, Augsburg

Renaissance and Mannerism

The Renaissance reached Bavaria from Italy via Augsburg, where in 1510 the Renaissance chapel of the Fugger family was built. This set the style for town houses (as at Neuburg and Augsburg). At the end of the century, Renaissance style was overtaken by Mannerism, which departed from Classical forms. One of the key Mannerist architects was Elias Holl.

The window is set under a broken pediment.

Carvings contrast with the austere façade.

The façade of the Arsenal at Augsburg, designed by Josef Heintz the Elder in 1607, is a fine example of Mannerism, distinguished by a flat façade and the rejection of Classical proportions.

The Archangel Michael overcoming Satan, a bronze sculpture by Hans Reichle, displays dramatic poses typical of Mannerism.

Baroque

No architectural style left such a strong impression on southern Bavaria as did the Baroque. Its highly decorated, almost theatrical style held a special appeal, and it was expressed in skilfully articulated spaces to which abundant ornamentation was added. The first Baroque buildings were by Italian architects, but a local school was soon producing work of the highest quality. The Bavarian Baroque reached its greatest heights with the Asam brothers *(see pp70 & 72–3)*.

The vaulting of Passau Cathedral is a fine example of late Baroque forms derived directly from Italy. Despite the excessive stuccowork and elaborate fresco decorations, the main architectural elements are still discernible.

The façade of the church of Berg am Laim illustrates the typical Baroque rhythm of architectural elements, accentuated by cornices, pilasters and columns.

The windows of the Neues Schloss in Schleißheim are framed and decorated with rosettes and mock-antique masks. Doorways and windows with exuberant ornamentation were highly characteristic of Baroque architecture.

Neo-Classicism

The Neo-Classical style developed in France in the 18th century. After 1806, when Bavaria proclaimed itself a kingdom, it was adapted to serve the purposes of the Napoleonic Empire style. Neo-Classicism reached the peak of its splendour after 1816, but was confined to Munich. Ludwig I intended to rebuild the city to turn it into "Athens on Isar". To this end the court architect Leo von Klenze designed many fine buildings, with references to ancient Greece and the Italian Renaissance.

The Prinz-Carl-Palais, by the architect Karl von Fischer, is a typical example of early Neo-Classical architecture. It is fronted by an imposing portico with Ionic columns supporting a tympanum.

This capital of a column in the portico of the Glyptothek is decorated with typically Ionic scrolled volutes.

An akroterion is a decorative element often used in Classical architecture.

The tympanum of the Propyläen contains sculptures of Otto I among kings of the Greeks. Otto I abdicated before the building was completed. The people mocked: "Do not glorify the day before the sun is down – the proof is the Propyläen."

Sculptures in a style evoking the glory of ancient Greece were carved by Ludwig Schwanthaler.

Monasteries and Abbeys

A surprising feature of the Bavarian Alps is the large number of monasteries and abbeys that can be found here. The first Benedictine monastery was founded in the early Middle Ages. In the 11th and 12th centuries monastic establishments were built in the foothills of the Alps. The next period in which building activity flourished was the Baroque, when medieval abbeys were rebuilt and new ones, such as Ottobeuren and Ettal, were constructed. In the 18th century, with the spirit of the Enlightenment, fine libraries with valuable collections of books were built. The secularization of more than 160 monasteries in 1803 led to the destruction of a large part of Bavarian monastic culture.

Altarpieces often take the form of large statues of saints or of one of the Church Fathers. They are a prominent feature of church interiors.

Heilig-Kreuz-Kapelle
The Chapel of the Holy Cross is one of the few monastic chapels open only to monks. Such chapels were used for gatherings and for silent prayer away from the outside world. Their decoration is no less lavish than that of the rest of the monastery.

The church interior is graced by numerous altars, and the architectural features, mouldings, paintings and furniture combine to form a unified whole.

The Library reflects the scientific and cultural aspirations of Bavarian churches. The walls are lined with decorated shelves that harmonize with the leather-bound volumes they hold.

The Kaisersaal, or imperial hall, was one of the abbey's countless reception rooms. It underlines the abbey's close association with the concept of a Christian Empire.

The ceremonial hall was designed for official gatherings.

Ottobeuren Abbey

Ottobeuren, which has been described as the "Swabian Escorial", is one of the largest monastic establishments in Europe. The church is attached to a vast complex with rows of rooms built around three courtyards, as well as numerous ancillary buildings.

Ottobeuren Abbey blends with the sub-Alpine landscape in a way that is characteristic of many Bavarian monasteries, with their red roofs and their tall belfries. In spring and summer, the entire building stands in striking contrast to the lush greenery with which it is surrounded.

The staircase, a feature of conscious pomp and elegance, shows the importance that abbeys attached to the appearance of public reception areas.

Art of the Bavarian Alps

Art in the region developed against the background of the major trends in European art. The ecclesiastical and ducal protectorate, and later that of free cities, led to the development of important artistic centres in Munich, Augsburg, Landshut and Passau. Schools of painting, sculpture and craftsmanship developed as early as the Gothic period, and the Renaissance and Mannerism also left their mark. But it was in the Baroque period that the arts of fresco, stucco and sculpture reached their peak. Folk elements meanwhile were always a feature of Bavarian art, taking the form of votive images, roadside shrines and murals on village houses.

This man with a shield is a late Gothic figure from Ottobeuren Abbey.

Romanesque and Gothic Art

Romanesque art is characterized by a stylization rooted in Byzantine art. As well as the crafts and sculpture, southern Bavaria has interesting examples of mural painting. The windows of Augsburg Cathedral are among the finest in Europe. The Gothic period, which continued until about 1520, brought in a new style, primarily in the way that human figures were depicted, with flowing garments and expressive gestures. By about 1,500 Gothic painting and sculpture had their greatest exponents in Jan Polack and Erasmus Grasser.

Masks are placed at the intersections between panels.

Bas-reliefs are of allegorical and Old Testament subjects.

Door handles take the shape of lions' masks.

The Moriskentänzer is one of ten expressive carvings by Erasmus Grasser of Moriskentanz, a court dance. According to custom, the men would dance in sophisticated poses, and capture the ladies' attention with elegant gestures. These sculptures are a rare example of secular subject matter in Gothic art.

The bronze doors of Augsburg Cathedral show the influence of Byzantine art. They initially consisted of four wings, with a total of 224 reliefs. Only 35 remain today.

1400	1450	1500	1550
	1450–1518 Erasmus Grasser	**c.1540–99** Friedrich Sustris	**c.1570–1634** Hans Krumpper
	c.1460/65–1524 Hans Holbein the Elder	**c.1500–62** Christoph Amberger	
		1516–73 Hans Mielich	**c.1570–1642** Hans Reichle
One of Erasmus Grasser's Moriscos	**c.1435–1519** Jan Polack	**1473–1531** Hans Burgkmair	
		c.1548–1628 Peter Candid de Witte	
		c.1550–1620 Hubert Gerhard	

Renaissance and Mannerism

The southern Bavarian Renaissance was influenced by Italy and the Netherlands, but it developed its own elements. The crafts flourished, and in sculpture and painting new themes, such as genre scenes, classical mythology and portraiture, appeared. The most prominent artists of the time were the Augsburg painters Hans Holbein the Elder, Hans Burgkmair and Christoph Amberger. Mannerism developed in the mid-16th century, its most outstanding exponents in southern Bavaria being Hans Krumpper and Hans Reichle.

This ornamental cup dating from 1570–80 was made in one of Augsburg's famous goldsmiths' workshops. The work of Augsburg goldsmiths graced many churches and grand houses in Europe.

This portrait of Felicitas Welser by Christoph Amberger is typical of Renaissance portraiture in that it shows a certain rigidity of pose combined with a care to capture the sitter's individuality and accurately depict the costume. The coloration reveals a Venetian influence.

Baroque

During the Baroque period the walls of churches, monasteries and palaces were lavishly covered with stucco mouldings and trompe l'oeil paintings. An important centre for such art was Wessobrunn. From the 18th century the prominent Asam brothers began working in Bavaria *(see p70)*. *Lüftlmalerei*, paintings on the walls of houses *(see p216)*, is a typically Bavarian phenomenon. Fine Rococo sculpture was produced by Ignaz Günther and Johann Baptist Straub, while the court artist François Cuvilliés refined the art of Rococo decor to perfection.

This traditional wardrobe is from the renowned furniture-making centre in Bad Tölz. The distinctive furniture made here was covered in folk paintings. Sideboards, beds and the carts associated with the St Leonard's Day festival can be seen in the town's local history museum.

This amber sculpture from the Bürgersaal in Munich by Ignaz Günther embodies all the elements of the late Baroque: pathos, levity and dynamism.

1692–1750 Egid Quirin Asam

1601–34 Georg Petel

1680–1758 Johann Baptist Zimmermann

Guardian angel by Ignaz Günther

1600	1650	1700

1609–84 Johann Heinrich Schönfeld

Portrait of Cosmas Damian Asam

1686–1739 Cosmas Damian Asam

1695–1768 François Cuvilliés

1697–1776 George Desmarées

1704–84 Johann Baptist Straub

1725–75 Ignaz Günther

Traditions of the Bavarian Alps

Bavaria is a land where old local traditions and folklore are cultivated and revered. Almost every town and village has its own local holiday, with folk bands, beer-drinking and general merriment in the streets. These events variously involve folk dancing and firework displays. The Catholic tradition is strong in the region and the countless religious feast days and church processions often coincide with fairs. Many places also commemorate local historical events.

Passion Plays

Once every ten years (next in 2020), the mountain village of Oberammergau becomes the centre of the Easter mystery plays *(Passionsspiele)* that are performed over four months from late May to early October. This tradition dates back to 1633.

At that time, so as to ward off the plague, the villagers vowed to act out scenes from the Passion of Christ. Initially these were staged outside the church, but since 1930 they have been held in a special open-air theatre with seating for 4,800. The performances, lasting from morning until late afternoon with a break in between, take place five days a week. According to tradition, the actors must be residents of Oberammergau by birth. The lavish decorations and the costumes, of which there are over 1,000, are provided by the local populace. The scenes, accompanied by a choir and music, are performed by amateur actors in a natural and expressive way. Set against the backdrop of mountains, they have the realism of *tableaux vivants*.

The Passion plays are world renowned, and tickets must be booked years in advance. A similar tradition exists in certain other Bavarian villages.

The Maypole

On 30 April each year, small groups of people can be seen beside fires, drinking beer and watching over a long, barkless tree trunk. Recovering a tree trunk stolen by the inhabitants of the neighbouring village is rewarded by a large number of barrels (or today, cases) of the Bavarians' favourite drink. Next day the trunk is decorated and ceremonially raised in the village square.

According to tradition, the maypole, the pride of every local community, ensures a successful year. The custom of raising the maypole ("the tree of life") goes back to medieval times. Usually painted in the Bavarian colours of white and blue, maypoles are decorated with the emblems of local crafts and crowned with a large wreath. Traditions include dancing round the maypole and climbing up it to reach the prizes tied to the wreath.

Residents of a small town joining forces to raise the maypole

Landshut Wedding

In 1475, Landshut saw the wedding of Georg, son of Ludwig the Rich, and Princess Jadwiga of Poland, daughter of Casimir Jagiellon. The celebrations lasted eight days, and went down in history as one of the most sumptuous in medieval Bavaria.

Since 1903 the Landshut Wedding (Landshuter Fürstenhochzeit) has been re-enacted every four years (next in 2021) on three weekends in June and July. About 100,000 visitors come to enjoy this historic drama. Medieval costumes are worn during the young couple's triumphal procession, which is accompanied by court dances and by tests of the skills of knights and squires.

Christ stumbling under the Cross during the Oberammergau Passion play

The Oktoberfest

This famous folk festival, the world's largest, began in 1810, when Princess Therese von Sachsen-Hildburghausen married Ludwig (later to become King Ludwig I), the heir to the Bavarian throne. Horse races were organized in a meadow on the edge of Munich, which was named the Theresienwiese in honour of the young lady. It was decided to make this a regular event, and gradually it became customary to organize agricultural shows, which were combined with equestrian events and shooting contests. To these were added roundabouts, beer tents and fireworks, thus giving rise to the present Oktoberfest (it was moved from October to late September due to the weather).

Today the Oktoberfest attracts around 6.5 million visitors from all over the world. Year after year the record for amounts of beer, sausages and roast chickens consumed at the festival is broken. The Oktoberfest opens with a grand procession of wagons of the city's seven main breweries accompanied by folk bands. On the stroke of noon, the city's mayor broaches a barrel of beer to open the two-week revelry surrounding the city's fair.

Traditional dress at the world-renowned Oktoberfest

The Christmas Fair

Advent, which comes from the Latin *adventus*, "the coming", is the period in the Christian calendar leading up to Christmas. It starts on the fourth Sunday before 24 December. In Bavaria this period is marked with a number of rituals.

Advent candles are lit in churches and in people's houses, and special biscuits known as *Plätzchen* are baked. In larger towns and cities, market stalls are set up for the Christmas fairs, which are known as *Christkindlmarkt* or *Weihnachtsmarkt*. They begin with the ritual raising of a huge Christmas tree in the brightly illuminated market squares.

Wooden decorations, Nativity figures and all sorts of delicacies and gifts are displayed for sale round the tree. The air is filled with the delicious aroma of freshly baked gingerbread and roasted almonds. The celebrations include drinking mulled wine (*Glühwein*) in the frosty air. St Nicholas, accompanied by Knecht Ruprecht or Krampus, distribute apples and nuts to children, and the holiday atmosphere is heightened by the joyful singing of carollers. The best Christmas fairs in southern Bavaria are those held in Nuremburg, Munich and Augsburg.

Bavarian Folk Costume

To many people, traditional Bavarian folk costume epitomizes Bavaria. It is among one of the most widely celebrated and recognisable of the European national costumes. The traditional men's *Tracht* includes: *Lederhosen*, leather shorts held up by leather braces and sometimes tied up at the knees; the *Janker*, a waistcoat of rough cloth with bone buttons; the *Gamsbart*, a hat with a goat's hair tassel, and asymmetrically tied shoes. Women wear the *Dirndl*, a blouse with puffed sleeves, a corsetted waistcoat, a crimped skirt and an apron. Jewellery and ornaments are an important element of Bavarian costume. Men's trousers are decorated with chains and pendants, and their shirts are embroidered with letters, medallions and coats of arms. Women wear intricate necklaces and richly decorated chokers.

St Nicholas figures and decorations at a Bavarian Christmas market

Bavarian in national costume

MUNICH & THE BAVARIAN ALPS THROUGH THE YEAR

The Bavarian calendar is filled with picturesque rituals, historical spectacles, festivals and trade fairs. The type of event depends on the season, and in Bavaria they are varied indeed. The snowy winter is the season for skiers and tobogganists, while hikers enjoy walking along the scenic and well-marked trails. From springtime onwards, colourful paragliders can be spotted as they soar over mountain peaks, and the appearance of sails heralds the start of the yachting season on the lakes. The summer attracts mountaineers, hikers and watersports enthusiasts. Almost everyone can be seen during the famous Oktoberfest, which starts in the middle of September.

Spring

Spring comes early here. At the beginning of April, fruit trees are in blossom, Alpine meadows become carpeted with flowers and the melting Alpine snow creates rushing streams. Numerous festive ceremonies mark the Easter period in Bavaria. Easter traditions centre on the symbolism of the egg. Houses are decorated with ornamental twigs with Easter eggs hanging from them, while excited children are up early searching for eggs. In May, the blossom of chestnut trees forms a canopy over reawakening beer gardens.

March

Starkbierfest *(between Ash Wednesday and Good Friday)* Munich. The Festival of Strong Beer commemorates the ale that was drunk by Pauline monks as they observed the Lenten fast.
Internationale Jazzwoche *(last two weeks in March)*, international jazz festival that takes place in Burghausen.

April

Biennale *(every two years; two weeks in April/May; next in 2018, 2020)*, Munich. Germany's largest contemporary music festival.
Augsburger Plärrer *(twice a year: two weeks after Easter and two weeks end of August, start of September)*, Augsburg. Biannual event. The largest folk festival in Swabia, a small counterpart to the Oktoberfest.
Auer Dult (Maidult) *(nine days from last Sat in April)*, Munich. Renowned fair held in the Mariahilfplatz in the Au district.

May

Maibockausschank *(end of April/beginning of May)*, Munich. Celebration marking the occasion when the strong Bockbier is broached. It begins in the Hofbräuhaus to the sounds of a children's orchestra.
Maibaumaufstellen *(May 1)*. Virtually every Bavarian community honours the custom of Raising the Maypole *(see p32)*.
Trachten-und Schützenzug *(first Sunday in May)*, Passau. A large procession of folk groups and bands from all over Bavaria and Austria opens this annual fair.
Lange Nacht der Musik *(Sat in May, varies)*, Munich. Over 400 live music events are held at 100 venues for one long night.
Fronleichnam *(Thursday after Trinity Sunday)*. According to Catholic tradition, this religious festival in honour of Corpus Christi is marked by countless processions. The most picturesque are in Lenggries and Bad Tölz.

Typical Fronleichnam (Corpus Christi) procession

Summer

On summer days the blue skies over Bavaria reach an almost Mediterranean intensity. Cascades of flowers hang from balconies and window boxes. Bathers and watersports enthusiasts are drawn to the crystal-clear rivers and lakes. Almost every resort has its

Antiques for sale at the famous Auer Dult fair in Au

Average Hours of Sunshine

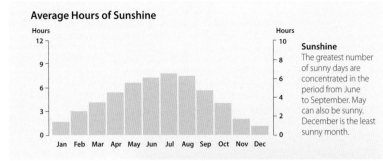

Sunshine
The greatest number of sunny days are concentrated in the period from June to September. May can also be sunny. December is the least sunny month.

own summer festival, and these celebrations are particularly impressive when they are held by a lakeside. They feature regattas, firework displays and angling contests.

June

Stadtgeburtstag *(weekend after 14 June)*, Munich. Festival commemorating the foundation of the city (14 June 1158).
Filmfest München *(end of June/ beginning of July)*, Munich. One of Europe's liveliest and most important film festivals.
Tollwood Festival *(four weeks June–July)*, Munich, Olympic Park. Festival of jazz, rock and theatre, with lots of food stalls.
Münchner Opernfestspiele *(four weeks in June/July)*, Munich. Festival of classical opera, ballet, singing and music.

Agnes-Bernauer-Festspiele in Straubing

July

Kaltenberger Ritterspiele *(first 3 weekends in July)*, Kaltenberg Castle, near Landsberg. Jousting tournaments re-enacting medieval traditions.
Landshuter Hochzeit *(every four years, the next in 2017)*, Landshut. Spectacle commemorating the marriage of Georg, son of Ludwig the Rich, and Princess Jadwiga *(see p32)*.
Schwäbischwerder Kindertag *(mid-July)*, Donauwörth. Children dressed in historical costume re-enact events in the history of the town.
Agnes-Bernauer-Festspiele *(every four years, the next in 2021)*, Straubing. Historical theatre festival telling the story of

Poster for the Auer Dult fair

Duke Albrecht III and Agnes Bernauer, an Augsburg barber's daughter.
Memminger Fischertag *(second half of July)*, Memmingen. Trout-angling competition.
Auer Dult (Jakobidult) *(nine days in July/ August)*, Munich. One of three annual fairs held in the Au district.
Schleißheimer Schloss-konzerte *(July/August)*, Schleißheim. Classical music concerts in the stunning baroque splendour of Schloss Schleißheim.

August

Gäubodenfest *(around mid-Aug)*, Straubing. Folk festival combined with an agricultural and industrial fair, Bavaria's second largest after the Oktoberfest.
Allgäuer Festwoche *(mid-August)*, Kempten. Exhibition of the Allgäu region's economic and cultural achievements with over 400 exhibitors and a packed programme of events.
König-Ludwig-Feuer *(24 Aug)*, Oberammergau. Fire festival commemorating the death of Ludwig II, who drowned in Starnberger See.

Decorated house in Oberammergau, where the König-Ludwig-Feuer is held

Average Precipitation

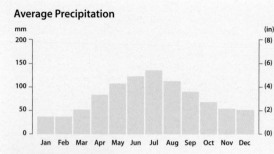

Rain and Snowfall
Although the autumn drizzle is the most unpleasant, the heaviest rainfall occurs in summer. Intensive snowfall is common in winter, particularly in the Alps and the foothills.

One of the vast beer tents at the Oktoberfest

Autumn

Bavarian autumns are often warm and sunny. The forests turn every shade of red and gold, and mushroom-pickers return with baskets filled with many species of edible fungi. The mountain pastures echo to the sounds of herded cows and sheep.

In autumn the sky becomes dull and overcast, and the shortening days are chilly and damp. The first overnight frosts set in, and mornings often start with a blanket of thick fog, which causes problems for road and air traffic.

September

Oktoberfest (16 or 17 days leading up to the 1st Sunday in October), Munich. The city's world-famous folk festival, held in the Theresienwiese fairground. Sample Wiesnbeer, especially brewed for the Oktoberfest, accompanied by traditional Bavarian entertainment (see p33).
Viehscheid (second half of September). Traditional celebration of the cattle being brought down from summer pastures in many areas, including Hindelang, Oberstdorf and Königssee.

October

Oktoberfest (see September).
Lange Nacht der Museen (one night in October, date varies), Munich. About 90 of the city's galleries and museums open late for one evening of tours and parties.
Medientage München (second half of October), Munich. Fair dedicated to the mass media. Discover the latest trends in multimedia and communications.
Auer Dult (Herbst Dult) (9 days at the end of October), Munich. The third of the annual fairs held in the Au district of Munich.

November

Leonardifahrten und Leonardiritte (1st Sunday in November) throughout Bavaria. In many areas, such as Bad Tölz, Schliersee, Murnau and Benediktbeuern, processions on horseback or in painted carts take place in honour of St Leonard, regarded by Bavarians as the patron saint of horses. In Bad Tölz the horses re-enact Christ's journey on the road to Calvary in a procession after receiving a blessing.
St Martin's Day (11 November) throughout Bavaria. In almost every town and village processions are held in which children take part, carrying lanterns. Pretzels that they have been given hang from the lanterns. The processions are often led by a horse-rider in a long cloak who represents St Martin.

Bavarian women in a painted cart on St Leonard's Day

Average Monthly Temperatures

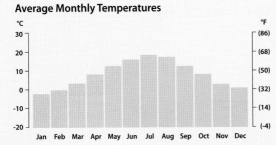

Temperatures
Temperatures are highest in the summer, although they rarely exceed 30°C (86°F). Winters are frosty and snowy, although they can be mild. The coldest temperatures are naturally in the mountains.

Winter

As autumn draws to a close, people light the candles on the Advent wreaths in their homes every week to mark the countdown to christmas. At the beginning of December skiers set out on excursions, and if the lakes and canals are sufficiently thickly frozen, they are soon covered with skaters.

Winters in southern Bavaria are unpredictable. They may be icy and snowy, or mild and snowfree. December is marked by the carnival spirit. Village carnivals are colourful affairs. At events associated with driving off winter with witchcraft, masks and costumes are a common sight.

December

Winter-Tollwood (end of November to New Year's Eve), Munich. A major music and arts festival held in Theresienwiese.

The Skifasching (skiing carnival) in Firstalm

Christkindlmarkt (end of November to Christmas Eve), throughout southern Bavaria. A Christmas fair inaugurating the festive Christmas season with the ritual raising of the Christmas tree in the town or village square.

Oberstdorf in winter during the Four Ski-Jump Tournament

Sylvester (31 December). Sumptuous balls and receptions mark the New Year, which is ushered in with lavish firework displays.

January

Four Ski-Jump Tournament (turn of the year), Oberstdorf, Garmisch-Partenkirchen (and Innsbruck and Bischofshofen in Austria). Famous ski-jumping tournament.

Schäfflertanz (Epiphany to Shrove Tuesday), Munich. The Dance of the Coopers street festival held every seven years (the next in 2019) to commemorate the passing of the plague in the 15th century.

February

Skifasching (last Sunday of Carnival), Firstalm. Bavaria's renowned skiing carnival. Also held in Garmisch-Partenkirchen.

Tanz der Marktfrauen (Shrove Tuesday), Munich. Market women of the Viktualienmarkt dress up and perform a dance.

Public Holidays

Neujahr New Year

Epiphany (6 January)

Karfreitag Good Friday

Ostern Easter

Maifeiertag May Day

Christi Himmelfahrt Ascension

Pfingsten Whitsun

Fronleichnam Corpus Christi

Mariä Himmelfahrt Assumption (15 August)

Nationalfeiertag German Reunification Day (3 October)

Allerheiligen All Saints (1 November)

Weihnachten Christmas (25/26 December)

THE HISTORY OF MUNICH AND BAVARIA

Over the centuries, and despite its location in the heart of Europe, southern Bavaria gradually built up its own distinct character, becoming a geographically and culturally unified entity. Although it never played a leading role, it was one of the strongest duchies in Germany. The Wittelsbach dynasty ruled Bavaria until 1918, when the Free State of Bavaria (Freistaat Bayern) was proclaimed. After World War II Bavaria opposed centralization.

Early Settlement

The first farming communities settled in southern Bavaria in the 4th millennium BC. Traces of their presence, in the form of the foundations of peasant huts, were found near Kelheim in the 1960s. During the period of the Altheim culture (about 3900–3500 BC), peasant settlements were often surrounded by fortified ditches. During the Bronze Age (1800–1200 BC) the pace of cultural development accelerated, and a wealth of items from burials and many everyday tools of that period have been discovered. During the Hallstatt period, iron began to be used in preference to bronze.

The Celts

The Hallstatt period was marked by the appearance in Bavaria of the Celts, whose origins are not clear to this day. The Celts were distinguished by their loose tribal and family ties. The Vindelici tribe of Celts settled in the territory between the rivers Inn and Lech, and their capital was Manching, near Ingolstadt. The Bavarian Celts maintained links with the Mediterranean world, particularly with the Etruscans. They imported Etruscan, and sometimes Greek, luxury goods. Many later Bavarian towns, among them Regensburg (Ratisbon), Kempten, Straubing and Passau, were founded by the Celts.

The Roman Empire

In 15 BC the Roman army, under Drusus and Tiberius, conquered the Celts and reached the Danube. This became the frontier of the Roman Empire and a fortified wall was constructed to defend it. Southern Bavaria was divided into the provinces of Raetia and Noricum. The city of Vindelicorum, today Augsburg, was founded by the Emperor Augustus, whose name it still bears. It became the administrative centre of this part of the Roman Empire.

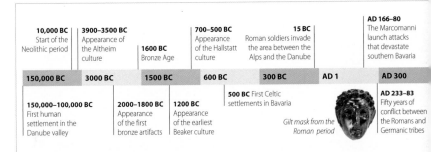

10,000 BC Start of the Neolithic period	3900–3500 BC Appearance of the Altheim culture	1600 BC Bronze Age	700–500 BC Appearance of the Hallstatt culture	15 BC Roman soldiers invade the area between the Alps and the Danube	AD 166–80 The Marcomanni launch attacks that devastate southern Bavaria

150,000 BC	3000 BC	1500 BC	600 BC	300 BC	AD 1	AD 300

150,000–100,000 BC First human settlement in the Danube valley	2000–1800 BC Appearance of the first bronze artifacts	1200 BC Appearance of the earliest Beaker culture	500 BC First Celtic settlements in Bavaria	Gilt mask from the Roman period	AD 233–83 Fifty years of conflict between the Romans and Germanic tribes

◀ Portrait of Ludwig I, king of Bavaria (1786–1868)

The End of the Roman Empire

After two centuries of peaceful development, Raetia and Noricum were attacked by two Germanic tribes, the Marcomanni and the Alamanni. The first attacks were repulsed by Emperor Marcus Aurelius, but the province suffered destruction in the mid-3rd century by invasions and civil war. Towards the end of the 3rd century stability returned for about 100 years, but after AD 400 a new wave of Germanic invasions toppled Roman control. From those war-torn and troubled times there are records of the activities of the early Christians – St Afra, the martyr who was burned in Augsburg, and St Severinus, who revived missionary activity in the region.

Roman stele from Augsburg

The Great Migration and Early Christianity

The origins of the Bavarians are still not fully understood. Most historians believe that a new tribe, whom the Romans knew as the Baiovarii, appeared south of the Danube, in the area of present-day southern Bavaria, in 450–550. They are thought to have orig-inated from a Germanic tribe centred in Boiohaemum, what is today the Czech Republic. The Baiovarii were joined by remnants of other Germanic and Celtic tribes and by Romanized people. At the same time, settlers started appearing to the west of the River Lech. The Alamanni tribes became the neighbours of the Baiovarii to the west, while to the north, the region a few dozen kilometres beyond the Danube was conquered by the Franks. This situation continued virtually unchanged to the present day, with the addition of the territories beyond the River Lech and Bavaria's acquisition of the Franconian lands after 1803.

Most of the inhabitants of the region retained their pagan beliefs for some time, and Christianity took hold very slowly. Irish, Anglo-Saxon and Frankish missionaries started preaching in the region in the early 7th century. At the turn of the 7th century, numerous bishops were active in Bavaria: Emmeram in Ratisbon, Korbinian in Freising, and Rupert in Salzburg. In 739 there were bishoprics in Ratisbon, Freising, Passau and present-day Salzburg. They were set up and run by the Anglo-Saxon missionary bishop, St Boniface. It is noteworthy that the importance of their sees continued for the next millennium. A key role in the establishment of Christianity and the nurturing of cultural

Roman mosaic with hunting scenes from a villa near Westerhofen

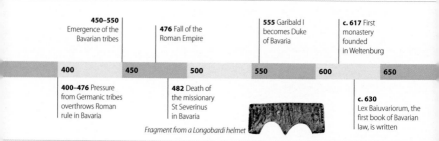

450–550 Emergence of the Bavarian tribes

476 Fall of the Roman Empire

555 Garibald I becomes Duke of Bavaria

c. 617 First monastery founded in Weltenburg

| 400 | 450 | 500 | 550 | 600 | 650 |

400–476 Pressure from Germanic tribes overthrows Roman rule in Bavaria

482 Death of the missionary St Severinus in Bavaria

Fragment from a Longobardi helmet

c. 630 Lex Baiuvariorum, the first book of Bavarian law, is written

development from the late 7th century and throughout the 8th century was played by the many Benedictine monasteries, particularly by those of Weltenburg and Benediktbeuern.

Rule of the Bavarian Tribes

The Duchy of Bavaria was founded in the mid-6th century. The ruling Agilolfing dynasty probably originated from the territories of the Merovingian state to the west, and was its vassals. The first known Duke of Bavaria was Garibald I (555–591). According to the *Lex Baiuvariorum,* the first legal code issued in those lands, the ducal throne was to belong to the Agilolfing dynasty for all time.

Being dependent on the powerful Merovingians and weaker than the Frankish dukes to the north, Bavaria's Agilolfing rulers were forced to resort to constant manoeuvring to retain their position. One of the ways they preserved their rule was by strategic marriages with the Allaman, Longobardi and Frankish dynasties. Their activity within the state was limited to military leadership, while in peacetime they took charge of the judiciary. Despite this, the Agilolfing dukes played a major role in Bavaria's development. Not only did they lay the foundations of the future state of Bavaria by ensuring territorial unity, but they also championed Christianity.

The main centre of ducal and ecclesiastic power was Ratisbon, on the River Danube. The duchy itself grew slowly and by

The Cross of Tassilo from the church in Polling

peaceful means, and almost unnoticed it expanded into what was later to become Austria. Under the rule of Tassilo III (748–88), the last ruler of the Agilolfing dynasty, the duchy extended as far as Carinthia. However, the growing might of the Agilolfing dynasty and of its state alarmed the Frankish ruler Charlemagne, who defeated Tassilo in 788 and put an end to the Bavarian tribes' first state. Bavaria lost its independence and became part of the Frankish state, while Tassilo was confined to a monastery.

After the division of the Frankish empire under the terms of the Treaty of Verdun in 843, Bavaria became one of the centres of the East Frankish Empire (which was the embryo of the later Germany). The Emperor Arnulf of Carinthia resided in Ratisbon at the end of the 9th century.

Initial from an illuminated manuscript, depicting the martyrdom of St Emmeram, Bishop of Ratisbon

---

A fibula decorated with a geometric pattern

907 Hungarian tribes overrun Bavaria

788 Tassilo III is overthrown by Charlemagne

938 Emperor Otto's campaign against Duke Eberhard of Bavaria

| 750 | 800 | 850 | 900 | 950 | 1000 |

739 Bishoprics established in Freising and Passau

843 Division of the Frankish empire

899 Death of Emperor Arnulf leads to a period of instability

954 Hungarian tribes invade Swabia

738 St Boniface begins evangelizing Bavaria

Friedrich Barbarossa, who transferred power from the Welfs to the Wittelbachs

Wittelsbach. This powerful dynasty was to rule Bavaria right up until 1918, a record length of time for any German dynasty. The Wittelsbachs gradually built up their family possessions in central Bavaria, repelling successive attacks by rival families. In 1214 they annexed part of the Rhineland Palatinate, and by 1253 Bavaria was one of the largest ducal territories in the fragmented German empire.

The Early Middle Ages

At the end of the 8th century, rulers proceeded to unify the Bavarian tribes and founded a new duchy. Throughout the 9th century the Bavarian dukes were in conflict with the Saxons, who took the Bavarian throne in 919. These conflicts ended in their defeat, and in the 10th century the German kings decided to appoint their own vassals to the Bavarian ducal throne, or to rule the duchy directly.

The following centuries brought a degree of stability with the rule of the Welf dynasty. Duke Henry the Lion founded Munich in 1158 and with the support of Bavaria and his possessions in Saxony waged a war against the Emperor Friedrich Barbarossa. He was finally defeated in 1180, and Bavaria lost the lands east of Salzburg. The same year, Friedrich Barbarossa conferred the title of Duke of Bavaria on Otto I

The Late Middle Ages

Under Ludwig IV of Bavaria, the duchy was at the height of its powers. Ludwig added the Margravate of Brandenburg, the Tyrol and part of the southern Netherlands to Bavaria. In 1314 he became king of Germany, and 14 years later he was crowned Holy Roman Emperor. External glory was reflected in internal changes. The Emperor introduced civic and land laws, and built up an administrative system with new central institutions.

From the end of the 14th century, tax affairs were decided by representatives of three ranks: knights, clergy and burghers. From the 15th century this group assumed the form of an assembly called the Landtag or Landschaft. After the death of Ludwig IV, Bavaria was shaken by an endless succession of conflicts and local wars.

Late Gothic sculpture from Ottobeuren Abbey

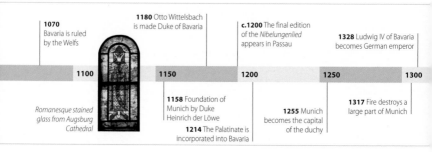

1070 Bavaria is ruled by the Welfs

1180 Otto Wittelsbach is made Duke of Bavaria

c.1200 The final edition of the *Nibelungenlied* appears in Passau

1328 Ludwig IV of Bavaria becomes German emperor

Romanesque stained glass from Augsburg Cathedral

1100 **1150** **1200** **1250** **1300**

1158 Foundation of Munich by Duke Heinrich der Löwe

1214 The Palatinate is incorporated into Bavaria

1255 Munich becomes the capital of the duchy

1317 Fire destroys a large part of Munich

The sons of Ludwig IV attempted to divide the state into small duchies ruled by each of them. In spite of the poverty and sacrifice brought by the resulting wars, this situation had a positive aspect. The division and rivalry of the various ducal courts encouraged the development of culture.

Landshut underwent a period of splendour and in 1475 it was the venue of the sumptuous wedding of the daughter of Casimir Jagiellon, king of Poland (*see p32*). However, in the Swabian territories on the River Lech, territorial disintegration continued in the 15th century. A leading role was played by the empire's principal city, Augsburg. The territory under the control of the Bishop of Augsburg also held a prime position.

Renaissance tombstone from the church in Oettingen

The Renaissance and Counter-Reformation

In 1506 the Bavarian states forced the adoption of a regulation that forbade the division of duchies: from then on, the throne passed to the eldest son. The Bavarian duchies were strengthened by the fact that their lands were not affected by the German peasants' wars of 1524–6.

The rulers of Bavaria were firmly opposed to the Protestantism that was spreading through the territories of Swabia and Franconia.

In 1530, at the imperial parliament in Augsburg, the Protestants presented the articles of their faith, known as the Confessions of Augsburg, to the Emperor. Some Bavarian Protestants were forced to renounce their faith, while the following edict of 1571 finally removed all supporters of the reformation from Bavaria. In the war of 1546–7 between Karl V and the Protestant dukes, Bavaria took the Emperor's side. The first Bavarian Jesuits fought actively against the Reformation. The great Michaelskirche in Munich was built in the late 16th-century as a symbol of Bavarian Catholicism.

In return for their allegiance to Rome, the younger sons of the Wittelsbachs were given sees in the west and north of the Empire, thus further strengthening the position of the Wittelsbachs on the German political scene.

Handing the Confessions of Augsburg to Emperor Karl V

(see p32)

1385 The first residence in Munich is built by Duke Stephan III

1369 The population of Munich exceeds 10,000

1516 The dukes of Bavaria issue the Reinheitsgebot, the world's first decree, enforced to this day, on brewing beer

Martin Luther, father of the Reformation

1506 The states of Bavaria issue a decree forbidding the division of the country

1517 Luther's 95 "theses" launch the Reformation

1530 Protestants submit the Confessions of Augsburg to Karl V at the imperial parliament

1555 The imperial parliament declares the Religious Peace of Augsburg

1350   1400   1450   1500   1550

The Age of Maximilian I

Duke Wilhelm V, who came to the throne in 1579, brought the state to the edge of bankruptcy, abdicating in 1598 in favour of his son Maximilian I (1573–1651). During his 54-year reign, Maximilian reorganized the administration of the state and the military, streamlined the fiscal system and reigned in a kind of early absolutism. In the

Maximilian I, painted by Dürer

face of worsening religious and political conflicts in the empire, which ultimately led to the outbreak of the Thirty Years' War, Maximilian I took charge of the Catholic camp. In 1618 he supported the Habsburgs against the rebellious Bohemian state, and Bavarian troops played a decisive role in the defeat of the Bohemians at the Battle of White Mountain in 1620.

As a reward for his part in this victory, Maximilian I was given the title of Prince Elector in 1623. The lands of the Upper Palatinate, which were added to Bavaria, were subjected to a brutal regime of re-Catholicization.

During the second part of the Thirty Years' War, attacks by Swedish and Franco-Swedish forces caused a great deal of devastation and severely impoverished the country.

Finally, thanks to French support, Maximilian succeeded in retaining all conquered lands and the title of Elector at the peace congress in Münster. Pro-French policy would dominate Bavarian policy from then up until German Unification in 1871.

Maximilian's style and method of rule were emulated by later Bavarian leaders, including Duke Maximilian Montgelas and Franz Josef Strauß. Bertel Thorvaldsen's equestrian statue of Maximilian in Munich commemorates his achievements.

Dreams of Power

Maximilian II Emanuel, who married the daughter of the Polish king Jan III Sobieski, was known as the "White Knight". One of the most colourful figures in Bavaria's history, he had dreams of great conquests and of winning the crown. He allied himself with the Viennese court, and took part in the Battle of Vienna, where the Turks were defeated, in 1683. He was rewarded with the regency of the southern Netherlands. Entangled in the Wars of the Spanish Succession, he changed sides and in 1702 formed an alliance with Louis XIV. However, in 1704 the Franco-Bavarian army was defeated by Habsburg troops and Maximilian II Emanuel fled to France. Bavaria then suffered ten years of harsh Austrian rule

Maximilian Emanuel receiving a Turkish emissary after his victory at Vienna

during which protests by desperate peasants were suppressed with bloodshed.

Maximilian II Emanuel did not return to the elector's throne until a peace treaty was signed in 1714. Although he was a prominent patron of the arts and a popular leader, his lengthy and turbulent rule had weakened Bavaria's position.

Rococo window arch at the Residenz in Munich

Reform, Annexation and Enlightenment

In 1740–45, despite Maximilian II Emanuel's disastrous anti-Habsburg policy, his son Karl Albrecht made a further attempt to become involved in the Austrian succession. As Karl VII, Emperor of the Holy Roman Empire, he

Rococo monstrance from Passau

was, however, unable to repel the troops of Maria Teresia. At the Treaty of Füssen in 1745, his successor Maximilian III Joseph was forced to renounce claims to the Austrian throne.

During the long and peaceful reign of Maximilian III Joseph, in which the ideology of enlightened absolutism was put into practice, there were important agricultural reforms, as well as the foundation of the Bavarian Academy of Sciences in 1759. Another development was the famous Nymphenburg porcelain factory.

The king's death in 1777 ended the direct Wittelsbach line. Emperor Joseph II's orders to annex Bavaria caused Prussian objections and led to the accession of Karl Theodor, an indirect descendant of the ruling family of the Palatinate. Karl Theodor continued his predecessor's policy of enlightenment, while the spirit of scientific enquiry was cultivated in Bavarian abbeys, which contributed to knowledge and culture.

With the outbreak of the Napoleonic Wars (1799–1815), Bavaria tried to remain neutral but was unable to protect its possessions in the Palatinate from French occupation.

Ornamental interior of the church of Weltenburg Monastery, one of many built in the Baroque period

The Wittelsbach Dynasty

In 1180 Bavaria was given in lien to Otto I Wittelsbach, whose family ruled Bavaria until 1918. In 1329 the family was divided into a Bavarian and Palatinate line, which branched out even further. The Wittelsbachs occupied the German imperial throne on two occasions (in 1328 and 1742). In 1806 Napoleon proclaimed Maximilian I Joseph king. The family traditionally patronized the arts, which reached their apogee in the 19th century. The decline of the Wittelsbach dynasty began with Ludwig II, the "dilettante" king, and finally ended with the abdication of Ludwig III.

Wilhelm IV (1508–50) periodically shared his rule with his brother, Albrecht IV.

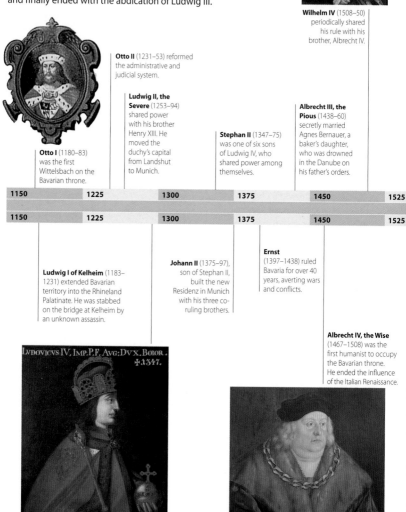

Otto II (1231–53) reformed the administrative and judicial system.

Ludwig II, the Severe (1253–94) shared power with his brother Henry XIII. He moved the duchy's capital from Landshut to Munich.

Otto I (1180–83) was the first Wittelsbach on the Bavarian throne.

Stephan II (1347–75) was one of six sons of Ludwig IV, who shared power among themselves.

Albrecht III, the Pious (1438–60) secretly married Agnes Bernauer, a baker's daughter, who was drowned in the Danube on his father's orders.

1150	1225	1300	1375	1450	1525
1150	1225	1300	1375	1450	1525

Ludwig I of Kelheim (1183–1231) extended Bavarian territory into the Rhineland Palatinate. He was stabbed on the bridge at Kelheim by an unknown assassin.

Johann II (1375–97), son of Stephan II, built the new Residenz in Munich with his three co-ruling brothers.

Ernst (1397–1438) ruled Bavaria for over 40 years, averting wars and conflicts.

Albrecht IV, the Wise (1467–1508) was the first humanist to occupy the Bavarian throne. He ended the influence of the Italian Renaissance.

Ludwig IV of Bavaria (1294–1347) was crowned king of Germany in 1314. He became Emperor in 1328, and this brought him into conflict with the Pope.

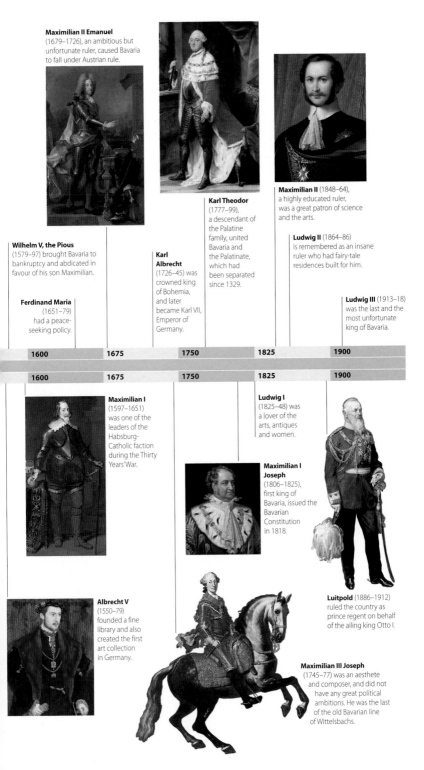

Maximilian II Emanuel (1679–1726), an ambitious but unfortunate ruler, caused Bavaria to fall under Austrian rule.

Wilhelm V, the Pious (1579–97) brought Bavaria to bankruptcy and abdicated in favour of his son Maximilian.

Ferdinand Maria (1651–79) had a peace-seeking policy.

Karl Albrecht (1726–45) was crowned king of Bohemia, and later became Karl VII, Emperor of Germany.

Karl Theodor (1777–99), a descendant of the Palatine family, united Bavaria and the Palatinate, which had been separated since 1329.

Maximilian II (1848–64), a highly educated ruler, was a great patron of science and the arts.

Ludwig II (1864–86) is remembered as an insane ruler who had fairy-tale residences built for him.

Ludwig III (1913–18) was the last and the most unfortunate king of Bavaria.

1600 1675 1750 1825 1900

1600 1675 1750 1825 1900

Maximilian I (1597–1651) was one of the leaders of the Habsburg-Catholic faction during the Thirty Years' War.

Ludwig I (1825–48) was a lover of the arts, antiques and women.

Maximilian I Joseph (1806–1825), first king of Bavaria, issued the Bavarian Constitution in 1818.

Albrecht V (1550–79) founded a fine library and also created the first art collection in Germany.

Luitpold (1886–1912) ruled the country as prince regent on behalf of the ailing king Otto I.

Maximilian III Joseph (1745–77) was an aesthete and composer, and did not have any great political ambitions. He was the last of the old Bavarian line of Wittelsbachs.

Panel with portraits of the Wittelsbach rulers of Bavaria, painted by Franz Xaver Thallmaier, 1880

Golden Age of The Wittelsbachs

The modern state of Bavaria was established at the beginning of the 19th century and it has survived more or less intact to this day. In 1803 Napoleon dissolved the German Empire's old territorial structures, and with his approval in 1803–06 Bavaria doubled its territory, incorporating the Swabian lands up to Ulm, and the Franconian lands. In 1806 Maximilian Joseph, again with Napoleon's approval, was crowned king, acquiring the title of Maximilian I Joseph.

Territorial expansion was accompanied by far-reaching internal reforms. In 1803 Maximilian I Joseph and his aide Count Maximilian Montgelas disbanded the

Maximilian I Joseph, king of Bavaria

monasteries and reorganized the country's administration. In late 1813 they deftly switched allegiance from Napoleon to the anti-Napoleonic coalition. Thus, at the Congress of Vienna they were able to retain the bulk of the territory that they had acquired with Napoleon's aid.

From 1815 to 1866 the Bavarian kings manoeuvred between the Prussians and Austrians, managing to conduct an independent foreign policy. This ended when the Prussians defeated the Bavarian-Austrian alliance.

In the latter half of the 19th century Bavaria made significant cultural and political advances. Education was developed and the re-established University of Munich flourished. Thanks to Ludwig I, Munich acquired impressive new parks, gardens and buildings. The visual arts and drama flourished, briefly overtaking those of Vienna and Berlin. Maximilian I Joseph's reign saw great progress in science and industry, and the emergence of "Maximilian" architecture. Ludwig I's patronage of the arts was continued by his grandson Ludwig II. In 1866 Bismarck forced Bavaria to join the Prussian camp, which was supported by groups from the state bureaucracy and Franconian Protestant quarters.

Cartouche with Bavarian crest

1803 Montgelas dissolves the Bavarian monasteries

1813 Bavaria joins the anti-Napoleonic coalition

1818 Bavaria becomes a constitutional monarchy

1848 The revolution in Munich leads to the abdication of Ludwig I

1866 Prussian War against Austria and Bavaria

1800   **1815**   **1830**   **1845**   **1860**

1805 Bavaria forms an alliance with Napoleon

1815 At the Congress of Vienna, Bavaria retains almost all its territorial gains from the Napoleonic period

1806 Bavaria becomes a kingdom

The dancer Lola Montez, mistress of Ludwig I

After the Unification of Germany

Their country's participation on the victors' side in the Franco-Prussian war of 1870–71 won many Bavarians over to the idea of a unified Germany. Ludwig II, who ruled Bavaria at the time, increasingly avoided any involvement in politics and escaped more and more into the world of Wagner's music, tales of chivalry and fairy-tale castles. The day-to-day running of the country was left to an anonymous group of government officials in Munich.

When the regency was taken over by Prince Luitpold after Ludwig II's tragic death, little changed. Luitpold, a popular ruler, attempted to offset political dependency on Berlin with a liberal cultural policy which contained a distinct anti-Prussian element. Under Luitpold's rule, Munich enjoyed the highest period of cultural and artistic development that it has ever experienced. Luitpold's son and heir, Ludwig III, who was thoroughly pro-Prussian, quickly lost his popularity.

After Germany's defeat at the end of World War I, on 7 November 1918 the rule of the Wittelsbachs in Munich was overthrown, and the Free State of Bavaria (Freistaat Bayern) was proclaimed. This has been Bavaria's official name ever since. Between February and May 1919 the far left Bavarian Soviet Republic ruled Munich and part of Bavaria. This weakened Bavaria's moderate forces and radicalized the right, which started to embrace extremist groups, such as Hitler's. In the

Old postcard painted by Fritz Bergen depicting King Ludwig II, much admired among Bavarians

general ferment of the Weimar Republic, Bavaria became a bastion of stability, with a slightly dictatorial rightwing government. The failure of Hitler's attempted putsch in 1923 helped to stave off Nazism for a while, but the mild sentences imposed on the leaders of the fascist Brownshirts only helped to increase their popularity.

From 1923 to 1933 the country was ruled by the Bavarian People's Party, whose policy was to oppose that of liberal and "red" Berlin. However, attempts to weaken Prussia's position in the Reich were unsuccessful, and political and cultural decline ensued. From 1918 to 1933 Munich's position as a cultural metropolis was taken over by Berlin.

Cartoon from a 1908 issue of the satirical journal *Simplicissimus*

1870–1871 Franco-Prussian War, in which Bavaria takes part	**1900** Population of Munich reaches 500,000	*Art Nouveau decoration on a house in Munich*	**9 November 1923** Hitler's attempted putsch in Munich
1875	**1890**	**1905**	**1920**
Frieze from the Propyläen in Munich	**1886** Tragic drowning of King Ludwig II in Starnberger See	**1 August 1914** Outbreak of World War I	**7 September 1918** Revolution in Munich overthrows the Wittelsbach dynasty. Bavaria is declared Freistaat Bayern

The Castles of Ludwig II

King Ludwig II of Bavaria, fondly known as "Kini" to his subjects, has remained a cult figure to this day. With his ambitious building projects and lack of interest in affairs of state, he was a controversial figure. The king's passions were architecture and music, and his friendship with Richard Wagner influenced his entire life. He dragged the country to the edge of financial ruin as he built one magnificent country home after another, all the while dreaming of new ones. Gradually he became withdrawn and, deemed insane, was finally removed from power. At the age of 42 he drowned in Starnberger See in mysterious circumstances.

This turret is reached by a spiral staircase leading from a picturesque gallery.

Ludwig II's Night Sleigh Ride
This painting by Richard Wenig, and the actual sleigh, can be seen in the Marstall-museum in Nymphenburg. The king adored his nocturnal escapades, which helped him avoid the harsh realities of daylight.

Throne Room of Neuschwanstein Castle
The Throne Room was designed in Byzantine style. It is decorated with gilded mural paintings, mosaics and a huge chandelier. A splendid gold and ivory throne planned for Ludwig II (see p234) was never made.

The Minstrels' Room is a lavishly painted official reception room.

Neuschwanstein Castle

The castle was built in 1868–86. Assisted by the painter and designer Christian Jank, Ludwig II fulfilled his vision of an old German castle, although he only lived here for 172 days.

The Linderhof Grotto
Built in the park, complete with stalactites, the grotto covers a lake 3 m (10 ft) deep. Ludwig II reached it in a gilded barge, which rocked on artificially created waves (see pp220–21).

Hall of Mirrors in Herrenchiemsee Palace
This showcase gallery was built in 1879–81 along the side of the palace facing the garden. Almost 100 m (328 ft) long, it outstrips the Hall of Mirrors at Versailles, on which it is based. The ceiling frescoes glorify Louis XIV, and night-time concerts *(see p206)* were illuminated with 1,848 candles placed in the gilded candelabras and chandeliers.

Turkish Hall in Schachen
With its fountain, rich carpets, ottomans, gilded candelabra and vases, the hall of this palace conjures up *The Tales of the Thousand and One Nights (see p221)*.

The upper courtyard leads into the main part of the castle, containing the reception room and apartments.

The gatehouse, flanked by turrets and set with crenellations, is decorated with the royal coat of arms.

Ludwig's Castles

Ludwig II was obsessed with creating the perfect residence. In Alpine surroundings he built Neuschwanstein Castle *(see p244)*. His fascination with the world of the Bourbons was expressed in the Linderhof *(see pp220–21)* and Herrenchiemsee *(see p206)* palaces.

Adolf Hitler signing the Munich Agreement

In the Shadow of the Nazis

The rulers of Bavaria underestimated the danger of the burgeoning Nazi movement. The participants in Hitler's 1923 putsch were given light sentences, with Hitler spending only eight months behind bars. In 1925 the NSDAP (Nazi Party) was reactivated, and in 1926 the ban on public speeches by Hitler was lifted. By 30 January 1933 Hitler had seized power, and in March he overthrew the Bavarian government and stripped Bavaria of its autonomy. Munich became Capital of the Movement; the Führer wanted it to become the Reich's ideological and cultural centre. The first concentration camp was built in nearby Dachau. During the Winter Olympics in Garmisch-Partenkirchen and the Summer Olympics in Berlin in 1936, the Nazis were at pains to present a positive image to the world. In 1937 Hitler embarked on an overt

clampdown in cultural policy. An exhibition of Degenerate Art was held in Munich, and later in other cities, its aim being to stigmatize modern "degenerate" art. The Haus der Kunst was built for annual exhibitions of German art. The large-scale redevelopment of Munich began, and the Königsplatz became the venue for Nazi rallies. In 1938 the Munich Agreement, by which Czechoslovakia was partitioned, was signed and four years later the first Allied bombs fell on Munich. Hitler was associated with Bavaria until the end of his life, frequently visiting its capital and his residence near Berchtesgaden. Relatively few Bavarians spoke out against Hitler, a notable exception being the White Rose student group, and the opposition movement did not play a significant role here. In April 1945 an attempt was made to organize the final resistance here, but Hitler's "Alpine Fortress" ultimately proved to be of no use.

Concentration camp prisoner's shirt

Hikers at the Kehlsteinhaus restaurant, the surviving part of Hitler's residence

1934 Hitler abolishes independence of German states, including Bavaria

1 September 1939 German attack on Poland launches World War II

30 April 1945 American troops enter Munich

1 October 1946 The first elections in Bavaria bring victory to the CSU

1974 Five FIFA World Cup matches are played in Munich, including the final

14 June 1958 Celebrations mark Munich's 800th anniversary

1972 The 20th Olympic Games are held in Munich

| 1930 | 1935 | 1940 | 1945 | 1950 | 1955 | 1960 | 1965 | 1970 | 1 |

29 September 1938 Munich Agreement

30 January 1933 Hitler becomes Chancellor of the Reich

February 1936 – the 4th Winter Olympics are held in Garmisch-Partenkirchen

1957 The population of Munich reaches 1 million

14 September 1949 Appointment of the government of the Federal Republic of Germany

1966 Construction of the Munich U-Bahn and S-Bahn network begins

Pageant at the Oktoberfest below *Bavaria*, a bronze statue cast by Ferdinand von Miller

Modern Bavaria

The ravages of war were less severe in Bavaria than in other parts of Germany. In April and May 1945 Bavaria was occupied by American troops and until 1949 it formed part of the American occupation zone. Despite a great influx of displaced people, most of Bavaria's inhabitants were spared the worst of post-war deprivation because of the region's agricultural strength. The Federal Republic of Bavaria, set up in 1949, made efforts to take an independent position as the region with the best preserved sense of historical and geograph-ical identity, and opposed centralization. One manifestation of this trend towards autonomy was the success that the

local Christian Democrats had in keeping their own organization distinct from the CDU (Christian Democratic Union), and in setting up their own CSU (Christian Social Union). It has governed Bavaria virtually continuously from 1949. By contrast, the city of Munich itself has largely elected candidates from the centre-left SPD (Social Democratic Party) as mayor.

The CSU, appealing to regional tradition, skilfully pursued a policy of industrialization for Bavaria after 1960. Electronics and computer manufacture developed strongly, as did the car manufacturers BMW and Audi. During the 1972 Summer Olympics, the region glittered; the Olympic ideal of peace was, however, marred by bloodshed in an attack by Palestinian separatists.

In the years leading up to the reunification of Germany, Munich was regarded as "Germany's secret capital"; it remains the country's most vibrant city, and the one many Germans would like to move to, given the chance. In 2009 Munich announced that by 2025, it aims to become the world's first city powered entirely by renewable energy – an indication that, even with the economy and tourism thriving, the region remains ready to embrace new challenges.

One of Europe's finest stadiums, the Allianz Arena in Munich

1980 Pope John Paul II visits Altötting during his pilgrimage to Germany

1992 The opening of Munich's new airport

The BMW logo, one of the symbols of modern Bavaria

2008 Munich celebrates its 850th birthday

2014 Dieter Reiter of the SPD is elected mayor of Munich, succeeding Christian Ude (also SPD)

1980	1985	1990	1995	2000	2005	2010	2015	2020

1988 Death of Franz Josef Strauß

3 October 1990 Reunification of Germany weakens Bavaria's political role

2004 Munich hosts the EuroGames

2006 Germany hosts the FIFA World Cup. The opening ceremony is held in Munich's Allianz arena

2015 Population of Munich passes the 1.5 million mark

MUNICH AREA BY AREA

Munich at a Glance

Munich is Germany's third-largest city, and even after the fall of the Berlin Wall it continues to be regarded as Germany's "secret capital". Another name for it was the "village with a million inhabitants". Its metropolitan bustle, prosperity and high-tech industries exist alongside a rural, traditional atmosphere. The city has many parks, including the landscaped Englischer Garten, with the pretty River Isar that flows through it, and on fine days there are splendid views of the Alps, all of which combine to give the capital of Bavaria its unique atmosphere. It is also a city of culture. Munich has many historic monuments as well as outstanding museums and art galleries and several theatres.

Alte Pinakothek
Susanna and the Elders by Albrecht Altdorfer is one of the gallery's masterpieces of German Renaissance art *(see pp122–25)*.

The Glyptothek
Peace, a Roman copy of a sculpture by Cephisodotus, is one of the many classical sculptures on display in the Glyptothek, built by Ludwig I specifically to house such works of art *(see p119)*.

The Museums District
(See pp114–131)

Old Town (North)
(See pp74–

Old Town (South)
(See pp58–73)

SCHELLINGSTR.

BARERSTRASSE

BRIENNER STR.

ELISENSTRASSE

NORDENDSTRASSE

FR

GÄRTNE PLATZ

Theatinerkirche
This elegant Baroque church with its twin-towered façade is a prominent feature of the city's skyline *(see p83)*.

Asamkirche
The interior of the Church of St Johann Nepomuk exemplifies Baroque illusionism. Space, architectural elements, stuccowork, frescoes and the interplay of light and shadow combine to create the illusion of wave-like motion *(see pp70–71)*.

0 metres 750
0 yards 750

◀ Colourful roofscape of the city centre seen from the tower of Peterskirche

Siegestor
Based on the Arch of Constantine in Rome, this is a monument to the Bavarian army. It is crowned by a statue symbolizing Bavaria riding in a chariot drawn by four lions *(see p108)*.

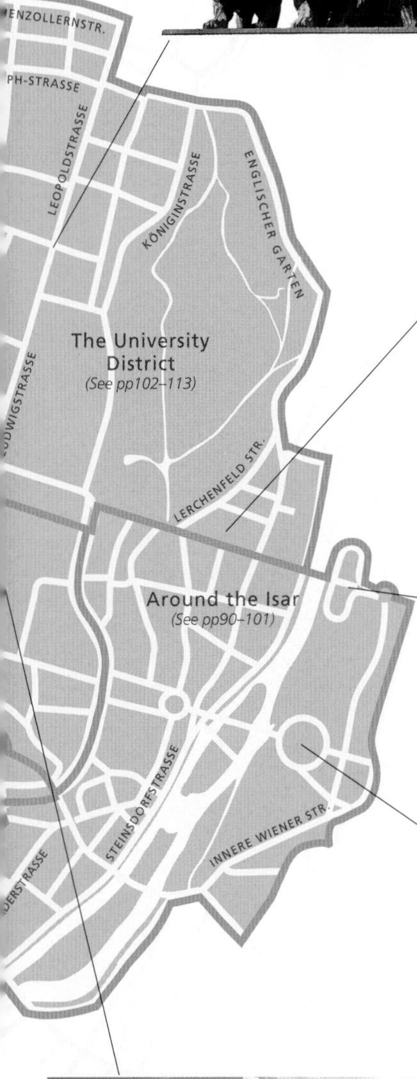

ENZOLLERNSTR.

PH-STRASSE

LEOPOLDSTRASSE

KÖNIGINSTRASSE

ENGLISCHER GARTEN

The University District
(See pp102–113)

LUDWIGSTRASSE

LERCHENFELD STR.

Bayerisches Nationalmuseum
This museum contains interiors taken from elsewhere in Bavaria and preserved in their entirety. An example is the Gothic Weberstube from Augsburg *(see pp112–13)*.

Around the Isar
(See pp90–101)

Friedensengel
The Angel of Peace, standing on the right bank of the Isar, can be seen from afar. The column, 18m (59 ft) high, is topped by a gilded bronze angel *(see p96)*.

STEINSDORFSTRASSE

INNERE WIENER STR.

ERSTRASSE

Maximilianeum
This building, in what is known as the Maximilian style, now houses the Bavarian parliament *(see p95)*.

The Residenz
The Brunnenhof is one of the seven courtyards in the Residenz. It takes its name from the Mannerist Wittelsbach Fountain (Brunnen) that stands in the centre *(see pp78–81)*.

OLD TOWN (SOUTH)

Three gates, the Karlstor, Sendlinger Tor and Isartor, mark the boundary of the southern part of the Altstadt (Old Town). Marienplatz is the main square in this district, and it is also the central point of the whole of Munich. Marienplatz was once a market square, and it has witnessed all of the most important events in Munich's history.

Both tourists and local people come to admire the many fine historic buildings,

including the Frauenkirche, with its distinctive outline, and Peterskirche, the city's oldest church. South of Marienplatz is the Angerviertel. Because it was safe from flooding by the River Isar, this area was chosen by the legendary monks who founded Munich and gave the city its name. Life in the Angerviertel centres around the Viktualienmarkt, which has been held here for almost 200 years.

Sights at a Glance

Buildings and Squares
1 Karlstor
7 Neues Rathaus
8 Marienplatz
11 Altes Rathaus
13 Isartor
15 Viktualienmarkt
16 Gärtnerplatz
17 Ignaz-Günther-Haus
19 Jüdisches Zentrum
21 Asamhaus
22 Sendlinger Tor

Museums
5 Deutsches Jagd- und Fischereimuseum
14 Bier- und Oktoberfestmuseum
18 Münchner Stadtmuseum

Churches
2 Bürgersaal
4 Michaelskirche
6 *Frauenkirche pp64–5*
9 Peterskirche
12 Heiliggeistkirche
20 *Asamkirche pp70–71*
23 Matthäuskirche
24 Allerheiligenkirche am Kreuz
25 Damenstift St Anna

Eateries
3 Augustinerbräu
10 Ehemalige Stadtschreiberei

☐ **Restaurants** *p276*
1 Augustinerbräu
2 Bratwurstherzl
3 Café Glockenspiel
4 Der Pschorr
5 Fisch Poseidon
6 Fraunhofer am Dom
7 Hofer – der Stadtwirt
8 Nürnberger Bratwurst Glöckl am Dom
9 Prinz Myshkin
10 Ratskeller
11 Riva Tal
12 Sushi Sano
13 Weisses Bräuhaus
14 Weinhaus Neuner
15 Yum

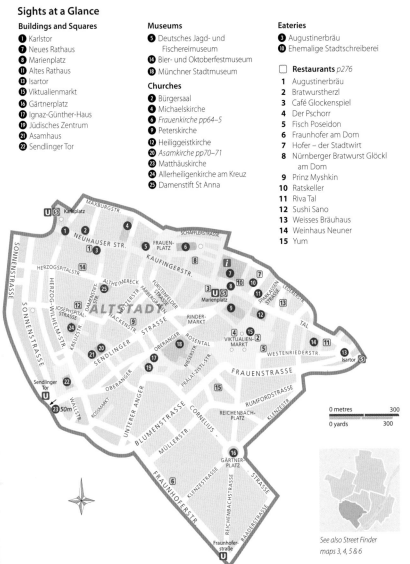

0 metres 300
0 yards 300

See also Street Finder maps 3, 4, 5 & 6

◀ Interior of the Asamkirche, Church of St Johann Nepomuk

For keys to symbols *see back flap*

Street-by-Street: Around Marienplatz

Ever since Munich was founded, Marienplatz has been the
city's architectural and commercial hub. The geographical
centre of the city is marked by the Mariensäule (Column of
the Virgin), from which all distances in Munich are measured.
The square and the streets around it, which have been
pedestrianized since the Munich Olympics in 1972, are
always lively. This area is Munich's busiest, bustling
with shoppers, visitors taking walking tours
and office workers going about their business.

❶ Karlstor
This gate was retained
when the old city walls
were demolished in 1791.

❷ Bürgersaal
The austere façade of this
church is decorated by a
statue of the Madonna and
Child by Franz Ableitner set
over the portal.

❸ Augustinerbräu
This pub, one of the
oldest in Munich,
has elaborate interior
decoration and a
picturesque beer-
garden courtyard.

Neuhauser Straße
is Munich's largest
shopping street. It is filled
with typical 19th-century
buildings and with cafés
and shops that are busy
from morning till night.

❹ ★ Michaelskirche
The nave of the Church
of St Michael, roofed by
impressive barrel vaulting, is
separated from the presbytery
by a triumphal arch.

Key

— Suggested route

❺ Deutsches Jagd- und Fischereimuseum
The German Hunting and Fishing Museum, located in a former Augustinian church, is reached from the presbytery side.

Locator Map
See Street Finder, maps 3, 5 & 6

❻ ★ Frauenkirche
The figure of the Madonna and Sorrowful Christ comes from a 13th-century basilica. The Baroque gates were carved by Ignaz Günther.

❼ ★ Neues Rathaus
The figures in the New Town Hall's chiming clock enact a joust and perform the Dance of the Coopers.

❾ Peterskirche
The high altar of the Church of St Peter is decorated with a figure of the saint carved by Erasmus Grasser. Around it are the four Church Fathers, by Egid Quirin Asam.

KAUFINGERSTR.

ROSENSTR.

Viktualienmarkt

MARIENPLATZ

RINDERMARKT

Heilig-Geist-Kirche

⓫ Altes Rathaus
The tower of the Old Town hall was reconstructed after World War II on the basis of plans dating from 1493.

❶ Karlstor
Karl's Gate

Karlsplatz 5. **Map** 3 A2 (5 A2). Ⓢ or Ⓤ Karlsplatz (Stachus). 🚋 16, 17, 18, 19, 20, 21, 22, 27, 28, N16, N19, N20, N27.

A vestige of the medieval town's fortifications, this gate stands at the western entrance to the Old Town. Originally known as the Neuhauser Tor, the gate received its present name in 1791 in honour of Elector Karl Theodor, who recommended the demolition of the old walls to enable the city to expand.

Initially, the Karlstor had three towers. The tallest of them, the central tower, was destroyed in 1857 when the gunpowder that was stored there exploded. The gate was rebuilt, to a Neo-Gothic design by Arnold Zenetti. The bronze figures in the walls of the arches were taken from the old fountain in Marienplatz in 1865.

The medieval Karlstor, seen from the Old Town

❷ Bürgersaal

Neuhauser Str. 14. **Map** 3 A2 (5 B3). **Tel** 21 99 720. Ⓢ or Ⓤ Karlsplatz (Stachus). 🚋 16, 17, 18, 19, 20, 21, 22, 27, 28, N16, N19, N20, N27. Lower church hall: **Open** 8am–7pm daily. Upper church hall: **Open** Daily, during mass.

The name of this church reflects its original purpose as the headquarters of the Marian congregation. It was designed by Giovanni Antonio Viscardi and consecrated in 1778. The rather austere façade fronts a two-storey interior. The **lower church** contains the tomb of

The dazzling interior of the Bürgersaal, featuring 19th-century frescoes

the beatified Rupert Mayer, a staunch fighter against the Nazis. The **upper church**, which was the main meeting place of the Marians, glitters with Rococo stuccowork by Joseph Georg Bader and paintings by Anton von Gumpp. During World War II the interior was damaged and some of the decoration has been restored. Surviving original features include the bas-relief on the high altar by Andreas Faistenberger, dating from 1710, the famous Guardian Angel of 1763 and the group of figures crowning the pulpit by Ignaz Günther.

❸ Augustinerbräu
Augustine Brewery

Neuhauser Str. 27. **Map** 3 A2 (5 B3). **Tel** 23 18 32 57. Ⓢ or Ⓤ Karlsplatz (Stachus). 🚋 16, 17, 18, 19, 20, 21, 22, 27, 28, N16, N19, N20, N27. **Open** 9am–midnight Mon–Sat, 10am–midnight Sun. 🚲

Two adjoining houses with picturesque 19th-century façades form part of the oldest

Alfresco seating outside the Augustinerbräu

brewery in Munich. The Augustinerbräu was founded by Augustinian monks and was mentioned as early as 1328. The historic interior of the brewery hall is a fine, and rare, example of the aesthetics and atmosphere of a Munich restaurant pre-dating World War I. An unusual feature is the Muschelsaal (Shell Hall), whose walls are lined with seashells, pebbles, busts and antlers. The brewery is divided into a restaurant and beer hall, with a delightful beer garden.

❹ Michaelskirche
St Michael's Church

Neuhauser Str. 6. **Map** 3 B2 (5 B3). Ⓢ or Ⓤ Karlsplatz (Stachus). 🚋 16, 17, 18, 19, 20, 21, 22, 27, 28, N16, N19, N20, N27. **Open** 10am–7pm Mon & Fri; 8am–8:15pm Tue; 8am–7pm Wed, Thu & Sat; 7am–10:15pm Sun.

The founder of this church, built for the Jesuit order, which was active in this area from 1559 onwards, was Duke Wilhelm V. Construction began in 1585, but when the tower collapsed in 1590, it was decided to enlarge the transept and to add a choir to designs by Friedrich Sustris. The Michaels-kirche, which aimed to bolster the Counter-Reformation and reinforce the Jesuits' presence, is the largest late-Renaissance religious building north of the Alps. It is remini-scent of the church of Il Gesú in Rome.

The three-tier façade, with its double doorway, is an outstanding example of Mannerist architecture. Between the pilasters there are windows and rows of niches containing the figures of Bavarian and imperial rulers engaged in the expansion and defence of Christendom. The ground floor is dominated by a bronze figure of St Michael slaying the Dragon, with a figure of Christ the Saviour on his shield, made by Hubert Gerhard in 1585. The two portals, designed by Friedrich Sustris, lead in to a strikingly spacious interior. The barrel vaulting over the nave spans the second-largest space after St Peter's Basilica in Rome. The elongated choir ends with the massive high altar, where a painting by Christoph Schwarz depicts the fall of the rebellious angels. In the crypt beneath the choir lie members of the Wittelsbach family, including Maximilian I and Ludwig II, and the church's founder. Beside the church is a monastery and a college. The latter was built in 1585–97, also by Sustris. It is known as the Alte Akademie.

Statue from the Michaelskirche

❺ Deutsches Jagd- und Fischereimuseum
German Hunting and Fishing Museum

Neuhauser Str. 2. **Map** 3 B2 (5 B3). **Tel** 22 05 22. Ⓢ or Ⓤ Marienplatz. 🚋 16, 17, 18, 19, 20, 21, 22, 27, 28, N16, N19, N20, N27. **Open** 9:30am–5pm Fri–Wed; 9:30am–9pm Thu. 🅿 🔳 jagd-fischerei-museum.de

The largest collection of field sports equipment in the world is displayed in a white Augustinian basilica. The building's ecclesiastical origins are concealed by the shops in the aisle, through which the museum is entered from the street. The church was built in the late 13th century. It was rebuilt several times, and became the first building in Munich to be decorated in the Baroque style. In 1911 it was converted into a concert hall, and in 1966 the collection of the German Hunting and Fishing Museum, founded in 1938, was moved here from Schloss Nymphenburg. The collection includes hunting weapons, bags and sleighs, 1,000 stuffed animals and birds in re-creations of their natural surroundings. There are also trophies and pictures of hunting scenes. The angling section illustrates the development of fishing tackle, and shows numerous specimens of fish.

❻ Frauenkirche
See pp64–5.

❼ Neues Rathaus
New Town Hall

Marienplatz 8. **Map** 3 B2 (6 D3). **Tel** 23 300. Ⓢ or Ⓤ Marienplatz. 🚋 🔳 Viewing tower: **Open** Nov–Apr: 10am–5pm Mon–Fri; May–Oct: 10am–7pm daily. Clock chimes: Nov–end Feb: 11am & noon; Mar–Oct: 11am, noon & 5pm.

In the second half of the 19th century, the civic authorities decided to build new headquarters for themselves. The chosen site was the north side of Marienplatz and 24 houses were demolished to clear a large plot of land. Construction lasted from 1867 to 1909. This monumental building with its six courtyards is a prime example of German pseudo-historical architecture, in this case mock-Netherlands Gothic. The decoration of the façade abounds in sculptures alluding to Bavaria's legends and history, images of local saints and many allegorical figures. The steeple is topped by a bronze figure of the Münchner Kindl (Munich Child), the symbol of the Bavarian capital. The clock in the tower is the fourth-largest chiming clock in Europe. Every day a concert is played on its 43 bells, with coloured copper figures dancing to its rhythms. The figures dance in two scenes: a knightly tournament of honour of the wedding of Duke Wilhelm V and Renata of Lotharingia, and the Schäfflertanz, or Dance of the Coopers *(see pp36–7)*, which is performed in the streets of Munich to this day to commemorate the passing of an epidemic of the plague in 1515–17. In the evening, in the bays of the tower's seventh storey, appear the figures of a night-watchman blowing on his horn and the Angel of Peace blessing the Münchner Kindl. The spectacular viewing tower commands a fine view of the city.

The Neues Rathaus, a highly ornamented 19th-century public building

⑥ Frauenkirche

The Frauenkirche, the largest Gothic building in southern Germany, was built in just 20 years from 1468–88, a record time for the period. It stands on the site of an earlier Romanesque parish church. The imposing triple-naved brick building was begun by Jörg von Halspach, and was continued after his death by Lucas Rottaler. The domes that crown the west towers, rising to a height of almost 100 m (330 ft), were not completed until 1525. Since 1821, the Frauenkirche has been the seat of the archbishopric of Munich and Freising.

View of the Church
With its twin towers, the church's distinctive silhouette is Munich's oldest and best-known symbol. By law, no new building that may obscure the view of the church is allowed.

★ Emperor's Tomb
A Mannerist canopy of black marble covers the tomb of Emperor Ludwig IV of Bavaria. The sarcophagus is surrounded by the figures of four kneeling knights, personifications of War and Peace, and putti.

KEY

① **The onion domes** crowning the towers are typical of the Renaissance.

② **The façade** has a rather severe aspect. The towers have blind windows at their angles and are pierced by arched doors and windows that echo the shape of the central portal.

Entrance

Chorhauptkapelle
This painting by Jan Polack (c.1510), in the main chapel of the choir, shows the Virgin protecting members of the patrician Sänftl family.

VISITORS' CHECKLIST

Practical Information
Frauenplatz 1.
Map 3 B2 (5 C3).
Open May–Sep: 7:30am–8:30pm daily; Oct–Apr: 7:30am–8pm daily. **Closed** to visitors during services. 🎧 May–Sep: 3pm Tue, Thu & Sun. 🖼

Transport
🄢 or 🅄 Marienplatz. 🚋 19. 🚌 52.

★ Statue of St Christopher
This carved statue, sculpted by Hans Leinberger (c.1525), is an example of the dramatic style of the late Gothic period.

★ Stalls
Like the other figures that decorate the stalls, this bust of St James was made by Erasmus Grasser.

Cathedral Interior
Legend tells that the cathedral's builder wagered with the Devil that no window could be seen from within. From the spot where the Devil made his footprint, only a wall of pillars is seen.

"Memminger Altar"
This altar was built in 1500, incorporating reliefs by Ignaz Günther and a Rococo Madonna.

The Neues Rathaus on Marienplatz, Munich's bustling and historic central square

❽ Marienplatz
St Mary's Square

Map 3 B2 (6 D3). Ⓢ or Ⓤ Marienplatz. 🎄 Dec.

Ever since the city was planned by Heinrich der Löwe, Marienplatz has been Munich's focal point. Until 1807 it was a marketplace. It acquired its present name in 1854, when Munich's citizens asked the Virgin Mary to protect them from a cholera epidemic. For centuries the square was the place where major public events, proclamations, tournaments and executions took place. Today it is the venue for the famous Christkindlmarkt (Christmas Fair), which is held in the days leading up to Christmas.

The square is dominated by the Neues Rathaus (New Town Hall). Crowds of tourists and local people gather in the square every day to watch the mechanical figures on the clock tower perform their concert. The Mariensäule (Column of the Virgin) in the square was erected in 1638 in gratitude for the end of the Swedish invasion.

The golden statue of the Virgin (1593) is by Hubert Gerhard and the four putti around the plinth (1639) are by Ferdinand Murmann. The putti are shown overcoming hunger, war, heresy and pestilence. Another attraction of the square is the 19th-century Fischbrunnen (Fish Fountain), which was rebuilt after being destroyed in World War II.

❾ Peterskirche
St Peter's Church

Rindermarkt 1. **Map** 3 C, D2 (6 D3). Ⓢ or Ⓤ Marienplatz. Church: **Open** 7am–7pm daily (closed Wed pm). Tower: **Open** 9am–7:30pm Mon–Fri, 10am–7:30pm Sat, Sun & public hols (to 5:30pm in winter); short-term closure during certain weather conditions.

St Peter's Church, standing on the highest point of the Old Town, is Munich's earliest public building. Built in the 12th century, the basilica formed part of the monastery from which the city received its name (*Mönchen* meaning "monks"). In 1278–94 it was replaced by a new church in the Gothic style. In the 14th century the twin towers were replaced with a single tower. In the 17th century the church was redecorated in Baroque style, and in the 18th

The Peterskirche, with its famous tower, Munich's oldest church

century was remodelled in the Rococo style. The stuccowork is by Johann Baptist Zimmermann and others. The church's famous tower, known as Alter Peter (Old Peter), has eight clocks, seven bells and a viewing gallery that offers a splendid view over the Old Town. The interior of the church has unusually lavish decoration. The high altar is crowned with a statue of St Peter (1492) by Erasmus Grasser, surrounded by the Church Fathers (1732) by Egid Quirin Asam. The choir contains five figures (1517) by Jan Polack with scenes from the life of St Peter.

Late Gothic side entrance to the Ehemalige Stadtschreiberei

❿ Ehemalige Stadtschreiberei
Former City Writers' Guild

Burgstraße 5. **Map** 3 C2 (6 D3). **Tel** 22 80 74 20. Ⓢ or Ⓤ Marienplatz. Restaurant: **Open** 10am–noon Mon–Sat.

A visit to Munich's oldest surviving town house is the perfect excuse to enjoy a beer and some food in a late Gothic cloistered courtyard. In 1510 the town council bought this pair of houses between Burgstraße and Dienerstraße. The house on Burgstraße, rebuilt in 1551–2, housed the offices of the city writers' guild (Stadtschreiberhaus) from 1552–1612. The house has an interesting façade with a large window in the centre. The perfectly preserved large main doorway conceals the entrance passage. To the right of the façade is a small late

Gothic side entrance framed by a donkey-back arch. The façade, which had been under restoration, was unveiled in 1964, revealing most of the restored Renaissance decoration executed by Hans Mielich in 1552. An attractive addition to the courtyard is a late Gothic tower with a spiral staircase.

⓫ Altes Rathaus
Old Town Hall

Marienplatz 15. **Map** 3 C2 (6 D3). Ⓢ or Ⓤ Marienplatz. **Closed** to visitors. Spielzeugmuseum: **Tel** 29 40 01. **Open** 10am–5:30pm daily.

The original Old Town Hall, dating from 1310, was replaced by a new one in 1464 which is known today as the Altes Rathaus (Old Town Hall). It was built by Jörg von Halspach, who also built the Frauenkirche. The town hall was rebuilt on many occasions, most recently in 1861–4, when it acquired its present Neo-Gothic character. In 1877 and then in 1934 two gateways were cut through in order to accommodate the increasing flow of traffic.

The oldest part of the building is the tower of 1180–1200, part of the original city fortifications. Since 1983 it has housed the **Spielzeugmuseum** (Toy Museum), which as well as antique doll's houses, tin cars and copper soldiers contains a display tracing the history of the Barbie doll.

The Gothic interior of the Altes Rathaus survives. The ceremonial hall occupying the ground floor has wide wooden barrel vaulting, and a wall with a frieze of 96 coats of arms dating from 1478. There are plans to use this hall to exhibit the Moriscos (Moriskentänzer) that Erasmus Grasser carved in 1480. The figures currently on display here are copies of the originals that can be seen in the Münchner Stadtmuseum.

The Pentecost, by Ulrich Loth, in the Heilig-Geist-Kirche

⓬ Heilig-Geist-Kirche
Church of the Holy Spirit

Prälat-Miller-Weg 3. **Map** 3 C2 (6 D3). Ⓢ or Ⓤ Marienplatz. **Open** 8:30am–7pm daily.

The Church of the Holy Spirit is one of Munich's oldest buildings, ranking in importance alongside the Cathedral and the Peterskirche.

It stands on the site of a chapel, a hospital and a pilgrims' hostel. In the mid-13th century a hospital church was built here. This was replaced by a church

Clock on the tower of the Altes Rathaus

in the 14th century. In 1724 the church was decorated in the Baroque style. The fine vaulting and stuccowork are by the Asam brothers. In 1729 a tower was added. Its Neo-Baroque façade dates from 1895, when the hospital next to the church was demolished.

The interior is a fine example of the combination of Gothic and late Baroque elements. The ceiling frescoes depict scenes from the hospital's history. The high altar was made by Nikolaus Stuber and Antonio Matteo in 1728–30 and rebuilt after World War II.

Original elements of the altar include the painting of the Pentecost (1644) by Ulrich Loth and the flanking angels by Johann Georg Greiff. The bronze figures in the vestibule (1608) by Hans Krumpper originally formed part of the tomb of Ferdinand of Bavaria.

⓭ Isartor
Isar Gate

Tal 50. **Map** 3 C3 (6 E4). Ⓢ Isartor. Valentin-Karlstadt-Musäum: **Tel** 22 32 66. **Open** 11am–5:30pm Mon, Tue & Thu, 11am–6pm Fri & Sat, 10am–6pm Sun.

Entry into the city from the southeast is through the Isartor. This gate is the only vestige of the city's original fortifications. The central tower was built in 1337, and in 1429–33 two eight-sided towers, connected by walls, were added. In the 19th century arcades were made in the towers. They were decorated with friezes representing the triumphal procession of Ludwig IV of Bavaria after his victory at the Battle of Ampfing (1322).

The southern tower houses the **Valentin-Karlstadt-Musäum**, a museum dedicated to the actor and comedian Karl Valentin (1882–1948), a master of the absurd who wrote theatre sketches and short films. The collections include many of his scenes, among them *The Vesuvius that Doesn't Smoke Because it is Forbidden in the Museum* and *The Hook on which the Artist Hung his Learned Profession.*

The central fortified tower of Isartor

⓮ Bier- und Okto-
berfestmuseum

Sterneckerstr. 2. **Map** 3 C3. **Tel** 24 23
16 07. Ⓢ or Ⓤ Isartor. 🚋 16, 18.
Open 1–6pm Tue–Sat. 🏷 🅿
ⓦ bier-und-oktoberfestmuseum.de

The building housing the Bier-
und Oktoberfestmuseum was
constructed under the city
expansion scheme, spear-
headed by Ludwig IV of Bavaria,
after the great fire of 1327.

The museum covers both the
history of beer and the Oktoberfest, telling the story of how the
festival is an important part
of Munich's tradition.
Visitors can learn how
beer was first made in
ancient Egypt, as well as
how the beer-making
process developed in
Munich itself. Up until
1870, beer was only
brewed in the city
during the winter
months, as ice from
the lakes was
necessary for the
cooling process. After the invention of refrigerators, beer began
to be brewed all year round,
with a rapid expansion in the
number of breweries in Munich.
At one time there were as many
as 70 breweries in the ancient
city; today just six remain.

There is also a collection of
artifacts from Oktoberfests over
the years, including a vast collection of tankards. The museum
has a restaurant serving beer
and typical Bavarian snacks.

A tankard from the Bier- und
Oktoberfestmuseum

⓯ Viktualienmarkt
Food Market

Between Petersplatz and Frauenstr.
Map 3 C3 (6 D4). Ⓢ or Ⓤ Marienplatz. 🚋 52.

This is Munich's oldest and most
picturesque market. Since the
beginning of the 19th century
food of all kinds has been sold
here – fruit and vegetables, milk,
meat, the finest French wines
and cheeses, fish and shellfish
and exotic delicacies from all
corners of the world, albeit at
fairly high prices. All sorts of
people, from ordinary shoppers

A colourful stall at the popular, lively and historic Viktualienmarkt

to tourists, can be seen here.
Local customs include eating
white sausage (Weißwürste),
sipping hot soup and
drinking beer in a beer
garden around a deco-
rated maypole. The last
day of the carnival is
famed for the masked
dance of the market
women. The fountain,
which was erected
to commemorate
various German
cabaret artists such
as Karl Valentin,
emphasizes the
popular nature of the square.

⓰ Gärtnerplatz

Road map 3 C3 (6 D5). Ⓤ Fraunhoferstr. 🚋 16, 17, 18. 🚌 132. Staatstheater am Gärtnerplatz: **Tel** 21 85 19
60. ⓦ gaertnerplatztheater.de

The hexagonal square lying at
the intersection of Reichenbachstraße, Corneliusstraße
and Klenzestraße is named
after the prominent 19th-
century architect Friedrich von
Gärtner. It is the focal point of
the district known as the Gärt-
nerplatzviertel, built in the

The 19th-century Gärtnerplatz, a green
space in the city

second half of the 19th
century. It was the first large
district of purpose- built apartment blocks in Munich to be
designed in a unified style.

In 1864–5 a theatre was built
on the south side of Gärtnerplatz.
It was designed by Franz Michael
Reiffenstuel and was known
as the **Gärtnerplatztheater**. It
was a slightly less upmarket res-
ponse to the courtly Nationaltheater. Its decorative façade
stands out among the somewhat monotonous architecture
that surrounds it and is considered by many to be the most
beautiful theatre in Munich.

The Gärtnerplatztheater
stages minor operas, operettas
and musicals. Rare works are
often staged, including operas
that have never been performed
in Munich before.

⓱ Ignaz-Günther-
Haus
Ignaz Günther House

St-Jakobs-Platz 15. **Map** 3 B3 (5 C4).
Ⓢ or Ⓤ Marienplatz. Ⓤ Sendlinger
Tor. **Closed** to public (staircase & hall
may sometimes be viewed during
business hours).

Ignaz Günther (1725–75) was
one of Europe's finest Rococo
sculptors. He worked throughout southern Germany, but
primarily in Munich. His work
can be seen in the Peterskirche,
Bürgersaal, Frauenkirche, the
grounds of Schloss Nymphenburg and Schleißheim Palace as
well as the churches and abbeys
of Upper and Lower Bavaria. In
1754 he became court sculptor
to the Wittelsbachs. He moved
into the house on St Jakob's
Platz in 1761.

The Ignaz-Günther-Haus is a very fine example of late Gothic residential architecture. It still has its small courtyard with a central fountain. The reception room on the first floor has an early 16th-century wooden ceiling. The façade on the side of the Oberanger contains a statue of the Virgin carved by Günther and known as the Hausmadonna. This is a copy of the original, which is housed in the Bayerisches Nationalmuseum in Munich.

Simple façade of the Synagogue Ohel Jakob at St. Jakobsplatz

⑱ Münchner Stadtmuseum

Town Museum

St-Jakobs-Platz 1. **Map** 3 B3 (5 C4). **Tel** 23 32 23 70. Ⓢ or Ⓤ Marienplatz. Ⓤ Sendlinger Tor. **Open** 10am–6pm Tue–Sun. 🅿 🆆 **muenchner-stadtmuseum.de**

Six adjoining buildings house the Münchner Stadtmuseum. Two of them, the Marstall (which was rebuilt after World War II), and the Zeughaus, were built in the 15th century as granaries but later became the city's stables and arsenal. During the rebellions of 1848, the citizens of Munich broke into the Zeughaus tower. However, the weapons that they found there had rusted and were useless.

In the second half of the 19th century, the Zeughaus

The house and studio of the renowned sculptor Ignaz Günther

was used as a display space for the museum of local history. At this time a major campaign was under way to collect antique objects from the city's inns and attics, hospitals, orphanages, churches and pawnshops. In addition to the 1,500 objects that were amassed in this way, a huge collection of etchings with a Munich theme, called the Maillinger Collection, was purchased. The Museum of History finally opened in 1888. As the collection grew, four additional wings were added to the original buildings in the following decades. The museum was given its present name – the Münchner Stadtmuseum – in 1954.

The museum consists of various collections of applied arts, photography, graphic art, fashion and urban culture. There are permanent exhibitions of the puppet theater/fairground attractions collection and the music collection, as well as those illustrating the history of Munich. The most valuable and intriguing items in the museum are the ten famous Moriskentänzer (Moriscos), made by Erasmus Grasser in about 1480. These were originally designed for the ceremonial hall of the Old Town.

The daily-changing program at the film museum features comprehensive retrospectives, selected premieres, and theme-related films including both German and international productions.

⑲ Jüdisches Zentrum

Jewish Centre

St-Jakobs-Platz 16. **Map** 3 B3 (5 C4). Ⓢ or Ⓤ Marienplatz. **Tel** 23 39 60 96. **Open** Jewish Museum: 10am–6pm Tue–Sun. 🅿 🆆 **juedischeszentrum jakobsplatz.de** 🆆 **juedisches-museum-muenchen.de**

The Main Synagogue Ohel Jakob, the Jewish Community Centre of Munich and Upper Bavaria, and the Jewish Museum, constitute a prestigious centre for the Jewish community at St Jakobsplatz. Commissioned with the design of the entire complex were the Saarbrücken based architects Wandel, Hoefer and Lorch.

The **Jewish Museum** is housed in a cube-shaped, free standing building. The transparent ground floor lobby, glazed on all sides, emphasizes the museum's role as a place for open discussion. Three floors of exhibitions, plus a library and a learning centre, all offer extensive information on Jewish culture and history and highlight important aspects of contemporary Jewish life.

The Synagogue, also cube-shaped, is crowned by a light-flooded roof. The Community Centre contains the administrative department, the rabbinate, conference rooms, a kindergarden, a public full-time school, a youth and arts centre and a kosher restaurant. It is a popular venue for events. With this combination it reflects the religious, cultural and social demands of contemporary life.

⑳ Asamkirche

The Asamkirche, or Church of St Johann Nepomuk, was built in 1733–46. It was funded, designed and executed by the Asam brothers, the most famous builders and decorators of the time. Drawing on the full effects of Baroque artistic expression, they created a mysterious theatrical illusion of another world. The façade, set upon a plinth that imitates natural stone, gives no hint of the splendour within. The nave, with its low-key lighting, is full of striking architectural details, rich stuccowork and masterpieces of fresco painting.

Count Zech's Epitaph
This fine Rococo epitaph, made by Ignaz Günther in 1758, depicts the Grim Reaper taking away someone's life. It stands in the church vestibule.

Statues above the Doorway
The arch over the doorway depicts St John Nepomuk surrounded by cherubs and two angels symbolizing the Secrecy of the Confession and the Profession of Faith.

Church Interior
The exquisite combination of architecture, painting, light and shadow draws attention away from the proportions of the interior. The nave is 28 m (92 ft) long and just 8.80 m (29 ft) wide, proportions that were dictated by the relatively small ground space available.

Bas-relief on the West Doors
The top left-hand carving on the doors of the west façade depicts St John Nepomuk being thrown into prison.

Entrance

★ Painted Ceiling
The ceiling is covered with accomplished trompe l'oeil paintings executed by Cosmas Damian Asam in 1735. They depict scenes from the life and martyrdom of St John Nepomuk.

Detail of the Gallery
The undulating gallery that encircles the interior divides the walls of the nave and the high altar into two distinct parts.

★ High Altar
The high altar contains a glass sarcophagus in which lies a robed wax figure of a prelate representing St John Nepomuk.

Pulpit
The pulpit is reached directly from the adjacent presbytery to the east. It is surrounded by a relief with scenes from the life of St John the Baptist and symbols of the Evangelists.

Façade of the Asamhaus, lavishly decorated with allegorical scenes

❹ Asamhaus

Asam House

Sendlinger Str. 34. **Map** 3 A3 (5 B4).
Ⓤ Sendlinger Tor. 🚋 16, 17, 18, 27, 28, N16, N27. 🚌 62. **Closed** to visitors.

It would be difficult to find a more unusual artist's home. While Cosmas Damian Asam decided to settle in the suburban Maria Einsiedel Palace, which he renovated, his brother Egid Quirin Asam purchased four adjoining properties on Sendlinger Straße in 1729–33. He converted them into his own residence, with a church and presbytery in addition.

This was the first time that an artist had built his own house next to a church of his own design (there was even an interior window looking from the house towards the high altar).

Egid Quirin Asam added stucco decorations to the medieval façades, depicting Christian and Classical motifs – personifications of the fine arts, poetry and music are watched over by St Joseph, patron saint of craftsmen, who is surrounded by symbols of Faith, Hope and Mercy. A relief depicting Perfection and the initials IHS crowning the entire imagery symbolize the Christian concept of heaven.

On the left the artist gives a vision of the world of Antiquity, whose ideals were adopted by Baroque artists. Thus Pallas Athenae leads a childlike figure into the world of art and science under the aegis of Pegasus, with Apollo watching over

The Asam Brothers

The fresco painter Cosmas Damian Asam (1686–1739) and the sculptor and stuccoist Egid Quirin Asam (1692–1750) were taught by their father, the painter Hans Georg Asam, and studied briefly at the Accademia di San Luca in Rome. Cosmas Damian married twice and had a total of 13 children, while Egid Quirin remained a bachelor. They worked in partnership in Bavaria from 1714 onwards, creating masterpieces of late Baroque art in Weltenburg, Rohr, Osterhofen and Munich. They were adept at

Portrait of Egid Quirin Asam in the Asamkirche presbytery

combining architectural, sculptural and paint effects, creating what was called *theatrum sacrum*. This was based on the interaction of shapes modelled by means of light and shadow.

them all. These visions are complemented by the world of sensations, which are represented by Cupid, satyrs and fauns.

❷ Sendlinger Tor

Sendlinger-Tor-Platz. **Map** 3 A3 (5 A4).
Ⓤ Sendlinger Tor. 🚋 16, 17, 18, 27, 28, N16, N27, N40, N41. 🚌 62.

The southern end of the bustling thoroughfare known as Sendlinger Straße passes through a large Gothic city gate that is overgrown with vines.

The Sendlinger Tor was first mentioned in 1318 and, with the Karlstor and Isartor, this gate is all that remains of the secondary city fortifications that were built in 1285–1347 during the reigns of Ludwig II the Severe and Ludwig IV of Bavaria. An important trade

route to Italy via Innsbruck once passed along here.

The tall gatehouse that formerly stood in the centre of the Sendlinger Tor was demolished in 1808. The octagonal tower which then functioned as a gatehouse dates from the end of the 14th century. In 1906, because of the increasing volume of traffic, the three arches were converted into a single large arch, with pedestrian arches made through the side towers.

Beyond the gate is Sendlinger Tor Platz, a square named after the gate. It is one of Munich's crossroads, with pedestrian subways leading to the metro station. The Sonnenstraße, which continues from here, was the first 19th-century thoroughfare to be built along the course of the old city walls.

The medieval Sendlinger Tor, now overgrown with vines

Its name, meaning "sun street", reflects its bright, open design compared with the narrow, shady passages of the Old Town. Sendlinger-Tor-Platz has a park on the west side with St Matthew's Church rising over it.

㉓ St-Matthäus-Kirche

Church of St Matthew

Nußbaumstraße 1. **Map** 5 A5. **Tel** (089) 54 54 16 80. **U** Sendlinger Tor. 🚋 16, 17, 18, 27, 28. 🚌 62. ✝ 12am Wed, 6:30pm Fri, 8:30am, 10am, 6pm Sun. **Open** 9am–4pm Tue–Fri.
w stmatthaeus.de

The original St-Matthäus-Kirche was built in 1827–33 at the junction of Stachus and Sonnen-straße, and was the earliest Protestant church in Munich. Known as "Stachuskirche" due to its original location, the church was demolished in 1938 by command of the National Socialists, who planned an expansion of the area on a scale of that found in Berlin.

The replacement church was built in 1953–5 to a design by Gustav Gsaenger at the southern end of the Sendlinger-Tor-Platz, between Nußbaum-straße and Lindwurmstraße. The modern, red-brick building is one of two Lutheran episcopal churches of the Protestant church in Bavaria (the other is the Lorenzkirche in Nuremberg).

St-Matthäus-Kirche is graced by a large Steinmeyer organ, which started with 65 registers and four manuals. Since 2014 the organ has gradually been restored and extended to 106 registers. The free-standing 51-m (167-ft) high tower has six bells, two of which hang at the level of the clock, while the other four sit a floor above.

In addition to being the ministry of the regional bishop, St-Matthäus-Kirche offers a wide range of activities, including services for motorcyclists, a healthcare chaplaincy, exhibitions of Munich church history, the "You Dare" children's circus, art installations and performances of church music by the Münchner Motettenchor.

Baroque tombstone set into the façade of the Allerheiligenkirche

㉔ Allerheiligenkirche am Kreuz

All Hallows' Church

Kreuzstr. 10. **Map** 3 A3 (5 B4). **U** Sendlinger Tor, Karlsplatz (Stachus). **Open** 8am–8pm daily.

All Hallows' Church was built in 1478 by Jörg von Halspach, and was the first cemetery church in the parish of St Peter. In the past, four streets converged here, hence the name "am Kreuz" ("at the crossing").

The church's bare brick walls, Gothic vaults and tall steeple make it a prominent landmark in Kreuzstraße. The interior was refurbished during the Baroque era, so that the only vestiges of its Gothic appearance are the web vaulting over the nave, fragments of a fresco of Christ in a mandorla and a crucifix made by Hans Leinberger in 1520.

Fine examples of the transitional style of art that developed between the Mannerist period and led into the Baroque can be seen in the tomb of the banker Gietz (1627) by Hans Krumpper, and in the depiction of the Virgin appearing before St Augustine on the high altar, which was created by Hans Rottenhammer in 1614. Today Allerheiligenkirche is a Uniate (Greek Catholic) church.

㉕ Damenstift St Anna

Church of St Anne

Damenstiftstr. 1. **Map** 3 A2 (5 B3). **U** Karlsplatz (Stachus), Marienplatz. **Open** 8am–8pm daily.

Princess Henrietta of Savoy, founder of the Theatine

Church, brought the Salesian order of sisters to Munich in 1667. During the 18th century the order acquired its own church, which was designed by the Gunetzrhainer brothers. In time the convent passed into the hands of an order of aristocratic ladies, hence the name "Damenstift". Today the building houses a high school for girls. The façade is in the late Baroque style, as is the opulent decoration of the interior, which was executed by the Asam brothers. After suffering total destruction during World War II, the painting inside the church was restored in sepia, as black-and-white photographs were the only existing record of the original decorative scheme. The paintings depict the oath of angels, the Glory of St Mary and St Anne, and the concert of angels (above the gallery). The realistic group of the Last Supper to the right of the high altar is unusually lifelike. The life-sized statues sitting at the table and gesticulating were probably copied from Spanish originals. This single-nave church, with side chapels behind mighty arches and a presbytery at one end, is a typically Baroque attempt to combine the centrally planned church with the elongated model.

The intersecting interior spaces of the Baroque Damenstift St Anna

OLD TOWN (NORTH)

The northern part of the Old Town (Altstadt) was once defined by the fortified city walls. Today it is enclosed by the Altstadtring (ring road). The principal thoroughfares traversing the Old Town are Theatinerstraße and Residenzstraße. West of Theatinerstraße is the old Kreuzviertel district, with Promenadeplatz its hub.

The Old Town has modern shopping streets, and also many fine 17th- and 18th-century palaces and churches – two of them being the Theatinerkirche and Dreifaltigkeitskirche.

To the east lies the former Graggenau district. At the Alter Hof (Old Court), the first seat of the Wittelsbach family, there is a maze of medieval streets and buildings, among which is the Hofbräuhaus, Munich's most renowned brewery. The majestic Residenz overlooks the Hofgarten (Palace Gardens).

Max-Joseph-Platz, a stately square surrounded by fine Neo-Classical buildings, marks the beginning of the grand Maximilianstraße, which is a practical example of 19th-century ideals of integral town planning.

Sights at a Glance

Churches
6 Theatinerkirche (St Kajetan)
7 Salvatorkirche
13 Dreifaltigkeitskirche

Museum
11 Literaturhaus

Garden
23 Hofgarten

Eatery
18 Hofbräuhaus

Theatres
20 Münchner Kammerspiele im Schauspielhaus

Historic Buildings
1 *Residenz (pp78–81)*
3 Eilleshof
4 Palais Preysing
5 Feldherrnhalle
8 Erzbischöfliches Palais
9 Palais Porcia
10 Palais Neuhaus-Preysing
12 Künstlerhaus
15 Palais Toerring-Jettenbach
16 Münzhof
17 Alter Hof
21 Marstall
22 Bayerische Staatskanzlei

Streets and Squares
2 Max-Joseph-Platz
14 Promenadeplatz
19 Maximilianstraße

Restaurants *pp276–8*
1 Austernkeller
2 Bar München
3 Dallmayr
4 Garden Restaurant
5 Kulisse
6 Le Stollberg
7 Matsuhisa Munich
8 Pageou
9 Pfälzer Residenz Weinstube
10 Refettorio
11 Restaurant Pfistermühle
12 Spatenhaus an der Oper
13 Tambosi
14 Tavernetta
15 Trader Vic's
16 Zum Franziskaner

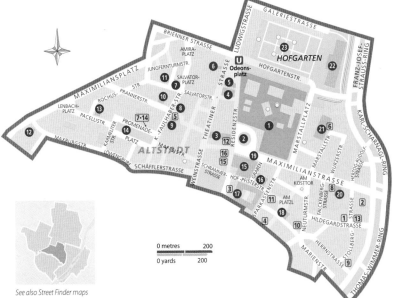

See also Street Finder maps 3, 4, 5 & 6

◀ The famed Hofbräuhaus brewery in Munich city centre

For keys to symbols *see back flap*

Street-by-Street: Around the Residenz

The Residenz is set in the most elegant part of Munich, an area characterized mainly by the Wittelsbach residences, numerous Baroque palaces and the fine silhouettes of the Theatinerkirche and the opera house. The streets leading to the Altstadtring are lined with cafés and shops selling luxury goods. This area is also the centre of Munich's cultural life, with several theatres as well as concert and banqueting halls within the residences themselves.

❼ Salvatorkirche
Until the end of the 18th century this old chapel stood in the middle of the city cemetery. It is now a Uniate church.

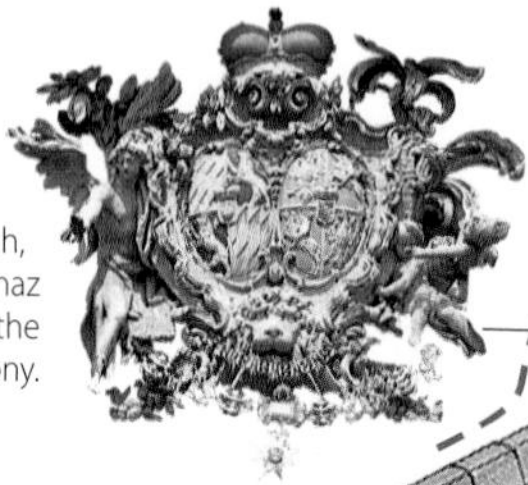

❻ ★ Theatinerkirche
The Baroque coat of arms on the façade of the Theatine Church, designed by Ignaz Günther, features the crests of Bavaria and Saxony.

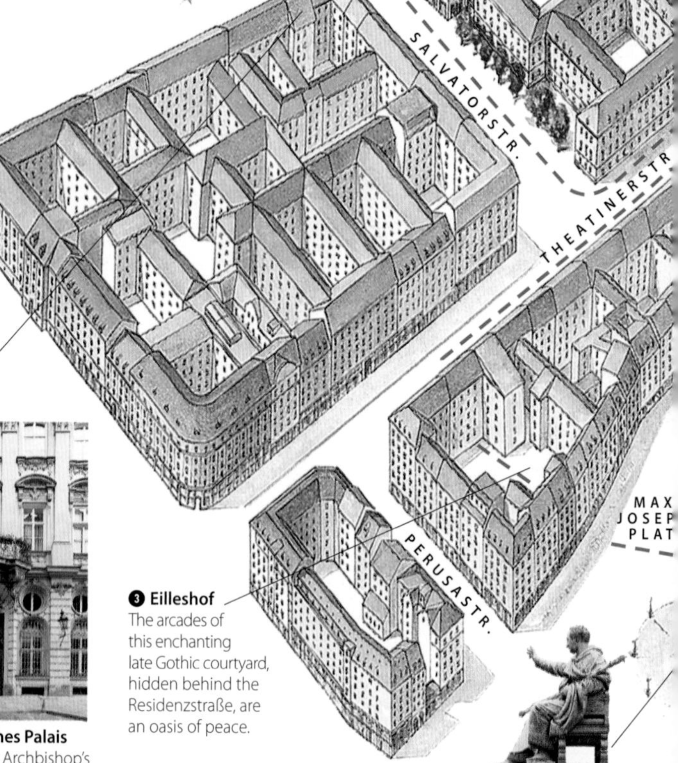

❸ Eilleshof
The arcades of this enchanting late Gothic courtyard, hidden behind the Residenzstraße, are an oasis of peace.

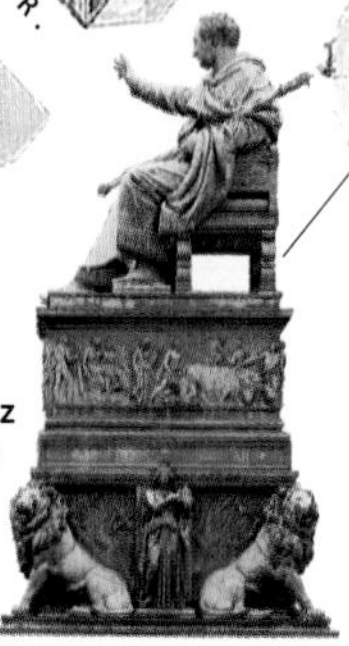

❽ Erzbischöfliches Palais
The façade of the Archbishop's Palace was decorated by the great stuccoist Johann Baptist Zimmermann.

Key

— Suggested route

❷ Max-Joseph-Platz
This monument to Maximilian I Joseph was erected in the square ten years after the king's death. He had opposed it, believing that the pose did not convey sufficient majesty.

MAX JOSEPH PLAT

Alter Hof

⑤ Feldherrnhalle
This hall was built in 1841–44 in honour of Johann Tilly and Karl Philipp von Wrede, the Bavarian field marshals after whom it is named. Their statues stand inside the loggia.

Locator Map
See Street Finder maps 3, 4, 5 & 6

④ Preysing-Palais
This was the first late Baroque palace in Munich to be decorated with Regency elements. It is also the first work of the court architect Joseph Effner.

① ★ Residenz
The wooden carvings that decorate the interior of the Residenz's Cuvilliés-Theater feature allegories of the arts and mythology.

| 0 metres | 50 |
| 0 yards | 50 |

The Nationaltheater doubles as the National Opera. It was famed for operas by Richard Wagner staged here for Ludwig II.

❶ Residenz

The Residenz was the home of the Wittelsbach dynasty up until 1918. The buildings date back to 1385, when the Neuveste was built in the part of Munich enclosed by city walls. In the 16th century the Antiquarium and another wing were added, creating the Grottenhof courtyard. The Kaiserhof was added in the 17th century. After rebuilding in the Baroque and Rococo periods, the ensemble was enclosed by Königsbau and Festsaalbau in the 19th century.

★ Hofkapelle
The Princely Chapel, with intricate ceiling stuccowork, was designed by Hans Krumpper in 1601–3.

Patrona Bavariae
The 17th-century façade is decorated with a bronze statue of St Mary, patron saint of Bavaria, by Hans Krumpper.

Grottenhof
The courtyard contains a grotto decorated with volcanic crystals and colourful seashells, and a gilded bronze sculpture of Mercury.

KEY

① **Kaiserhof**

② **Apothekenhof**

③ **Cuvilliés-Theater** is the Residenz's old theatre. It is one of the finest Rococo theatres in the world.

④ **Brunnenhof**

Nibelungensäle
This mural by Julius Schnorr von Carolsfeld, showing Hagen von Tronje defeating Siegfried, is one of the paintings of the *Nibelungenlied*.

★ Antiquarium
Built in 1569–71, this great hall is the largest Renaissance ceremonial hall north of the Alps, and the oldest surviving part of the Residenz.

②

③

④

Entrance

★ Schatzkammer
The crown and orb of the Bavarian kings were made by Martin Guillaume Biennais in 1806 when Bavaria was recognized as a kingdom and Maximilian I was proclaimed king. However, the coronation itself did not take place.

★ Schatzkammer
This 17th-century ornamental cup is made of rhinoceros horn and gold-plated silver. It can be admired here alongside numerous other works of art.

Exploring the Residenz

A thorough exploration of this unusual palace takes a few days. The first parts to see are the three monumental façades and the many courtyards that are open to the public. The interior of the Residenz is open to the public as the Residenzmuseum. There is separate admission to the Schatzkammer and the Cuvilliés-Theater. Due to on-going restoration, there are always some parts of the museum that are closed to the public.

The Grottenhof, which exudes an air of cool Mannerist elegance

The Courtyards

The courtyard that lies on the side of the Residenzstraße features two Mannerist doorways with figures representing the four cardinal virtues: Justice, Prudence, Fortitude and Temperance.

The south doorway leads into the Kapellenhof (Chapel Yard). It is enclosed by the Residenz's tower, built in 1615. The Grottenhof (Grotto Court) is visible through the gates to the right. This Mannerist courtyard, designed by Friedrich Sustris, encloses the Perseus Fountain.

The north doorway leads to the Kaiserhof, the centre of that part of the Residenz that was built in Maximilian style in the early 17th century. This leads in turn to the monumental Apothekenhof, which is closed on its northern side by the Festsaalbau (Ceremonial Hall Wing) of 1835–42.

Parallel to the Antiquarium is the elongated octagonal Brunnenhof, with the famous Wittelsbach Fountain by Hans Krumpper and Hubert Gerhard (1611–23). It shows Otto I surrounded by personifications of the rivers of Bavaria.

Museums and Rooms

Access to the Residenzmuseum is from Max-Joseph-Platz and through Königsbau, built by Leo von Klenze in 1826–35. Visits start from the vestibule and the two garden halls leading to the Ahnengalerie (Ancestral Gallery) with its lavish stuccowork. and 121 portraits of the Wittelsbachs. After passing François Cuvilliés' porcelain

Tureen from the Silberkammern

cabinet, visitors reach the Grottenhof and the Antiquarium, the oldest part of the Residenz, which was built in 1568–71 for Prince Albrecht V. The first floor once housed a library and a richly decorated reception hall containing classical sculpture. The final room on this floor is the Schwarzer Saal (Black Hall) of 1590, with trompe l'oeil paintings on the ceiling. It in turn leads to the Gelbe Treppe (Yellow Stairs), where there is a statue of Venus Italica by Antonio Canova, and rooms in which European and Oriental porcelain and Persian divans are displayed.

Beyond the bedrooms of Maximilian III Joseph and his wife, designed by Cuvilliés in 1763, is the Allerheiligengang (All Saints Passage). It is decorated with 18 paintings by Carl Rottmann, which were moved here from the Hofgarten arcades in 1966. The Charlottentrakt that leads away from here is named after Princess Karoline Charlotte Auguste von Bayern, daughter of Maximilian I Joseph, who once lived in the Residenz.

Next is the 17th century Trierzimmer (Trier Room). The ceiling was painted by Peter Candid and others and the walls are hung with tapestries dating from 1604–15. The St Georgs-Rittersaal (Knights' Hall) leads to the Reiches Zimmer (Rich Room), built in the 1730s to a design by Cuvilliés, with early Rococo decoration. These rooms also include the Grüne Galerie (Green Gallery), Paradeschlafzimmer (Parade Bedroom) and Spiegelkabinett (Mirrored Cabinet).

Other notable rooms include the Ahnengalerie (Ancestral Gallery) and Porzellankabinett (Porcelain Cabinet), Reiches Zimmer (Rich Room), Päpstliches Zimmer (Pope's Room), the Nibelungensäle and the large collections of European porcelain that are exhibited

The Grüne Galerie, an example of Rococo interiors at their finest

The Reiche Kapelle, a masterpiece of encrusted ornamentation

in the seven Porzellankammern (Porcelain Rooms). Also accessible is the lavishly decorated Hofkapelle, designed by Hans Krumpper in 1601–14. It is adjacent to the Paramentenkammern, a treasury of liturgical objects. The royal staircase leads to the Reliquienkammer, which contains an interesting collection of reliquaries from the different workshops of the Augsburg monasteries.

The Reiche Kapelle is a true masterpiece of religious Mannerist architecture. The private oratory of Maximilian I, it was built in 1607 by Hans Krumpper and sparkles with coloured marble, stuccowork, stone plaques and terracotta reliefs, and scagliola (imitation marble).

The Silberkammern and Hartschiersaal nearby house 3,500 pieces of silver plate from the Wittelsbach Service, made in the 18th and 19th centuries. The Steinzimmer (Stone Rooms) beyond are named after their stone walls.

A visit to the 17th-century part of the Residenz ends in the Vierschimmelsaal (Hall of the Four White Horses) and the Kaisersaal (Imperial Hall), where there is a statue of Tellus Bavarica (1594), which once crowned the circular church in the Hofgarten.

Schatzkammer

In 1565, Albrecht V ordered that the jewels of the Wittelsbachs were not to be sold after his death. This led to the creation of a treasure house. To it Elector Karl Theodor added the contents of the Palatinate treasury from Heidelberg, Düsseldorf and Mannheim. Later, religious works of art confiscated after the secularization of the knightly orders, and the insignia of the newly founded kingdom of Bavaria were added.

Highlights include the royal insignia, the cyborium (covered cup) of Arnulf of Carinthia (c. 890), the

Decorative chain made in 1575

Figure of St George (1597), inlaid with precious stones

Rappoltsteiner Cup (1540), a statue of St George (1597) and royal insignia of 1806.

Cuvilliés-Theater

Europe's finest surviving Rococo theatre, also known as the Altes Residenztheater, was designed in 1751–53 by François Cuvilliés in collaboration with Johann Baptist Straub and Johann Baptist Zimmermann.

The predominantly gold and red wood carvings on the balconies, royal loggia and proscenia still survive. The first performance of Mozart's *Idomeneo* took place here in 1781. Destroyed in World War II, the theatre was rebuilt using the surviving original carvings.

East Asian Collection

The collection of East Asian art comprises of over 500 porcelain objects and some lacquer items. Most of the pieces on display were acquired around 1700 by Elector Maximilian Emanuel.

The earliest porcelain wares in the collection are the blue and white bowls and plates made in China around 1600, during the period of the Ming dynasty. The collection also contains items of Japanese and Chinese Imari porcelain.

Among others, items with mounts of finely chased fire-gilt bronze are of special note. The mounts were commissioned from craftsmen in Paris and were intended to enhance the richness of the objects.

Coin Collection

The Residenz contains the largest coin collection in the world. Its nucleus originated in a collection formed by Albrecht V and Ludwig I. It contains coins and medals dating from all periods and originating from all over the world. Seals, weights and banknotes also form part of the display.

The Neo-Classical Nationaltheater at Max-Joseph-Platz

❷ Max-Joseph-Platz

Map 3 C2 (6 D2). Ⓢ Marienplatz.
Ⓤ Odeonsplatz, Marienplatz.
🚋 19. Nationaltheater: **Tel** 21 85 19
20. **Open** 10am–7pm Mon–Sat
(tickets for performances can also be
obtained). 🔲 guided tours only.

During the 1820s, Karl von
Fischer and Leo von Klenze laid
out a grand square outside the
Residenz, flanking it with the
monumental façades of Neo-
Classical buildings: Königsbau
to the north, the National
Theatre to the east, and the
arcaded Toerring-Jettenbach
Palace to the south. The latter is
now an exclusive residence and
also houses high-end stores.
   In the square is a statue of
Maximilian I Joseph, the first
king of Bavaria, who drew up the
Bavarian constitution, the first in
Germany, in 1818. The statue
was created by Leo von Klenze
and Christian Daniel Rauch.
   The building of the **National
Theatre**, which doubles as
the National Opera, is modelled
on a Greek temple. The interior
also obeys Classical canons.
The large circular auditorium
is decorated predominantly
in purple, gold, ivory and sky
blue. It is surrounded by five-
tiered galleries, with the royal
box in the centre. The National
Theatre became famous for
its performances of Wagnerian
operas. It was here that *Tristan
und Isolde*, *Die Walküre* and
Rheingold were first performed.
Today it is the venue for
opera festivals. Next door is
the Residenztheatre.

❸ Eilleshof

Residenzstr. 13 (also accessible from
the side of Theatinerstr. 40–42).
Map 3 C2 (6 D2). Ⓤ or Ⓢ
Marienplatz. Ⓤ Odeonsplatz. 🚋 19.

Between the Residenzstraße,
Perusastraße and Theatinerstraße
runs a network of narrow
passages that are filled with
small shops and cafés. The
peace in this area is broken
only by the music of
street musicians.
   One of the most impressive
courtyards in this part of the
city is the mid-16th century
Eilleshof, which once formed
part of a monastery. The yard
is surrounded by glazed arched
cloisters with late Gothic
balustrades. It is one of the
last surviving arcaded courtyards in Munich. Nearby is the
award-winning shopping area,
Fünf Höfe (see p144).

❹ Palais Preysing

Residenzstr. 27. **Map** 3 C1 (6 C2).

On an irregular plot
of land between
Theatinerstraße and
Residenzstraße, which
leads to Odeonsplatz,
Count Emanuel Graf
von Preysing built the
first Rococo palace in
Munich. It was
designed by the
court architect
Joseph Effner and
built in 1723–8.
Novel designs were
used for the three

sides of the palace (the fourth
adjoins Feldherrnhalle). For the
first time exuberant mouldings
covered the entire façade,
partially obscuring the architectural divisions of the building.
   The finest example of rich
Baroque design at the palace
is the grand staircase, in the
centre of the north wing. It
is reached today via an internal
passage that was once a hall
and is now lined with elegant
shops. The staircase has
decorative balustrades and is
supported by giant Caryatids,
and the walls are covered with
lavish stuccowork. No succeeding
late Baroque palace has such a
wealth of interior decor.

Palais Preysing, an example of early
Baroque exterior decoration

❺ Feldherrnhalle

Field Marshals' Hall

Odeonsplatz. **Map** 3 C1 (6 C2).
Ⓤ Odeonsplatz. 🚌 100.

On the site of the Schwabinger
Tor, a medieval watchtower,
the architect Friedrich von
Gärtner raised a building that
blends perfectly with the old
and new towns between
which it stands. The aim had
been to create a focal point
that would close off
Ludwigstraße and
give the irregular
Odeonsplatz a
more ordered
appearance. At the
request of Ludwig I
a loggia in honour of
the heroes of Bavaria
was built, modelled on
the famous Loggia dei
Lanzi in Florence.
   The Feldherrnhalle
was completed in

Statue of Count Tilly in the
loggia of the Feldherrnhalle

Hitler and the Feldherrnhalle

On 8 November 1923, Adolf Hitler announced the start of the "people's revolution" in the Bürgerbräukeller and ordered the takeover of the central districts of Munich. The following day, a march of some 2,000 people acting on his orders was stopped by a police cordon outside the Feldherrnhalle in Residenzstraße. Four policemen and 16 of Hitler's supporters were shot.

The marchers were dispersed, and Hitler fled to Uffing am Staffelsee, but was arrested and imprisoned. When Hitler finally came to power in 1933, he turned what became known as the *Hitler-Putsch* ("revolt") into a central element of the Nazi cult.

The accused in the trial against the participants in the *Hitler-Putsch* of 1923

Cuvilliés and his son, who finished the work in 1765. The distinctive form of the church brought considerable variety to Munich's cityscape. The huge domes of the towers are 70 m (230 ft) high. The volutes on the towers are inspired by those of Santa Maria della Salute in Venice.

The Cuvilliés' late Baroque façade is brought forward and broken up by pilasters and scrolled cornices. It also has niches with the figures of Ferdinand and Adelaide, Maximilian and Kajetan, the patron saint of the church. The portico contains a cartouche with coats of arms, including those of Bavaria and Saxony.

The white interior, which contrasts with the black confessionals and pulpit, is decorated with stuccowork, allegorical figures and putti. The main altar is flanked by twisted columns.

The crypt contains the tombs of the dukes and kings of Bavaria, among them the founders of the church and their son Maximilian Emanuel and his wife Therese Kunigunde Sobieska.

1844. It consists of an open hall 20 m (65 ft) high with a triple arcade approached by a stairway in the central span. The statues of lions flanking the stairway were added in 1906. The niches in the arcade contain statues of Count Tilly, a renowned military leader in the Thirty Years' War, and of Count von Wrede, a marshal of the Bavarian Napoleonic era. There is also an allegorical memorial to the Bavarian army of Ferdinand von Miller the Younger, built in 1892.

❻ Theatinerkirche (St Kajetan)

St Cajetan's Church

Theatinerstr. 22. Ⓢ Marienplatz. Ⓤ Odeonsplatz. 🚋 19. **Open** 6:30am–8pm daily.

To celebrate the birth of their long-awaited son in 1662, the Elector Ferdinand Maria and his wife Henriette Adelheid von Savoyen ordered the construction of a church and monastery for the Theatine order. It was designed by Agostino Barelli of Bologna, who wanted it to be the finest and most highly decorated temple.

Work began in 1663. The church was also designed for use as a court chapel. It was based on Sant' Andrea della Valle in Rome. Thus a building of pure Roman Baroque form

rose in Munich. It is a barrel-vaulted cruciform basilica with an apse, a dome over the crossing and arcades opening onto side chapels. From 1675 work was supervised by Enrico Zucalli, who completed the dome, designed the interior and added twin towers which had not formed part of Barelli's original design. Almost 100 years later, the completion of the façade was entrusted to

The Baroque Theatinerkirche, one of Munich's finest buildings

The Salvatorkirche, with the Literaturhaus in the foreground

🕖 Salvatorkirche
Church of the Saviour

Salvatorplatz 17. **Map** 3 B1 (5 C2).
Ⓤ Odeonsplatz. 🚋 19. 🚌 100.
Open 10am–8pm daily.

In the late 15th century, the population of Munich increased greatly, and the existing cemeteries at Frauenkirche and Peterskirche were no longer sufficient. A new cemetery was created near the city walls, and cemetery chapels were built – the Allerheiligenkirche am Kreuz for the parish of St Peter and the Frauenkirche for that of St Mary.

Salvatorkirche was completed in a single year (1493–4). It was built by Lukas Rottaler, who brought the Gothic style to Munich. The combination of brick, stone and terracotta, the intricate fan vaulting and the delicate division of the walls give the church a distinctive elegance. It is complemented by

a slender tower ending in a steeple. Vestiges of late Gothic frescoes can be seen over the north door.

In 1829 Ludwig I donated the church to the Orthodox community. The iconostasis (screen) at the end of the nave is in Romanesque style, and the combination of Gothic architecture with Greek Orthodox furniture creates a unique effect. A plaque on the outer wall commemorates those who lie in the cemetery. They include the painter Hans Mielich, the composer Orlando di Lasso, and the architects François Cuvilliés and Johann Baptist Gunetzrhainer.

🕗 Erzbischöfliches Palais
Archbishops' Palace

Kardinal-Faulhaber-Str. 7. **Map** 3 B1 (6 D2). Ⓢ Ⓤ Marienplatz, Odeonsplatz. 🚋 19. **Closed** to visitors.

This palace, which consists of four wings enclosing a courtyard, was commissioned by the Elector Karl Albrecht and built by François Cuvilliés in 1733–7. It became the seat of the archbishops of Munich and Freising in 1821. It is the only surviving urban palace built by Cuvilliés.

The building is fronted by finely moulded pilasters. The tympanum contains the crest of Count von Holnstein, Karl Albrecht's illegitimate son, the division across the coat of arms indicating his illegitimate status.

A bas-relief over the doorway depicts the Virgin surrounded by cherubs.

The interiors of the palace were completed in about 1735 by Johann Baptist Zimmermann to a design by Cuvilliés. They are among the finest examples of late Baroque decoration in Munich. The courtyard contains a statue of Venus by Johann Baptist Straub.

Monumental sculpture on the façade of the Palais Porcia

🕘 Palais Porcia

Kardinal-Faulhaber Str. 12.
Map 3 B2 (5 C2). Ⓢ Marienplatz.
Ⓤ Marienplatz, Odeonsplatz. 🚋 19.
Closed to visitors.

The Palais Porcia was Munich's first four-winged Italianate Baroque palace. It was built for the Fugger family in 1693–4 by the architect Enrico Zucalli.

The façade is based on that of Bernini's Palazzo Odescalchi in Rome. The rusticated lower storey, which is pierced by a columned doorway, is surmounted by two upper storeys that are divided by pilasters.

In 1733 the Elector Karl Albrecht dedicated the palace to his sweetheart, Princess Porcia. The interior was remodelled in the Rococo style to a design by François Cuvilliés, with the involvement of Johann Baptist Zimmermann. The balustrade of the balcony was replaced by an ornamental grille.

In 1819 the palace was acquired by the Museum

Medallion with the Virgin above the entrance to the Erzbischöfliches Palais

Literary Society, and in 1820 the rear wing was extended by the addition of a ballroom and a concert hall designed by Leo von Klenze.

Over the following century the building was an important centre of musical life in Munich. In 1934 it housed the Bayerische Hypotheken- und Wechselbank. Bombing raids in 1944 unfortunately destroyed the Rococo interior. However, the general design of the vestibule was restored in 1952, and the Rococo statue of Bellony was moved here from the Archbishops' Palace.

❿ Palais Neuhaus-Preysing

Prannerstr. 2. **Map** 2 B1 (5 C2).
Ⓢ Marienplatz. Ⓤ Marienplatz, Odeonsplatz. 🚋 19.
Closed to visitors.

This palace was built in 1737, probably by Karl Albrecht von Lespilliez. A small attic was added during the Neo-Classical period.

The building is currently owned by Hypo Vereinsbank. The interior was completely destroyed during World War II, although the façade somehow survived. The palace was restored and renovated in 1956–8.

A little further along the same street are two fine late Baroque palaces, also probably designed by Lespilliez: the Palais Seinsheim at No. 7, built in 1764, and the Palais Gise at No. 9, built in 1765.

The SiemensForum

The SiemensForum is a showcase that the electronics giant Siemens has built in Munich, and also in Berlin, Zurich, Vienna and Milan. Its purpose is to provide a forum for discussion and information on modern technological advances. As well as organizing congresses, events and exhibitions, the Munich SiemensForum contains a permanent exhibition taken from the Siemens-Museum. The museum was built in 1916 in Berlin to commemorate the 100th anniversary of the birth of Werner von Siemens, the inventor and engineer who founded the company. The museum moved to Munich in 1954.

The history section includes exhibits of the first telegraphic devices, such as the Morse transmitter. The modern section displays modern electronics and microelectronics, which are presented using the latest multimedia technology.

The SiemensForum, an impressive display of modern technology

⓫ Literaturhaus

Salvatorplatz 1. **Tel** 29 19 340. During exhibitions: **Open** 11am–7pm Mon–Fri (to 9:30pm Thu), 10am–6pm Sat–Sun.

Munich's great literary traditions and its influential position in the European publishing market were marked by the opening of the Literaturhaus in 1997.

This monumental building, which blends with the closely aligned façades of town houses and the outline of the Salvatorkirche, dominates Salvatorplatz. Until the beginning of the 20th century this was the site of the city market. In 1887 a large school building designed by Friedrich Löbel was built here, its open ground floor fulfilling the function of a market hall up until 1906.

In 1993 the building, which had been partially destroyed during World War II, underwent renovation and re-opened as the Literaturhaus.

The present building skillfully combines the period style of the lower storeys with a light steel and glass structure for the two upper storeys. These provide a breathtaking view on to the dome of the Theatinerkirche and the city's rooftops.

The Literaturhaus is the home of literary institutions and foundations that organize literary conferences and seminars as well as readings, concerts and receptions.

Part of the ground floor hall is occupied by an interesting display area where temporary exhibitions are held. There is a library on the first floor.

One of the institution's great attractions is the literary café. Its decor includes an impressive installation by the American artist Jenny Holzer devoted to the Bavarian poet and novelist Oskar Maria Graf.

Façade of the Palais Neuhaus-Preysing with its rich Rococo stuccowork

The Künstlerhaus, built in northern German Renaissance style

⑫ Künstlerhaus
Artists' House

Lenbachplatz 8. **Map** 3 A1 (5 B2).
Tel 59 91 840. Ⓢ or Ⓤ Karlsplatz
(Stachus). 🚊 19, 20. 🚌 N40, N41.
Inner Courtyard: **Open** only during
events.

The Künstlerhaus, on the
southern side of Lenbachplatz,
was designed by Gabriel von
Seidl and built in 1892–1900. This
attractive building, with wings
set around an inner courtyard,
is in mock northern German
Renaissance style, which is
characterized by stepped gables
and bronze decoration.

The Munich painter Franz von
Lenbach made a great contribu-
tion to its completion. Having
collected funds, he set to work
on the interior. The rooms are
decorated in Italian Renaissance
and Art Nouveau styles.

Despite wartime destruction,
the vestibule and the Venetian
Room – which today houses a
restaurant – have been preserved.
The Künstlerhaus is now the
headquarters of an art
foundation with the same name.
Small exhibitions, workshops
and concerts are also held here.

⑬ Dreifaltigkeits-kirche
Church of the Holy Trinity

Pacellistr. 6. **Map** 3 B1 (5 B2). Ⓢ &
Ⓤ Karlsplatz (Stachus). 🚊 19.
Open 7am–7pm daily.

In the war of the Spanish
Succession (1700–14) the
townswoman Anna Maria
Lindmayr had a vision in
which the city was consumed
by the flames of war. To ward
off such disaster, the burghers
pledged to build a church.

Work began in 1711, and the
result is an unusually interesting
piece of architecture. The design,
inspired by the Roman architecture of Francesco Morrominiego,
is by Giovanni Antonio Viscardi,
and construction was supervised
by Enrico Zucalli and Johann
Georg Ettenhofer. It was
completed in 1718.

The broken façade is set
with a multitude of columns,
pilasters and cornices, and
windows of different shapes
are set in surprising places.
A niche in the upper storey
contains a statue of St Michael
by Joseph Fichtl. The plan
combines elongated and
centralized schemes.

High altar of the Dreifaltigkeitskirche

The interior is profusely
decorated with stuccowork
and with paintings by Cosmas
Damian Asam. The high altar
(1717) has a painting of the Holy
Trinity, to whom the church is
dedicated, by Andreas Wolff
and Johann Degler. The Rococo
tabernacle of 1760 is by Johann
Baptist Straub.

⑭ Promenadeplatz

Map 3 B2 (5 C2). Ⓤ Marienplatz. 🚊 19.

This elongated rectangular
square, whose origins date back
to the Middle Ages, was once
the site of the salt market, and
storehouses for salt and the
customs house stood here. At
the end of the 18th century, the
buildings were demolished and
the square was planted with
linden trees. Fine palaces and
town houses also rose up all
round the square.

The square, whose present
name dates from 1805, is
decorated with 19th-century
statues of well-known local
and regional figures.

On the northern side is the
Bayerischer Hof, a high-class
hotel, where many famous
people have stayed. In addition
to the main building, in the
Maximilian style, the adjoining
Palais Montgelas also forms part
of the hotel. It was designed for
the king's minister and the
creator of modern
Bavaria by the architect
Emanuel Joseph von
Herigoyen (1811–13).
The decoration is by
Jean-Baptiste Métivier.
The grand interior has
been preserved,
including the Royal
Hall, Montgelas Hall
and Library, all in Empire
style. It was beside the
building on Kardinal-
Faulhaber-Straße that
Kurt Eisner, first president
of the Bavarian Republic,
was shot in 1919.
Situated on the other
side of the square,
at No. 15, is the house
belonging to the
architect Johann Baptist
Gunetzrhainer.

Bayeriches Nationalmuseum). The new arcade-style loggia was painted in ochre, contrasting with the red walls behind. This aristocratic palace, once home to a post office, is now an exclusive residence and also houses high-end stores.

⑯ Münzhof
State Mint

Hofgraben 4. **Map** 3 C2 (6 E3). Ⓢ or Ⓤ Marienplatz. 🚊 19. Courtyard: **Open** 8am–4:15pm Mon–Thu, 8am–2pm Fri.

Two ducal seats in Munich are associated with Albrecht V – the Alter Hof and the mid-14th century Neuveste (now destroyed), which were separated by a stable building. Designed by the architect Bernhard Zwitzel of Augsburg, they were built by Wilhelm Egkl.

The courtyard was surrounded by a three-storey loggia housing the stables and coach-houses. They also contained Albrecht V's library and some of the earliest collections of art in Europe. Despite a marked adherence to the Italian Renaissance, the building shows Albrecht's own interpretation.

When it was rebuilt in the 19th century as the state mint, it was given a Neo-Classical east façade. The north façade, meanwhile, is in the Maximilian style.

The Neo-Renaissance loggia of the Palais Toerring-Jettenbach

⑮ Palais Toerring-Jettenbach

Residenzstr. 2. **Map** 3 C2 (6 D2). Ⓢ or Ⓤ Marienplatz. Ⓤ Odeonsplatz. 🚊 19.

The Baroque palace that originally stood on this site was at odds with ideas of town planning that had inspired the creation of Max-Joseph-Platz, particularly after the Neo-Classical wing of Königsbau and the Opera House were built.

In 1835–8 Ludwig I commissioned Leo von Klenze to rebuild the original palace, extending it and creating a façade based on that of the Ospedale degli Innocenti in Florence. The Baroque doorway was moved inside, as were two of the nine sculptures by Johann Baptist Straub (the remaining seven are in the

⑰ Alter Hof
Old Residence

Burgstr. 8. **Map** 3 C2 (6 D3). Ⓢ or Ⓤ Marienplatz. 🚊 19.

The first fortified residence built for the Wittelsbachs within the walls of Munich was constructed in 1253–5. The purpose was to protect them not only from outside invaders, but also from rebellious citizens. In 1328–47 the Alter Hof was the residence of Emperor Ludwig IV of Bavaria. In the second half of the 14th century construction began on a larger residence, and gradually the seat of power was moved there.

From the 14th century the Alter Hof only housed the duchy's administrative offices. This delightful residence is a rare example of medieval secular architecture. The west wing ends with a gatehouse decorated with the crests of the Wittelsbachs, and it retains its original Gothic character. Another original feature is the distinctive bay window known as the Monkey Tower. According to legend, when Ludwig IV was a baby he was carried off by a monkey from the royal menagerie. The monkey climbed to the top of the tower, and it took a long time for it to be coaxed into returning the child.

Monkey Tower in Alter Hof

Renaissance triple-tier arcades create an orderly sense of space in the Münzhof

The Hofbräuhaus – the best-known address in Munich

⑱ Hofbräuhaus

Platzl 9. **Map** 3 C2 (6 E3). **Tel** 29 01 36 100. Ⓢ Isartor or Ⓤ Marienplatz. 🚋 19. **Open** 9am–11:30pm daily. 🅿

Munich's greatest tourist attraction, and the epitome of the Bavarian lifestyle, is the Hofbräuhaus. An inn, it formed part of the Royal Brewery that was founded by Wilhelm V in 1589. The opening ceremony of the inn in 1830 was attended by Ludwig I. Extended on numerous occasions, the building was given its present Neo-Renaissance exterior in 1896.

The ground floor contains the Schwemme, a large hall with a ceiling painted in 1971. The hall can hold 1,000 drinkers seated at long tables, strains of folk music audible over the talking and laughter.

On the first floor is the vaulted Festsaal, a ceremonial hall seating 1,300, and many smaller side-rooms known as *Trinkstuben*. In summer the beer garden, with chestnut trees and a bubbling fountain, is a popular place. Every day 10,000 litres (17,600 pints) of beer are consumed here.

⑲ Maximilianstraße

Map 3 C2 (6 D, E2). Ⓤ Odeonsplatz. Ⓢ or Ⓤ Marienplatz. 🚋 19.

When he came to power, Maxmilian I Joseph continued the passion for building that had gripped his father Ludwig I. His wish to make his own archi-tectural mark on Munich manifested itself in Maximilianstraße. Built in 1852–5, this was a reaction to the outmoded Neo-Classicism of Ludwig-straße. Maximilianstraße was built to connect the Residenz and the Old Town with the green areas along the banks of the Isar. It is divided into two parts, the showpiece square closed off by the Maximilianeum, and the commercial part within the Old Town. The division is further accentuated by the modern ring road. Today, this luxurious boulevard is one of the world's most exclusive and expensive streets.

Friedrich Bürklein, who designed the thoroughfare, created a novel architectural and decorative scheme that combined English Gothic with Italianesque arcades and depended on new skeleton construction methods. The arcades of the imposing Neo-Gothic buildings contain Munich's luxury shops such as Bulgari, Laroche, Hermès, Armani and the eccentric local men's fashion designer the late Rudolph Moshammer.

The famous Kempinski Vier Jahreszeiten hotel and the Ethnographic Museum are the only buildings not designed by Bürklein.

The opera house, the theatre, the many art galleries, where private views are a social event, and the clientele of the bustling cafés combine to create a thriving urban atmosphere in the area.

⑳ Münchner Kammerspiele im Schauspielhaus

Munich Chamber Theatre

Maximilianstr. 28. **Map** 4 D2 (6 F3). **Tel** 23 39 66 00. Ⓤ Lehel. 🚋 19. Box office: **Open** 10am–6pm Mon–Fri, 10am–1pm Sat.

The Schauspielhaus is one of the few surviving Art Nouveau theatres in Germany. It was built in 1900–01 and adjoins the backs of two buildings in Maximilian style. The architect was Richard Riemerschmid and the modern stage equipment was created by Max Littmann.

The interior is also in Art Nouveau style. The walls of the auditorium are bright red with ornamental outlines. The green ceiling has six stucco beams and imaginative floral strands lit by spotlights in the shape of flower buds. The typical Art Nouveau device of softening lines with floral motifs can be seen everywhere – around the stage and the balconies and on door handles. The deco-rative stage curtain was made in 1971. Equally imaginative and colourful are the foyers on the two floors and the ticket office.

The theatre, which was originally named the Schau-spielhaus (Playhouse), was renowned for the controversial works performed there, such as Frank Wedekind's *The Awakening of Spring*. The theatre's avant-garde traditions continued in the postwar period.

The interior of the Art Nouveau-style Munich Chamber Theatre

The imposing façade of the Bavarian State Chancellery

㉑ Marstall
Royal Stables

Marstallplatz 4. **Map** 3 C1 (6 E2). **Tel** 21 85 19 40. Ⓤ Odeonsplatz. 🚋 19.

Leo von Klenze's first major work on the Residenz was the royal stables, on which he worked from 1817 to 1822. The large hall-like building is based on Renaissance and Baroque palace architecture.

The row of semi-circular windows is topped by medallions depicting horses' heads. Busts of Castor and Pollux, the sons of Zeus who (particularly in the case of Castor) were excellent horsemen, crown the columns at the entrance. The reliefs on the gates depicting the epic battle between the Lapiths and the Centaurs were made by Johann Martin von Wagner in 1821.

Today the Marstall houses the Marstalltheater, which is known for its experimental performances combining theatre with dance and music.

Medallion from the Marstall

㉒ Bayerische Staatskanzlei
Bavarian State Chancellery

Map 4 D1 (6 F1). Ⓤ Odeonsplatz. 🚌 100.

After a dispute between the city council and the government that went on for almost 30 years, the Bavarian State Chancellery

was finally completed in 1992. A design proposed in the 1980s, by which the ruins of the former army museum at the end of the Hofgarten would be linked to a modern architectural complex, seemed too invasive to most of Munich's residents. It interfered with green areas, and the wings of the new building would mean the demolition of the 16th-century garden wall. After protests and litigation brought by the town council, supported by art historians and building conservationists, the government altered the original plans.

㉓ Hofgarten
Palace Garden

North side of the Residenz. **Map** 3 C1 (6 E1). Ⓤ Odeonsplatz. German Theatre Museum: Galeriestr. 4a. **Open** 10am–4pm Tue–Sun.

The Hofgarten is one of the largest Mannerist gardens north of the Alps. It was laid out in front of the north wing of the Residenz in 1613–17. The geometrically designed gardens are divided by two straight main paths that intersect at right angles. At the intersection is the polygonal Hofgartentempel, or Temple of Diana, built by Heinrich Schön in 1615. The figure of Diana crowning the cupola was completed by Hubert Gerhard in 1594 (the present one is a copy). In 1623 Hans Krumpper

remodelled the figure, transforming it into a symbol of Bavaria and adding putti bearing the ducal insignia.

The garden is bounded to the west and north by a gallery built in the reigns of Albrecht V and Maximilian I. The art gallery built in the north of the garden in 1781 was the precursor of the present Alte Pinakothek and Neue Pinakothek. The rooms now house an art gallery and the **German Theatre Museum**, the oldest of its kind in Europe. Its collections illustrate the history of drama in all parts of the world.

The triumphal arch of the entrance gate is Leo von Klenze's first work in Munich. The carvings are by Ludwig Schwanthaler and the frescoes, by Peter von Cornelius, depict the history of the Wittelsbachs and Bavaria. The northern arcades feature landscapes by Richard Seewald of 1962. South of the gardens rises the imposing Festsaalbau, with von Klenze's huge doorway of 1835–42.

The Mannerist Temple of Diana in the centre of the Hofgarten

AROUND THE ISAR

The Isar, the river that flows through Munich, is quite attractive in the stretch between two bridges, the Luitpoldbrücke (Prinzregentenbrücke) and Corneliusbrücke. The Praterinsel and Museumsinsel, two islands linked to the city by several foot-bridges, also contribute to a striking townscape.

The main attractions that draw visitors to this part of Munich are in the area of the Luitpoldbrücke, Maximiliansbrücke and Ludwigsbrücke. On the steep right bank of the Isar are the Maximiliansanlagen, green

areas densely planted with trees and favourite places for walks and cycle rides.

The Maximilianstraße leads to the Maximilianeum, the great parliament building, which appears to be drawn like a theatre curtain across this wide thoroughfare. Everything exudes an air of dignity. Here is the monument to Maximilian II, the Ethnographical Museum and the Upper Bavarian government building. This section of Maximilianstraße is flanked by Lehel, one of Munich's prettiest districts.

Sights at a Glance

Churches
1 Pfarrkirche St Anna
2 Klosterkirche St Anna
10 St-Lukas-Kirche

Museums and Galleries
4 Museum Fünf Kontinente
6 Alpines Museum
8 Villa Stuck
14 *Deutsches Museum*
    see pp98–101

Historic Buildings and Monuments
3 Regierung von Oberbayern
5 Monument to Maximilian II
7 Maximilianeum
9 Friedensengel
12 Müllersches Volksbad
13 Ludwigsbrücke

Other Sights
11 Gasteig

Restaurants *pp277–8*
1 Café Dukatz
2 Crêperie Bernard et Bernard
3 Gandl
4 Goa
5 Käfer-Schänke
6 Königsquelle
7 Nero
8 Wirtshaus in der Au

0 metres 200
0 yards 200

See also Street Finder maps 4 & 6

◀ The impressive Müllersches Volksbad, Munich's first public baths, next to the Isar   **For keys to symbols** *see back flap*

Street-by-Street: Along Maximilianstraße

Maximilian II, with the aid of his court architect Friedrich Bürklein, translated his vision of urban planning into reality in the Maximilianstraße. Designed in what became known as the Maximilian style, it opens out from the Old Town into a kind of forum flanked by monumental buildings. It is completed by a circus with a monument of the king contemplating his creation. The scheme is dominated by the Maximilianeum, the Bavarian parliament building, on the opposite side of the river.

Haus der Kunst

ST-ANNA-STR.

BÜRKLEINSTR.

❸ **Regierung von Oberbayern**
These Neo-Gothic buildings house the government of Upper Bavaria.

ST-ANNA-STR.

PFARRSTR.

Residenz

MAXIMILIANSTR.

❷ ★ **Klosterkirche St Anna**
The niche in the finial of St Anne's church holds a statue of its patron saint.

❺ **Monument to Maximilian II**
This statue, 13 m (42 ft) high, was carved by Ferdinand von Miller, to a design by Kaspar von Zumbusch, in 1875. The king, whose great ambition was to be a professor rather than a monarch, is surrounded by figures symbolizing Peace, Liberty, Justice and Strength.

❹ **Museum Fünf Kontinente**
The rich collection of the Ethnographical Museum illustrates the culture and everyday life of non-European peoples.

STEINSDORF

0 metres		100
0 yards		100

Key

— Suggested route

The Isar, although flanked by embankments, retains its woodland charm.

❶ Pfarrkirche St Anna
The monumental apse of St Anne's Church, built in Neo-Romanesque style, was painted by Rudolf von Seitz in 1892. It shows the Holy Trinity surrounded by St Mary, St Anne and the Apostles.

Locator Map
See Street Finder maps 4 & 6

The Maximiliansbrücke
was built in 1904–6 to a design by Friedrich von Thiersch that incorporates Neo-Romanesque decoration. The figure of Athena expresses the idea of Munich as Athens on the Isar.

❼ ★ Maximilianeum
This tympanum in the façade of the Maximilianeum contains scenes of the foundation of the abbey and the knight house in Ettal by Ludwig IV of Bavaria in 1330.

Friedensengel

MAXIMILIANSBRÜCKE

❻ Alpines Museum
This museum is dedicated to the Alps and mountaineering displays, including equipment from 1900.

Neo-Romanesque doorway of Pfarrkirche St Anna

❶ Pfarrkirche St Anna

Parish Church of St Anne

St-Anna-Platz 5. **Map** 4 D2. Ⓤ Lehel.
🚋 18, 19. **Open** 8am–6pm daily.

A competition for the design of a parish church for the Lehel district was held in 1885. The winner was Gabriel von Seidl. Work began in 1887, continuing until 1892. The design of the church is based on that of the Romanesque imperial cathedrals of the Rhineland, in the great German nationalist style that was prevalent after 1871.

The monumental triple-nave basilica has a square plan, the transept and apse ending in a chapel and the west front having a large tower and a Neo-Romanesque doorway. The interior is decorated with late 18th- to early 19th-century wall paintings. An interesting feature is the hybrid iconography in the figure of Christ on the west front, dating from 1910, in which He is depicted on horse-back holding a bow and an olive branch.

❷ Klosterkirche St Anna

Abbey Church of St Anne

St-Anna-Platz 21. **Map** 4 D2 (6 F2).
Ⓤ Lehel. 🚋 18, 19. **Open** 6am–7pm daily.

In 1725 Lehel, then still a suburb, was settled by an order of Hieronymite monks. A monastery church was built here in 1727–33. Designed by Johann Michael Fischer, it was a real architectural jewel for the city: Munich's first Rococo religious building. The oval interior is lined with scalloped niches that are separated by arches supported on pilasters. The interior decoration was executed by the Asam brothers. The ceiling paintings, which glorify St Anne, were executed by Cosmas Damian Asam and completed in 1730. In 1737 the Asam brothers completed the high altar and most of the side altars, their stuccowork and paintings harmonizing with the fluid forms of the interior. The pulpit and tabernacle, by Johann Baptist Straub, date from around 1756.

After suffering war damage, the interior was restored on the basis of a record of colour photographs.

Cartouche from the Klosterkirche St Anna

❸ Regierung von Oberbayern

Upper Bavaria Government Building

Maximilianstr. 39. **Map** 4 D2 (6 F3).
Ⓢ Isartor. Ⓤ Lehel. 🚋 18, 19.

This monumental building, the seat of the government of Upper Bavaria, is one of the finest examples of the Maximilian style.

The eponymous king, Maximilian II, strove to create a new architectural style, distancing himself from the severe Classicism of his father, Ludwig I. The result was an eclectic mixture of elements drawn from such diverse styles as English Gothic and Moorish architecture.

Solid and imposing, the Regierung von Oberbayern was built in 1856–64 to a design by Friedrich Bürklein. The façade, 170 m (558 ft) long, was conceived as part of the grand new city plan. It is vertically divided into 17 bays of arched windows arranged above an imposing arcade. Its strong horizontal lines and its ornamentation are highly reminiscent of those of English Gothic cathedrals. Indeed, the pseudo-ecclesiastical appearance of the building was designed to underline its civic importance and dignity. This symbolism is further reinforced by the large statue of Justice that crowns the building.

❹ Museum Fünf Kontinente

State Museum of Ethnography

Maximilianstr. 42. **Map** 4 D2 (6 F3).
Tel 21 01 36 100. Ⓢ Isartor. Ⓤ Lehel.
🚋 18, 19. **Open** 9:30am–5:30pm
Tue–Sun. ♿ 🅦 **museum-fuenf-kontinente.de**

The building that was eventually to become the State Museum of Ethnography was built in 1859–65 to a design by Eduard Riedel. It is in the Maximilian style and the façade is set with eight figures personifying the virtues of the Bavarian people: Patriotism, Diligence, Magnanimity, Piety, Loyalty, Justice, Courage and Wisdom.

The building was originally intended to house the collections of the Bavarian National Museum. From 1900 to 1923 it served as the first main building of the Deutsches Museum.

Part of the façade of the Upper Bavaria Government building

Telamones flanking the entrance to the Museum Fünf Kontinente

Since 1926 it has been the home of the State Ethnographic Museum, the second largest in Germany after that in Berlin.

The collection dates from 1782, when curiosities from the collections of Bavarian rulers were displayed in the galleries of the Residenz. The museum collection now consists of some 150,000 pieces relating to the life and culture of non-European peoples. The Far East (China and Japan), South America (Peru) and East and Central Africa are particularly well represented.

Because of the size of the collection, many exhibits are displayed on a rotating basis.

❺ Monument to Maximilian II

Rondo Maximilianstr. **Map** 4 D2. 18, 19.

As you walk along Maximilianstraße you pass a circus that has at its centre a statue of Maximilian II, patron of the arts and industry, and inspirer of the new architectural style to which he gave his name. Maximilian II conceived the urban planning of this part of the city. The monument was erected by the citizens of Munich in homage to their ruler and in honour of the monarchy.

The bronze statue, designed by Kaspar Zumbusch and cast in 1875, stands on a red marble plinth surrounded by personifications of the four royal virtues. Four putti hold the coat of arms of the four tribes of Bavaria: the Franconians, Bavarians, Swabians and Palatines.

❻ Alpines Museum
Museum of the Alps and Mountaineering

Praterinsel 5. **Map** 4 E3. Lehel. 18. **Tel** 21 12 240. **Open** 10am–6pm Tue–Sun.

The museum stands in scenic parkland in the southern part of Praterinsel, one of the islands in the Isar in central Munich. The building that it occupies, dating from the late 19th century, was presented to the German-Austrian Mountaineering Association in 1938.

The museum's exhibits illustrate both the scientific and the aesthetic aspects of the Alps. The displays, with a geological section on Alpine rocks and minerals, relate to their exploration and study, and include many paintings and drawings of Alpine scenery.

The museum also houses the world's largest library of books on Alpine subjects, and has a mountaineering archive. An information centre serves the needs of mountaineers intending to set out on expeditions into the Alps.

A book from 1897, Alpines Museum

❼ Maximilianeum

Max-Planck-Str. 1. **Map** 4 E2. Max-Weber-Platz. 15, 16, 19, 25. 190, 191.

The largest building on Maximilianstraße is, not surprisingly, the monumental Maximilianeum. It was built as a commission from Maximilian II by Friedrich Bürklein in 1857–74 and stands on an elevation on the right bank of the Isar.

The building is the headquarters of a royal fund that gave gifted school students the opportunity to study at university without paying fees. Since 1949 it has also been the seat of the Bavarian parliament (and until 1999 the Bavarian senate).

It took 17 years to complete the Maximilianeum, progress being hampered by the sloping terrain of the river bank. The focal point of the slightly concave façade is the tall, triple-arched projecting entrance, topped by the figure of an angel. Wings, arcaded in their lower storey, extend on either side. The terracotta façade is decorated with busts and statues, while coloured mosaics on a gold background fill the semi-circular blind windows over the upper storey. The interior is decorated with historical and allegorical paintings by Wilhelm and Friedrich von Kaulbach.

The Maximilianeum, seat of the Bavarian parliament

Die Sünde, a portrait of sin by Franz von Stuck, in the Villa Stuck

❽ Villa Stuck

Prinzregentenstr. 60. **Map** 4 F1. **Tel** 45 55 510. Ⓤ Prinzregentenplatz, Max-Weber-Platz. 🚊 16, N16. 🚌 100. **Open** 11am–6pm Tue–Sun 📷 (6–10pm 1st Fri of month free). 🌐 **villastuck.de**

Franz von Stuck (1863–1928), the talented son of a miller from Lower Bavaria, made a giddy career for himself in Munich. He not only achieved great success as a painter, sculptor and graphic artist, but also became a professor at the Academy of Fine Arts, was given an aristocratic title and earned himself the nickname "prince of art".

In 1897–8 Stuck built himself a magnificent home, to which a large studio was added in 1913–14. Both the architectural conception and the interior decoration of the house were his own work. In it, he combined Neo-Classical, Art Nouveau and Symbolist elements, thus underlining his tenet that art and life were connected.

The house contains finely decorated reception rooms which, after the artist's death, were used for meetings by Munich's high society. The walls of the drawing rooms and studios are covered with mosaics and paintings in a Pompeian style. As well as ostentatious furniture, there are examples of Stuck's own sculpture. The museum also has an Art Nouveau display and hosts visiting exhibitions.

❾ Friedensengel
Angel of Peace

Prinzregentenstr. **Map** 4 F1. 🚊 16. 🚌 100.

High on the right bank of the Isar stands the Angel of Peace, a monument raised to mark 25 years of peace after the Franco-Prussian War of 1870–71, in which Germany was victorious.

Commissioned by the city council, the monument was designed by the architect Jacob Möhl in 1891 and built in 1896–9 by Heinrich Düll, Max Heilmeier and Georg Pezold. It stands on the Maximilian Terraces, which are supported by a wall pierced by three niches. The central niche is in the form of a grotto that acts as a backdrop to the fountain. The monument is flanked by a stairway with a decorative balustrade. The plinth, on a tall podium, is in the form of an open hall with caryatids and columns. It contains portraits of the rulers and generals of the Franco-Prussian War.

The monument was modelled on the Erechtheum on the Acropolis in Athens. Inside the hall, gold mosaics depicting the allegories of Peace, War, Victory and Culture cover a pedestal from which rises a Corinthian column 38 m (125 ft) high. The golden figure of the angel, 6 m (19 ft) high and crowning the column,

The Angel of Peace

imitates the Greek statue of Nike Paioniosa on Mount Olympus.

❿ St-Lukas-Kirche
Church of St Lukas

Mariannenplatz. **Map** 4 D3. **Tel** (089) 21 26 860. 🚊 18. Ⓢ Isartor. Ⓤ Lehel. 🕙 10am Sun. **Open** 8am–6pm daily.

St-Lukas-Kirche is located on the banks of the Isar, between Steinsdorfstraße and Mariannenplatz and near the Isartor (*see p67*). Its 64-metre (210-ft) high dome dominates the cityscape at the Isar. The church was built between 1893 and 1896 in historicist style, to a design by Albert Schmidt.

The layout is based on the shape of a Greek cross. Initially the Catholic Bavarian dynasty resisted this building, but the church overcame both the war and the following purifications, and from 1945 was used by the US army.

There is a vast Steinmeyer organ and in the northeast tower there are four bells. Music is important at St-Lukas-Kirche. In addition to traditional Protestant church music, there are concerts, as well as gospel, dance and contemporary music performances, and the church has been awarded a cultural prize by the Evangelical Churches in Germany.

St-Lukas-Kirche, close to the Isar

The Modernist, fortress-like Gasteig Cultural Centre

⓫ Gasteig

Rosenheimer Str. 5. **Map** 4 E4. **Tel** 48 09 80. Ⓢ Rosenheimer Platz. 🚋 16, N16. **Open** 8am–11pm daily. Library: 10am–7pm Mon–Fri, 11am–4pm Sat. ⓦ **gasteig.de**

Gasteig Cultural Centre is one of the largest of its kind in Europe. Built from 1978 to 1985, it covers more than 23,000 sq m (247,300 sq ft) and stands on the site of the Bürgerbräukeller, the beer hall where Hitler survived an attempt on his life when a bomb was planted there in 1939. The beer hall was demolished in the 1970s.

The modern glass, steel and brick building dominates the surrounding area like a fortress. It houses three major institutions: the Volkshochschule (an adult education centre), the municipal library, the Munich Philharmonic Orchestra and the Academy of Music and Theatre Munich.

The semicircular concert hall, with seating for 2,400, is lined with wood to enhance the acoustics. Besides the three other halls – the Carl Orff performance hall, the Small Concert Hall and the Black Box chamber theatre – there are smaller auditoriums, workshops and rooms, which offer huge scope for variety and are a focal point in the cultural life of Munich.

The complex contains a large forum where performances often take place, and where there are shops, restaurants and cafés. The main entrance is graced by a fountain in the shape of an enormous wind instrument.

⓬ Müllersches Volksbad
Müller Baths

Rosenheimer Str. 1. **Map** 4 E3. **Tel** 23 61 50 50. Ⓢ Isartor. 🚋 16, 18. 🚌 132. **Open** 7:30am–11pm daily (to 5pm Mon); sauna: 9am–11pm daily. ♨ ⓦ **swm.de**

Anyone who is keen on swimming or interested in interior design should visit this complex. It was built in 1897–1901 by the engineer Karl Müller to an architectural design by Carl Hocheder. At the time the baths – the first public baths in Munich – were considered to be the finest in Germany.

The men's and women's pools were originally separate. In addition to the many relaxation rooms, showers and baths, there is also a barrel-vaulted men's swimming pool, a domed ladies' swimming pool, a Roman bath and an Art Nouveau café that should not be missed.

The whole building reflects the new concepts of hygiene that were coming into vogue in the late 19th century, together with an interest in Roman bathing traditions. From an architectural point of view, the building is notable for the Neo-Baroque, Art Nouveau and Moorish elements that it incorporates.

The tower of the Müllersches Volksbad

⓭ Ludwigsbrücke

Zweibrückenstr./Rosenheimer Str. **Map** 4 D3 (6 F5). Ⓢ Isartor. Ⓤ Rosenheimer Platz, Isartor. 🚋 16, 18.

The history of Munich began at Ludwigsbrücke in 1158, when Heinrich der Löwe destroyed the toll bridge over the Isar belonging to the Bishop of Freising. Prince Heinrich wished the Salzstraße, the salt route that had existed since Roman times, to cross the Isar near the place where Benedictine monks had established a settlement. He therefore built a new toll bridge, and the settlement became a centre of trade, having trading rights and issuing its own coinage.

The present bridge dates from 1935. It is decorated with figures personifying Industry and River Navigation (these were made in 1892 for the previous bridge) and Art (made in 1979).

Beside the bridge, on Museumsinsel, is the Fountain of Father Rhine, built in 1897–1902 by the sculptor Adolf von Hildebrand. The bronze statue of Father Rhine originally formed part of the fountain that stood outside the theatre in Strasbourg. When it was brought to Munich, it was placed in the centre of a fountain and was surrounded by putti standing on plinths.

⓮ Deutsches Museum

The Deutsches Museum, one of the world's oldest and largest museums of technology and engineering, draws over 1.4 million visitors each year. It was founded in 1903 by Oskar von Miller, an engineer. The collections cover most aspects of technology and the museum is also home to the world's largest library of technology. There are two other branches in Munich – the Verkehrszentrum for urban transport and the Flugwerft Schleißheim on the history of aviation.

Exterior of the Museum
The building combines Neo-Baroque, Neo-Classical and modern elements.

Decorative Arts
This plate with the portrait of a lady from Ludwig I's "Gallery of Beauties" is an example of reproduction techniques applied to porcelain. The ceramics section illustrates the development of faience, stoneware and porcelain.

Second floor

★ Physics
Galileo's workshop features a large collection of the scientific equipment used by the famous astronomer and physicist to establish the basic laws of mechanics.

First floor

★ Pharmaceuticals
Among the exhibits in this section is a model of a human cell magnified 350,000 times and graphically illustrating how it functions.

Main entrance

Museum Guide

The museum's 20,000 exhibits are displayed over six floors. While those on the lower floors include sections on chemistry, physics, and aeronautics, those on the middle floors relate to the decorative arts. The upper floors are devoted to astronomy, computers and microelectronics.

Ground floor

Sixth floor
Fifth floor
Fourth floor

Third floor

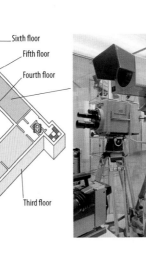

VISITORS' CHECKLIST

Practical Information
Museumsinsel. **Map** 4 D4. **Tel** 2179 333. **Open** 9am–5pm daily; until 2025 some sections may be closed during restoration. 🅿 ♿ 🖥 🚻 🛍 by arrangement (2179 252). **W** **deutsches-museum.de**

Transport
Ⓤ Fraunhoferstr. Ⓢ Isartor. 🚋 16. 🚌 132.

Telecommunications
The Philips camera of 1967 was one of the first colour television cameras in the world.

★ **Musical Instruments**
The keyboard instruments room contains the earliest southern German organ and a 17th-century highly decorated harpsichord.

Key to Floorplan

☐ Design and Technology
☐ Centre for New Technology
☐ Kids' Kingdom
☐ Physics, Chemistry and Pharmaceuticals
☐ Musical Instruments
☐ Decorative Arts
☐ Time, Weights and Measures
☐ Automation, Microelectronics and Telecommunications
☐ Astronomy
☐ Agriculture and Geodesy
☐ Aviation
☐ Miscellaneous

Kinderreich, "Kids' Kingdom", is an area where children aged 3–8 can learn about science and technology in a fun and imaginative way. There are many exciting exhibits, including a giant guitar, a fire engine and an electric light cinema. It lives up to its name because adults can only enter with a child's permission.

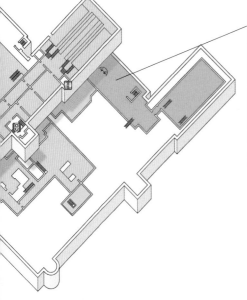

Exploring the Deutsches Museum

To view all the exhibits on every floor in detail would take a whole month since the entire route through the museum is 17 km (10.5 miles) long. With more than 50 sections on offer, it is best to concentrate on just a few areas. The attractive way in which the exhibits are laid out is very effective, and there are plenty of items that visitors can operate themselves, so this is a museum that children will enjoy too. There are also regular demonstrations of working machinery and film shows.

Design and Technology

The museum contains displays of such classic aspects of engineering as machine-building, mining, metallurgy, and hydraulic and civil engineering. The display of machines and turbines features many pro-totypes and the first diesel engine. The demonstrations of high-voltage currents and artificial lightning are particularly impressive, as is the re-creation of a mine.

Figures of miners at work in a re-created coal mine from c.1925

Physics, Chemistry and Pharmaceuticals

The physics and chemistry section is outstanding. There are fascinating reconstructions of the laboratories of great scientists and also a collection of the original instruments used in some of the greatest scientific discoveries, as well as many pieces of prototype apparatus.

The exhibits are complemented by interesting demonstrations of the latest technology in optics, nuclear physics and chemistry. In the pharmaceuticals section the exhibits graphically illustrate the different biochemical processes that take place in the human body.

Musical Instruments

This section is displayed in chronological order, with over 1,800 instruments on display. The centrepiece of the keyboard instruments section is the earliest harpsichord, which was made in 1561.

On the first floor are wind, stringed and percussion instruments. There are also music machines and modern electronic keyboards located on the second floor, displayed in a walk-in storage area. Regular tours take place, as well as concerts on specific musical themes.

Decorative Arts

The decorative arts are illustrated by a number of thematic displays. The section opens with glass and ceramics manufacturing techniques from the earliest times to the present.

There is an exhibition of paper manufacturing and printing technology, including an impressive display of industrial textile machinery.

The exhibition of the development of film and photography begins with Daguerre's original equipment from 1839 and ends with digital technology.

The display of technical toys goes all the way from simple building blocks to the most sophisticated modern modelling kits. On the same floor is a realistic re-creation of Altamira Cave, in Spain, with its Stone Age paintings.

A quadrant (an instrument for measuring azimuths) made in 1760

Time, Weights and Measures

A fine display of clocks and watches illustrates the problems of measuring time. The clocks begin with the simplest forms, such as sundials and sand-clocks, and progress to highly intricate and lavishly decorated mechanical clocks. There are also gigantic clock-tower mechanisms and elaborately ornamented grandfather clocks from various periods, as well as more modern clocks and watches.

The weights and measures section illustrates the unification of measurements, and shows various types of measuring equipment.

An Augsburg clock with the figure of a dancing bear, 1580–90

Astronomy

With over 180 exhibits, the astronomy section explores such major and still incompletely understood questions as the structure of the universe and the nature of solar energy. It also charts the development of this field of human enquiry with a variety of measuring instruments and models of spaceships, and with models of solar systems and galaxies. It also addresses the problems of radiation and the enigma of black holes. In the observatory visitors can view the stars through giant telescopes.

A highly ornamental brass calculating machine from 1735

Automation, Microelectronics and Telecommunications

The purpose of this section is to illustrate the genesis and development of modern technology. It opens with the first calculating machines, developed by Blaise Pascal (1642), Gottfried Wilhelm Leibniz (1700) and Anton Braun (1735), and the first computer, the earliest built by Konrad Zuse in 1941. There is also an interesting display of the latest information technology.

The development of microelectronics is illustrated with models of the simplest diodes, transistors, resistors, condensers and semiconductors. The importance of crystals in semiconductors and other aspects of modern electronics is also illustrated.

For non-specialists, the use of high-tech applications in everyday life is of particular interest. Broadcasting and the disseminating of information, by means of radio, television, fibre optics and computers, also have important displays.

The Zeiss Planetarium

One of the world's best-equipped planetariums occupies the sixth floor of the museum. An artificial sky is created by a Zeiss computer-controlled projector. The dome, 15 m (49 ft) across, is used for the projection of images of the sun, the moon and the planets, along with 8,900 stars and 25 constellations and nebulae. You can watch the movements of heavenly bodies as they change position through the year and view them from different points on the earth, and listen to detailed explanations of the universe. It is a treat to experience a clear, starry sky. Presentations available vary and tickets for the Zeiss Planetarium are sold separately.

Agriculture and Geodesy

This section illustrates the development of farming equipment from the simplest tools to ploughs and modern farm machinery. The geodesic displays show methods of measuring the earth and the development of topography, from early surveying equipment and maps and globes to modern satellite surveying.

Centre for New Technology

The Centre is a platform from which technological experts can share their knowledge with a wider public on subjects as diverse as research on climate change to biomedical discoveries and inventions. The Centre hosts permanent exhibitions as well as temporary presentations. An exhibition on permanent display is Nanotechnology and Biotechnology. This exhibition examines the ultra-miniscule side of our world, looking at genome research and cancer treatments amongst other subjects. There is also a small exhibition on Robotics, which illustrates the development and potential of modern robots.

The Centre for New Technology also contains three laboratories. At the interactive DNA visitors' laboratory you can take part in modern research and even examine your own genetic matter.

Due to the nature of the technological world, the exhibits here are ever-changing, aiming to provide an up-to-date resource on the very latest discoveries.

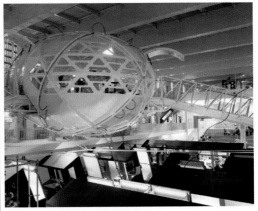

A laboratory pod in the Centre for New Technology

THE UNIVERSITY DISTRICT

The area to the north of the Old Town is a varied district in terms both of its architecture and its atmosphere. Ludwigstraße is lined exclusively with elegant Neo-Classical buildings, most of them government offices and public buildings, including the Bavarian State Library and the university.

However, west and north of Ludwigstraße the atmosphere changes completely. The buildings here span a variety of styles from the 19th and 20th centuries. The area abounds in trendy boutiques, bookshops and pubs, and it is filled with crowds of young

students. Full of history and local colour, this area, known as Schwabing, is fascinating. Leopoldstraße, its bustling main boulevard, comes as a great contrast to Ludwigstraße.

To the east of Schwabing is the Englischer Garten, with the museums of Prinzregentenstraße on its southern side. The park is a welcome oasis to the weary tourist and to those seeking a moment's peace. Here you can rest among abundant greenery, soak up some sunshine, cool off in the water or enjoy a cold beer in the beergarden at the Chinese Tower.

Sights at a Glance

Churches
5 Ludwigskirche

Museums and Galleries
11 Archäologische Staatssammlung
12 Sammlung Schack
13 Bayerisches Nationalmuseum pp112–13
14 Haus der Kunst

Historic Buildings
4 Bayerische Staatsbibliothek
6 Ludwig-Maximilians-Universität
7 Siegestor
8 Akademie der Bildenden Künste
9 Pacelli-Palais
10 Jugendstilhaus in der Ainmillerstraße

Streets and Squares
1 Wittelsbacherplatz
2 Odeonsplatz
3 Ludwigstraße

☐ **Restaurants** p278
1 Alter Simpl
2 Atzinger
3 Bei Mario
4 Café Puck
5 Reitschul

0 metres 400
0 yards 400

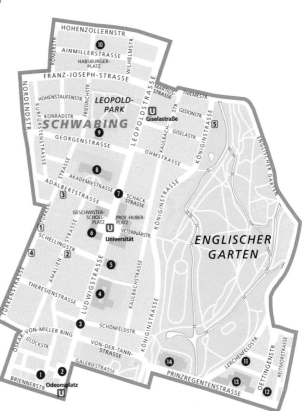

See also Street Finder maps 2, 3, 4 & 6

◀ Magnificent frescoes adorn the interior of Ludwigskirche

For keys to symbols *see back flap*

Street-by-Street: Along Ludwigstraße

Sightseeing in this part of the city is fascinating for some but can be less appealing for others. The district's monumental Neo-Classical architecture was designed to a unified urban plan. There are no shops or pubs. Instead the Ludwigstraße is lined with palaces whose façades are reminiscent of Italian Romanesque or Renaissance architecture, and the long avenue is punctuated by large squares. It is hard to imagine that the bustling and culturally varied Schwabing district is just next door.

⑥ Ludwig-Maximilians-Universität
The university building, looking onto Amalienstraße, has an eclectic façade with an arcaded lower storey.

❶ ★ Wittelsbacherplatz
The Palais Ludwig Ferdinand on Wittelsbacherplatz was built by Leo von Klenze and was his residence for 25 years. Today, it serves as the headquarters of Siemens AG.

The Monument to Maximilian I
by the Danish sculptor Bertel Thorvaldsen is based on the style of equestrian statues of the Italian Renaissance.

❷ Odeonsplatz
The focal point is the Feldherrnhalle on the south side.

❸ Ludwigstraße
This stretch of the street is flanked by monochrome façades in Italian Renaissance style.

For hotels and restaurants in this region see pp266–7 and pp276–9

Schwabing

The 19th-century architecture between Ludwigstraße and the Englischer Garten is as varied as the colourful Schwabing district.

ADALBERTSTR.

LUDWIGSTR.

VETERINÄRSTR.

UNIVERSITY DISTRICT

Locator Map
See Street Finder maps 2, 3, 4 & 6

❼ **Siegestor**
This triumphal arch is decorated with bas-reliefs depicting scenes of battles fought by the Bavarian army. The reliefs, by Johann Martin von Wagner, show the Bavarian troops dressed in the uniforms of Classical antiquity.

❺ ★ **Ludwigskirche**
St Ludwig's Church was built in the Italian Romanesque style. The façade, with its triple-arched entrance, is watched over by figures of Christ and the four Evangelists by Ludwig Schwanthaler.

Key

— Suggested route

❹ **Bayerische Staatsbibliothek**
A long flight of steps leads to the entrance of the Bavarian State Library. The balustrade is decorated with statues of Thucydides, Homer, Aristotle and Hippocrates by Ludwig Schwanthaler.

0 metres		100
0 yards		100

The Palladian façade of Arco-Zinneberg Palace on Wittelsbacherplatz

❶ Wittelsbacherplatz

Map 3 C1 (6 D1). **U** Odeonsplatz.
🚌 100.

This square is situated on Briennerstraße, one of the city's most elegant streets, which leads off from Odeonsplatz. Wittels-bacherplatz was laid out in the 1820s to a design by Leo von Klenze, and is one of Munich's finest squares. It is lined on three sides by Neo-Classical palaces, and the square itself is laid with paving slabs and stones arranged to form various patterns.

Von Klenze lived in the Ludwig-Ferdinand Palais on the north side of the square. From 1878 the palace belonged to Duke Ludwig Ferdinand, after whom it was named. It is now owned by the Siemens corporation.

On the west side of the square is Arco-Zinneberg Palace, also designed by Leo von Klenze, which today houses upmarket shops. To the east is the Odeon and the Palais Méjean, which was rebuilt after being destroyed in World War II.

In the centre of the square stands a monument to the Elector Maximilian I. It was designed by the prominent Danish Neo-Classical sculptor Bertel Thorvaldsen and was unveiled in 1839.

❷ Odeonsplatz

Map 3 C1 (6 D1). **U** Odeonsplatz.
🚌 100.

In the early 19th century, when the Schwabinger Tor was demolished, a decision was made to impose order on the haphazard arrangement of buildings to the north of the Residenz and the Theatinerkirche. In 1817 Maximilian I Joseph approved Leo von Klenze's plan for the Odeons-platz, unaware that its originator was in fact his son, Ludwig I. The heir to the throne wished to create a magnificent square marking the start of the main thoroughfare to the northern districts and also acting as a triumphal entry point into Munich.

The Odeonsplatz takes its name from the Odeon, a concert hall built by Leo von Klenze in 1826–8 as a counterpart to the Leuchtenbergpalais of 1816–21. Set back from the square, both buildings serve to elongate it.

The equestrian statue of Ludwig I flanked by personifications of Religion, Art, Poetry and Industry in the centre of the square was created by Max Widmann in 1862. It faces the side of the square containing the Market Hall of

Monument to Ludwig I
on Odeonsplatz

❸ Ludwigstraße

Map 2 D5, 2 E5. **U** Odeonsplatz, Universität. 🚌 100, 154.

One of the most splendid city streets in Europe is Ludwigstraße. It was built from 1815 to 1852, the general plan and the first group of buildings being designed and completed by Leo von Klenze. The street begins at Odeonsplatz, whose Italian Renaissance-style palaces harmonize perfectly with the buildings at the beginning of Ludwigstraße. In 1827 the project was taken over by Friedrich von Gärtner, who was responsible for the buildings north of Theresienstraße, which he gave Romanesque and Byzantine elements.

The principal buildings on this part of the street are the Bavarian State Library, Ludwigskirche and university buildings. In the mid-19th century, the Feldherrnhalle and Siegestor were added, at the south and north ends of the street respectively. In building this triumphal route, Ludwig I departed from the city's planning rules to satisfy his aesthetic and political ideals.

1825–6 and the arch leading to the palace court. On the side of the Old Town, the square is bounded by the Feldherrnhalle.

The Odeon concert hall before it was destroyed in 1944

The fountain in the centre of Professor-Huber-Platz at Ludwig-Maximilians-Universität

❹ Bayerische Staatsbibliothek

Bavarian State Library

Ludwigstr. 16. **Map** 2 E5. **Tel** 28 63 82 322. Ⓤ Odeonsplatz, Universität. 🚌 100. **Open** 8am–midnight Mon–Sun. ♿ phone in advance.
🅦 bsb-muenchen.de

The Bayerische Staatsbibliothek, Germany's second largest library after the German national library in Leipzig, has its origins in the collections of books that were amassed by Duke Albrecht V and Wilhelm V in the 16th century. It was enhanced from 1663, when the Elector Friedrich Maria ordered that one copy of every new book published in Bavaria or published by a Bavarian abroad should be kept in the library. An enormous addition to the royal collection of books – particularly of early editions – was made when the Jesuit order was disbanded in 1773 and again when the monasteries were dissolved in 1803.

Today the Bayerische Staatsbibliothek contains almost 10 million volumes, including 95,900 manuscripts, 29,000 maps and over 62,000 current periodicals.

The library was the first architectural project started by Friedrich von Gärtner, who started in 1832 and completed it in 1843. The building echoes the style of Italian Renaissance palaces. The great interior staircase is flanked by figures of Classical sages carved by Ludwig Schwanthaler and

overlooked by figures of the library's founders, Albrecht V and Ludwig I.

❺ Ludwigskirche

St Ludwig's Church

Ludwigstr. 20. **Map** 2 E5. Ⓤ Universität. 🚌 154. **Open** 8am–8pm daily (except during services).

Its façade set with pointed twin steeples, St Ludwig's Church is in sharp contrast to the neighbouring Staatsbibliothek. It was built in the Italian Romanesque style by Friedrich von Gärtner in 1829–43. The niches in the façade contain figures of Christ and the four Evangelists. The wings connect the church to the presbytery and to Friedrich von Gärtner's house. The interior is decorated with Italian Renaissance-style paintings by Peter von Cornelius and his pupils. The painting of the Last Judgment is the second largest in the world after Michelangelo's in the Sistine Chapel.

Statue of Hippocrates outside the library

❻ Ludwig-Maximilians-Universität

Ludwig Maximilian University

Geschwister-Scholl-Platz/Professor-Huber-Platz. **Map** 2 E4. **Tel** 21 800. Ⓤ Universität. 🚌 154. **Open** 6:15am–10pm Mon–Fri, 8am–6pm Sat. ♿

This institute of higher education is named in honour of its first sponsors. In 1472 Ludwig der Reiche (the Rich) founded a Jesuit Studium Generale in Ingolstadt. In 1771 it became a university. Maximilian I Joseph moved it to Landshut in 1800 and in 1826 Ludwig I transferred it to Munich. The university has been located on Ludwigstraße since 1840.

Today there are some 52,000 students. The noisy crowds of young people ensure that the streets in the vicinity are always full of life. The university's assembly hall and seminar rooms are set round two quadrangles. The latter are named after Hans and Sophie Scholl and Professor Kurt Huber, who together founded the White Rose movement that opposed Hitler. In 1943 members of the group distributed anti-Nazi leaflets at the university. The group was arrested and most of its members were executed. The event, and the movement, are commemorated with a free exhibition on the ground floor.

The Neo-Romanesque façade of St Ludwig's Church

The monumental Siegestor, crowned by the personification of Bavaria

❼ Siegestor
Victory Gate

Ludwigstr. **Map** 2 E4. Ⓤ Universität. 🚌 154.

Following the early 19th-century fashion for erecting triumphal arches, Friedrich von Gärtner designed the Siegestor for Ludwig I. The monument was built in 1843–50, and with its three grand arches it echoes the architecture of the Feldherrnhalle *(see pp82–3)*. The building stands on Ludwigstraße at the junction with Leopoldstraße, Schwabing's fine main street.

The design of the Siegestor is based on the Arch of Constantine in Rome. It honours the Bavarian army and its role in the country's victory against Napoleon. The arch is covered in bas-reliefs depicting battle scenes, medallions, personifications of the Bavarian provinces, and figures of Victory at the top of the columns. The arch is crowned by the figure of Bavaria riding in a chariot drawn by four lions. The inscription that was added in 1958 states that the arch, which is "dedicated to victory, destroyed during the war", appeals for peace.

Passing through the Siegestor and entering Leopoldstraße,

there is a notable change of atmosphere. The architectural uniformity of Ludwigstraße is replaced by stylistic variety in houses of the late 19th and early 20th centuries. The cafés, restaurants, music shops, bookstores, cinemas and discos here make for a vibrant atmosphere that persists into the small hours. This is the heart of the renowned Schwabing district.

❽ Akademie der Bildenden Künste
Academy of Fine Arts

Akademiestr. 2–4. **Map** 2 E4. **Tel** 38 520. Ⓤ Universität. 🚌 154. ♿ **Closed** to the public.

During the 19th century Munich was one of the most important centres of painting, although it was regarded as being rather conservative.

Munich's artistic community developed around the Academy of Graphic Arts, which was founded in 1808. Many painters who subsequently became famous studied here, including the Germans Wilhelm Leibl and Franz Marc, the German-Swiss Paul Klee, the Russian-born Wassily Kandinsky, and the Italian Giorgio de Chirico.

The Academy of Graphic Arts was originally housed in the Jesuit College of Michaelskirche, moving to its present location in 1886. The architect of the new building was Gottfried Neureuther, who based his design on that of a three-storey Italian palazzo.

The imposing façade is pierced by a series of arched windows and the building is approached by a driveway leading to a grand staircase, with equestrian statues of Castor and Pollux.

❾ Pacelli-Palais

Georgenstr. 8–10. **Map** 2 E3. Ⓤ Universität, Giselastr. **Closed** to the public.

This grand city palace provides an opportunity to compare two distinct architectural styles that were prevalent in Munich around 1900. The right-hand half of the building is in a late historical style, with columns, tympanums, small towers, carved loggias and sculptures. The flat but colourful Neo-Classical decoration on the left-hand half is typical of the Munich Art Nouveau style. It is now a private residence.

Art Nouveau decoration on the Pacelli-Palais

❿ Jugendstilhaus in der Ainmillerstraße
Art Nouveau House

Ainmillerstr. 22. **Map** 2 E2. Ⓤ Giselastr. 🚌 154, N40, N41. 🚃 27, 28, N27. **Closed** to the public.

The house at Ainmillerstraße 22 was the first residential building in Munich to be given an Art Nouveau (Jugendstil) façade. It was designed by Ernst Haiger and Henry Helbig in 1899–1900. The intricate scheme features decorative floral and mock-antique motifs.

Highly ornamental terracotta frieze on a window at the Akademie der Bildenden Künste

Schwabing

At the end of the 19th century Schwabing was well known as a bohemian district inhabited by writers and avant-garde artists. *Simplicissimus*, an anti-authoritarian satirical magazine, and the Elf Scharfrichter cabaret associated with it, were both located here. Many writers' cafés determined the atmosphere of the district. It had its heyday in the years preceding World War I, when the writers Thomas Mann and Frank Wedekind and the artists Wassily Kandinsky and Paul Klee lived here. Paradoxically, after 1918, it became the favourite haunt of Adolf Hitler, who set up the offices of the *Völkischer Beobachter* newspaper here. After 1945, the district strove to revive its former glory with the help of local artists and students.

Art Nouveau window decoration on the house at Leopoldstraße 77 is a fine example of the trend for geometrical Art Nouveau typical of houses in Schwabing.

The suburbs of Munich are seen here in a painting by Wassily Kandinsky. The Russian-born painter lived in Schwabing from 1902 to 1914, becoming a German citizen in 1927.

Artists from Schwabing formed the avant-garde Neue Künstlervereinigung in Munich in the early 1900s. This photograph was taken on the balcony of Kandinsky's house at No. 36 Ainmillerstraße. It shows, from left to right: Maria and Franz Marc; Bernhard Koehler, Kandinsky (seated), Heinrich Campendonk and Thomas von Hartmann. In 1911, a group called Der Blaue Reiter was established in Munich, with Kandinsky at the forefront.

This front door decoration on the Jugendstilhaus in Ainmillerstraße shows Art Nouveau asymmetry and symbolism. It reflects local artistic bohemian culture, in which the legendary Countess Reventlow, who propounded a free, erotic lifestyle, was a leading figure.

Englischer Garten

The Englischer Garten (English Garden) is so named because it is naturalistically laid out, in the manner of English landscaped grounds. One of Europe's largest city parks, it owes its existence to the vision of Sir Benjamin Thompson, an American officer on whom the Elector Karl Theodor bestowed the title Count von Rumford. As Bavaria's Minister of War, he ordered that the swampy terrain around the Isar be developed for military use. It became a municipal park, with many landscaped features designed by Rumford, Reinhold von Werneck and Friedrich Ludwig von Sckell, in 1789. Today the park is a valued green area for residents and tourists alike.

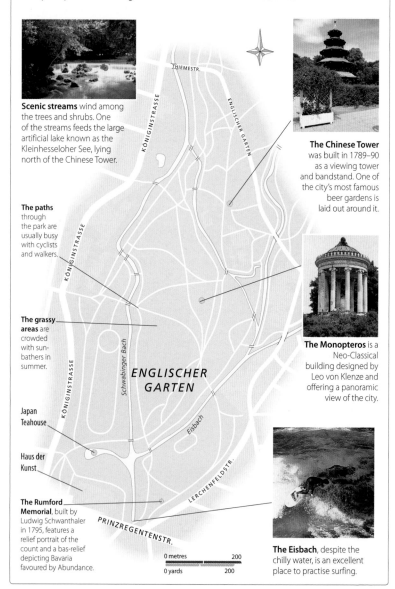

Scenic streams wind among the trees and shrubs. One of the streams feeds the large artificial lake known as the Kleinhesseloher See, lying north of the Chinese Tower.

The Chinese Tower was built in 1789–90 as a viewing tower and bandstand. One of the city's most famous beer gardens is laid out around it.

The paths through the park are usually busy with cyclists and walkers.

The Monopteros is a Neo-Classical building designed by Leo von Klenze and offering a panoramic view of the city.

The grassy areas are crowded with sun-bathers in summer.

Japan Teahouse

Haus der Kunst

The Rumford Memorial, built by Ludwig Schwanthaler in 1795, features a relief portrait of the count and a bas-relief depicting Bavaria favoured by Abundance.

THIEMESTR.

KÖNIGINSTRASSE

ENGLISCHER GARTEN

Schwabinger Bach

Eisbach

LERCHENFELDSTR.

PRINZREGENTENSTR.

0 metres	200
0 yards	200

The Eisbach, despite the chilly water, is an excellent place to practise surfing.

⓫ Archäologische Staatssammlung
Archaeological Museum

Lerchenfeldstr. 2. **Map** 4 E1.
Tel 21 12 402. 🚊 18. 🚌 100.
Closed until 2020. ♿

The Archaeological Museum, at the southern end of the Englischer Garten, is a modern glass and steel construction consisting of six blocks arranged in chequer-board formation. Formerly known as the Museum of Prehistory, it is one of the largest regional museums of archaeology in Germany.

The collections date back to the foundation of the Bavarian Academy of Sciences in 1759. The exhibits, which span a period of time from as early as 100,000 BC to AD 800, are chronologically pre-sented in three separate sections: Prehistoric, Roman and Early Medieval.

Implements and jewellery, coins and religious artifacts illustrate the history of human settle-ment in Bavaria. There is a rich collec-tion of Roman exhibits, including bronze masks from Eining, the Straubing Treasure and many mosaics. A popular but grisly attraction is the mummified body of a 16th-century woman.

A Celtic staff, probably for use in rituals

⓬ Sammlung Schack

Prinzregentenstr. 9. **Map** 4 E1.
Tel 23 80 52 24. 🚌 100. 🚊 18.
Open 10am–6pm Wed–Sun (to 8pm 1st and 3rd Wed in month). 📷
W pinakothek.de

This interesting collection of 19th-century paintings was formed by Friedrich von Schack (1815–94), a wealthy baron from Mecklenburg. As well as an art collector, he was a man of letters, a translator and a traveller. In 1857 Schack bought a palace near the Propyläen, where he housed his art collection. Von Schack's main interest lay in contemporary Munich painters, and he often sponsored

Façade of the Neo-Classical Haus der Kunst

young artists. Under the terms of his will, von Schack's art collect-ion was bequeathed to Emperor Wilhelm II, who then decided to give the collection a home in Munich, commissioning a building especially for it. Designed by Max Littmann and completed in 1910, the Schack-Galerie has a Neo-Classical façade and is similar to the Berlin castle of the collection's founder, who is praised in an inscription on the façade.

In 1939, the Sammlung Schack was merged with the Bavarian State Art Collection. In 17 halls, it presents German painting from the late Romantic period. Among the 270 paintings are works by Moritz von Schwind, including Turnip-counter and King Olch, and Anselm Feuerbach's Portrait of a Roman Woman and Paolo and Francesca. Also of interest are the paintings by Karl Spitzweg, Franz von Lenbach and Hans von Marées.

Façade of the Schack-Galerie, based on von Schack's Berlin castle

⓭ Bayerisches Nationalmuseum
See pp112–13.

⓮ Haus der Kunst
Art House

Prinzregentenstr. 1. **Map** 4 D1. **Tel** 21 12 71 13. 🚌 100. **Open** 10am–8pm daily (until 10pm Thu). **Closed** 24 & 31 Dec. ♿ **W** hausderkunst.de

At the end of World War II, the palatial Haus der Kunst housed a collection of modern art. Built between 1933 and 1937, the Neo-Classical building is the work of architect Paul Ludwig Troost; Adolf Hitler laid the foundation stone and the building became the model for the nascent National Socialist architecture.

The museum, known as the House of German Art under the Nazi regime, opened its doors in July 1937 with a display of propaganda art, proclaimed by the Nazis as "truly German". At the same time "The Exhibition of Degenerate Art", opened in the Hofgarten Arcades, now the German Theatre Museum *(see p89)*. Several of the masterpieces were denigrated and ridiculed by the public during the opening. The "Great German Art Exhibition", housed here, displayed the work of officially approved artists.

In 2002, the National Collection of Modern and Contemporary Arts moved into the Pinakothek der Moderne *(see pp120–21)*. Today, with no permanent collections, the museum show-cases temporary exhibitions of the world's major contemporary artists and photographers.

⓭ Bayerisches Nationalmuseum

In architectural terms, the Bavarian National Museum was intended to embody the idea of a 19th-century artistic shrine. It was built by Gabriel von Seidl in 1894–1900, and features a mixture of styles that expresses the richness and variety of the collections within. The decoration of the interior was devised with the exhibits in mind. The nucleus of the collection is that of the Wittelsbachs, which Maximilian II donated to the country in 1855. One of Germany's largest history museums, its collections span Classical antiquity to the 19th century.

Model of Munich
Commissioned by Albrecht V, this wooden model was made by Jakob Sandtner in 1570.

First floor

Bauernstube (Farmhouse Parlour)
These pieces of traditional furniture were made by Anton Perthaler of Lower Bavaria in the late 18th century.

Ground floor

★ **Judith with the Head of Holofernes**
This alabaster figure was made by Conrad Meit in 1515, with the figure of Judith being depicted as a nude.

Main entrance

★ **Christmas Crib**
This 18th-century Neapolitan crib forms part of the largest and most important collection of its kind in the world.

Basement

Harpsichord
This harpsichord in the Musical Instruments Hall was made in Paris in 1754 by Jean Henri Hemsch.

★ St Mary Magdalene
This statue of the saint borne by angels was made by Tilman Riemenschneider in 1490–92 for an altarpiece.

VISITORS' CHECKLIST

Practical Information
Prinzregentenstr. 3. **Map** 4 E1.
Tel 21 12 42 16. **Open** 10am–
5pm Tue–Wed & Fri–Sun, 10am–
8pm Thu. ⬛ ⬛ 6pm Thu, 11am
Sun, or by arrangement (phone
ahead). ⬛ by arrangement.
🆆 bayerisches-
nationalmuseum.de

Transport
Ⓤ Lehel. ⬛ 100. ⬛ 18.

Museum Guide

The collections are laid out on three floors connected by grand staircases. The basement contains a collection of Christmas cribs and a section devoted to folk art. Painting, sculpture and crafts up to the 18th century are exhibited on the ground floor. The upper floor contains collections of musical instruments, porcelain and Biedermeier art.

Gothic Hall
Laid out like a church, the hall contains religious art and tombstones of around 1500, including paintings by Jan Polack.

Romanesque Sculpture
Sculpture and architectural details dating from the first half of the 13th century and originating from the Wessobrunn Benedictine monastery fill this sculpture hall.

Key to Floorplan

- ⬜ Ethnographic, Pottery and Furniture
- ⬜ Cribs
- ⬜ Gothic
- ⬜ Renaissance
- ⬜ Thematic exhibition, including musical instruments and porcelain
- ⬜ 19th-Century Art and Jugendstil
- ⬜ Baroque and Rococo
- ⬜ Non-exhibition space

THE MUSEUMS DISTRICT

A competition for an architectural design to embellish the area along the Royal Route between the Residenz and Schloss Nymphenburg was announced in 1807. The winning design was jointly produced by Friedrich Ludwig von Sckell and Karl von Fischer, although it was later modified by Leo von Klenze.

The axis of this area, known as the Maxvorstadt, is Briennerstraße. Maximilian I

Joseph and Ludwig I dreamed of turning Munich into a city of the arts, commissioning the Alte Pinakothek and Neue Pinakothek, and grand buildings on Königsplatz. The 19th-century painter Franz von Lenbach had an imposing villa (now an art gallery) built on the square. The omnipresence of art here is underscored by the district's many private galleries, antique shops and bookstores.

Sights at a Glance

Museums and Galleries
3 Staatliche Antikensammlungen
5 Glyptothek
6 Städtische Galerie im Lenbachhaus
7 Paläontologisches Museum
8 *Alte Pinakothek pp122–5*
9 *Neue Pinakothek pp126–9*
10 Museum "Reich der Kristalle"
11 Pinakothek der Moderne
12 Museum Brandhorst
19 Staatliches Museum Ägyptischer Kunst

Historic Buildings
4 Propyläen
13 Palais Pinakothek
16 Justizpalast

Churches
2 Basilika St Bonifaz

Streets and Squares
1 Karolinenplatz
14 Lenbachplatz
15 Karlsplatz

Gardens
17 Alter Botanischer Garten

Other Sights
18 Löwenbräukeller

☐ Restaurants *p278*
1 Königshof
2 Rilano No. 6
3 Schmock

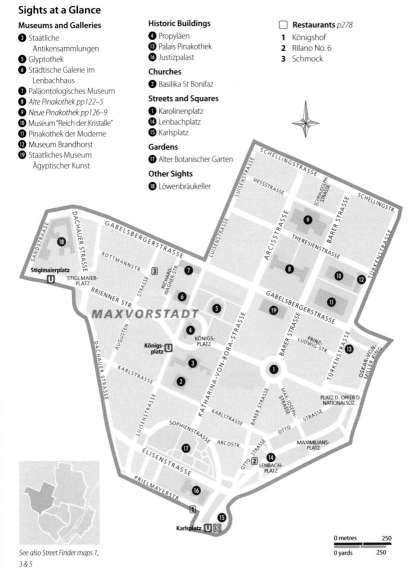

See also Street Finder maps 1, 3 & 5

◀ Classical statuary and mosaics in the Glyptothek

For keys to symbols *see back flap*

Street-by-Street: Around Königsplatz

Several days are needed for a thorough exploration of this part of the city. The many museums here contain world-class art – from prehistoric to modern. On Königsplatz, Greek and Roman sculpture can be seen in the Glyptothek, and Classical and other antiquities in the Antikensammlungen. The Alte Pinakothek, Neue Pinakothek and Pinakothek der Moderne nearby contain some of the richest collections of European painting in the world, while the Lenbachhaus is renowned for works by the Blaue Reiter group. Those interested in natural history will enjoy the Palaeontology Museum.

⑦ Paläontologisches Museum
One of the most impressive exhibits in the museum is the cast of a mammoth skeleton from the early Tertiary period.

⑥ Städtische Galerie im Lenbachhaus
The Lenbachhaus interior sets in its context the bourgeois lifestyle of Franz von Lenbach, the famous late 19th-century portraitist.

④ Propyläen
The frieze decorating the side towers of the Propyläen, with motifs and scenes from the Greek War of Independence, is by Ludwig Schwanthaler.

③ Staatliche Antikensammlungen
Among the museum's treasures is a collection of antique art and artifacts.

② Basilika St Bonifaz
This church contains the tomb of Ludwig I.

⑤ ★ Glyptothek
The Glyptothek's Ionic colonnade with pediment is flanked by statues of great artistic figures from Classical antiquity: Hephaestus, Prometheus, Daedalus, Phidias, Pericles and Emperor Hadrian.

For hotels and restaurants in this region see pp266–7 and pp276–9

❾ ★ Neue Pinakothek
After viewing this modern museum's impressive collection of paintings ranging from 1780 to 1910, visitors can relax on the terrace, with its pools of water.

Locator Map
See Street Finder map 1

❽ ★ Alte Pinakothek
Giovanni Battista Tiepolo's painting *The Adoration of the Magi* is one of the most important 18th-century works of Viennese art.

❶ Karolinenplatz
In the centre of this square, which was named in honour of Karolina, stepmother of Ludwig I, stands a large obelisk commemorating the 30,000 Bavarian soldiers in Napoleon's army who died during his Russian campaign.

Old Town

0 metres	100
0 yards	100

Key

— Suggested route

The Amerika Haus on Karolinenplatz

❶ Karolinenplatz

Map 1 C5, 3 A1. 🚋 27, 28, N27.

Maximilian I Joseph, who continued the development of Munich that was begun by his predecessor Karl Theodor, focused his attention on the area around Briennerstraße. The Royal Route connecting the Residenz with Schloss Nymphenburg was opened up, and it became the focal point of the development of this suburb, which was named Maxvorstadt in the king's honour.

In 1809–12 a square was built at the junction of Briennerstraße and Barer Straße. This square was Karolinenplatz, the first star junction in Munich. Designed by Karl von Fischer, it was modelled on the Place de l'Étoile in Paris. In the centre of the square stands a bronze obelisk 29 m (95 ft) high, designed by Leo von Klenze and cast from Turkish guns captured at the Battle of Navarino in 1827. The obelisk commemorates the 30,000 Bavarian soldiers who died during Napoleon's Russian campaign of 1812.

On the south side of the Karolinenplatz is the Staatssammlung für Anthropologie und Paläoanatomie, the only anthropological collection of its kind in Germany, with a curious assortment of skulls. On the southwestern side is the Amerika Haus, an American cultural centre, which was built in 1955–7.

❷ Basilika St Bonifaz

Basilica of St Boniface

Karlstr. 34. **Map** 3 A1, 5 A1. **Tel** 55 17 10. **Open** 7am–7pm daily. 🚋 27, 28, N27.

The Basilica of St Boniface, which was commissioned by Ludwig I, functioned as the parish church of the Maxvorstadt but was later dedicated to the Benedictine monks who moved to Munich. The church, which takes the form of an early Christian basilica, was built in 1835–48 by Georg Friedrich Ziebland. Behind the portico, which is supported by Ionic columns, are three arched doorways. The central one is flanked by statues of St Peter and St Boniface, and the arch is crowned by a portrait of the architect himself – a rare occurrence – in medieval dress. The location of the church and monastery at the rear of the Kunstausstellungsgebäude (now the Antikensammlung) illustrates contemporary ideas about architecture, in which religion was to be linked with art and science, as represented by the Benedictine order.

The basilica, which was built after the destruction brought by World War II, carries no memory of the original

double-aisled church, which had colourful paintings and an open-beam roof supported on 66 monolithic columns. Of its furnishings, the white marble tomb of Ludwig I survives, with the tombstone of his wife Therese behind it.

❸ Staatliche Antikensammlungen

The National Collection of Antiquities

Königsplatz 1. **Map** 1 B5. **Tel** 28 92 75 02. Ⓤ Königsplatz. 🚋 27, 28, N27. 🚌 100. **Open** 10am–5pm Tue–Sun (to 8pm Wed). ♿ Ⓦ antike-am-koenigsplatz.mwn.de

In 1838 Ludwig I, temporarily at loggerheads with the court architect Leo von Klenze, commissioned Georg Friedrich Ziebland to design the southern side of the Königsplatz. The king wished for an exhibition hall that would adjoin the Benedictine monastery and Basilica of St Boniface at the rear. The building, completed in 1848, was modelled on the design of a late Classical Greek temple, its proportions differing from those of the Glyptothek on the opposite side of the square. Over the large colonnaded portico is a tympanum containing a figure of Bavaria as patroness of art and industry. From 1898 to 1916 the hall housed the gallery of the Munich Secession (Art Nouveau movement), after which it was taken over by the Neue Staatsgalerie. Since 1967 it has housed the National Collection of Antiquities. This impressive collection includes an important assemblage of Greek and Etruscan vases, plus fine pottery and glass, bronze and terracotta figures and jewellery. The core of the collection was donated by Ludwig I, a passionate collector and an ardent admirer of the ancient world.

Greek kylix (drinking vessel), Staatliche Antikensammlung

Central section of the façade of the Basilika St Bonifaz

❹ Propyläen

Map 1 B5. 🆄 Königsplatz.
🚋 27, 28, N27. 🚌 100.

From 1815, Ludwig I and Leo von Klenze planned the layout of the Royal Square, or Königsplatz, west of Karolinenplatz. The latter was laid out as an almost perfect square, with the Glyptothek and what is now the Antikensammlungen facing one another on opposite sides. To the west of the square was a gate built by Leo von Klenze in 1854–62, named the Propyläen.

According to the designs of the king and the architect, the buildings on three sides of the square would each represent one of the orders of architecture. The Propyläen would represent the Doric order, the Glyptothek the Ionic, and the exhibition hall the Corinthian.

The Propyläen was based on the Propylaeum in Athens, which consists of a central entrance way crowned by a grand tympanum and flanked by towers. Munich's Propyläen was intended to function as the western gate into the city, the Neo-Classical equivalent of the medieval Isar Gate.

When, however, the city's development rendered it superfluous, Ludwig I and von Klenze emphasized the Hellenistic character of the Propyläen, turning it into a kind of monument to the Greek War of Liberation against Turkey (1821–9). In so doing they strove to underline the connection between Bavaria and the newly independent Greek state (Otto I Wittelsbach, son of Ludwig I, was its first ruler).

Leo von Klenze (1784–1864)

After Karl Friedrich Schinkel, Leo von Klenze is considered to be the most prominent representative of the Neo-Classical movement in 19th-century German architecture. In the reign of Ludwig I, his constant if fussy patron, von Klenze was responsible for the new face of Munich, designing such buildings as the Alte Pinakothek, the forum of the Königsplatz, the Residenz, the Ruhmeshalle and Ludwigstraße. He was responsible for planning Munich as the new Athens, as well as the Walhalla near Ratisbon, the Befreiungshalle in Kelheim and the New Hermitage in St Petersburg.

Bust of the architect crowned with laurel

❺ Glyptothek

Glyptoteca

Königsplatz 3. **Map** 1 B5. **Tel** 28 92 75 02. 🆄 Königsplatz. 🚋 27, 28, N27. 🚌 100. **Open** 10am–5pm Tue–Sun (to 8pm Thu). 🅿 🌐 **antike-am-koenigsplatz.mwn.de**

The idea of building a museum to house Greek and Roman sculpture originated in 1805, when Ludwig I, the future king, was on his first tour of Italy. In 1816, Leo von Klenze was given the task of designing a museum for his collection. It was named the Glyptothek, from the Greek word *glypte*, meaning "carved stone". It is regarded as von Klenze's finest Neo-Classical work.

The museum's hall contains the world's finest collection of antique sculpture. Prize exhibits include Archaic figures from the Temple of Aphaia on Aegina of 500 BC, the famous Barberini Faun of 220 BC and the Rondanini Alexander of 338 BC.

❻ Städtische Galerie im Lenbachhaus

Lenbachhaus Art Gallery

Luisenstr. 33. **Map** 1 B5. **Tel** 23 33 20 00. 🆄 Königsplatz. 🚌 100. **Open** 10am–8pm Tue, 10am–6pm Wed–Sun. **Closed** 24 Dec. 🅿 🌐 **lenbachhaus.de**

The portraitist Franz von Lenbach (1836–1904) commissioned Gabriel von Seidl to build him a grand residence behind Königsplatz. Completed in 1891, the house and its garden are in the style of an Italian suburban villa, with Renaissance and Baroque elements.

In 1924 the property was bought by the municipality for use as an art gallery. The exhibition area contains galleries of Munich painting from the Gothic to the Art Nouveau periods, the 19th and early 20th centuries being well represented with works by Karl Spitzweg, Wilhelm Leibl and Lovis Corinth. The museum is also renowned for its fine paintings by artists of the Blaue Reiter group, which was active in Munich from 1911 to 1914 (see p219). In 1957 Gabriele Münter, Wassily Kandinsky's partner up to 1914, gave her collection of art from his defining Munich and Murnau period. A building designed by Norman Foster has been added to the gallery. An exhibition hall, which is part of the gallery can be seen at the Kunstbau space under Königsplatz U-Bahn station.

Propyläen, Leo von Klenze's grand city gate in the Neo-Classical style

❼ Paläontologisches Museum
Palaeontology Museum

Richard-Wagner-Str. 10. **Map** 1 B5. **Tel** 21 80 66 30. Ⓤ Königsplatz. 🚌 100. **Open** 8am–4pm Mon–Thu, 8am–2pm Fri, 10am–4pm first Sun of the month. ♿

Since 1950, the Bavarian palaeontological collection has occupied an eclectic building dating from 1899–1902. Built by Leonhard Romeis as a crafts school, there are decorative motifs in the main entranceway. The main hall is an arcade with a glass roof, where skeletons of large animals are exhibited.

The displays are divided into various thematic groups. Skeletons found in Bavaria include a mastodon, woolly rhinoceros and giant tortoise. Fossilized palm trees show the existence of a tropical climate here in prehistoric times.

❽ Alte Pinakothek
See pp122–25.

❾ Neue Pinakothek
See pp126–9.

❿ Museum "Reich der Kristalle"
Mineralogy Museum

Theresienstr. 41 (entrance in Barer Straße). **Map** 1 C5. **Tel** 21 80 43 12. Ⓤ Theresienstr. 🚋 27. 🚌 100. **Open** 1–5pm Tue–Sun. **Closed** 31 Dec & Shrove Tue. 🐾 📷 ♿ 🖿 **mineralogische-staatssammlung.de**

The exhibits here are part of the great collection of the Mineralogische Staatssammlung, which originated with collections of rocks and minerals found in the 18th century. The museum owes its valuable collection to Duke Maximilian von Leuchtenberg, who supervised mineral extraction in Siberia. His collection was added to that of the Bavarian Academy of Sciences in 1858.

The present museum is in a modern building. Visitors can enjoy colourful mineral formations from all over the world.

⓫ Pinakothek der Moderne

The Pinakothek der Moderne opened in 2002 as one of the world's largest museums of modern art. Its vast collection contains works from the 20th and 21st centuries and is intended to complement the nearby Alte Pinakothek and Neue Pinakothek. The museum has outstanding artworks, from Cubism (with works by Pablo Picasso and Georges Braque), the Neue Sachlichkeit and paintings by Giorgio De Chirico and Max Beckmann through to Pop Art, Photorealism and the Junge Wilde movement of the 1980s. The gallery also houses Die Neue Sammlung – The International Design Museum.

★ **Still Life with Geraniums** (1910)
This painting is by Henri Matisse and shows his bold use of colour and lack of detail, which is typical of his style.

★ **The Falling Man** (1915)
This bronze cast of a naked youth by Wilhelm Lehmbruck mirrors the artist's shocked feelings about World War I. It was originally part of a monument entitled *Suffering of Mankind.*

Ground Floor

Proust's Armchair (1978)
Designed by Alessandro Mendini, this piece is one of 60,000 objects that illustrate the history of design.

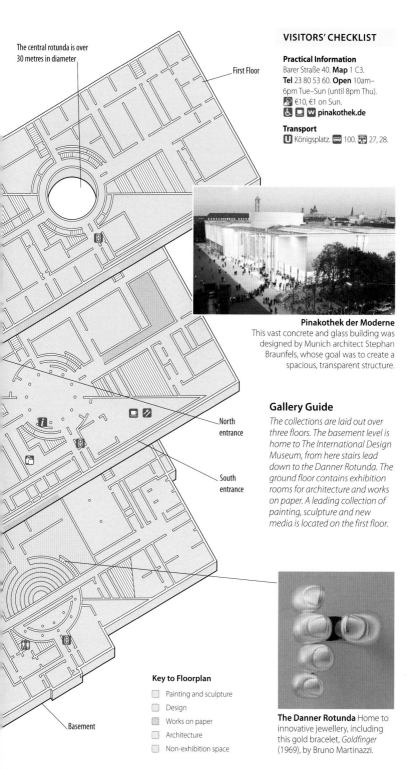

The central rotunda is over 30 metres in diameter

First Floor

North entrance

South entrance

Basement

VISITORS' CHECKLIST

Practical Information
Barer Straße 40. **Map** 1 C3.
Tel 23 80 53 60. **Open** 10am–
6pm Tue–Sun (until 8pm Thu).
€10, €1 on Sun.
pinakothek.de

Transport
Königsplatz. 100. 27, 28.

Pinakothek der Moderne
This vast concrete and glass building was designed by Munich architect Stephan Braunfels, whose goal was to create a spacious, transparent structure.

Gallery Guide

The collections are laid out over three floors. The basement level is home to The International Design Museum, from here stairs lead down to the Danner Rotunda. The ground floor contains exhibition rooms for architecture and works on paper. A leading collection of painting, sculpture and new media is located on the first floor.

Key to Floorplan

- Painting and sculpture
- Design
- Works on paper
- Architecture
- Non-exhibition space

The Danner Rotunda Home to innovative jewellery, including this gold bracelet, *Goldfinger* (1969), by Bruno Martinazzi.

❽ Alte Pinakothek

The Alte Pinakothek, one of the world's most famous art galleries, opened in 1836. It is a building in the Italian Renaissance style, designed by Leo von Klenze. The history of its collections goes back to the Renaissance, when Wilhelm IV the Steadfast (ruled 1508–50) decided to adorn his residence with historic paintings. His successors were equally keen art collectors and, by the 18th century, an outstanding collection of 14th- to 18th-century paintings had been amassed.

St Luke Painting the Madonna (c.1484)
This painting by the Netherlandish artist Rogier van der Weyden is one of his most widely copied works.

★ **The Battle of Issus** (1529)
This famous painting by Albrecht Altdorfer depicts the decisive moment in Alexander the Great's victory over the Persians.

★ **Pietà** (c.1490)
The rich, contrasting colours, strong effects of light and shadow and homogeneous composition of this painting are typical of the later work of Sandro Botticelli.

Portrait of Karl V (1548)
This portrait of the emperor in Augsburg, once attributed to Titian, was in fact painted by Lambert Sustris who worked in his studio.

Ground floor

Main entrance

Key to Floorplan

- 🔲 German painting
- 🔲 Netherlandish painting
- 🔲 Flemish painting
- 🔲 Dutch painting
- 🔲 Italian painting
- 🔲 Spanish painting
- 🔲 French painting
- 🔲 Non-exhibition space
- 🔲 Special exhibition space

Gallery Guide

The collections are laid out on two floors. The ground floor is occupied mainly by Flemish painting from the 16th and 17th centuries. On the first floor are works by German painters as well as Dutch, Netherlandish, Flemish, French, Italian and Spanish paintings.

Peasants Playing Cards
(c.1625–49)
This is an expressive, semi-satirical scene from Flemish peasant life painted by Adriaen Brouwer.

VISITORS' CHECKLIST

Practical Information
Barer Straße 27. **Map** 1 C5. **Tel** 23 80 52 16. **Open** 10am–6pm Wed–Sun (to 8pm Tue); some rooms closed for renovation to 2018. €4, €1 on Sun, children under 18 free. **pinakothek.de**

Transport
Königsplatz. 100. 27, 28, N27.

★ The Deposition
(c.1633)
In this dramatic painting, Rembrandt consciously challenges Rubens' idealised version of Christ's sacrifice by focusing on the pained expressions of the other figures in the composition.

Italian Baroque painting
is represented by such masters as Tiepolo and Guido Reni.

Portrait of the Marquise de Pompadour (1756)
One of the finest French Rococo paintings by François Boucher.

First floor

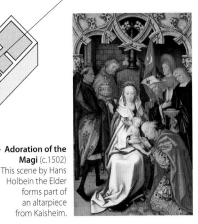

Adoration of the Magi (c.1502)
This scene by Hans Holbein the Elder forms part of an altarpiece from Kaisheim.

Land of Cockaigne (1567)
The Flemish artist Pieter Bruegel painted this visual satire on the mythical land of plenty, condemning gluttony and indolence.

Exploring the Alte Pinakothek

After World War II, the Alte Pinakothek was rebuilt by Hans Döllgast. The entrance hall, ticket office, bookshop and cafeteria are on the ground floor, as are the section on German Gothic painting, the Breughel Room and the temporary exhibitions gallery. The collections on the first floor are grouped according to the great national schools. Larger paintings are exhibited in the main rooms, with smaller ones in the side galleries.

The Abduction of the Daughters of Leukippos (1618) by Rubens

Four Apostles (1526), a pair of panels by Albrecht Dürer

German Painting

The Alte Pinakothek is renowned for its important collection of German late Gothic and Renaissance art. The section opens with a collection of paintings by the Cologne School, from the Master of St Veronica (c.1420), to the fine altar of St Bartholomew (1500–10), which anticipates the Renaissance. Late 15th-century painting is represented by Michael Pacher's *Altar of the Church Fathers*, with a bold handling of perspective.

The collection of paintings by Albrecht Dürer documents the development of his work from a *Self-Portrait* of 1500 to the *Four Apostles* of 1526. Two paintings by Matthias Grünewald show a strong Renaissance influence, as does the *Crucifixion* (1503) by Lucas Cranach the Elder. Albrecht Altdorfer of Regensburg, a painter of the Danube School, is represented by his *Battle of Issus* with its pioneering use of landscape.

Mannerism is exemplified by the allegories by Hans Baldung Grien and Hans von Aachen's

Allegory of Truth. Painting of the 17th century includes works by Adam Elsheimer and Johann Liss.

Netherlandish Painting

This school, which split into the Flemish and Dutch schools at the end of the 16th century, is introduced by the fine works of Rogier van der Weyden, particularly his Cologne Altarpiece with the famous *Adoration of the Magi*.

Hans Memling's *Seven Joys of the Virgin* depicts scenes from the life of Christ in an extensive symbolic landscape. A glimpse of the grotesque world of Hieronymus Bosch is given by a fragment of his *Last Judgement*, while a completely different climate bathes Pieter Breughel's *Land of Cockaigne*. An outstanding example of the assimilation of Italian Renaissance style is *Danae* by Jan Grossaert.

Flemish Painting

The largest collection of works by the great 17th-century painter Peter Paul Rubens can be seen here. They range from the intimate *Rubens and Isabella Brandt in the Honeysuckle Bower* (1609), painted to celebrate the artist's marriage, to *The Abduction of the Daughters of Leukippos* and *The Battle of the Amazons* in the High Baroque style. Here also are the large-scale *Last Judgement*, *Fall of the Rebel Angels* and *Women of the Apocalypse*, as well as sketches for the scenes from the life of Marie de Medici.

This section also includes paintings by Rubens' pupils Anthony van Dyck and Jacob Jordaens, and the peasant scenes of Adriaen Brouwer, the most notable of which is *Peasants Playing Cards*.

The Adoration of the Magi (c.1455) by Rogier van der Weyden

Dutch Painting

The gallery's rich collection of 17th-century Dutch art represents the Golden Age of Dutch painting. It includes an outstanding series of Passion scenes by Rembrandt that were executed in the 1630s and are important examples of the Baroque style.

Outstanding among the wealth of portraits is a self-portrait by Carel Fabritius and the *Portrait of Willem van Heythuysen* by Frans Hals.

Landscape painting is represented by the work of Jacob van Ruisdael and by the townscapes and river scenes of Jan van Goyen. Among the genre painters, Jan Steen, Gabriel Metsu and Gerard Terborch are particularly noteworthy names.

Portrait of Willem van Heythuysen (1625–30) by Frans Hals

Italian Painting

Such is the comprehensive nature of the gallery's collection that it is possible to make a thorough study of Italian painting here. Most of the early works came to the gallery thanks to Ludwig I's infatuation with the art of this particular period.

Paintings of the 14th century include Giotto's *Last Supper*. Florentine art, which flowered a century later, is represented by the religious paintings of Fra Filippo Lippi and Dominico Ghirlandaio. Other highlights include Leonardo da Vinci's *Madonna and Child* (c.1473), Perugino's *Vision of St Bernard* and works by Raphael,

The Annunciation (c.1473) by Antonello da Messina

outstanding among which is the *Madonna dei Tempi* (1507).

The Venetian School is represented by Titian's *Crown of Thorns* and Tintoretto's series of battle scenes glorifying the Gonzaga family. Great works of the 18th century include the religious canvases of Tiepolo and the fascinating Venetian townscapes of both Canaletto and Francesco Guardi.

Spanish Painting

Although it is smaller than other sections in the gallery, the collection of Spanish painting is no less interesting and includes works by the major masters of the Spanish School. The dramatic *Disrobing of Christ* by El Greco is one of three versions of this famous work. There are also paintings by Diego Velázquez, as well as the Mannerist scenes from the *Legend of St Catherine* by Francisco de Zurbarán, one of his finest works.

Also of interest are Murillo's paintings, in particular his genre scenes depicting street urchins in Seville. Other notable works include studio paintings by the lesser-known Claudio José Antonílez of about 1670.

French Painting

Despite their political connections with France, the Wittelsbachs did not collect French art on a large scale. The museum has three small paintings by Nicolas Poussin that, as early works, are not representative of his mature style. The work of Claude Lorrain is better documented, exhibits including his melancholic *Banishment of Hagar*.

By contrast, 18th-century French painting is well represented, most of the works having been acquired with the help of various banks. Noteworthy among them are paintings by Jean-Baptiste Pater and Nicolas Lancret, followers of Antoine Watteau, and Jean-Marc Nattier's excellent *Portrait of the Marquis of Baglion*. The work of François Boucher is generously represented, from the exquisite *Portrait of the Marquise de Pompadour* to his intimate study of the young Louise O'Murphy, mistress of Louis XV.

The eroticism of the Rococo age is illustrated by sketches by Jean-Honoré Fragonard, while Jean-Baptiste Greuze's moralistic *Grievance of Time* heralds the sentimentality of Neo-Classicism.

Disrobing of Christ (c.1585) by El Greco

9 Neue Pinakothek

The Neue Pinakothek, which contains 19th-century paintings displayed in a building designed by August von Volt, opened in 1853. From 1909 to 1914, under the curatorship of the art historian Hugo von Tschudi, the collection of academic paintings was extended in an avant-garde direction. The building itself was destroyed during World War II, and between 1976 and 1981 a new gallery, designed by Alexander von Branca, was constructed. Today the museum's exhibits consist primarily of German, French and English paintings dating from 1780 to 1910.

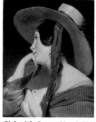

Girl with Straw Hat (1835)
This portrait is typical of Friedrich Von Amerling's work of the Biedermeier period.

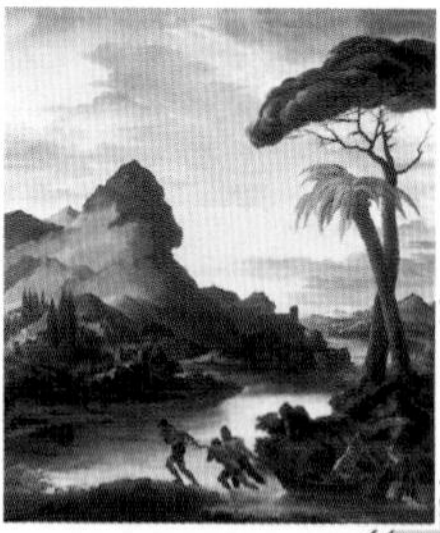

Heroic Landscape with Fishermen (1818)
In this Romantic painting by Théodore Géricault, the Neo-Classical landscape is bathed in a romantic light.

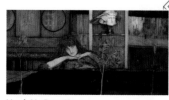

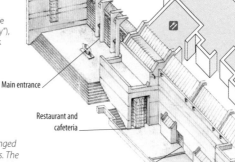

I Lock My Door Upon Myself (1891)
This evocative painting by Fernand Khnopff, a co-founder of the Groupe des XX ("Group of Twenty"), was inspired by the work of Christina Rossetti.

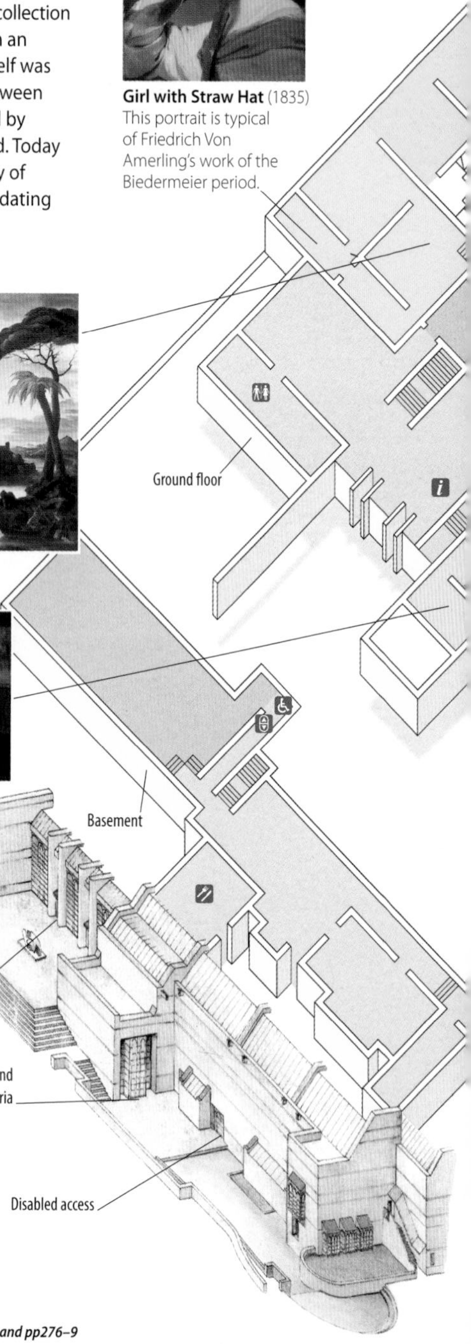

Ground floor
Basement
Main entrance
Restaurant and cafeteria
Disabled access

Gallery Guide

The collections are arranged in 22 halls and 11 rooms. The recommended route for visitors, tracing a figure of eight, takes the collections in chronological order. The halls, of varying size, height and level, are arranged around two inner courtyards.

For hotels and restaurants in this region see pp266–7 and pp276–9

★ **Italia and Germania** (1828)
This painting by Friedrich Overbeck looks back to the Renaissance.

Still Life with Asparagus
(c.1885/90)
The artist Karl Schuch remains underrated to this day. His painting of asparagus spears was influenced by the work of Édouard Manet.

★ **Seni before the Corpse of Wallenstein** (1855)
This illustration by Carl Theodor von Piloty of a scene from Schiller's famous play enjoyed enormous popularity during the 19th century.

Play of the Waves (1883)
Arnold Böcklin interpreted this mythological scene in a subtly erotic Neo-Baroque manner.

★ **Breakfast in the Studio** (1868)
This outstanding painting by Édouard Manet, with strongly constrasting dark and light tones, dates from the end of his pre-Expressionist period.

Key to Floorplan

- ▢ Neo-Classicism
- ▢ Art at the Court of Ludwig I
- ▢ Early Romantic Art
- ▢ History painting
- ▢ Böcklin, Marées and late Realism
- ▢ Impressionism
- ▢ Symbolism and Art Nouveau
- ▢ Art from 1800
- ▢ French Romanticism and Realism
- ▢ Biedermeier and Early Realism
- ▢ Temporary exhibitions
- ▢ Non-exhibition space

Exploring the Neue Pinakothek

The Neue Pinakothek is admirably designed for visitors. The recommended route for viewing the collections starts and ends in a large hall, and can easily be extended or shortened. Glass roofs allow the rooms to be illuminated by natural light. The varied rhythm of the itinerary and the size and height of the rooms, which are situated at different levels, keep the experience interesting and full of stimulating variety.

Don Quijote (1868) by French artist Honoré Daumier

Church Ruins in the Forest (1831) by Caspar David Friedrich

Neo-Classicism and Early Romanticism

The sculptures of Paris by Antonio Canova and of Adonis by Bertel Thorvaldsen show these artists' different approaches to Neo-Classicism. Ascetic Neo-Classicism was also shaped by Jacques-Louis David with his Portrait of the Comtesse Sorcy de Thélusson (1790). Neo-Classical landscape painting is represented by German painters including Jacob Philipp Hackert.

Also on display is a series of melancholy landscapes by the German Romantic painter Caspar David Friedrich. The Dresden school of landscape painters is represented by Carl Gustav Carus and Johan Christian Dahl, among others. Heroic Landscape with Fishermen by Théodore Géricault imbues the Neo-Classical landscape with a Romantic atmosphere. The paintings of Eugène Delacroix, such as Valentine Dying (c.1826) and The Death of Ophelia (1838) treat the Faustian and Shakespearean themes so beloved of the Romantic painters.

The Nazarenes and Biedermeier

The gallery's body of Nazarene paintings formed the basis of its collection when it first opened in 1853. Italia and Germania, the allegory by Friedrich Overbeck in which the two figures sit in a sisterly embrace, expresses the artistic relationship between the two nations. Joseph Anton Koch's paintings Heroic Landscape with Rainbow (1812) and View of the Environs of Olevano (1830) combine Romantic impulses with the religious mood characteristic of the Nazarenes.

Although they are artistically quite different, the genre paintings of the Austrian artist Ferdinand Waldmüller and the fairy-tale cycles of Moritz von Schwind (such as Symphony) both express a specific urban view of happiness in line with the Biedermeier style's Gemütlichkeit (domestic harmony).

Realism and Late Romanticism

In the early 20th century the Neue Pinakothek started to acquire French paintings of the Realist school, whose origins date from about 1850.

The Poor Poet (1839) by Carl Spitzweg

The gallery's acquisitions from that time include studies by Camille Corot, notably some of his Italian vignettes. There is also a collection of works by Gustave Courbet, among which images of rocks in landscapes predominate. The contrast between different paintings by the caricaturist Honoré Daumier is superb: while Dramatist on Stage (1860) shows the world of Parisian theatre, his incomparable Don Quijote (1868) conveys the symbolic character of the knight from La Mancha. With his satirical The Poor Poet (1839), Carl Spitzweg created almost a cult character in Germany.

History Painting

Historical subjects were a favourite theme in the 19th century. This section opens with Wilhelm von Kaulbach's vast canvas The Destruction of Jerusalem (1846), in which the sacking of the city by the Emperor Titus is given an allegorical setting. Kaulbach also painted canvases showing the virtues of Ludwig I, who was a prominent patron of the arts. Historical painting is represented to a significant degree by Carl Theodor von Piloty, with his famous Seni before the Corpse of Wallenstein (1855) and the much later *Thusnelda in the Triumphal Procession of Germanicus* (1873), a Neo-Baroque vision of what was seen as Germanic virtues.

Böcklin, Marées and Late Realism

After the unification of the German Empire in 1871, German art fragmented into various movements. Hans von Marées of the Rhineland sought new ways of treating Classical themes. The Neue Pinakothek houses his principal works, including the triptych *Hesperides II* (1884) and *Three Riders* (1887).

Anselm Feuerbach's superb handling of colour expresses a tragic interpretation of Classical themes, as in his *Medea* (1870), while Arnold Böcklin's world of Classical mythology is in harmony with Neo-Baroque trends (as in his *Play of the Waves*). Here also is a substantial collection of works by the Munich Realist Wilhelm Leibl, including *Portrait of Mrs Gedon* (1869), as well as paintings by Carl Schuch and Wilhelm Trübner.

Hesperides II (1884/87) by Hans von Marées

Boys on the Beach (1898) by Max Liebermann

Impressionism and Post-Impressionism

With regard to Impressionist painting, what the Neue Pinakothek lacks in quantity it makes up for in the importance of its collection. Mention should be made of masterpieces by Édouard Manet, such as *Barque at Argenteuil* (1874), Claude Monet's *Bridge at Argenteuil* (1874) and in particular of Paul Cézanne's *The Railway Cutting* (1870). In the latter, a milestone in his artistic development, the

artist shows for the first time his tendency to endow natural forms with geometric shapes. Edgar Degas' delightful *Woman Ironing* (1869) is accompanied by a number of his portraits and statuettes of dancers. The gallery also has paintings by Auguste Renoir, Camille Pissarro and Alfred Sisley.

German Impressionists are also well represented. On display are early works by Adolph von Menzel and paintings by Lovis Corinth, Max Slevogt and Max Liebermann, including his carefree *Boys on the Beach*. The room containing paintings by Paul Signac inaugurates the gallery's Post-Impressionist section. Paul Gauguin is represented by works from his Breton period as well as by *The Birth* (1896), a classic painting from his Tahitian period. Most notably, the Neue Pinakothek has a representative collection of works by Vincent van Gogh. Prominent among them are *Sunflowers* (1888) and two landscapes: *View of Arles* (1889) and *Plain at Auvers* (1890). All three paintings express the artist's delight in the beauty of the sun, the sky, flowers and crops.

Symbolism and Art Nouveau

The interaction between the two artistic movements Symbolism and Art Nouveau is illustrated by *I Lock My Door Upon Myself* by Fernand Khnopff. James Ensor's expressive *Masks* and paintings by Edvard Munch and Maurice Denis can also be seen here.

Of equal interest are works by artists such as Pierre Bonnard and Édouard Vuillard who continued the Impressionist tradition. The erotic and eschatological themes typical of Symbolism can be seen in Egon Schiele's *Agony* (1902), for example. The *Portrait of Margarethe Stonborough-Wittgenstein* (1905) by Gustav Klimt comes at the end of the Neue Pinakothek's exhibits.

Sunflowers (1888) by famous painter Vincent van Gogh

The modern and colourful façade of Museum Brandhorst

⑫ Museum Brandhorst

Theresienstr. 35a. **Map** 1 C5.
Tel 23 80 52 286. Ⓤ Universität.
🚊 2, 28, N27. 🚌 100.
Open 10am–6pm Tue–Sun
(until 8pm Thu).
Ⓦ museum-brandhorst.de

Opened in 2009, Museum Brandhorst is home to the Brandhorst collection; an extensive and important collection of modern and contemporary art. Commissioned by the Bavarian government, the museum lies adjacent to the Pinakothek der Moderne.

Many of the leading art figures of the late 20th century – among them Joseph Beuys, Gerhard Richter and Damien Hirst – are shown here. With more than 60 works by abstract painter Cy Twombly, the gallery provides a retrospective of this artist's development. The museum building is impressive, with 23 different coloured panes of glass.

⑬ Palais Pinakothek

Türkenstr. 4. **Map** 3 B1. Ⓤ Odeonsplatz.
🚌 100. **Closed** to the public.

Formerly known as Dürckheim Palais, the palace was built in 1843–4 for the chief steward of the court, Count Georg Friedrich von Dürckheim-Montmartin, the palace was designed by Friedrich Jakob Kreuther. Up until 1909 the building housed the Prussian Embassy. The modern building of the bank next door to the palace creates a strong sense of aesthetic dissonance.

The façade of the palace, with its distinctive brick and terracotta reliefs, makes reference to early Italian Renaissance architecture. The main entrance, which was originally centrally placed on the building, was moved to the right in 1912. The palace is a classic example of the transitional style of architecture that links the work of Friedrich von Gärtner and the Maximilian style.

Statue on the Wittelsbacher Brunnen on Lenbachplatz

⑭ Lenbachplatz

Map 3 A1. Ⓢ and Ⓤ Karlsplatz
(Stachus). 🚊 16, 17, 18, 19, 20, 21, 27, 28, N27.

This irregularly shaped square lies between Maximiliansplatz, the Alter Botanischer Garten and Karlsplatz. The buildings that line it are typical of the late 19th century and are laid out irregularly around the square, creating a set of contrasting perspectives.

On the west side stand the law courts (Justizpalast) and on the south side rises the bizarre outline of the Künstlerhaus. On the north side is the **Stock Exchange** (Börse). Built in 1868–98, it is an example of pompous Neo-Baroque, its splendour reflecting the power of the financial institution within. The neighbouring **Bernheimer Haus**, at No. 6, was built in 1889. It was regarded as the ultimate residential building in Munich, a novelty at the time being the exposed iron structure of the ground floor and the huge picture windows.

On the east side of the square is Munich's finest fountain, the **Wittelsbacher Brunnen**, built by Adolf von Hildebrand in 1893–5 to commemorate the completion of the city's new water-supply system. The fountain symbolizes both charity and the destructive power of water. It is dominated by two allegorical figures – a youth on a steed, and a woman seated on a bull.

⑮ Karlsplatz

Karlsplatz (Stachus). 🚊 16, 17, 18, 19, 20, 21, 22, 27, 28, N16, N19, N20, N27.

After the city's fortifications were blown up in 1791 on the orders of Karl Theodor, a vast square was laid out on the western side of the Old Town. It was named Karlsplatz in honour of the ruler, as was the gate called the **Karlstor**. The square also had a popular name – Stachus – which is still used today. It refers to the most popular inn in Munich, which

People relaxing beside the fountains of Karlsplatz

since 1759 has stood on the southwest side of the square. In 1899–1902 the architect Gabriel von Seidl added two wings, known as the Rondelbauten, to the Karlstor. These Neo-Baroque buildings, with two tower-shaped projections, have shops in their ground-floor arcades.

The large fountain in the centre of the square is a favourite meeting place, and there is a major shopping centre beneath the square.

Detail of the ornamental attic of the Justizpalast

⓰ Justizpalast
Law Courts

Elisenstr. 1a. (Karlsplatz) Prielmayerstr. 7. **Map** 3 A1 (5 A2). **Tel** 55 97 03. Ⓢ and Ⓤ Karlsplatz (Stachus). 🚋 16, 17, 18, 19, 20, 21, 27, 28, N16, N19, N20, N27.

On the northwest side of Karlsplatz stands one of the best-known late 19th-century landmarks in Munich. The law courts, built in 1891–98 by Friedrich von Thiersch, are an example of pure Neo-Baroque architecture, with discreet Neo-Mannerist elements.

The building's great novelty at the time was its vast steel and glass dome, which acted as a skylight. The interior – particularly the main hall and the main stair-way, which are directly beneath the dome – has an extraordinary wealth of detail in its design.

West of the Justizpalast are the Neues Justizgebäude (New Law Courts). Built in 1906–08, also by Thiersch, they are in the Neo-Gothic style and have a clocktower and gables.

⓱ Alter Botanischer Garten
Old Botanical Garden

Map 3 A1 (5 A1). Between Elisen- and Sophienstr. Ⓢ and Ⓤ Karlsplatz (Stachus), Hauptbahnhof. 🚋 16, 17, 18, 19, 20, 21, 27, 28, N27, N28. 🚌 100.

Visitors to Munich who find them-selves in need of respite from the bustle of the city centre will find a sanctuary in the Old Botanical Garden north of the Justizpalast. Laid out on a semi-circular plan in 1804–14, they were designed by Friedrich Ludwig von Sckell, who was also responsible for the Englischer Garten.

The entrance to the garden is through an early Neo-Classical gate built by Emanuel Joseph von Herigoyen in 1811 and bearing a Latin inscription by Goethe. In 1854 the greenhouse was demolished to make space for the Glaspalast. Modelled on London's Crystal Palace, it was built to house the First Industrial Exhibition. The Glaspalast burned down in 1931, destroying at the same time an exhibition of German Romantic painting.

In 1914 a new botanical garden was laid out in Nymphenburg, and the Old Botanical Garden was converted into a municipal park. A restaurant (today the Park Café) was built in 1935–7, as well as an exhibition hall designed by Oswald Bieber. The sculptor Josef Wackerle created the Neptune Fountain, which has a figure based on Michelangelo's David. The café garden, shaded by exotic trees, is an ideal place to relax and enjoy a cold beer.

⓲ Löwenbräukeller

Stiglmaierplatz 2/Nymphenburger-straße. **Map** 1 A5. **Tel** 54 52 42 44. Ⓤ Stiglmaierplatz. 🚋 20, 21, 22, N20. **Open** 10am–midnight daily.

Visitors entering the city from the west along Nymphenburgerstraße will see from afar the marble statue of the lion that crowns the Löwenbräukeller on Stiglmaierplatz. This famous Munich brewery has its own inn, which is large enough to hold 4,000 drinkers.

The Neptune Fountain in the Old Botanical Garden

The picturesque brewery and inn were built in 1883 by Albert Schmidt and were refurbished by Friedrich von Thiersch at the turn of the 19th and 20th centuries. The sides of the octagonal tower are decorated alternately with the brewery's emblem – a white griffin – and the city's coat of arms. The tower rises above an arcaded entrance hall with a roof terrace.

In summer drinkers are drawn to the beer garden shaded by large chestnut trees.

⓳ Staatliches Museum Ägyptischer Kunst
State Museum of Egyptian Art

Gabelsbergerstr. 35. **Map** 1 C5. **Tel** (089) 28 92 76 30. Ⓤ Königsplatz. 🚋 27. **Open** 10am–6pm Tue–Sun (Tue until 8pm). ♿ Ⓦ **smaek.de**

The State Museum of Egyptian Art is located below the building of the University of Television and Film Munich. Visitors enter the exhibition rooms down a ramp and through a monumental walled portal sunk into the ground like a pharaoh's tomb.

The exhibits are thousands of years old so the highest levels of conservatorial protection are essential. Items are displayed in three large halls and smaller, darker catacombs, organised into themes such as The Pharoah, Realm of the Dead and Egypt in Rome.

FURTHER AFIELD

Many of Munich's attractions lie outside the city centre and, thanks to a highly efficient transport system, they can be easily reached. To the north, for instance, is the famous Olympiapark and the BMW factory's modern complex of buildings. To the west lies the Nymphenburg district, with its palace, park and botanical gardens. Southwest of the Old Town is Theresienwiese, where the famous Oktoberfest is held, and unfailing attractions to the south are the Hellabrunn Zoo, in Thalkirchen, and the Bavaria Film Museum, in Geiselgasteig. To the east are some masterpieces of religious architecture – the great Mariä Himmelfahrtskirche in Ramersdorf, and Michaelskirche in Berg am Laim.

Sights at a Glance

Palaces and Historic Buildings
1 Nymphenburg pp134–7
11 Grünwald
12 Asam-Schlössl
16 Blutenburg

Museum
4 BMW Museum and BMW Welt
13 Deutsches Museum Verkehrszentrum

Districts
7 Westend
8 Haidhausen

Parks and Open Spaces
2 Botanischer Garten
3 Olympiapark
9 Tierpark Hellabrunn
14 Theresienwiese

Others
5 Neuhausen
6 Au
10 Bavaria-Filmstadt
15 Neue Messe München
17 Allianz Arena

Key
- Central Munich
- Outskirts of Munich
- Motorway
- Major road
- Minor road
- Railway line

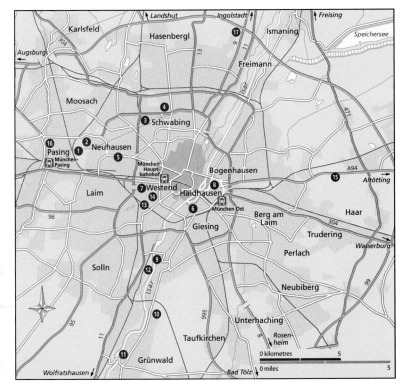

◄ The ultramodern BMW administration tower and museum

For keys to symbols see back flap

❶ Nymphenburg

After the birth in 1679 of Maximilian Emanuel, the heir to the throne, his father, Duke Ferdinand Maria, presented his wife with a suburban palace. The queen named it Nymphenburg (Nymphs' Castle) and supervised the building work that ensued. Max Emanuel continued his mother's work, creating with architects Joseph Effner and Enrico Zucalli one of the finest palaces and gardens in Europe. Later, buildings were added around the courtyard fronting the palace. In the 1800s the formal French gardens were converted into a landscaped park incorporating the existing canals.

★ Amalienburg
Built by François Cuvilliés, the Amalienburg was a small hunting lodge. Its circular hall was covered with fine shellwork, and the windows and mirrors created the illusion of great space.

★ Marstallmuseum
This museum contains coaches, carriages and sleighs that once belonged to Bavarian rulers, including Ludwig II's coronation coach, and portraits of his favourite horses.

KEY

① **The Porzellanmanufaktur** has produced fine porcelain since 1761. The factory's chief designer was Franz Anton Bustelli.

② **The façade of the Palace** is 600 m (1,968 ft) wide and broken up in typically Baroque style. It is perfectly complemented by the geometric layout of the formal gardens.

③ **The Museum Mensch und Natur** is dedicated to the structure of the earth and the workings of the human body.

④ **The orangery** was, at the time it was built, the first in Germany to be heated by hot water.

Garden
The formal French garden at the rear of the palace, with an 18th-century canal, forms the main axis of the entire palace and its gardens.

VISITORS' CHECKLIST

Practical Information
Nymphenburg: **Tel** 17 90 80.
W schloss-nymphenburg.de
Open 1 Apr–15 Oct: 9am–6pm daily; 16 Oct–31 Mar: 10am–4pm daily. Museum Mensch und Natur: **Open** 9am–5pm Tue–Fri (until 8pm Thu); 10am–6pm Sat, Sun & public hols.
W mmn-muenchen.de

Transport
Rotkreuzplatz, then 12. 51.

Badenburg
The bathing hall and the first heated tiled pool are surrounded by a viewing gallery.

★ Pagodenburg
This pavilion was used for receiving visitors and for relaxation. The ground floor is covered with 2,000 Dutch Delft tiles depicting figures and landscapes.

Magdalenenklause
This folly, built as a chapel in a grotto with hermits' cells, reflects the Baroque idea of withdrawal from courtly life into a world of peace and contemplation.

Schloss Nymphenburg

The oldest part of the palace is the central section, built in 1675 in the form of an Italianate villa. In 1702 Maximilian Emanuel commissioned the construction of side pavilions, which were connected to the villa by galleries. Soon after 1715, when Joseph Effner took charge of building work on the palace, the Steinerner Saal (Audience Hall) with stunningly lavish interior decoration was built, along with the other rooms in the wings, and the stables and orangery.

Italianate Villa
The façade of the oldest, 17th-century wing of the palace, facing the garden, is fronted by a double stairway supported on three arches.

★ Royal Bed
The royal bedchamber in the south wing of the palace is decorated with fine paintings and filled with mahogany furniture, including the Royal Bed, where Ludwig II was born.

★ Schönheitengalerie
Ludwig I commissioned Joseph Stieler to paint portraits of the city's beautiful women. The Gallery of Beauties was hung with portraits of noblewomen, dancers, towns-women and "Helene Sedlmayr, the Beauty of Munich", a cobbler's daughter.

Portrait of Karl Albrecht
The prince-elector of Bavaria became Holy Roman Emperor in 1742. Under his reign Nymphenburg was completed, with a series of Baroque mansions – the Kavaliershäuschen – that surround the palace.

KEY

① **Balustrades** decorated with vases line the stairways leading to the palace gardens.

Paintings
The walls and ceilings of the palace halls are covered with colourful paintings framed with stuccowork. The finest is the ceiling of the Steinerner Saal, in which mythological scenes are shown in idyllic garden settings.

VISITORS' CHECKLIST

Practical Information
Schloss Nymphenburg: Eingang 1.
Tel 17 90 80. **Open** 1 Apr–15 Oct:
9am–6pm daily; 16 Oct–31 Mar:
10am–4pm daily. 🖼 🖼 🖼
w schloss-nymphenburg.de

Transport
🚇 Rotkreuzplatz, then 🚋 12.
🚌 51.

Lackkabinett
This corner cabinet with Chinese motifs is exquisitely decorated with black lacquer on wood panelling. The Chinese theme is reinforced by the Rococo painting of the ceiling.

Entrance

Vorzimmer
This anteroom in the north part of the palace is richly decorated in French Regency style. Paintings, stuccowork and wood carvings cover the walls, while the ceiling is decorated with Classical subjects.

★ Steinerner Saal
Upon entering the palace, visitors walk into a spacious hall with windows on either side decorated in a resplendent Rococo style.

❷ Botanischer Garten
Botanical Garden

Menzingerstr. 12. **Tel** 17 86 13 10. 🚋 17.
Open Feb, Mar & Oct: 9am–5pm; Apr
& Sep: 9am–6pm; May–Aug: 9am–7pm;
Nov–Jan: 9am–4:30pm. Greenhouses:
Open 9am–30 minutes before garden
closing time. 🌐 botmuc.de

North of the gardens of Schloss
Nymphenburg, new botanical
gardens were laid
out in 1909–14.
Covering 0.22 sq km
(0.08 sq mile) and
containing over
14,000 species of
plants growing in
artistic arrangements,
this is one of the
finest botanical
gardens in Europe.

Entry to the garden
is through the
Botanical Institute, which is
fronted by the colourful
Schmuckhof (Decorative Yard).
Passing through it visitors see a
section on ecology and genetics,
followed by a rose garden and a
plantation of rhododendrons
and protected species, and of
medicinal plants and crops.
There is also an arboretum with
rare trees. Beyond this is a
section illustrating the vegetation
of meadows, plains, swamps and
sandy and arctic environments.

The impressive greenhouses
shelter tropical plants, cacti
and fruit trees, unusual orchids
and giant water lilies.

The Botanical Garden with its stunning
variety of plants

Inside the futuristic BMW Welt building

❹ BMW Museum and BMW Welt

Olympiapark 2. **Tel** (089) 1250 16001.
🚇 Olympiazentrum. Museum:
Open 10am–6pm Tue–Sun. 🅿 ♿
BMW World: Olympiapark 1. **Open**
7:30am–midnight Mon–Sat, 9am–
midnight Sun. 🌐 bmw-welt.com

In the early 1970s, the BMW car
manufacturing group built a
series of ostentatious structures
that went some way to rival the
architectural development of
the neighbouring Olympiapark.

The designer in charge of the
concept, Karl Schanzer of Vienna,
used the idiom of architectural

❸ Olympiapark

Munich's Olympic Park was built for the 20th
Olympic Games, which the city hosted in 1972.
The modern complex of sports facilities overlies
an area formerly used as drill grounds and later
as an airfield. The artificial lake is fed by the
Nymphenburg Canal and the hills were made
from the rubble removed from the city after
World War II. The whole complex is dominated
by the Olympic Tower.

⑥ BMW Museum and BMW Welt
A must for all motor and
architecture enthusiasts.

② Olympiahalle
The sweeping roofs,
designed by the architect
Günter Behnisch, form a
canopy of steel netting
and acrylic slabs
supported on masts up
to 80 m (260 feet) high.

① Olympiastadion
The main Olympic
stadium can hold
60,000 spectators.

GEORG-

Olympiahalle

Olympia-stadion
①

OLYMPIAPA

SPIRIDON-LOUIS-RING

ERNST-CURTIUS-WEG

Werner-von-Linde-Halle

TONI-MERKENS-WEG

symbolism. He envisaged the 19-storey office building that dominates the complex as resembling the four cylinders of a car engine. The building, clad in silver aluminium, has a ground plan in the form of a clover leaf.

At the foot of the building, and counterbalancing its imposing structure, is what could be described as a shrine – the BMW Museum. Built in concrete and taking the form of a bowl 41 m (135 ft) across, this window-less, silver-painted structure contains exhibits illustrating the history of the factory's production. A spiral ramp connects five platforms where the first cars, including the famous Dixi, are displayed, along with motorbikes, racing cars of the 1950s and 1960s, the modern BMW range and futuristic prototypes. There are also film and slide shows.

Linked to the museum is **BMW Welt** (BMW World), an ultra-modern showroom containing exhibitions, a café and the Esszimmer gourmet restaurant.

❾ Neuhausen

Map C E3 – 6. 🆄 Rotkreuzplatz.
🚊 12, 16, 17. 🚌 53.

Neuhausen is located west of the city centre, between Maxvorstadt and Nymphenburg. It ranges from the railway line in the south across Arnulfstraße

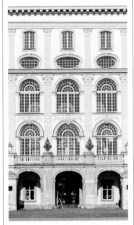

Façade of the Nymphenburg Palace and Park in Munich

and Nymphenburger Straße to Dachauerstraße and the Westfriedhof. The centre of Neuhausen is the Rotkreuzplatz. The district north of the Nymphenburger Schlosskanal is called Gern.

The village of Neuhausen was first mentioned in 1170. Industrialization (especially railway and locomotive manufacturing) led to a growth in population. It was incorporated into Munich in 1890, and in 1992 it fused together with the district of Nymphenburg.

Most of the buildings in Neuhausen date from the Gründerzeit after the Franco-Prussian War of 1870–71 and the Art Nouveau era. Neuhausen is also the setting for Munich's most modern church – Herz-Jesu-Kirche (1997–2000). Other attractions include the large Dantebad pool and spa complex, the popular Taxisgarten (beer garden) and the excellent Sarcletti ice cream parlour.

③ Schwimmhalle
The Swimming Hall is one of the finest in Europe. The complex comprises five pools, saunas, a jacuzzi and a diving platform, as well as a grassed relaxation area.

⑤ Olympia-Eissportzentrum
Like the Swimming Hall, the skating rink and ice-hockey stadium is open to the public.

⑦ Sea Life Olympiapark
Visitors can view seahorses, sharks, tropical fish and turtles.

Tips for Drivers

Getting there:
🆄 Olympiazentrum.
Start: Hans-Braun-Brücke.
Length of tour: 2 km (1.25 m).
Stopping-off places: At Olympiahalle and Olympiaturm.

④ Olympiaturm
The Olympic Tower commands a fine view over the city and – when the weather is fine – a panoramic view over the Bavarian Alps.

| 0 metres | 150 |
| 0 yards | 150 |

Key

— Suggested route

Colourful Italian crockery at the Auer Dult fair

❻ Au

Map 4 D5. 🚋 17. 🚌 52. 🚆 Auer Dult: Mariahilfplatz. Maidult: starts around 1 May; Jakobidult: starts Sat after 25 Jul; Herbstdult: starts third Sat in Sep.

Up until the 15th century, the district of Au was part of the floodplain of the River Isar, and it was only after the river was controlled that people started to settle here. Au was incorporated into Munich in 1854. Until the early 20th century, the poorer population of the city lived in Au, and picturesque cottages typical of old Munich can still be seen there today.

Three times a year, for nine days, the heart of the Au transforms into Munich's biggest traditional fair for household articles, antiquities and old books. This local event goes back to the 14th century. The atmospheric **Auer Dult** starts on the first weekend in May, at St Jacob's Day and in the week after Kermess. In addition to the many stalls with antiquities, books, pottery and every kind of household stuff there are some nostalgic shooting galleries, merry-go-rounds, and food stalls, as well as a beer tent.

The square with the fair is dominated by Maria-Hilf-Kirche, a Neo-Gothic brick church built by Joseph Ohlmüller and Georg Friedrich Ziebland in 1831–39. It was the first instance of the Gothic revival in southern Germany.

❼ Westend

Map D E7–8. 🚇 Schwanthalerhöhe. 🚋 18. 🚌 53.

The Westend, or Schwant-halerhöhe, is located at the western fringe of the city

centre, between Theresienwiese (Oktoberfest), Landsberger Straße, Donnersberger- und Hackerbrücke and the railway line to the south. The name originates from the sculptor Ludwig Schwanthaler, creator of the Bavaria figure (see p143). This densely built district is home to Munich's oldest brewery (Augustiner), a branch of the KPMG company, the former chief customs office and several beautiful green public spaces, such as the Bavariapark with its many statues and figures. After the relocation of the Alte Messe in 1998, parts of the Theresienhöhe were innovatively redesigned, including Steidle-Hochhaus and the Bavaria beer garden. Old Art Nouveau exhibition halls house the Verkehrsz-entrum of the Deutsches Museum (see p142). The old congress hall is now used for events.

Most of the attractive houses, many in Art Nouveau style with bay windows and sgraffito, were built before 1919. The Westend district incorporates a large number of cooperative flats. Also remarkable is the 1920s Ledigenheim building designed by Theodor Fischer and located near Gollierplatz.

The Westend is one of Munich's most vivid and

Danish-Icelandic architect Ólafur Elíasson's Endless Stair, Westend

colourful multicultural districts, with one third of residents coming from all over the world. The area is also popular with young Germans. The many dining options include Greek, Italian and Croatian restaurants.

Glaspalastbrunnen, the Glass Palace Fountain, in Weißenburger Platz

❽ Haidhausen

Map 4 E4. 🚇 🚇 Ostbahnhof. 🚇 Rosenheimer Platz. 🚇 Max-Weber-Platz. 🚋 15, 16, 19, 25. 🚌 63, 100.

Haidhausen is a residential district to the east of the city centre. It is bounded by the Isar, the railway line at Ostbahnhof, Prinzregentenstraße and Rosenheimer Straße. The French quarter, built after 1872, stretches from the Orleansplatz around Wörthstraße with Bordeauxplatz as its centre line.

Haidhausen was first mentioned as early as 808 and incorporated into Munich after 1854. It was once thought of as a poor district, but today it is one of the most popular parts of Munich. It offers a multitude of shops, cafés, restaurants and charming squares like the Weißenburger Platz with its beautiful fountain or the Wiener Platz with its daily food market. Excellent beer gardens have been opened here by the Hofbräu and Bürgerbräu breweries.

The Maximilianeum, the state parliament of Bavaria, is located in Haidhausen (see p95), as is the Müllersches Volksbad (see p97) and the Gasteig Cultural Centre (see p97). There is much worth seeing and hearing at the Prinzregententheater (see pp146–7) and at the Villa Stuck (see p96).

Tierpark Hellabrunn

Munich's zoo was established in 1911. It has almost 5,000 animals representing 480 species and covers an area of 3.6 sq km (1.38 sq miles). The species are arranged by continent and by their geographical occurrence. The design of the enclosures, which recreate natural environments, makes Hellabrunn one of the most beautiful zoos in the world. The zoo specializes in breeding animals that are under threat of extinction.

VISITORS' CHECKLIST

Practical Information
Tierparkstr. 30. **Tel** 62 50 80.
Open 9am–6pm daily (Nov–Mar: 9am–5pm).
W **hellabrunn.de**

Transport
U Thalkirchen. 52.

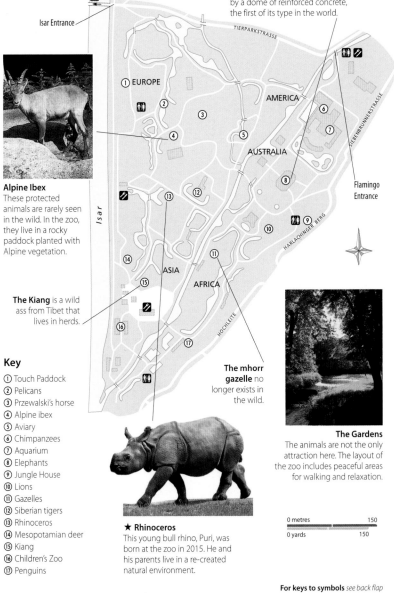

Elephants
The elephants live in a hall covered by a dome of reinforced concrete, the first of its type in the world.

Isar Entrance

1.2km (0.75 miles)

TIERPARKSTRASSE

① EUROPE

AMERICA

AUSTRALIA

SIEBENBRUNNERSTRASSE

Flamingo Entrance

HARLACHINGER BERG

ASIA

AFRICA

HOCHLEITE

Isar

Alpine Ibex
These protected animals are rarely seen in the wild. In the zoo, they live in a rocky paddock planted with Alpine vegetation.

The Kiang is a wild ass from Tibet that lives in herds.

The mhorr gazelle no longer exists in the wild.

The Gardens
The animals are not the only attraction here. The layout of the zoo includes peaceful areas for walking and relaxation.

Key

① Touch Paddock
② Pelicans
③ Przewalski's horse
④ Alpine ibex
⑤ Aviary
⑥ Chimpanzees
⑦ Aquarium
⑧ Elephants
⑨ Jungle House
⑩ Lions
⑪ Gazelles
⑫ Siberian tigers
⑬ Rhinoceros
⑭ Mesopotamian deer
⑮ Kiang
⑯ Children's Zoo
⑰ Penguins

★ Rhinoceros
This young bull rhino, Puri, was born at the zoo in 2015. He and his parents live in a re-created natural environment.

| 0 metres | 150 |
| 0 yards | 150 |

For keys to symbols see back flap

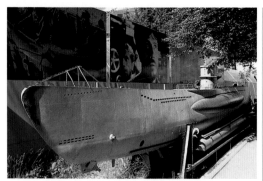

The realistic reconstruction of the U-boat from the film *Das Boot*

⑩ Bavaria-Filmstadt

Geiselgasteig. Bavariafilmplatz 7.
Tel 64 99 20 00. **U** Silberhornstr,
Wettersteinplatz (some distance
away). 🚌 25. **S** Rosenheimer
Platz (some distance away), then
🚌 25. **Open** Apr–Oct: 9am–6pm;
Nov–Mar: 10am–5pm, daily. 🌐 📷
W filmstadt.de

Commonly known as Holly-
wood on the Isar, Bavaria-
Filmstadt is one of Europe's
major film studios.

Set up in 1919, they were
originally located in the Stachus
district. Among the prominent
people who have worked here
have been famous directors
such as Orson Welles and
Ingmar Bergman. Every year
scores of films for the big screen
and television are made at
the Filmstadt ("cinema city"),
which opened to the public
in 1981.

The 90-minute tour of the
studios takes visitors on a
miniature railway and on foot,
through some fascinating
film sets.

Entering the 57 m (187 ft)
reconstruction of the U-boat
used in the Oscar-winning
film *Das Boot* is an unforgettable
experience. Another lasting
impression is made by the backdrops used in the production
of *Asterix and Obelix*, set in the
age of the Romans and Gauls.

Another major attraction is
Bullyversum, an interactive,
3-D adventure into the world
of film. The attraction is named
after, and stars, the German
comedian, actor and director,
Michael "Bully" Herbig.

⑪ Grünwald

Grünwald Burg. Grünwald Zeillerstr. 3.
U Silberhornstr. 🚌 25.
S Rosenheimer Platz, then 🚌 25.
Open 10am–5pm Wed–Sun.
Closed 31 Oct–mid-Mar.

Grünwald, on the southern
outskirts of Munich, is one
of the city's most exclusive
villa suburbs. It is also a good
starting point for walking
and cycling tours. The district's
greatest attraction is Burg
Grünwald, a well-preserved
medieval castle whose origins
go back to the 12th century.
In 1270 the building came into
the possession of the Wittelsbachs. In the 15th century a
gatehouse was constructed:
its stepped gable is set with
11 coats of arms, those of
Bavaria at the apex and those
of Poland and Jerusalem
among the others further
down. From 1602 to 1857
the castle accommodated a
prison and a gunpowder store.

Grünwald Burg's Gothic gatehouse, set with
coats of arms

The archaeological collections
housed here illustrate the
history of the castle and of
Roman art in Bavaria. There
are lapidariums and frescoes,
a kiln and a reconstruction
of a Roman kitchen.

⑫ Asam-Schlössl

Thalkirchen. Maria-Einsiedel-Str. 45.
Tel 72 363 73. **U** Thalkirchen.
🚌 135. **W** asamschloessl.de

In 1724 Cosmas Damian Asam
acquired a 17th-century
property in the Isar valley. He
intended to use it as an out-of-
town residence and studio.

With the help of his brother
Egid Quirin Asam, Cosmas
Damian rebuilt the house
that he had bought, con-
verting the second floor
into a spacious studio lit by
a huge semicircular window.
The house was named Maria
Einsiedel in honour of the
Swiss pilgrimage church that
the brothers had decorated.
The artist covered the façade
of his new home with paintings. He decorated the third
floor with a statue of Moses
bearing the Ten Command-
ments, and a painting of the
antique sculpture known as
The Borghese Fencer.

The building now houses an
excellent restaurant serving
interesting takes on local food.

⑬ Deutsches Museum Verkehrszentrum

Am Bavariapark 5. **Tel** 21 79 333.
U Schwanthalerhöhe. **Open**
9am–5pm daily. **Closed** 1 Jan, Good
Friday, 1 May, 1 Nov, 24, 25 & 31 Dec.
🌐 **W** deutsches-museum.de/
verkehrszentrum

The historic exhibition halls
on Theresienhöhe house t
he transport section of the
Deutsches Museum. This huge
collection ranges from the
very first motorcar to the ICE-
Experimental train and features
interactive displays that illustrate
the past, present and future of
worldwide travel and mobility.

⑭ Theresienwiese

Theresienhöhe 16. Ⓤ Theresienwiese.
Ruhmeshalle, Bavaria: **Tel** 29 06 71.
Open Apr–15 Oct: 9am–6pm daily
(until 8pm during Oktoberfest).
🎪 Oktoberfest Sep–Oct (16/17 days).

The events that took place in
Munich on 17 October 1810
had far-reaching consequences.
This was the day on which
the marriage of Therese von
Sachsen-Hildburghausen and
Ludwig I, the future king, took
place. To mark the occasion,
horse races, a cattle fair and
a folk festival were held in
meadows outside the city. The
folk celebrations were repeated
in following years, and this
custom continued to grow
and eventually became the
Oktoberfest (see p33), the
largest folk festival in the world.
The festival grounds were
named Theresienwiese in
honour of the bride.

The folk festival is not, however,
the only attraction of Theresienwiese. On an elevated ridge with
a grand stairway stands the Neo-
Classical **Ruhmeshalle** (Hall of
Fame), built by Leo von Klenze
in 1848–53. It is an open hall
fronted by 48 Ionian columns
and containing the busts of 77
prominent Bavarians. In front of
the hall stands a gigantic figure
of Bavaria as a Germanic goddess
carrying a sword and an oak
wreath and accompanied by a
lion. This unusual work by Leo von
Klenze and Ludwig Schwanthaler,
which stands 18 m (59 ft) high,
was the first monumental cast
iron figure to be made. It predates
New York's Statue of Liberty by
some 30 years. Visitors can view
the city from a platform in the
figure's head.

The great statue of Bavaria fronts the
Ruhmeshalle in Theresienwiese

The main entrance to the Neue Messe,
with the flags of many nations

⑮ Neue Messe München

Am Messesee 2. Ⓤ Messestadt-
West, Messestadt-Ost. 🖿 **messe-
muenchen.de**

In 1992 the international
airport at Riem was closed and
the site, where building work
took place from 1995 to 1998,
was transformed into a huge
exhibition area.

This was the Neue Messe
München, which came to
stand as an example of
modern functional yet elegant
architecture. It was designed by
Bystrup, Bregenhoj & Partners,
architects from Copenhagen,
the winners of the inter-
national competition that
was announced in 1991.

A sequence of 17 halls
is arranged along the
Atrium, an arterial axis
600 m (1,968 ft) long. The
main entrance is flanked
by the multi-functional
ICM (International
Congress Centre
Munich) building. The
entire covered area of
200,000 sq m (50 acres)
stands in front of a large
lake. Major international events
that are held in the Neue Messe
include an information and
telecommunications fair, a
fashion show, a crafts show and
a mineralogy congress.

⑯ Blutenburg

Blutenburg. Ⓢ Obermenzing
(some distance away). 🚌 143, 160.
Internationale Jugendbibliothek:
Tel 89 12 110. **Open** 2–6pm Mon–Fri.
🖿 **blutenburg.de**

On a man-made island in
the River Würm stands
Blutenburg, a small hunting
lodge surrounded by greenery
and water. From 1425 the
lodge belonged to the
Wittelsbachs and its residents
included Duke Albrecht III, his
son Sigismund, the later
Princess Henriette Adelaide,
Therese Kunigunde Sobieska
and Maximilian I Joseph.

The lodge now houses the
**Internationale Jugend-
bibliothek**. Containing over
500,000 volumes in 110
languages, the library is the
largest collection of children's
and young people's literature
in the world and is under the
patronage of UNESCO.

The only original part of
the lodge that still stands is St
Sigismund's Chapel (1488), built
by the architects of Munich's
Frauenkirche. The frescoes on its
exterior walls are among the few
surviving examples of late Gothic
mural painting. The interior of the
chapel, covered with intricate rib
vaulting, contains some treasures of religious art, including
altarpieces of 1491 by Jan Polack
and late Gothic sculptures and
stained glass.

The doorway
of Blutenburg's
Gothic chapel

⑰ Allianz Arena

Werner-Heisenberg-Allee 25.
Tel (089) 69 93 12 22.
Ⓤ Fröttmaning.
Open 10am–6pm daily
(except match days).
🚫 (except match days).
🖿 **allianz-arena.de**

Since May 2005 the
Allianz Arena has been
home to the two
Munich football clubs – FC
Bayern München and TSV 1860
München. The stadium was
designed by the Swiss
architects Jacques Herzog and
Pierre de Meuron and can now
house more than 70,000
visitors. The distinctive exterior
consists of 2,760 rhombic air
cushions, which can be
illuminated in red, blue or
white, depending on whether
Bayern (red), TSV (blue) or the
German national team (white)
are playing. The arena covers
6,000 sq m (64,600 sq ft), has a
partial roof that shelters all
seats, and includes a fan shop
and various catering options.

SHOPPING IN MUNICH

Munich often claims to be Germany's richest and most sophisticated city and when it comes to shopping you are sure not to be disappointed. The key shopping areas are dotted around the centre of the city. You can conveniently walk around the pedestrianized central area, with numerous options for taking a break

for lunch or a coffee. Not to be missed is the visual and gourmet treat of the Viktualienmarkt food market, the classic department store Ludwig Beck and some of the smaller speciality shops tucked away in side streets. In the less commercial shopping streets, shops tend to open late morning or in the afternoon only.

Main Shopping Areas

Munich's key luxury shopping street is Maximilianstraße and those streets connected to it, Theatinerstraße, Briennerstraße and Residenzstraße. Here you will find all the top international brands and jewellery shops. For more affordable shops head to the central pedestrianized area between Kaufingerstraße, Neuhauser Straße and Marienplatz. Here you will find family shops, large chains, mid-market fashion, souvenirs and department stores. For less conventional areas with small specialist boutiques and local designers seek out the Glockenbach-viertel around Hans-Sachs-Straße, or streets radiating out from Gärtnerplatz, home to the Art Nouveau State Theatre and relaxed cafés. Schwabing is the young Bohemian area with a variety of casualwear and streetwear shops, plus fashion boutiques and plenty of laid-back bistros and coffee bars.

Department Stores and Shopping Centres

The most famous department store in Munich is **Ludwig Beck**, which has a particularly impressive Christmas decorations department in December. **Galeria Kaufhof** is another large national department store chain offering several floors of goods. Shopping Centres (*Einkaufspassagen*) are also aplenty. **Fünf Höfe** (the five courtyards) is central and upmarket. It sits between Theatiner, Maffei, Kardinal-Faulhaber and Salvator streets and mixes shopping, art and culture with cafés. Munich has several other large shopping centres. The **Stachus Passagen** is Europe's largest underground mall with 58 high street names. **Olympia-Einkaufszentrum** (OEZ) is vast with over 140 shops on two levels, **Pasing Arcaden** has more than 100 shops and the **Riem Arcaden** is home to the largest branch of H&M, a huge Lego store, C&A and Ludwig Beck Fashion.

Pedestrianized shopping area in central Munich

Fashion

Munich has a wide variety of shops for clothes and accessories. For Munich-style chic try boutiques such as **Theresa** which has the best choice of designer fashion and accessories, **Trachten Angermaier** at the Viktualienmarkt, which offers the pick of top brands and **Off & Co** in Schwabing for fashion items for both men and women.

Hohenzollernstraße in Schwabing is a good place to shop for youth-styled street fashion and trainers. For traditional Bavarian Loden costumes take a look in **Lodenfrey**.

Children's Shops

Munich is a stylish and expensive city and parents love to dress their children accordingly. This means there are some good shopping opportunities for kids' clothing and toys, mainly in the department stores and C&A. A large central shop for mother and

The exclusive shopping centre, Fünf Höfe

One of the city's regularly held flea markets

baby is **Schlichting**, as well as **Thierchen Kindermode** for original hand-made clothing. **Engel & Bengel** sells traditional-style clothing for children, as well as furniture, buggies, bedding and baby equipment.

Flea Markets

Flea markets are popular, especially at the weekends. Most take place on Saturday, some every two weeks and most only from spring to late autumn. The key ones around Munich are **Zenith Flohmarkt** (open 6am–6pm Thu–Sat) at Lilienthalallee, **Flohmarkt Riem**,

the largest flea market in Bavaria, at the trade show grounds, and **Riesenflohmarkt auf der Theresienwiese**, which takes place in the middle of April.

Food Shopping

Viktualienmarkt *(see p68)* is a huge produce market, selling fruit, vegetables, spices, meat, poultry, fish, preserves and flowers. Open daily, it is a feast for all the senses and a permanent fixture. *Bio* is the German word for organic and Germans have always been enthusiastic about organic produce. **Basic Bio** is a good organic supermarket in the city centre. For a selection

of gourmet treats head to **Dallmayr** or **Käfer**, the city's top delicatessens, while butchers' shops sell the famous Bavarian white sausages.

Christmas Market

Munich holds a traditional Christmas market *(Christkindlmarkt)* from the first week of Advent until Christmas Eve. The market is a great tourist attraction and special trips are organized from all over Europe. Wooden stalls sell a huge variety of handcrafted decorations, in particular delicately carved wooden mangers and tree decorations, in addition to candles, ornaments, food and mulled wine *(see p37)*.

Christkindlmarkt, Munich's Christmas market

DIRECTORY

Department Stores and Shopping Centres

Fünf Höfe
Theatinerstraße. Map 3 B1–2. ⓦ fuenfhoefe.de

Galeria Kaufhof
Kaufingerstraße 1–5. Map 3 B2. Tel (089) 231851. ⓦ galeria-kaufhof.de

Ludwig Beck
Marienplatz 11. Map 3 C2. Tel (089) 236910. ⓦ ludwigbeck.de

Olympia Einkaufszentrum (OEZ)
Hanauer Straße 68. ⓦ olympia-einkaufszentrum.de

Pasing Arcaden
Pasinger Bahnhofsplatz 5. ⓦ pasing-arcaden.de

Riem Arcaden
Willy-Brandt-Platz 5. ⓦ riem-arcaden.de

Stachus Passagen
Karlsplatz. Map 3 A2. ⓦ stachus-passagen.de

Fashion

Lodenfrey
Maffeistraße 7. Map 3 B2. ⓦ loden-frey.com

Off & Co
Promenadeplatz 1. ⓦ offandco.com

Theresa
Maffeistraße 3. Map 2 B4. ⓦ mytheresa.com

Trachten Angermaier
Rosental 10. Map 3 B3. ⓦ trachten-angermaier.de

Children's Shops

Engel & Bengel
Innere Wienerstraße 61. Map 4 F3. ⓦ engelundbengel.com

Schlichting
Maximilianstraße 35. Map 4 D2. ⓦ schlichting.de

Thierchen Kindermode
Hans-Sachs-Straße 15. ⓦ thierchen.net

Flea Markets

Flohmarkt Riem
Am Messeturm. Tel (089) 960 51632. ⓦ flohmarkt-riem.com

Riesenflohmarkt auf der Theresienwiese
Theresienwiese.

Zenith Flohmarkt
Lilienthalallee. Tel 0176 628 76374. ⓦ zenith-muenchen.de/flohmarkt

Food Shopping

Basic Bio
Westenriederstraße 35. Map 3 C3. ⓦ basic-ag.de

Dallmayr
Dienerstraße 14–15. Map 3 C2. ⓦ dallmayr.de

Käfer
Prinzregentenstraße 73. ⓦ feinkost-kaefer.de

Viktualienmarkt
Petersplatz-Frauenstraße. Map 3 B–C3.

ENTERTAINMENT IN MUNICH

Munich is perhaps best known for the Oktoberfest, the Olympic grounds and Hofbräuhaus, but it also has an international reputation as a city of culture. There are more than 50 theatres, three large orchestras and one opera house. Munich has the rich and the powerful of its past to thank for creating and preserving its many splendid venues. This cultured metropolis on the Isar caters to all tastes, from traditional to modern, whether in theatre, music or film. There are several festivals during the year, as well as various sporting events, when the city attracts thousands of visitors from all over the world.

Entertainment Guides and Tickets

Munich Found is the best events magazine and the **Munich Tourist Board** has comprehensive listings of events happening all over Munich. Also, be sure to check the Thursday edition of *Süddeutsche Zeitung* and the daily *Münchner Merkur*.

Tickets can be booked at box offices, by phone or in person. There are also two **Zentraler Kartenverkauf** ticket kiosks in the Marienplatz underground concourse, or use the **Nationaltheater** at Marstallplatz for tickets to the state opera, ballet and orchestra, or the Munich Opera Festival.

Theatre, Opera and Classical Music

State theatres are subsidized and tickets, therefore, are very reasonably priced. The Bavarian State Orchestra, Opera and Ballet all perform at the **Nationaltheater**. The **Deutsches Theater** offers musicals and shows, while the **Prinzregententheater** is home to the Bavarian State Opera and a concert hall. The Art Nouveau

Staatstheater am Gärtnerplatz presents opera, ballet, operetta, musicals and the Symphony Orchestra. **Gasteig Culture Center** is a world-class concert hall, home to the Munich Philharmonic Orchestra. The city also hosts an opera festival in July.

Music and Dance

The **Pasinger Fabrik** offers a good programme of jazz, chansons and café theatre. There are numerous dance events and dance clubs. Big name artists, such as Elton John, Adele and The Rolling Stones, tend to perform at the **Circus Krone Bau**, **Zenith Kulturhalle**, **Olympiahalle** and the **Olympic Stadium**.

Film

As the centre of the German film industry Munich offers 76 cinemas and a college for film and television. The **Bavarian Film Studios** offers tours of their studios daily. The **Munich Film Festival** in July boasts over 200 films on 15 screens, almost all of them German, European or world premieres.

Munich's world-famous folk festival, Oktoberfest

Festivals

Munich's most famous festival is the **Oktoberfest**. For the last two weeks of September it takes over a dedicated fairground, Theresienwiese, with beer tents, traditional Bavarian brass bands, people dressed in traditional Bavarian costume (*Trachten*), fairground rides and the famous iced gingerbread hearts, *Lebkuchenherzen*.

There is also the **Tollwood Festival** in July and December, which has music, food, a circus, performances in tents and a craft fair.

Munich also celebrates the *Dult* on three occasions throughout the year. *Dult* is the old word for street fair or market and there are traditional stalls and merry-go-rounds all over the city. Carnival or *Fasching* is celebrated throughout Munich with parties, processions and dressing up, but it is not as important here as in other cities.

The imposing Nationaltheater on Max-Joseph-Platz

Munich's ultramodern Allianz Arena

Sport

Most Münchners love the outdoors. Many make regular trips to the not too distant Alps. Running, skiing, rollerblading, cycling, Nordic walking and football are all very popular. The English Garden in the city centre is a huge park where people cycle, run or go walking.

Munich has two football teams: FC Bayern Munich and TSV 1860 München, also known as "the Lions". The **Allianz Arena** is the fantastic stadium built for the 2006 World Cup. It is an architectural marvel which lights up in various colours. For Bayern Munich merchandise head to the **FC Bayern Shop** in the Arena. The shop website gives details of other stores located at Central Station and the Hofbräuhaus.

Other key sporting events are the Bavarian International Tennis Championships (ATP tournament), the BMW International Golf Open and Munich Blade Night, on Monday evenings from April to September, when rollerbladers take over the streets.

Runners will enjoy the Media Marathon and also the Münchner Stadtlauf (city run). A sport unique to Munich is surfing on the River Isar at the weirs.

Kids' Entertainment

Children will love Kids' Kingdom – **Kinderreich** – in the Deutsches Museum *(see pp98–101)*. The area is designated for children and has giant interactive water games, plus a real fire engine. Adults can only enter with their children. Several playgrounds can be found along the River Isar in the city centre, but the best is **Spielzone Ost Westpark Sendling** which can be reached by the underground. The **Sea Life Olympiapark** centre is also an excellent outing, as is the zoo at **Tierpark Hellabrunn**.

Close encounter at Sea Life Olympiapark, Munich

DIRECTORY

Entertainment Guides and Tickets

Munich Tourist Board
W muenchen.de

Nationaltheater
(box office)
Marstallplatz 5. **Map** 3 C2.
Tel 21 85 19 20.

Zentraler Kartenverkauf
Tel (089) 54 818181.
W muenchenticket.de

Theatre, Opera and Classical Music

Deutsches Theater
Schwanthalerstr. 13. **Map** 1 E4. **Tel** (089) 552 340.

Gasteig Culture Center
Rosenheimer Str. 5.
Tel (089) 480980.

Nationaltheater
Max-Joseph-Platz. **Map** 2 B4. **Tel** (089) 21851920.

Prinzregententheater
Prinzregentenstr. 12. **Map** 3 D3. **Tel** (089) 21851920.

Staatstheater am Gärtnerplatz
Gärtnerplatz 3.
Tel (089) 202411.

Music and Dance

Circus Krone Bau
Marsstraße 43. **Map** 1 E3.
Tel (089) 5458000.
W circus-krone.de

Olympiahalle and Olympic Stadium
Spiridon-Louis-Ring 21.
Tel (089) 54 818181
(tickets).
W olympiapark.de

Pasinger Fabrik
August-Exter-Str. 1.
Tel (089) 82929079.

Zenith Kulturhalle
Lilienthalallee 29.
W zenith-die-kulturhalle.de

Film

Bavarian Film Studios
W filmstadt.de

Munich Film Festival
W filmfest-muenchen.de

Festivals

Oktoberfest
W oktoberfest.de

Tollwood Festival
W tollwood.de

Sport

Allianz Arena
W allianz-arena.de

FC Bayern Shop
W shop.fcbayern.de

Kids' Entertainment

Kinderreich
Deutsches Museum, Museumsinsel 1. **Tel** (089) 21791. W deutsches-museum.de

Sea Life Olympiapark
Willi-Daume-Platz 1.
Tel (089) 45 00 00.
W visitsealife.com

Spielzone Ost Westpark Sendling
Preßburger Straße.

Tierpark Hellabrunn
Tierparkstr. 30. **Tel** (089) 625 080. W hellabrunn.de

MUNICH STREET FINDER

Map references given for historic buildings and other sights throughout the chapter on Munich refer to the maps included on the following pages only.

The key map below shows the area of Munich covered by the *Street Finder*. Buildings and monuments in pink are star sights that are covered in detail in the chapter; those in brown are sights and places that are worth seeing. Streets shown in yellow are closed to traffic.

The *Street Finder* maps include U-Bahn and S-Bahn stations as well as main car parks, hospitals, police stations, tourist information centres and taxi ranks in Munich. The word *Straße (Str.)* indicates a street, *Platz* a square, *Brücke* a bridge and *Bahnhof* a railway station.

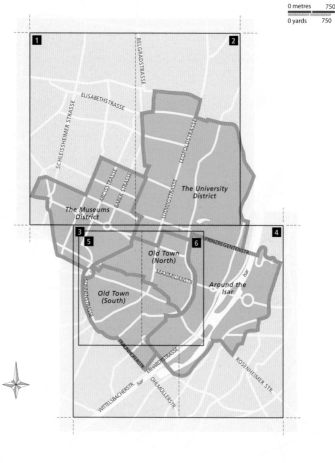

Key

▓ Major sight	✚ Hospital	
░ Place of interest	✝ Church	
Ⓤ U-Bahn station	✡ Synagogue	
Ⓢ S-Bahn station	— Pedestrianized street	
🚓 Police station		
🛈 Tourist information		

Scale of Maps 1–4

0 metres 200
0 yards 200 — 1:11,750

Scale of Maps 5–6

0 metres 150
0 yards 150 — 1:7,000

Street Finder

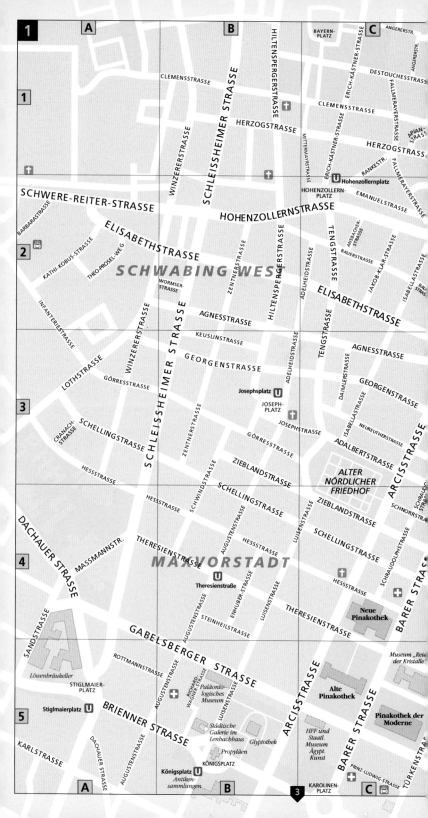

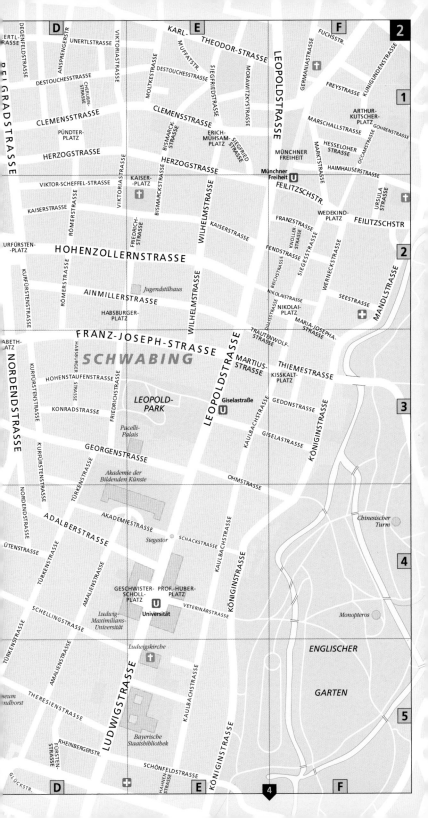

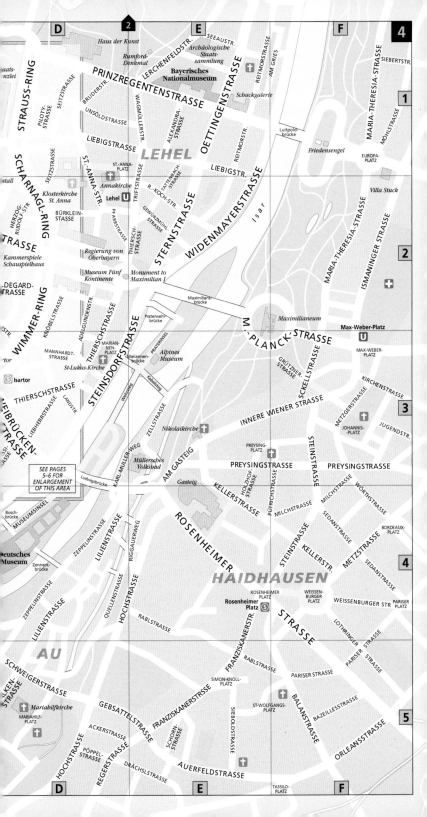

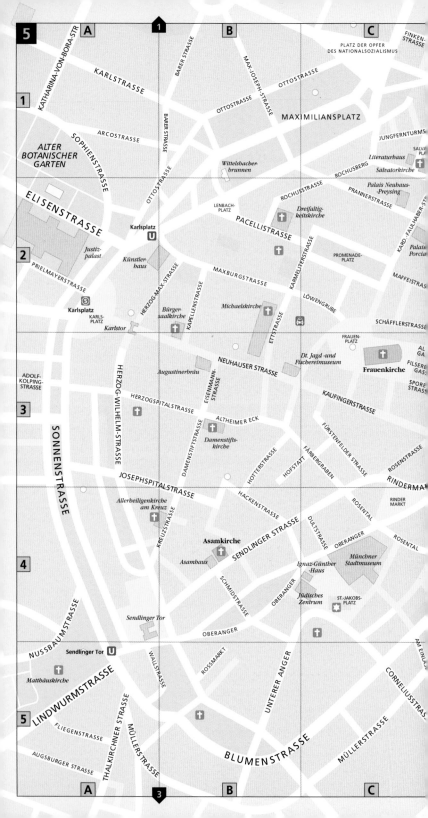

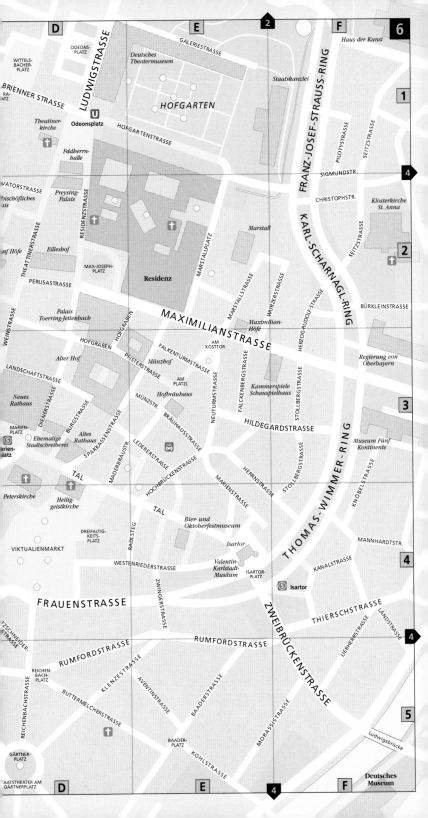

THE BAVARIAN ALPS AREA BY AREA

The Bavarian Alps at a Glance

The Bavarian Alps have much to offer tourists. Well endowed with ski lifts and shelters, the Alps offer ideal conditions for skiers, while the many lakes draw watersports enthusiasts and ice-skaters. The mountainous regions of the Bavarian Forest are a delight, both for their primeval natural surroundings and for the affordable prices to be found here. Many of the region's towns and villages contain buildings of great splendour and architectural importance.

Augsburg
Because of its many canals which are crossed by bridges, this town is known as the Venice of the North (*see pp252–7*).

Ottobeuren
The Rococo stalls of this renowned Benedictine church are part of the overall decorative scheme (*see p232*).

Wallerstein

Nördlingen

Monheim

Donauwörth

Rain

Lauingen

Höchstädt

SOUTHERN SWABIA
(*See pp242–59*)

Leipheim

Neu-Ulm

Gersthofe

Augsburg

Neuschwanstein
This castle is the embodiment of Ludwig II's idea of a romantic seat of power. It has a fantastical setting, and its design, particularly that of the towers, was the model for Disneyland's fairy-tale castle (*see pp234–5*).

Fürstenfeldb

Memmingen

Landsberg am Lech

THE ALLGÄU
(*See pp226–41*)

Kempten

Marktoberdorf

Schongau

Murnau

Wasserburg

Garmisc
Partenki

Linderhof
The gardens surrounding Ludwig II's favourite palace were modelled on those of Versailles. The fountains and cascades add a magical dimension (*see p220*).

Oberammergau
Like many others here, this house, built in 1775, is covered with *Lüftlmalerei*. Oberammergau is the centre of this type of trompe l'oeil decoration (*see p220*).

◀ Picturesque view of Burghausen with its castle in the background

Altmühl
Picturesquely set on a hill, Prunn Castle overlooks the River Altmühl with its wooden bridge – the oldest and longest in Europe *(see p187).*

Hallertau
This region is renowned for its hop plantations, which supply the country's brewing industry, so satisfying the demand for beer from both home and export markets *(see p163).*

Viechtach

Zwiesel

Bogen

Regen

Metten

Deggendorf

Tittling

Kelheim

Abensberg

Ingolstadt

Dingolfing

Vilshofen

Oberznell

LOWER BAVARIA
(See pp178–97)

Landshut

Passau

UPPER
ARIA (NORTH)
(See pp162–77)

Moosburg

Freising

Eggenfelden

Pfarrkirchen

Pocking

terschleißheim

Erding

Garching

Dorfen

Mühldorf

München

Haag

UPPER BAVARIA
(EAST)
(See pp198–209)

mering

Ebersberg

nberg

Rott am Inn

Traunreut

ER BAVARIA
(SOUTH)
See pp210–25)

Miesbach

Bernau

Freilassing

Anger

Bad Tölz

Lenggries

0 kilometres   30

0 miles   30

Herrenchiemsee
Bavaria's largest palace, with the most extensive grounds, features sculpture created for Ludwig II *(see p206).*

Schwarzeck
Schwarzeck is one of the many hiking and skiing stations around Berchtesgaden, reached by a steep and winding road *(see p204).*

UPPER BAVARIA (NORTH)

Consisting of flat countryside traversed by the river valleys of the Danube and its tributaries the Isar, Iller, Paar and Altmühl, this region of Upper Bavaria (Oberbayern) is not as varied as the south. However, it has plenty of historic monuments, as at Eichstätt and Freising, and architectural gems such as the palace at Schleißheim.

During the Jurassic period 150 million years ago, a lagoon existed at the northern edges of this region. This became what is today the valley of the meandering River Altmühl, the location of the third largest nature reserve in Germany. Many Jurassic fossils have been unearthed here, particularly in the area around Eichstätt.

More recent history concerns Dachau, a charming little town just 25 km (15.5 miles) northwest of Munich. Its name has become synonymous with one of the earliest concentration camps to be set up in Germany, in 1933. The camp is still surrounded by barbed wire and guard towers still stand. The site functions as a museum of the Nazis' cruel system of forced labour and extermination in which millions of victims of the Third Reich lost their lives. It is preserved as a memento and a warning to present and future generations.

The northern part of Upper Bavaria is mainly farmland. Extensive asparagus plantations stretch out around Schrobenhausen, while in a region between the rivers Amper and Danube, an area known as Hallertau, endless forest-like plantations indicate the large-scale production of the hops that are used in the brewing of beer, Bavarians' top tipple. Hallertau forms part of the Hopfenstraße, or German Hop Trail. Along the way lies Ingolstadt, whose main claim to fame nowadays is the Audi car plant.

Here, too, are many fine historic buildings. The imposing outlines of castles tower over towns such as Beilngries, Eichstätt, Ingolstadt and Neuburg, on the northern fringes of this region. There is also a wealth of ecclesiastical buildings, the most prominent among which are the churches and abbeys at Scheyern, Indersdorf and Fürstenfeldbruck.

The imposing Baroque façade and formal gardens of the Neues Schloss in Schleißheim

◀ Painted ceiling of the Great Hall in Neues Schloss, Schleißheim

Exploring Upper Bavaria (North)

Any exploration of the northern part of Upper Bavaria should take in the Baroque Neues Schloss at Schleißheim, the grandest building in the area, set in extensive parkland. Equally interesting is the town of Freising, with its fine cathedral and the Diözesanmuseum, which contains one of the most resplendent collections of religious art in Germany. Nature-lovers looking for particularly beautiful countryside should head for the Altmühltal or the region of Hallertau, where hop plantations stretch to the horizon.

Getting Around

Several roads traverse northern Upper Bavaria. Motorways A9 and A93 lead to the north of Germany via Nuremberg and Regensburg. Motorway A8 leads west to Stuttgart, the A92 heads east to Lower Bavaria, and the A96 leads to the southwest. The S-Bahn local rail network and Deutsche Bahn national rail network provide links between towns. Franz-Josef-Strauß Airport, near Freising, provides air links with other cities in Germany and the rest of the world.

Nürnber
Würzburg
Titting
Fränkische Al
Atm
🏠🏛️🏥
❶ EICHSTÄTT
Adelschlag
Tauberfeld

🏠🏛️🏥 Danube (Dona
NEUBURG AN ❹
DER DONAU
Donauwörth
Burgheim
Hag
16
D o n a u m o o s
Niederarnbach
Hauptkanal
Schrobenhausen
300
Gerolsbach
Altomünste
Augsburg
Glonn
Egenhofen
8
Bergkirchen
2
Maisach
🏠
FÜRSTENFELDBRUCK ❶❸
Gröbenze
Germer
Memmingen
96

The grand Baroque staircase of the Neues Schloss in Schleißheim

For keys to symbols see back flap

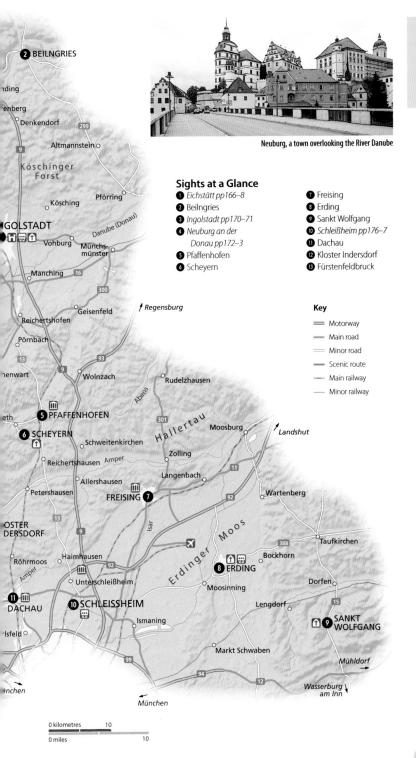

Neuburg, a town overlooking the River Danube

Sights at a Glance

1 *Eichstätt pp166–8*
2 Beilngries
3 *Ingolstadt pp170–71*
4 *Neuburg an der Donau pp172–3*
5 Pfaffenhofen
6 Scheyern

7 Freising
8 Erding
9 Sankt Wolfgang
10 *Schleißheim pp176–7*
11 Dachau
12 Kloster Indersdorf
13 Fürstenfeldbruck

Key

▭▭▭ Motorway
▬▬▬ Main road
····· Minor road
▬▬▬ Scenic route
▬▬▬ Main railway
──── Minor railway

❶ Eichstätt

Eichstätt, a centre of religious life since 741, is probably one of the prettiest towns in Bavaria. It stands in an exceptionally scenic location in the valley of the River Altmühl. The town's appearance was largely determined by 30 years of work by Maurizio Pedetti and Gabriel de Gabrieli, a prominent architect of the first half of the 18th century who was also active in Vienna. The town's unique atmosphere is further enhanced by the Catholic university and its students.

Tenement houses lining Marktplatz

🏛 Marktplatz

Marktplatz, north of the cathedral, is the focal point of the burghers' district. It is surrounded by the houses of prominent merchants, and these magnificent abodes alternate with modest craftsmen's houses. On the west side of the square stands the town hall, whose tower dates from 1444. The façade and upper part of the tower were built in 1823–4.

Eichstätt's other squares – Residenzplatz, Domplatz and Leonrodplatz – were also key elements in the urban planning of the town. Residenzplatz is

The magnificent tomb of St Willibald in the cathedral

one of the finest squares in the whole of Germany. It lies south of the cathedral and has a trapezoid shape. The two-storey buildings that line the square were originally part of the chapterhouses that were designed by Gabriel de Gabrieli.

Domplatz, with the cathedral on its southern side, is laid out on the site of the former cemetery.

On Leonrodplatz stands the church and former Jesuit abbey, as well as the former cathedral deaconry.

🏛 Dom St Salvator und St Willibald

Domplatz.

Eichstätt's cathedral has a late-Gothic nave and presbytery, the latter flanked by twin Romanesque towers. The Baroque façade was built by Gabriel de Gabrieli in 1716–18.

The Gothic cloisters on the south side of the cathedral adjoin the presbytery. The west wing of the cloisters contains a double-naved moratorium containing the Gothic tombs of priests, chaplains and benefactors of the cathedral. Distinctive among the many works of art to be seen in the

cathedral is the statue of St Willibald, who became the first bishop of Eichstätt in the 8th century. The statue, carved in the late Gothic style, was made in 1514 by Loy Hering. In 1745 Matthias Seybold built the two-sided Pappenheimer altar with a canopy to cover the statue of the saint and the tomb containing his relics. This altar is located on the elevated part at the west end of the cathedral.

🏛 Fürstbischöfliche Residenz

Residenzplatz 1. **Tel** (08421) 700.
🕐 7:30am–noon & 2–4pm Mon–Wed, 2–5:30pm Thu, 7:30am–noon Fri.

The former bishop's residence, which adjoins the cathedral on its southern side, was built in 1700–27 to a rectangular plan with a central courtyard. The interior has decorative stuccowork and Rococo frescoes, and features a fine Rococo staircase and Hall of Mirrors, from the 1700s. The Residenz houses the district administration.

The main staircase of the former bishop's residence

🏛 Schutzengelkirche

Ostenstr.

This former Jesuit church was built in 1617–20 under the direction of Hans Alberthal. Having suffered destruction in 1634, in the course of the Thirty Years' War, it was rebuilt in 1660. The interior was lavishly decorated by Franz Gabriel and Johann Rosner, among others, in the first half of the 18th century.

For hotels and restaurants in this region see pp267–8 and p279

Romanesque rotunda inside
the Kapuzinerkirche

To the south of the church are
the buildings of the former
Jesuit College, dating from the
17th and 18th centuries, with
two courtyards and cloisters. The
college is now used as a seminary.

🏠 Kloster Notre Dame du Sacré Cœur

Notre Dame 1. **Open** Apr–Oct: 9am–
5pm Mon–Fri, 10am–5pm Sat & Sun;
Nov–Mar: 9am–noon & 2–4pm Mon–
Thu, 9am–noon Fri. Informationszentrum
Naturpark Altmühltal: **Tel** (08421) 98
760. 🇼 **naturpark-altmuehltal.de**

This convent was built for a
foundation established in 1711
for the education of young girls.

Work on the convent began in
1712, and on the church in 1719,
both to designs by the architect
Gabriel de Gabrieli.

The church has a centralized
plan. The façade is divided by
huge pilasters and decorated with
a sculpture of the Immaculate
Conception above the portal. The
headquarters of the information
centre for Altmühl Valley National
Park are housed in the church.

🏠 Kapuzinerkirche Kreuz und zum Heiligen Grab

Kapuzinergasse 2. **Tel** (08421) 6001
400. **Open** Daily during daylight

This modest church of the
Capuchin monks was built
in 1623–5 and enlarged in
1905. To the south of the
nave stands an oval stone-
built Romanesque rotunda
crowned by an open gallery
and a dome supported on
tall, slender columns. It was
built in 1160 in imitation of
the Church of the Holy
Sepulchre in Jerusalem.

VISITORS' CHECKLIST

Practical Information
Road map C2. 📊 13,400.
ℹ️ Domplatz 8, (08421) 600
1400. 🇼 **eichstaett.de**
📅 Fliegerfest (May/Jun),
Burgfest auf der Willibaldsburg
(Jul/Aug), Brauereifest (Aug),
Volksfest (Aug/Sep).

Transport
🚌 🚆 Bahnhofplatz 17.

🏠 Fürstbischöfliche Sommerresidenz

Ostenstr. 24.
The former bishop's summer
residence, also designed by
Gabriel de Gabrieli, dates from
1735–7. The ground and upper
floors and narrow side galleries
now house the offices of the
Catholic university. The residence
is set in geometrically laid out
parkland that merges into a
landscaped park descending in
terraces to the River Altmühl.

The Baroque façade of the former bishop's summer residence

Eichstätt Town Centre

① Marktplatz
② Dom St Salvator
   and St Willibald
③ Fürstbischöfliche Residenz
④ Schutzengelkirche
⑤ Kloster Notre Dame
   du Sacré Cœur

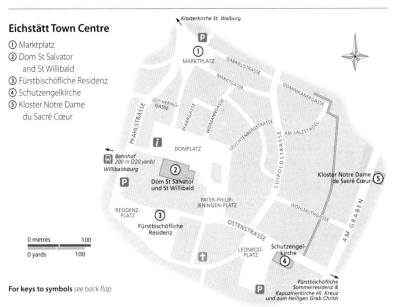

Klosterkirche St. Walburg

① MARKTPLATZ
GABRIELISTRASSE
MARKTGASSE
DOMINIKANERGASSE
LOY-HERING-GASSE
PFARRGASSE
WIDMANNGASSE
PFAHLSTRASSE
LEUCHTENBERGSTRASSE
AM SALZADEL
DOMPLATZ

Bahnhof
200 m (220 yards)
Willibaldsburg

② Dom St Salvator
und St Willibald
LUIPOLDSTRASSE

⑤ Kloster Notre Dame
de Sacré Cœur

PATER-PHILIP-
JENINGEN-PLATZ
WOHLMUTHGASSE
AM GRABEN

RESIDENZ-
PLATZ
③ Fürstbischöfliche
Residenz
OSTENSTRASSE

LEONROD-
PLATZ
④ Schutzengel-
kirche

0 metres   100
0 yards   100

Fürstbischöfliche
Sommerresidenz &
Kapuzinerkirche Hl. Kreuz
und zum Heiligen Grab Christi

⬆ Klosterkirche St Walburg
Westenstr.

This church was built on the spot where the relics of St Walburg were buried in 875. The present monastery dates from 1629–31. In the chapel behind the high altar is St Walburg's tomb, the church's most holy feature and the object of pilgrimages. The chapel, which contains numerous votive images placed there in gratitude to the saint, is decorated with intricate wrought-iron grilles. The altarpiece consists of Gothic carvings depicting St Walburg, his parents and his brother, St Willibald.

🏛 Willibaldsburg
Burgstr. 19. Jura-Museum: **Tel** (08421) 29 56, (08421) 47 30. **Open** Apr–Sep: 9am–6pm, Tue–Sun; Oct–Mar: 10am–4pm Tue–Sun. Museum für Ur- und Frühgeschichte: **Tel** (08421) 89 450. **Open** Apr–Sep: 9am–6pm Tue–Sun; Oct–Mar: 10am–4pm Tue–Sun.

This castle, on a hill northwest of the town centre, overlooks the Altmühl river valley. It can be reached by car through a tunnel 63 m (206 ft) long. The castle has an elongated design and is surrounded by 17th century fortifications. From 1353 to 1725 it was the seat of bishops but was partly demolished in the 19th century. The present approaches to the castle were built in the first half of the 17th-century. The castle walls contain the ruins of a residence built for

Bishop Martin von Schaumberg (1560–90).

The western section of the hill is occupied by a three-winged building with central cloisters, and a main building with small towers. Both were built by Elias Holl, who was brought to Eichstätt by Bishop Konrad von Gemmingen in 1609. Together with Augsburg town hall, they are regarded as Germany's most important late Renaissance buildings.

The north wing houses the **Jura-Museum**, with a rich collection of fossils from the Jurassic period. The south wing contains the **Museum für Ur- und Frühgeschichte** (Museum of Prehistory and Early History), with fascinating displays.

❷ Beilngries

Road map D2. 🚉 9,300. 🚌 🚆
ℹ Hauptstr. 14, (08461) 84 35.
🔲 beilngries.de

The best way to reach Beilngries is by road or boat from Kelheim along the scenic Altmühl valley. The town still has a section of its defensive walls, which are set with nine towers and reinforced by a fosse (moat). Among the historic buildings on Hauptstraße is the late 16th-century house at No. 25,

Romanesque tower, a vestige of the medieval castle outside Beilngries

known as the **Kaiserbeckhaus**, which has a cantilevered upper storey supported on corbels.

The imposing Neo-Baroque **Pfarrkirche St Walburga** was built in 1912–13 to a design by Wilhelm Spannagl. The span of its vaulting and the ingenuity of its circular windows are impressive.

On a steep hill outside the town once stood a medieval castle, vestiges of which are two tall Romanesque **towers** flanking the gatehouse. In 1760–4 the castle was converted into the **Bishop's hunting lodge**. Its main decorative motifs are deer, which led to its being called Schloss Hirschberg ("Deer Mountain"). The Imperial Hall and the Knights' Hall are decorated with paintings by Michael Franz and have Rococo stuccowork. The palace chapel, built with material from the walls of the Romanesque castle chapel, was designed by Alexander von Branca in the 1980s.

❸ Ingolstadt
See pp170–71.

❹ Neuburg an der Donau
See pp172–3.

Fossils from the Jurassic Era

About 150 million years ago, the region of the Altmühl river valley in northern Upper Bavaria and southern Franconia lay beneath a shallow lagoon that was separated from the open Jurassic sea by a reef of

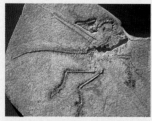

corals and sponges. Today collectors search quarries for fossils of ammonites, small crustaceans, insects and marine plants. For a modest sum impressive specimens can also be purchased from the quarry workers. A rich collection of fossils is on view in the Jura-Museum in Willibaldsburg castle in Eichstätt.

A fossil of *Archaeopteryx lithographica* in the Jura-Museum in Eichstätt

❺ Pfaffenhofen

Road map D3. 🔼 4,500. 🚌 🚊
ℹ️ Hauptplatz 47, (08441) 78 22 50.
🌐 **pfaffenhofen.de**

The town, situated on the
River Ilm, lies at the western
extremity of the hop-growing
region. It was once surrounded
by fortifications set with 17
towers and pierced by four
gates. Around the pleasant
square stands the Gothic
St Johannes-Baptist-Kirche
and a Neo-Gothic **town hall**.
A tall, square tower with a
steeple stands beside the
church presbytery. The
Mesnerhaus, a
residential house
dating from 1786,
contains a **museum**
with a sizeable
collection of art
dating from the 16th
to the 19th centuries.

🏛️ **Museum im
Mesnerhaus**
Scheyrer Str. 5. **Tel**
(08441) 27 442 or
(08441) 18 362.
Open only by prior
arrangement.

Soaring Gothic tower of St Johannes-
Baptist-Kirche, Pfaffenhofen

❻ Scheyern

Road map D3. 🔼 4,800. 🚌 🚊 in
Pfaffenhofen. ℹ️ Ludwigstr. 2, (08441)
80 640.

Scheyern lies southwest of
Pfaffenhofen. In 1119, when the
seat of the Scheyern family was
converted into a monastery, it
was occupied by monks of the
Benedictine order. After the first
wave of the dissolution of the

Façade of the Benedictine monastery in Scheyern

monasteries, the Benedictines
left but returned in 1837 at the
request of Ludwig I.

The triple-nave basilica
of **Mariä Himmelfahrt** was
remodelled in the Baroque
style in 1768–9, with decorative
mouldings by the Wessobrunn
stuccoists. The Chapel of the
Holy Cross contains a Baroque
altar with a late Renaissance
crucifix of 1600. The centrepiece of the tabernacle is a
Byzantine relic of the True Cross,
which is kept in a magnificent
monstrance made by Johann
Georg in 1738.

❼ Freising

Road map D3. 🔼 47,000. 🚌 🚊 Ⓢ
ℹ️ Rindermarkt 20, (08161) 54 44 111.
🌐 **freising.de**

The seat of a bishopric from 720,
the town was for centuries the
residence of the bishops of
Freising and Munich. The hill
on which the **cathedral** stands is
known as Mons Doctus (Learned
Mount). The cathedral dates
from the mid-13th century,
with the cloisters added
in the 15th century. It
was remodelled in
1723–4 with the
involvement of the
Asam brothers (see p72).

An outstanding
feature of the interior
is a Pietà of 1492 by
Erasmus Grasser and
Gothic stalls dating
from 1485–8. The
Romanesque crypt
contains a column
known as the
Bestiensäule, which
is decorated with
carvings symbolizing

Oriel window of
Freising town hall

the fight against evil. Beside the
crypt is the Maximilianskapelle,
with stuccowork and paintings
by Hans Georg Asam.

The late Gothic **cloisters**
feature paintings by Johann
Baptist Zimmermann of 1717
and tombstones dating from
the 15th to the 18th centuries.
The cloisters are linked to the
Gothic **Benediktuskirche** of
1345, and a stunning Baroque
cathedral library designed by
François Cuvilliés.

The Gothic **Johanniskirche**, in
front of the cathedral, is linked
to the **bishop's residence**,
which has fine Renaissance
cloisters. On the cathedral hill
is the **Diözesanmuseum**, the
largest museum of religious
art in Germany.

In the town at the bottom
of the hill are the church of
St Peter und Paul, designed
in the early 18th century by
Giovanni Antonio Viscardi,
with paintings by Johann
Baptist Zimmermann, and
the late Gothic **St-Georg-
Kirche**, with a Baroque tower,
as well as the Neo-
Renaissance **town
hall** of 1904–05.

On Weihenstephan
hill stands the world's
oldest **brewery**,
founded in 1040.
The Benedictine
monastery now
houses certain
departments of
Munich's Technical
University.

🏛️ **Diözesanmuseum**
Domberg 21. **Tel** (08161)
48 790. **Open** check
website for details.
🌐 **dimu-freising.de**

❸ Ingolstadt

Ludwig the Rich founded Bavaria's first university here in 1472. Initially a centre of humanism, it later became a focal point of the Counter-Reformation. In the 16th century Ingolstadt was the largest fortified town in southern Germany, and was defended by Swedish soldiers during the Thirty Years' War. It suffered severe bomb damage during World War II but was restored soon after. Today Ingolstadt is known principally for Audi cars, which are manufactured here, and for its oil refinery. However, it also has some noteworthy buildings.

Alte Anatomie, now the Deutsches Medizinhistorisches Museum

The Baroque interior of the Asamkirche Maria de Victoria

🏛 Museum Mobile

Audi Forum Ingolstadt, Ettinger Straße 60. **Tel** (0800) 283 4444. **Open** 9am–6pm daily. 🅿 **w** audi-mediacenter.com

With its "museum mobile", the Audi Forum is a delight for car enthusiasts. More than 80 Audi cars, motorbikes and bicycles are on display and the history of the automobile is documented in fascinating detail.

⬆ Asamkirche Maria de Victoria

Neubaustraße. **Open** Nov–Feb: 1–4pm Tue–Sun; Mar–Oct: 9am–5pm Tue–Sun (May–Oct: daily). Organ concerts, Apr–Oct: noon Sun. 🅿

This hall was built in 1732–6 as the meeting place of the Marian students' association. The stuccowork is by Egid Quirin Asam, and the painting by his brother Cosmas Damian Asam, who exploited the various points of perspective as he covered the ceiling with extensive frescoes. The sacristy contains a famous monstrance of 1708 by the Augsburg goldsmith Johannes Zeckl, depicting the defeat of the Turks at the Battle of Lepanto in 1571.

🏰 Kreuztor and City Walls

The city walls, together with their semicircular towers, were built from 1362 to 1440. Of the four original city gates, only the western one, known as the Kreuztor, survives. It is considered to be one of the finest of its kind in Germany.

The Taschenturm, a tower with stepped gables, also survives. Of the fortification towers, built from 1539 to 1579 and demolished in 1800, only the ruins of casemates and bastions still stand today. Fortifications begun in 1823 are dotted around the town.

⬆ Liebfrauenmünster

Bergbräustr./Kreuzstr. 1.

This great 15th-century church with diagonally set twin towers is one of the largest Gothic brick buildings in Bavaria.

The high altar, completed in 1572, commemorates the centenary of the foundation of Ingolstadt's university. The altar, 9 m (30 ft) high, incorporates 91 paintings by Hans Mielich. Other features of the interior are the Renaissance stalls and pulpit, the Gothic and Renaissance stained glass, and the monument to Johannes Eck, Martin Luther's greatest opponent, who died in 1543.

🏰 Alte Anatomie

Anatomiestr. 18/20. Deutsches Medizinhistorisches Museum: **Tel** (0841) 305 2860. **Open** 10am–5pm Tue–Sun. 🅿 **w** dmm-ingolstadt.de

This fine Baroque building, completed in 1723, originally housed the university's Department of Medicine and is now home to a museum of medical history. The pleasant courtyard has a garden where medicinal herbs are grown.

The Gothic Kreuztor, Ingolstadt's western gate

For hotels and restaurants in this region see pp267–8 and p279

🏰 Neues Schloss

Paradeplatz 4. Bayerisches
Armeemuseum: **Tel** (0841) 93 77 222.
Open 9am–5:30pm Tue–Fri,
10am–5:30pm Sat & Sun. 🚫
🌐 **armeemuseum.de**

The Neues Schloss (New Castle)
was built in the first half of the
15th century. Set with corner
towers, the two-storey castle
appears to be an impregnable
stronghold. A Renaissance gateway leads into an inner courtyard.
The castle houses the **Bavarian
Army Museum**, displaying items
from the wars against the Turks.

🏰 Herzogskasten

Hallstr. 4.

This ancient castle, standing on
the southeastern corner of the city
walls, was built in 1255. The oldest
secular building in Ingolstadt, it

The Neo-Renaissance Altes Rathaus, with
its elaborate gable

was a ducal residence until it was
superseded by the Neues Schloss,
which was built in the 15th
century. The castle then was
converted into a granary. Rising
two storeys high, it has a very tall
roof with a Gothic stepped gable.
It now houses a library.

VISITORS' CHECKLIST

Practical Information
Road map D2. 🚗 132,500.
ℹ️ Altes Rathaus, Rathausplatz
2, (0841) 30 53 030.
email: touristinformation@
ingolstadt.de
🎪 Ingolstädter Bürgerfest
(first weekend in Jul).
🌐 ingolstadt-tourismus.de

Transport
🚌 🚊 (0841) 93 41 825.

🏛 Altes Rathaus

Rathausplatz 2.

The elegant town hall was
lavishly remodelled in the
Neo-Renaissance style by
Gabriel von Seidl in 1882–3.
Its sculptural decoration was
designed by Lorenz Gedon. The
building incorporates a
former residence.

⛪ Moritzkirche

Hieronymus Str. 3.

Begun in the mid-14th century
and completed in 1489, the
church is a Gothic basilica with
a 14th–15th-century watchtower known as the Pfeifturm.
  The hospital nearby,
completed in 1434, served as
the main university building
from 1472 to 1800.

The Neues Schloss, an elegant and imposing residence

Ingolstadt City Centre

① Asamkirche Maria de Victoria
② Kreuztor and City Walls
③ Liebfrauenmünster
④ Alte Anatomie
⑤ Herzogskasten
⑥ Neues Schloss
⑦ Altes Rathaus
⑧ Moritzkirche

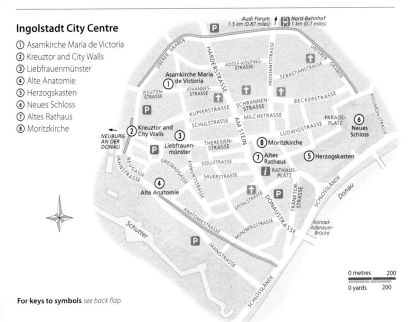

❶ Neuburg an der Donau

Situated on the River Danube (Donau), Neuburg is considered to be one of Bavaria's most beautiful towns. The atmosphere from the time when it flourished as a ducal residence lives on in the streets and squares of the Obere Stadt (Upper Town). These are rivalled by the Obere Vorstadt, an early centre of the Counter-Reformation, which has an Ursuline convent as well as patricians' town houses and the palaces of the court elite. Along the Danube lies the Englischer Garten, a park traversed by the road to the 16th-century castle of the Wittelsbachs in nearby Grünau.

Oberes Tor, gateway to the Upper Town

🏛 Oberes Tor and Town Walls

In the 14th century Obere Stadt was enclosed by walls, towers and galleries. Considerable vestiges of the upper town remain, notably Oberes Tor, the main gate. It was rebuilt in 1530, when it was flanked by circular towers and topped with a Renaissance gable.

🏰 Peterskirche

Amalienstr. 40.

The church stands on the site of the oldest church in Neuburg, first mentioned in 1214. It was designed by Johann Serro of Graubünden and built in 1641–6. The triple-nave open interior is decorated with Baroque painting and stuccowork.

🏛 Amalienstraße

Of the many fine gabled houses that line this street, two are especially worthy of note. One is the Eybhaus, the old post office, built in 1720 and located next to Weveldhaus, and the other the Court Pharmacy, first mentioned in 1713. Both have ornamental gables. Equally elegant are the 17th and 18th-century houses that can be seen in Herrenstraße.

🏛 Stadtmuseum im Weveldhaus

Amalienstr. A47. **Open** Mar–Dec: 10am–6pm Tue–Sun. **Closed** Jan–Feb.
🌐 **stadtmuseum-neuburg.de**

The two-storey late Gothic Weveldhaus was built in the 16th century, and was redecorated in 1715 by Gabriel de Gabrieli, who added a fine Baroque portal. The building houses a museum displaying artifacts relating to the history of the town and the surrounding area.

🏛 Karlsplatz

There are few town squares in Bavaria more charming than Karlsplatz. Surrounded by trees, it has a Mariensäule (Column of the Virgin) and a fountain in the centre. The square is dominated by the façade of Hofkirche, which occupies its entire eastern side. The square boasts exquisite proportions and fine, elegant

Baroque doorway of the Weveldhaus on Amalienstraße

buildings. On the northern side of the square stands the Renaissance town hall of 1603–09. Its double exterior stairway leads to the grand entrance on the first floor. Beside it stands the Taxishaus (named after the von Thurn und Taxis family). It was completed in 1747 and its façade is decorated with elaborate poly-chrome stuccowork. Further on is the Zieglerhaus, with fine wrought-iron grilles and an elegant gate.

On the west side of the square is the pleasantly proportioned and decorated Lorihaus and the library building, its Rococo façade facing onto Amalienstraße. Built in 1731–2, it was furnished in 1802 with furniture from the Kaisheim monastery library.

Mariensäule on Karlsplatz

🏰 Hofkirche

Karlsplatz 10.

The former Hofkirche (Court Church) was founded by the Protestant rulers of Neuburg in reaction to the building of the Jesuit Michaelskirche in Munich. Work began in 1608 but was interrupted by the death of Philip Ludwig. In 1617 his Catholic successor brought the Jesuits to Neuburg and donated the church to them. It was completed in 1627.

The late Renaissance building, with a flat façade and a central octagonal domed tower, was decorated with fine stuccowork in 1616–18. The paintings by Peter Paul Rubens that once graced the altar are now in the Alte Pinakothek in Munich. Some particularly interesting features of the presbytery are the ducal loggia and the stairway to the crypt, the dukes' final resting place. A passage connects the church to the neighbouring castle.

For hotels and restaurants in this region see pp267–8 and p279

Ornate interior of Pfarrkirche Mariä Himmelfahrt

🏛 Schloss

Residenzstr. 2. **Tel** (08431) 64430.
Open 10am–5pm Tue–Sun. 🎫
Schloss museum: **Open** Apr–Sep:
9am–6pm Tue–Sun; Oct–Mar:
10am–4pm Tue–Sun.

The history of Neuburg Castle goes back to Roman times, when the fort of Venaxa-modorum stood here. It has been in the possession of the Wittelsbach family since the 13th century. The present-day castle was built in 1530–45 and was redecorated in the Renaissance style in 1667–70. It has a pentagonal outline and is set with two circular towers that look onto the Danube.

The attractive Renaissance courtyard is surrounded by a double-tiered gallery. The west side of the courtyard has sgraffito decorations and two stone figures of dukes, probably dating from the second half of the 17th century. The west wing has a Renaissance chapel with galleries and ceiling frescoes painted by Hans Bockberger in 1543. These were plastered over in 1616, when Protestant fervour celebrated its triumph over Catholicism, but they were uncovered again in 1934–51.

An underground passage beneath Neuer Bau, the north wing, leads from the Danube to Obere Stadt. The Baroque grottoes are open to visitors.

VISITORS' CHECKLIST

Practical Information
Road map C2. 🚉 29,200.
ℹ️ Ottheinrichplatz A118,
(08431) 55 240. 🎭 Schlossfest
(in odd years, Jun/Jul); Volksfest
(Jul); Kartoffelwochen (Oct).
email: tourist@neuburg-donau.de
🌐 **neuburg-donau.de**

Transport
🚌

🏛 Former Jesuit College

Am Unteren Tor.
This 17th-century college building has a modest but imaginatively designed façade. On the third floor is the former assembly hall, which is renowned for its excellent acoustics.

Stone figures in the arcaded courtyard of the Schloss

Neuburg Town Centre

① Oberes Tor and Town Walls
② Peterskirche
③ Amalienstraße
④ Stadtmuseum Weveldhaus
⑤ Karlsplatz
⑥ Hofkirche
⑦ Schloss
⑧ Former Jesuit College

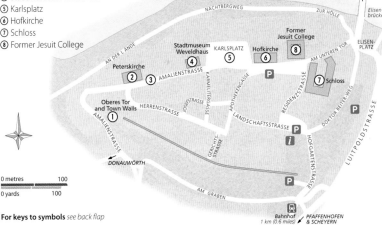

0 metres   100
0 yards   100

For keys to symbols *see back flap*

The Landshuter Tor in Erding, crowned by a Baroque dome

❽ Erding

Road map D3. 🏔 36,200. 🚌 🚃 ⑤
ℹ Landshuter Str. 1, (08122) 40 80.
🇼 erding.de

Known primarily for its beer, this town is bounded by the rivers Fehlbach and Sempt, which join to its south. The historic buildings are grouped along two intersecting axes: Landshuterstraße, which culminates in the elongated Schrannenplatz, and the streets of Lange Zeile.

At the west end of Schrannenplatz is the Gothic **Johanneskirche**, built in the late 14th to early 15th centuries. It has an unusual layout, with the presbytery facing the square. Outside the presbytery stands a tall, 10-storey **belfry**, its façade decorated with friezes and blind windows. Inside the church the most interesting feature is the larger-than-life figure of Christ on the Cross, carved by Hans Leinberger in about 1525.

On the opposite side of Landshuterstraße stands the Gothic town gate known as the **Landshuter Tor**, or Schöner Turm. Flanked by towers, its façade is divided by rows of arched blind windows and it is covered by a shingle-clad Baroque dome, making it one of the most outstanding town gates in southern Bavaria. At Landshuterstraße 1 is the former **residence** of the counts

of Preysing, dating from 1648, which is now the town hall. Opposite stands the Gothic **Hospital Church of the Holy Spirit**, while at No. 3 Schrannenplatz is the 14th-century **Frauenkirche**.

❾ Sankt Wolfgang

Road map E4. 🏔 4,400. 🚌 🚃 St Wolfgang. Hauptstr. 9, (08085) 18 80.
🇼 st-wolfgang-ob.de

The town is named in honour of St Wolfgang, the Bishop of Ratisbon (Regensburg), who was canonized in 1052. According to legend the saint, while on his way to Mondsee monastery, discovered a spring with miracle-working waters here.

In the early 15th century a **chapel** was built over the spring. **Wolfgangskirche** was built to the south of the chapel in 1430–77. This two-nave, web-vaulted church is an outstanding example of late Gothic Bavarian brick architecture. The foundations contain the Stone of St Wolfgang, a piece of red marble bearing what is said to be the saint's footprint. Substantial fragments of the original Gothic altar of about 1485 also remain. There is also a carving of St Wolfgang with St George and St Sigismund by Heinrich Helmschrot of Landshut (or his studio), and

Statue of St Wolfgang

paintings of scenes from the life of St Mary. In the elongated northern nave, and a few steps higher up, is the original **chapel** with the miracle-working spring, which attracts pilgrims. In the early 18th century it was decorated with fine stuccowork with acanthus motifs. The small figure of St Wolfgang that stands on the Rococo altar was made in 1470 and is said to have miraculous powers. Before the altar is a deep covered well. Visitors can lie down beside it and drink its curative water using a ladle.

The town hall is another interesting building. It was originally a presbytery, built by Johann Baptist Gunetzrhainer.

❿ Oberschleißheim

Road map D3. 🏔 11,600. ⑤
ℹ Freisinger Str. 15, (089) 315 61 30.
🇼 oberschleissheim.de

This town is best known for its three impressive **palaces** (see pp176–7), set in the gardens of the Hofgarten. But also of interest is the **Flugwerft Schleißheim**, a museum located on one of the oldest aerodromes in Germany. Part of the Deutsches Museum, the museum is located in restored buildings dating from 1912–19, in an exhibition hall and on the apron. Some 50 aircraft and helicopters are on display. There is also an exhibition illustrating the development of flight and of space flight.

Otto Lilienthal's aeroplane, built in 1894, Flugwerft Schleißheim

The gardens of the Renaissance castle in Dachau

⓫ Dachau

Road map D4. 🏛 45,600. Ⓢ 🚆
ℹ️ Konrad-Adenauer-Str. 1, (08131) 75 286 or 75 287. 🎭 Dachauer Volksfest (Aug). 🖥 **dachau.de**

Set on a steep hill, this picturesque little town on the River Amper has a panoramic view of nearby Munich, although it is best known as one of the sites of the Holocaust.

In 1933 the first Nazi **concentration camp** was set up here and it was in use up until 1945, during which time 30,000 prisoners perished here. The site of the camp was opened to the public as a place of remembrance in 1965.

One of the buildings contains the **KZ-Gedenkstätte Dachau**, a museum which documents the history of the concentration camps and the crimes against humanity that were committed here before and during World War II.

On the hill at the edge of the town, a **palace** was built on the site of a 15th-century castle as a summer residence for the Wittelsbachs. Of the original four wings constructed in 1558–77, only the southwest wing remains. The ceremonial hall on the first floor, which survives, was decorated in 1564–5 by Hans Wissreuter.

The focal point of the town is a triangular plaza on which the town hall and the church stand. Hans Krumpper's late Renaissance **Jakobskirche** was built in 1624–5. It incorporates an earlier presbytery with a fine tower dating from about 1425 and extended in 1676–8 with the addition of a dome.

⓬ Kloster Indersdorf

Road map C3. 🚌 Ⓢ 🚆 Markt Indersdorf. ℹ️ Markt Indersdorf, Marktplatz 1, (08136) 93 40. 🖥 **markt-indersdorf.de**

This former Augustinian abbey built in the early 11th century stands on the north bank of the River Glonn. Vestiges of a 12th century triple-nave Romanesque basilica with a twin-towered façade and Gothic remodelling are discernible in the later **Klosterkirche Mariä Himmelfahrt**. The latter was lavishly furnished during the 18th century. Franz Xaver Feichtmayr the Elder added the interior Rococo stuccowork in 1754–6, and the paintings of scenes from the life of St Augustine were executed by Matthäus Günther, assisted by Johann Georg Dieffenbrunner.

The extensive **abbey buildings** of 1694–1704, designed by Antonio Riva, are set around two courtyards south and east of the church.

Gate and guard tower of Dachau concentration camp

Gothic Madonna in Fürstenfeldbruck's Baroque church

⓭ Fürstenfeldbruck

Road map C4. 🏛 35,700. Ⓢ 🚆 ℹ️ Hauptstr. 31, (08141) 280. 🖥 **fuerstenfeldbruck.de** 🎭 Volks- und Heimatfest (Jun–Jul); Brucker Altstadtfest (Jul); Leonhardifahrt (Oct–Nov); Christkindlmarkt (Dec); Lucien-Häuschen-Schwimmen (13 Dec).

The finest and most important building in the town is the former **Cistercian abbey**, situated on the way to Augsburg and built in 1263–90. Its establishment was funded by Ludwig II, the Severe, after the execution of his wife Maria of Brabant, who was unjustly accused of infidelity. In 1691–1754, remodelled by Giovanni Antonio Viscardi, it became one of the largest Baroque abbeys in Bavaria.

The monumental façade of **Klosterkirche Mariä Himmelfahrt** conceals an interior of fine stuccowork by Pietro Francesco Appiani, vaulting lavishly painted by Cosmas Damian Asam and a high altar of 1760–62 designed by his brother Egid Quirin Asam.

The monastery, its interior decorated with stuccowork and painting in 1924, now houses a police college and museum. Many historic town houses line the main street. The old town hall, refurbished in 1866–8, features paintings dating from 1900.

On St Lucy's Day, in memory of the flood of 1725, children float model houses illuminated with candles across the Amper, which flows through the town.

Schleißheim Palace

Originally intended to rival the splendour of Versailles, the palace at Schleißheim was the architectural setting for the imperial ambitions of Maximilian Emanuel. The architect was Enrico Zucalli, and work started in 1701. It was then interrupted, but restarted in 1717 under the direction of Joseph Effner, who deviated from the original plans. The 330-m (1,082-ft) long Neues Schloss has an overpoweringly lavish interior, which was decorated by Cosmas Damian Asam and Johann Baptist Zimmermann. Today, as well as admiring the elaborate interior decoration, visitors can see the palace's outstanding gallery of Baroque painting.

Doors
The doors leading into the vestibule were carved by Ignaz Günther in 1736 and are counted among his masterpieces.

Altes Schloss
In the late 16th century Wilhelm V built himself Altes Schloss. Heinrich Schön the Elder remodelled it in 1616–23, with mouldings and paintings by Peter Candid. It was rebuilt after World War II and houses two branches of the Bavarian National Museum.

KEY

① **A gateway with clock tower** built in about 1600 leads into the courtyard in front of the Altes Schloss.

② **Canals** of Lustheim form the axis of the park layout. In front of Neues Schloss the water flows into a basin with a cascade and fountains.

★ **Neues Schloss**
The vestibule, decorated with fine stuccowork and frescoes, leads into a Rococo dining room on one side and to a grand staircase on the other.

VISITORS' CHECKLIST

Practical Information
Map D3. Altes Schloss, Neues
Schloss & Schloss Lustheim:
Tel (089) 31 58 720.
Open Apr–Sep: 9am–6pm
Tue–Sun; Oct–Mar: 10am–4pm
Tue–Sun.
w schloesser-schleissheim.de

★ Schloss Lustheim
This small Baroque palace was built as a love
nest for Maximilian Emanuel and his first
wife. It now houses a collection of
Meissen porcelain.

②

★ Park
This is the only Baroque park in
Germany that has survived in its
original form. It is characterized by
canals and pathways that mark out
geometrical patterns of greenery.

0 metres   150
0 yards   150

Maximilian Emanuel

In 1701 the Elector Maximilian
Emanuel ordered the extension of
Schleißheim and the rebuilding
of Nymphenburg. Defeat in the war
against Austria caused work to be
temporarily suspended, so that he
did not see its completion. Despite
this his patronage brought Bavaria
into the mainstream of the high
Baroque, giving the Wittelsbach
family a name for splendour
and prestige.

LOWER BAVARIA

Lower Bavaria (Niederbayern), bordering Austria and the Czech Republic in the east, is both a distinct cultural entity and a separate administrative area. With an agriculture-intensive south and mountainous north and east, its forests and fields are oases of tranquillity. Its fine Baroque buildings leave an indelible impression on the visitor. With none of the bustle of big cities, towns like Landshut and Passau have retained an old-world flavour.

Lower Bavaria encompasses most of the Bayerischer Wald (Bavarian Forest), which includes a nature reserve and a national park. This is part of a larger forested area that spreads over the border into the even wilder Czech Republic. As recently as the 1960s, out-of-the-way villages delighted visitors with their tumbledown thatched cottages. Today such sights are confined to the open-air museums of the Museumsdorf Bayerischer Wald and the Freilichtmuseum Finsterau.

The local people, known for their hospitality and friendliness, work in the region's forestry, tourist and glassware industries. Calm and restrained, they have a strong sense of their own worth. When Franz Xaver Krenkl, a Lower Bavarian, beat the royal carriage on its journey to Munich in his own cart, his comment was simply "Wer ko der ko" ("He who can, can"). From the

Benedictine monastery at Weltenburg to the town of Kelheim the River Danube flows between high limestone cliffs overgrown with dense mixed foliage. On both sides of the river unique rock formations create fantastic shapes, and they have been named accordingly. Sailing along this stretch of the Danube is an unforgettable experience, as is the view down onto the river from the gallery around the Neo-Classical Liberation Hall in Kelheim. A canal completed in 1992 joins the Danube at Kelheim, providing a waterway link with the Main and the Rhine using a stretch of the River Altmühl. This valley is as magical as that of the Danube.

Initiatives to industrialize Lower Bavaria have resulted in the construction of two modern factories in Dingolfing, where the BMW produces some of its cars.

Passau's beautiful Old Town, on the banks of the River Danube

◄ Bold colours on the narrow medieval streets of Landshut

Exploring Lower Bavaria

Landshut is the capital of Lower Bavaria. Every four years tourists come for the Landshut Wedding, a great historical spectacle held at the foot of Trausnitz castle (see p35). Passau, at the confluence of the Danube, Inn and Ilz rivers, is equally picturesque. From here the "Asam Trail" begins, taking in the churches that the Asam brothers (see p72) decorated in Aldersbach, Osterhofen, Straubing, Rohr and Weltenburg. The piety of the local people can be seen in the many pilgrimage churches, the best known being at Bogenberg, known as the Mount Athos of Lower Bavaria, and Geiersberg, near Deggendorf.

Bavarian coat of arms on the town gate in Vilshofen

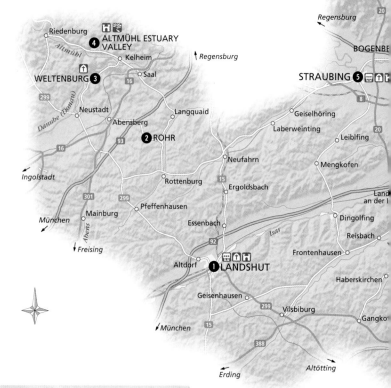

Getting Around

Lower Bavaria borders Austria and the Czech Republic. Three motorways pass through the region. The A92 links Landshut and Deggendorf, following the course of the River Isar, and the A3 links Regensburg and Passau, along the course of the River Danube. Regensburg can also be reached by A93. The railway network is sparse but there is a good bus service.

Barrage on the River Altmühl at Haidhof

For keys to symbols see back flap

Sights at a Glance

- **1** *Landshut pp182–5*
- **2** Rohr
- **3** Weltenburg
- **5** *Straubing pp188–9*
- **6** Bogenberg
- **7** Metten
- **8** Sankt Hermann

- **10** Museumsdorf Bayerischer Wald
- **11** *Passau pp192–3*
- **12** Fürstenzell
- **13** Ortenburg
- **14** Sammarei
- **15** Aldersbach

- **16** Vilshofen
- **17** Osterhofen

Tours

- **4** Altmühl Valley
- **9** Nationalpark Bayerischer Wald

Key

- Motorway
- Main road
- Minor road
- Scenic route
- Main railway
- Minor railway
- International border
- △ Summit

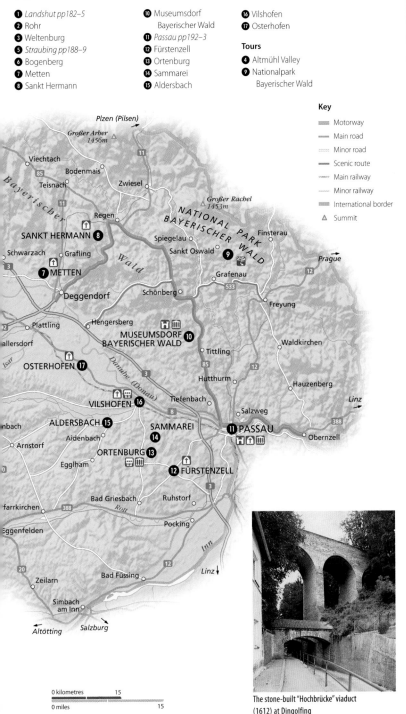

The stone-built "Hochbrücke" viaduct (1612) at Dingolfing

ⓞ Street-by-Street: Landshut

Landshut, the capital of Lower Bavaria, grew up around Trausnitz castle and flourished in the 14th and 15th centuries. In 1475 it was the scene of a grand and lavish wedding when Duke Georg of the House of Wittelsbach married the Polish Princess Jadwiga, daughter of Casimir Jagiellon. Wedding guests included the Emperor Frederick III and his son Maximilian. Today the event is commemorated every four years by a great spectacle, the Landshut Wedding *(see p35)*.

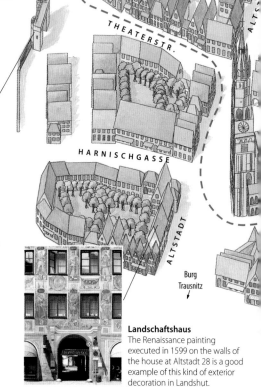

Emslander ←

★ Stadtresidenz
This palace, built for Duke Ludwig X in 1536–43, was the first Renaissance palace in Germany.

Ländtor
The Gothic gateway leading into the city from the side on the River Isar is a vestige of the old city fortifications.

Key

— Suggested route

Burg
Trausnitz ↓

Landschaftshaus
The Renaissance painting executed in 1599 on the walls of the house at Altstadt 28 is a good example of this kind of exterior decoration in Landshut.

★ Town Hall
The Gothic town hall has a fine Renaissance oriel window. The interior paintings and stained-glass windows on the theme of the Landshut Wedding date from 1860.

VISITORS' CHECKLIST

Practical Information
Map E3. 69,200. Altstadt 315, (0871) 92 2050.
landshut.de
Landshuter Hochzeit (Landshut Wedding) (Jul, every 4 years; next in 2017), Landshuter Hofmusiktage (Jul, every 2 years; next in 2020), Landshuter Flohmarkt (Jul or Aug), Altstadtfest (Jul), Bartlmädult (Aug), Haferlmarkt (Sep).

Transport
Bahnhofplatz.

STECKENGASSE

SCHIRMGASSE

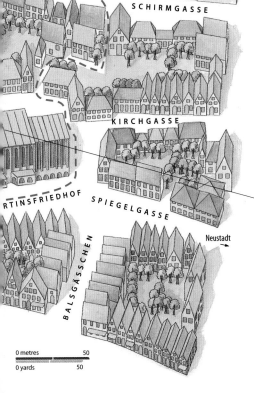

Grasbergerhaus
It was in this late Gothic house with stepped gables and street-level arcade that the betrothed Polish Princess Jadwiga stayed in 1475.

KIRCHGASSE

...RTINSFRIEDHOF SPIEGELGASSE

BALSGÄSSCHEN

Neustadt →

★ Martinskirche
The spacious interior of this triple-nave church, which took more than a hundred years to build (1389–1500), impresses with its height, its forest of columns and its fine vaulting.

0 metres 50
0 yards 50

Exploring Landshut

Landshut, like Munich, lies between a fork in the River Isar. It stretches out between Trausnitz castle, which is set on a vantage point, and the Cistercian abbey of Seligenthal. The central conurbation is concentrated around two wide parallel streets that function as squares lying on a north-south axis. They are known as Altstadt and Neustadt.

Landshut is perhaps the most quintessentially German of all Lower Bavarian towns. With its historic buildings spared damage during World War II, the town has retained the atmosphere of its earlier days of glory.

⛪ Jesuitenkirche
Spiegelgasse.

The Church of St Ignatius, located on the southern road leading out of Neustadt, was formerly part of a Jesuit monastery. Designed by the Jesuit architect Johannes Holl, it was built from 1631 to 1641. The interior features a fine Baroque high altar dating from 1663.

Side entrance to the impressive Gothic Jodokkirche

⛪ Jodokkirche
Jodokgasse.

This Gothic triple-nave brick basilica, built in 1338–1450, was dedicated to St Jodok, the son of a Breton duke who lived in the 7th century and who became a pilgrim and hermit. In the mid-19th century the church was restored to its original Gothic appearance and was furnished in Baroque style.

Stone reliefs on the Gothic altar in Martinskirche

⛪ Martinskirche
Altstadt 68. **Tel** (0871) 92 21 780.
Open 7:30am–6:30pm daily (to 5pm Oct–Mar). **Closed** 10:30am–3pm Mon & Fri.

Three architects collaborated on the building of this Gothic church. One of them was Hans von Burghausen, whose tombstone, dated 1432, is built into its southern wall. At 131 m (430 ft) high, the brick church tower is the tallest in the world; the steeple was added in 1500. The tower commands a splendid view of the town and of the castle and its gardens. The interior of the church abounds in priceless Gothic furnishings.

⛪ Dominikanerkirche
Regierungsplatz.

The Church of St Blasius, part of the former Dominican monastery, was built in 1271–1384 in the form of a triple-nave Gothic basilica. The interior was remodelled in the Rococo style by Johann Baptist Zimmermann and decorated with lavish stucco-work. The Neo-Classical façade was added in 1805.

⛪ Spitalkirche
Heilige-Geist-Gasse.

The late Gothic Church of the Holy Spirit and the building of the former hospital located opposite stand on the northern end of Altstadt. The triple-nave church was designed by Hans von Burghausen and built in 1407–61.

The interior features fan vaulting and there is an ambulatory around the presbytery.

On the northern side of the presbytery stands a large tower. The entrance to the church, in the west front, is a tall, ornamental portal fronted by a porch whose corners are set with low towers.

▥ Stadtresidenz
Altstadt 79. **Tel** (0871) 92 41 10.
Open Apr–Sep: 9am–6pm Tue–Sun; Oct–Mar: 10am–4pm Tue–Sun. 🅿

This residence, in the Italian Renaissance style, consists of two adjacent buildings.

The Deutscher Bau, built in 1536–7, has a Neo-Classical façade dating from about 1780 on the side looking onto Altstadt. A museum of local history was laid out here in 1935.

The Italienischer Bau, built in 1537–43, has a fine arcaded courtyard. The building's façade, looking onto Ländgasse, is decorated with a large cartouche bearing the coat of arms of Ludwig X of Bavaria, for whom it was built. Inside visitors can see the fine reception halls, which occupy two floors, and admire the beautiful Renaissance frescoes depicting mythological scenes.

Spitalkirche, on the road leading from Altstadt

Burg Trausnitz

This castle, whose history began in the year 1204, was the seat of the von Bayern-Landshut branch of the Wittelsbach family. It was extended in the 14th and 15th centuries, and was converted into a residence in 1568–79. In 1961 a fire destroyed the northwest wing, but painstaking restoration has allowed it to re-open to visitors. The late Romanesque chapel and the original staircase were spared.

VISITORS' CHECKLIST

Practical Information
Burg Trausnitz 168.
Tel (0871) 92 41 10. **Open** Apr–Sep: 9am–6pm daily; Oct–Mar: 10am–4pm daily.
W **burg-trausnitz.de**

Transport
7 (to Kalcherstraße).

★ Narrentreppe
The Fools' Staircase is decorated with lifesize figures from the Commedia dell'Arte painted in 1578 by Padovano. They commemorate the shows performed by an itinerant Italian theatre troupe for Wilhelm V.

St-Georgs-Rittersaal
The walls of this hall are hung with tapestries illustrating the exploits of Duke Otto Wittelsbach woven to designs by Peter Candid in Paris in 1618.

Arcaded courtyard

Alte Dürnitz
This spacious two-nave hall is situated on the ground floor and features arches supported on palmate pillars.

The Castle
A steep flight of steps leads up to the castle and its gardens. The castle commands a fine view of the whole town and the valley of the River Isar.

❷ Rohr

Road map D2. 🚍 🚆 Abensberg.
ℹ️ Marienplatz 1, (08783) 96 080.
Abbey: **Tel** (08783) 96 000.
Asamkirche: **Open** 6am–8pm daily.
📷 📷 🆆 **kloster-rohr.de**

This abbey dates from the 12th century. In the first quarter of the 13th century, when the church and **abbey** were transferred to the Benedictines, the buildings were remodelled in the Baroque style.

Asamkirche is renowned for its stuccowork and the high altar of 1723 by Egid Quirin Asam. The altar was built in the form of a theatrical stage with wings. The sculptural group on the altar depicts the Assumption of the Virgin. It embodies the idea of a *Theatrum Sacrum* and is one of Asam's masterpieces in this genre.

The high altar of the church of Mariä Himmelfahrt in Rohr

❸ Weltenburg

Road map D2. 🚍 🚆 Kelheim.
🚤 Monastery: **Tel** (09441) 20 41 32.
📷 Tours should be pre-booked. 📷
🆆 **klosterschenke-weltenburg.de**

This Benedictine **monastery** complex, dating from the early 7th century, stands in a picturesque setting on a terrace beside the Danube.

The Asam brothers added to the complex the splendid Baroque **Georgs- und Martinskirche**, which was completed in 1716. Cosmas Damian was responsible for the architectural designs and the paintings, and

A boat trip through the Danube Gorge from Weltenburg to Kelheim

Egid Quirin Asam built the fine high altar and the statue of St George slaying the Dragon.

There is a beer garden in the cloisters where visitors can sample the monastery's beer. Boat trips through the Danube Gorge to Kelheim also depart from a quay nearby.

❹ Straubing

See pp188–9.

❺ Bogenberg

Road map F2. 🔼 9,800. 🚍
🚆 Bogen. ℹ️ Bogen, Stadtplatz 56, (09422) 50 51 09. 🆆 **bogen.de**

Rising above the small town of Bogen, the Bogenberg, or "Mount Athos" of Lower Bavaria, was once a Celtic sacred place. Since the Middle Ages it has been a place of pilgrimage. Standing on the top is the Gothic **Hl. Kreuz und Mariä Heimsuchung**, which commands an excellent view

Angel and candles in the pilgrimage church of Bogenberg

over the Danube valley. Pilgrims come here to honour the miraculous statue of the pregnant Virgin Mary, dating from around 1400, which is clothed in a 17th-century dress and embroidered cloak. Dozens of votive candles flicker in the presbytery.

According to an ancient custom, at Pentecost the strongest man from the nearby village of Holzkirchen brings to the church a great candle – Die lange Stang – up to 100 kg (220 lb) in weight and 13 m (40 ft) long.

❻ Metten

Road map F2. 🔼 4,200. 🚍 🚆
ℹ️ Krankenhausstr. 22, (0991) 99 80 50. 🆆 **markt-metten.de**

The local **Benedictine abbey** was founded in about 766. In 1830, after it had been appropriated as a result of the dissolution of the monasteries, it was returned to its industrious owners.

Michaelskirche, which has been rebuilt several times since its foundation in the Romanesque period, was remodelled in 1712–29. The twin-towered façade outlines two circular chapels. The interior has paintings and a high altar by Cosmas Damian Asam.

The most exquisite part of the abbey is the library, built in 1722–9 and decorated with stuccowork by Franz Josef Holzinger. It is one of the finest library buildings in the world. A remarkable pair of Atlases support the low vaulted ceiling.

❹ Altmühl Valley

The River Altmühl winds scenically from central Franconia, meandering through the northern part of Upper Bavaria and through Lower Bavaria before flowing into the Danube. The Altmühltal Naturpark, in the river valley, is one of the largest and finest nature parks in Germany. This tour takes visitors along the estuary, ending with the famous canal that connects the River Danube with the Main and the Rhine.

Tips for Drivers

Tour length: About 20 km (12 miles).
Stopping-off points: There are cafés or bars at each of the places along the route. The larger towns have restaurants and some also offer accommodation.

⑤ Schloß Prunn
This castle, looking as if it had grown from the rocks, houses a museum. The longest wooden bridge in Europe, over the Altmühl, is visible from the terrace.

⑦ Rosenburg
This castle is a centre for the breeding of birds of prey and contains a museum of falconry equipment. Displays with birds of prey, including eagles, are held here every day.

⑥ Riedenburg
The local Crystals Museum is famous for having the world's largest cluster of rock crystal. It weighs 7.8 tonnes and comes from Arkansas in the United States.

Eichstätt

Altmühl

Donau

Kelheimwinzer

Saal

Regensburg

16

Ingolstadt

④ Essing
A narrow street leads to a delightful market square, while a medieval gate leads through to the wooden bridge (the longest in Europe) over the former course of the River Altmühl.

③ Randeck
A road running to the foot of the mountain leads to the ruins of an 11th-century castle, which was rebuilt several times, with the town of Essing at its feet.

① Kelheim
The Liberation Hall, built by Friedrich von Gärtner and Leo von Klenze in 1842–63, commemorates the defeat of Napoleon.

Key

▬ Suggested route

⋯ Other road

② Tropfsteinhöhle
These caves, off the road to Essing, were inhabited during the Stone Age. The temperature inside stays at a constant 9° C (48° F), regardless of external conditions.

0 kilometres 10

0 miles 10

❺ Straubing

Standing on the south bank of the Danube in the fertile Gäuboden, Straubing pulsates with life. The medieval buildings of the Old Town have survived basically unchanged, bearing a faithful resemblance to the wooden model made in 1568 by Jakob Sandtner and now on view in the Bayerisches Nationalmuseum in Munich (a copy can be seen in the Gäubodenmuseum). Every year in August the town holds the Gäubodenvolksfest, a folk festival second in size only to Munich's Oktoberfest.

The Stadtturm (city tower) in the centre of the town square

🏛 Ludwigsplatz and Theresienplatz

The pedestrianized market square resembles a long, wide avenue cutting through the heart of the Old Town. It is pleasant to wander through the large garden between closely packed stalls and crates full of colourful flowers, fruit and vegetables, and admire the historic buildings. The Stadtturm, or tower, offers a sweeping panorama of the town, the Gäuboden and the Bavarian Forest. A Neo-Classical gate built in 1810 divides the market square into two, with Ludwigsplatz on the eastern side and Theresienplatz on the western.

Ludwigsplatz and Theresienplatz have two fountains dedicated to the town's patron saints, St Jacob (1644) and St Tiburtius (1685). On Theresienplatz stands a column built in 1709, featuring gilt figures of the Holy Trinity.

Opposite the town gates on the south side of the square is the two-storey **town hall**, its two wings enclosing a courtyard. The town hall was created in 1382, when two adjacent Gothic houses were conjoined behind a single façade. The stepped gable, however, dates from the 19th century.

🏛 Karmelitenkirche
Albrechtsgasse 20.

This spacious triple-nave Gothic church with a tower was partly remodelled in about 1700 by Wolfgang Dientzenhofer. The lavish 17th and 18th-century furnishings successfully harmonize with the later Baroque decoration.

Baroque interior of Ursulinenkirche

In the church is the tomb of Duke Albrecht II. His son, Albrecht III, secretly married Agnes Bernauer, who was the beautiful daughter of a barber from Augsburg. When he found out Albrecht II ordered the drowning of Agnes in the Danube in 1435. Every four years in June/July amateur actors re-create this historical tragedy in the Agnes-Bernauer-Festspiele.

🏛 Ursulinenkirche
Burggasse 9.

This church, which forms part of an Ursuline convent, was built and decorated by the Asam brothers in 1736–41. In their inspired collaboration, Egid Quirin Asam created the architectural design and Cosmas Damian Asam painted the frescoes and the altarpieces (see p72).

🏰 Herzogsschloss
Schlossplatz 2B. **Tel** (09421) 94 43 07.
🔷 access for pre-booked guided tours only.

The castle, on the Danube, has an irregular plan and an inner courtyard. Its earliest parts date from the 14th century. The Bernauerturm on the north-western corner is the turret from which Agnes Bernauer is said to have been thrown into the Danube. The castle is home to tax offices, but special guided tours can be arranged.

🏛 Gäubodenmuseum
Fraunhoferstr. 9. **Tel** (09421) 94 46 32 14.
Open 10am–4pm Tue–Sun. 🔷
🔵 gaeubodenmuseum.de

This local history museum was founded in 1845. Its most renowned exhibit is the Römerschatz, or Roman Treasure, which was discovered in 1950 and which caused a sensation among academics. It is the largest collection of Roman parade armour to have been found anywhere in the former Roman Empire. The collection includes highly ornamental helmets with visors, shin-guards and metal masks for horses.

View of the Herzogsschloss from the Danube

↑ Basilika St Jakob
Pfarrplatz 1a.

This is one of Bavaria's largest and most magnificent Gothic churches. Building began in 1400 and was not completed for almost a century. The forest of columns in the extraordinarily tall interior support 18th-century barrel vaulting.

The church has preserved its Gothic statues and paintings, including an image of the Mother of God ascribed to Hans Holbein, Baroque paintings and sculptures by the Asam Brothers, and tombstones. The 15th-century stained-glass windows are the church's finest elements, giving the church interior a unique atmosphere.

↑ Kirche St Peter
Petersgasse. 50b.

Peterskirche, a Romanesque basilica dating from around 1200 whose steeples were

Gothic stained-glass window in Basilika St Jakob

enlarged in the 19th century, is one of the finest churches of its kind in Lower Bavaria. Among the interior features are a Romanesque Crucifix and a Gothic Pietà dating from about 1340.

The church cemetery is an interesting place to explore, as it is one of the oldest in Germany. It contains three Gothic chapels. One of them, the Bernauerkapelle, was built by Duke Ernst as penance for Agnes Bernauer's murder in 1435. Her symbolic tombstone can be seen within. The walls of the Totenkapelle, built in 1486, bear a cycle depicting the Dance of Death that was painted in 1763 by Felix Hölzl.

Straubing Town Centre

① Ludwigsplatz and Theresienplatz
② Karmelitenkirche
③ Ursulinenkirche
④ Herzogsschloss
⑤ Gäubodenmuseum
⑥ Basilika St Jakob

0 metres 50
0 yards 50

For keys to symbols *see back flap*

Wooden chapel and Baroque church at
Sankt Hermann

❽ Sankt Hermann

Road map F2. 🚌 🚊 Regen.
ℹ️ Bischofsmais, Hauptstr. 34 (09920)
94 04 44. 🌐 bischofsmais.de

Just outside Bischofsmais, on the
site of the oldest hermitage in the
Bavarian Forest, stands a group
of three ecclesiastical buildings.

In about 1320 St Herman,
a Benedictine monk from the
Niederalteich monastery, lived
here. His cult began in the 17th
century, when pilgrimages
were made to places that were
associated with him.

The **Brunnenkapelle**, a small
domed Baroque rotunda with
a niche for the miracle-working
spring, was built in 1611.
Hermannskirche, a Baroque
pilgrimage church, was built
in 1653–4.

The **Einsiedeleikapelle** was
added in 1690. It is a wooden
chapel built in memory of the
saint's hermitage. Its western
part, the Hermannszelle
(Herman's Cell), is full of wooden
legs and crutches left here by
pilgrims, in thanks for the
miracle cures they received.

❾ Museumsdorf Bayerischer Wald

Road map G2. 🚌 🚊 Tittling.
Tel (08504) 84 82. **Open** week before
Easter–Oct: 9am–5pm daily; Museum
grounds only: Nov–Mar: 9am–5pm
daily. 🌐 museumsdorf.com

Near Tittling, on the west side
of the road from Grafenau to
Passau, this open-air museum
is one of the largest in Europe.
Here over 140 buildings dating
from the 18th and 19th centuries
have been erected on a
200,000-sq m (50-acre) site. As
well as traditional cottages with
all their furnishings, visitors can

see mills, forges,
sawmills and also the
oldest public school
building in Germany.

Near the museum,
in an **inn** dating from
1829, traditional Bava-
rian specialities are
on offer. Visitors to the
inn include prominent
German figures, includ-
ing the former chan-
cellor Helmut Kohl and
the writer Friedrich
Dürrenmatt.

The museum is in
the Dreiburgenland, so
named after the three
castles, **Saldenburg**,
Fürstenstein and
Englburg. They are well
preserved but are not
open to the public.

❿ Passau

See pp192–5.

⓫ Fürstenzell

Road map G3. 🚊 8,000. 🚌
🚊 Passau. ℹ️ Marienplatz 7, (08502)
80 228. 🌐 fuerstenzell.de

Founded in 1274, the
Cistercian abbey here reached
the height of its artistic
development in the 18th
century (closed to the public).

Marienkirche, built in 1738,
was designed by Johann
Michael Fischer, with stuccowork
by Johann Baptist Modler and
Johann Georg Funk and
elaborate ceiling paintings

The 19th-century inn at the Museumsdorf
Bayerischer Wald

Marienkirche, Fürstenzell

by Johann Jakob Zeiller.
The interior features Baroque
and Rococo altars, the high
altar by Johann Baptist Straub,
and a fine Rococo pulpit.
The Gothic tombs of the
Cistercian abbots and the
abbey's founders, which
were transferred here from
the medieval church, are
also of interest.

The **monastery**, situated
south of the church, was
remodelled in 1674–87, and
extended after 1770. The
Festsaal (State Room), with
frescoes of 1773 in the late
Viennese Neo-Classical style,
is outstanding.

The monastery library was
decorated in about 1760.
Together with the monastery
library in the town of Metten
nearby, it is the finest example
of artistic patronage by the
Cistercian order in Germany.
The interior is lined with a
gallery supported on
alternating Tuscan columns
and herms (head of Hermes
on a stone pillar). The book-
cases are decorated with
Rococo putti, fencing figures
and Atlases carved by
Joseph Deutschmann.

🔼 Marienkirche
Tel (08502) 91 150. **Open** 8am–6pm
daily. 📷 by arrangement.

⑨ Nationalpark Bayerischer Wald

This excursion leads through the Nationalpark Bayerischer Wald, established in 1970 and the first national park in Germany. It is an extensive hilly area of forests, woodland, swamps and meadows, picturesque lakes and interesting rock formations that combine to create unique landscapes inhabited by many species of birds and animals. The Hans-Eisenmann-Haus is the main information centre in the area.

③ Finsterau
The Freilichtmuseum Finsterau is not far from Finsterau, a village with overflowing window boxes, where there is a working smithy and a bakery selling fresh bread.

④ Hans-Eisenmann-Haus
A scenic forest road leads to the house. From here visitors can go to the Pflanzenfreigelände, a reserve with over 500 plant species, or take a trip to the Tierfreigelände, a reserve for wild animals.

Nationalpark Bayerischer Wald

Zwiesel

Regen

Kleine Ohe

85

85

Grafenau

Passau

Reschbach

Reschbach

533

12

Passau

12 ①

⑤ St Oswald
The Waldgeschichtliches Museum illustrates the life and culture of the "forest people". The abbey and church of St Oswald were rebuilt in the Baroque style in 1876. The Brünnlkapelle stands beside a miracle-working spring.

② Mauth
The village glassworks, the Glasbläserhof Mauth, are fascinating. Glass-blowers can be seen at work and visitors may try their hand at this difficult art.

① Freyung
Schloss Wolfstein contains a hunting and fishing museum. The Schramlhaus (at Abtei-straße 6), with the Heimat-museum, is also worth a visit.

Tips for Drivers

Tour length: 50 km (31 miles)
Stopping-off points: There are bars and restaurants in Freyung, Finsterau, in the open-air museum and at Hans-Eisenmann-Haus.

0 kilometres 15

0 miles 15

Key

▬ Suggested route

╌ Other road

⑪ Passau

Passau is one of the oldest and most beautiful towns in Bavaria. Nestling in the hills at the confluence of three rivers, it is divided into three districts interconnected by 15 bridges. The Old Town lies on a peninsula between the Danube and the Inn, while Innstadt lies beside the Inn and Ilzstadt beside the Ilz. Passau's fine buildings give it its charm and magic, while the southern wind, felt both in the climate and the art, lends an Italian atmosphere.

Towers of the Dom St Stephan – Passau's great Baroque cathedral

▣ Domplatz

In 1155 the cathedral chapter acquired a plot of land between the cathedral and the western section of the city walls with the aim of building on it chapter-houses arranged around a large square. What were the originally modest chapterhouses were later remodelled in a more ostentatious Baroque style.

Distinctive among them is the Lamberg Chapterhouse, at No. 6 Domplatz, on the west side of the square. Rebuilt in 1724, the chapterhouse is also known as **Lamberg Palace** for its magnificent façade, which is decorated with fine mouldings. The old chapterhouses at Nos. 4 and 5, known as the Barbarahof and Kanonikatshof Starzhausen, today accommodate the presbytery and the seminary.

The square itself features a monument to the Bavarian king, Maximilian I Joseph, and was created by Christian Gorhan the Younger in 1824.

🏠 Dom St Stephan

Domplatz 1.

The original cathedral, set on the highest point in the town, was destroyed in the Great Fire of 1662. It was rebuilt in 1668–77 by Carlo Lurago, who created the largest Baroque church north of the Alps, incorporating the surviving Gothic presbytery and transept into the new scheme.

The elegant towers can be seen from afar. The interior contains a stunning wealth of stuccowork and other ornamentation added in 1677–85 by Giovanni Battista Carlone, and paintings by Carpoforo Tencalla.

The burial chapels on the north side of the cathedral include the Gothic Herrenkapelle, which was built in about 1300 for the members of the cathedral chapter and which contains an enormous Romanesque Crucifix dating from about 1190.

Passau Cathedral is famous for its magnificent organ, one of the largest in the world. Occupying the Baroque organ loft, it was built in 1924–8 and refurbished in 1979–81. Organ recitals take place every day at noon from May to October.

🏠 Neue Residenz

Residenzplatz 8. Treasury and Diocesan Museum: **Tel** (0851) 39 30.
Open 2 May–31 Oct: 10am–4pm Mon–Sat. 🅿

The new Bishop's residence, which occupies the south side of Residenzplatz, was built in 1713–30 to plans by Domenico d'Angeli and Antonio Beduzzi. It was refurbished in 1764–71 by Melchior Hefele of Vienna, with stuccowork by members of the local Modler family, the addition of a Neo-Classical façade and interior decoration in the late Baroque style.

The design and decoration of the vestibule and staircase are particularly successful. The reception rooms contain large collections of artifacts from the **Diocesan Museum** and Cathedral **Treasury**, some of which can also be seen in the cathedral.

The full splendour of the Dom St Stephan's Baroque interior

The pediment over the façade of the Neue Residenz

🏠 Alte Residenz

Theresienstr. 18.

The Old Residence, whose buildings are crowded into a small area between the cathedral and a hillside, is an important landmark visible from the River Inn. The residence probably stands on the site of a bishopric mentioned in 1188. The medieval buildings have been remodelled over the ages, and their present uniform appearance dates from 1680.

The reception rooms were decorated in the 18th century, but soon afterwards the bishopric was moved to the New Residence. The buildings now house the Landgericht, or provincial court.

🏛 Residenzplatz

This square acquired its grand stately character in the Baroque period. Later, stuccowork façades were added to the houses that line it. Particularly noteworthy are the houses at No. 1, built in 1725–30, and No. 13, built in about 1700. The Neo-Baroque fountain on the square was built by Jakob Bradl in 1906.

🏠 Michaelskirche

Michaeligasse 25.

In terms of architectural importance, the former Jesuit church is second only to Passau's cathedral. It was built and decorated in 1665–77 by members of the Carlone family. Its fine twin-towered façade makes it a distinctive feature

The Schaiblingsturm, part of Passau's medieval defences

of the city's skyline. The lavish interior includes a high altar of 1712 by Christoph Tausch of Breslau, side altars of about 1677 and a pulpit and organ loft built in 1717–20.

The former Jesuit college, which was built in 1613–25, is now used as a high school. The courtyard that is enclosed on three sides by the wings of the building has been closed off on its northern side by a glazed passage. At the end of the east wing is a tall octagonal tower that once housed an observatory.

🏛 Schaiblingsturm

The 14th-century Schaiblingsturm, on the bank of the River Inn, is a vestige of the old city fortifications. In centuries gone by the tower protected the port on the important salt route.

Passau City Centre

0 metres 200
0 yards 200

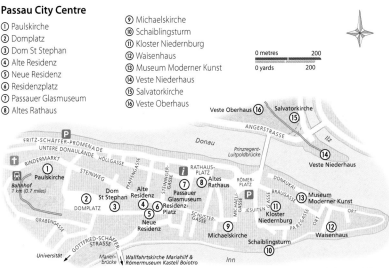

For keys to symbols *see back flap*

The Veste Oberhaus and below it the Veste Niederhaus, overlooking the Danube

🏛 Waisenhaus

Innkai.

This former orphanage, a two-storey building with an inner quadrangle, was built in 1750–62 to a design by Michael Schneitmann. The north wing contains a chapel whose façade and interior feature fine stuccowork executed by Giovanni Martin Luraghi in 1753.

🏛 Kloster Niederburg

Jesuitengasse.

Originally a Benedictine abbey, this was founded in about 740 on the site of the Roman Kastell Boiodurum. The present abbey church, which replaces an earlier one built in the early 11th century, is an example of an early Romanesque basilica with two towers and a transept. The presbytery was rebuilt in the Gothic style in the 15th century and the interior was redecorated in the Baroque style after it was damaged by fire in 1662 and 1680.

The south transept contains a Romanesque tombstone marking the tomb of the abbess, St Gisela, who was the sister of Emperor Henry II and widow of St Stephen, king of Hungary. In 1420 a sarcophagus with openwork sides was built over the tomb.

🏛 Salvatorkirche

Ferdinand-Wagner-Str.

Standing on the site of a synagogue, this former pilgrimage church is associated with a pogrom in 1477 against the

Jews, sparked off by their alleged sacrilege against the Host. On the west side the church is joined to the rock where the Veste Oberhaus stands. Before a tunnel was made between the upper and lower forts in 1762, the church was accessible only by boat. It is now used as a concert hall.

🏛 Veste Oberhaus and Veste Niederhaus

Oberhaus 125. Oberhausmuseum Passau: **Tel** (0851) 39 68 12.
Open mid-Mar–mid-Nov: 9am–5pm Mon–Fri, 10am–6pm Sat–Sun & public hols. **Closed** mid-Nov–mid-March (open 26 Dec–6 Jan: 10am–4pm). 🎫

Work on the imposing Oberhaus (Upper Castle) began in 1219, initiated by the bishop Ulrich II. It is set on a rocky outcrop known as St Georgsberg, on the bank of the Danube opposite the Old Town. The main castle consists of Gothic buildings and a chapel. The Niederhaus (Lower Castle) is connected to the Oberhaus by a gallery descending from the polygonal tower. Work on the Niederhaus,

on a spit of land between the rivers Danube and Ilz, began in 1250. Both castles, which have been extended and fortified over time, symbolize the power of the church over the town.

The Oberhaus now houses a historical museum. On the route to the Observatoriumsturm (observatory tower) is the Passauer Tölpel (Fool of Passau), a huge head with a mocking expression. This is the remains of a statue of St Stephen of about 1370 that fell from the cathedral during the Great Fire of 1662.

The Niederhaus, whose present apperance dates from about 1444, was the home of the painter Ferdinand von Wagner from 1890 to 1907. He filled the interior with antique furniture and his own paintings. A private residence, it is closed to visitors.

🏛 Altes Rathaus

Rathausplatz. **Tel** (0851) 39 60.
Open Apr–6 Jan: 10am–5pm daily. 🎫

The Town Hall stands on the site of the former Fish Market alongside the Danube. By the annexation of houses standing between Schrottgasse and Marktgasse, the town hall was constantly enlarged up until the 19th century. The original tower, which was demolished in 1811, was replaced in 1890–91 by a fine Neo-Gothic tower designed by Heinrich

The Altes Rathaus, with Neo-Gothic tower

von Schmidt. It is encircled by a gallery and has a steep sloped roof. Floodmarks on the façade show the high levels reached by the Danube at various times. Entering the building from the side facing Schrottgasse, visitors pass through a late Gothic carved portal of 1510.

The town hall's interior and three courtyards date from the 16th and 17th centuries. The halls, open to the public, contain historical paintings by Ferdinand von Wagner.

🏛 Passauer Glasmuseum

Höllgasse 1. **Tel** (0851) 35 071.
Open 9am–5pm daily. 📷

Housed in the Wilder Mann hotel, Passau's museum of glass contains over 30,000 pieces of decorative and household glassware from the 18th to the 20th centuries.

The large collection of Bohemian glassware and the glass made in the workshops of the Bavarian Forest are remarkable. There is also an interesting section on Art Nouveau glass.

Over the years the museum has attracted some eminent visitors, from Neil Armstrong to Mikhail Gorbachev. Photos in the entrance tell the story.

Art Nouveau vase in the Glasmuseum

🏛 Paulskirche

Rindermarkt.

The parish church of St Paul was built in 1663–78 on the site of a medieval church that was destroyed by the Great Fire of 1622. The stuccowork in the interior was executed in 1909. The façade's tall, picturesque tower, rising over the Rindermarkt, is a prominent Passau landmark.

🏛 Museum Moderner Kunst

Bräugasse 17. **Tel** (0851) 38 38 790.
Open 10am–6pm Tue–Sun.
Closed 24, 25, 31 Dec & Good Friday. 📷 🌐 mmk-passau.de

Located in one of the old town's most beautiful houses, Passau's Museum of Modern Art exhibits art from the 20th and 21st centuries. There are regular international exhibitions of different modern artists.

🏛 Universität

Innpromenade, Innstr., Augustinergasse.

In 1972 the buildings of the former **Augustinian monastery**, founded in about 1070 and turned into barracks in 1803, were converted into a newly founded university. Further buildings were added to the side of the monastery facing the river. These are joined by the **Geisteswissenschaften I** building, constructed in 1976–81 to a design by Werner Fauser. This reinforced concrete structure is rendered in red plaster and combines regional architectural elements with modern spatial concepts.

The **Nikolakloster**, today a seminary, still has its original Romanesque crypt, although the entire building was remodelled in the Gothic style in 1348 and again in the Baroque style in 1716–17. The church furniture was moved to the parish church in Vilshofen in 1803.

🏛 Wallfahrtskirche Mariahilf

Mariahilfberg 3.

This pilgrimage church, set on the hill known as Mariahilfsberg, dominates the River Inn and Passau's Innstadt district. It commands a fine view of the city and the Dreiflüsseeck – the confluence of the three rivers.

The Capuchin church and monastery, completed in about 1630, are reached by a covered flight of 321 steps. The object of pilgrimage is a copy of a painting of the

Picturesque houses on the banks of the Danube

Madonna and Child by Lucas Cranach the Elder which has been venerated since 1622. The original painting was acquired from a gallery in Dresden by Leopold, Bishop of Passau in 1611. In 1650 the painting was moved to the Jacobskirche in Innsbruck, where it remains to this day.

The strikingly austere interior of Wallfahrtskirche Mariahilf features a silver eternal lamp made by Lucas Lang and presented by the Emperor Leopold I in 1676 on the occasion of his marriage in Passau.

🏛 Römermuseum Kastell Boiotro

Lederergasse 43. **Tel** (0851) 34 769.
Open 10am–4pm Tue–Sun.
Closed mid-Nov–mid-Apr. 📷

This Roman fort was built in about AD 280. From then until 400 it was used by Roman soldiers, and in about 460 St Severinus built his cell in the ruins. Excavated in 1974, the ruins together with the finds unearthed here are open to visitors.

The imposing buildings of the Wallfahrtskirche Mariahilf

⓭ Ortenburg

Road map F3. 🏔 7,000. 🚌
🚉 Vilshofen or Passau. 🛈 Marktplatz
11, (08542) 16 421. 🆆 ortenburg.de

This Renaissance **palace**,
which is set on a ridge, was
built in about 1567 on the
site of a medieval castle
belonging to the Bavarian
von Krailburg-Ortenburg
family. Joachim, one of the
family members, brought
the Reformation to the town
in 1563, and ever since then
Ortenburg has been a
Protestant enclave within
Catholic, Counter-Reformation
Lower Bavaria.

The palace is today in private
ownership, but it contains a
museum that is open to the
public. Visitors can also see
such features as a fine late
Renaissance panelled ceiling
dating from around 1600 in
the castle chapel, the remnants
of trompe l'oeil frescoes on the
wall of the Knights' Hall and a
torture chamber. The well
outside the palace, which
descends to a depth of 55 m
(180 ft), supplied the townspeople with water until 1927.

The presbytery of the
late Gothic **church**, which
has been a Protestant
church since 1563, contains
the splendid tombs of the
owners of Ortenburg in
the 16th and 17th centuries.

🏛 **Schlossmuseum Ortenburg**
Tel (08542) 12 00. **Open** Apr–Oct:
10am–5pm Tue–Sun.
🆆 schloss-ortenburg.de

The chapel in Sammarei's church,
bedecked with votive images

⓮ Sammarei

Road map F3. 🏔 300. 🚌 🚉
Vilshofen or Passau. 🛈 Ortenburg,
Marktplatz 11, (08542) 16 421.
🆆 wallfahrtsland-sammarei.de

Sammarei has one of the
most remarkable pilgrimage
churches in the whole of
southern Germany.

An old wooden **chapel**
miraculously survived the
fire that destroyed the neighbouring house of Cistercian
monks from Aldersbach. The
chapel was subsequently
enclosed within the late Renaissance church of **Mariä
Himmelfahrt**, occupying part
of the presbytery. The construction of this stone-built
church was supervised by
Isaak Bader the Elder, a court
architect from Munich, and
work began in 1629. While
the church was completed in
1631, the interior decoration
was not finished until 1650.

The ambulatory that was
created between the walls of
the chapel and the presbytery
of the church are completely
covered with Baroque votive
images, as are the walls of the
chapel itself.

The chapel is separated
from the nave by a fine high
altar of 1645, which acts as a
kind of iconostasis.

The chapel's late Rococo
altar contains the miraculous
image that is venerated by
pilgrims to the church. It is a
copy of the original *Madonna
and Child* ascribed to Hans
Holbein the Elder in the church
of Jakobs- und Tiburtiuskirche
in Straubing.

Baroque façade of the Mariä Himmelfahrt
church, Aldersbach

⓯ Aldersbach

Road map F3. 🏔 4,200. 🚌
🚉 Vilshofen. 🛈 Klosterplatz 1,
(08543) 96 100. 🆆 aldersbach.de

Work on the **Cistercian
monastery** in the town began
at the end of the 17th century.
It was remodelled by Dominikus
Magzin in the first half of the
18th century, when it became
the church of **Mariä
Himmelfahrt**.

The interior, which is lit by
large windows, is decorated
with exquisite paintings and
stuccowork executed by Egid
and Cosmas Damian Asam in
1718–20, the first time that the
brothers had collaborated on
a project *(see p72)*. Among the
most outstanding features
are the choir borne by angels
in wide flowing garments, and
the trompe l'oeil paintings on
the ceiling over the nave.

The high altar, dating from
1723, is Matthias Götz' masterpiece. The pulpit, of 1748,
and the stalls, of 1762, are by
Joseph Deutschmann.

Courtyard of the Renaissance palace in Ortenburg

For hotels and restaurants in this region see p268 and p280

⑯ Vilshofen

Road map F3. 🏔 16,300. 🚍
🛈 Stadtplatz 27, (08541) 20 81 12.
Ⓦ **vilshofen.de**

Founded in 1206 where the Vils, Wolfach and Pfudrach meet the Danube, Vilshofen centres around Stadtplatz. This long street is lined with colourful houses that were built after the great fire that destroyed the town in 1794.

The parish church of **St Johannes der Täufer**, built in the late 14th century, with two naves, was rebuilt in 1803–04. Its fine Baroque decoration was executed in the 18th century, and was originally intended for the Nikolaikirche in Passau. The decoration was later transferred to this church.

Another notable feature of the town is the late Gothic **Barbarakirche**, built in the second half of the 15th century, and the **Mariähilfskirche**, a former pilgrimage church built in 1611 by Antonio Riva. The Mariähilfskirche is decorated with stuccowork and frescoes executed by northern Italian artists, among whom was Giovanni Pietro Camuzzi.

The **gate tower** was built in 1643–7. It was designed by Bartholomäus Viscardi in the Mannerist style and has greyish-white tones and an onion dome. It has come to symbolize the town.

The high altar at the Asambasilika in Osterhofen

The most prominent building in Vilshofen is the **Benedictine abbey** of Schweiklberg, designed by Michael Kurz and built in 1909–11. The church has two Art Nouveau steeples.

The gate tower at the end of the Straßenmarkt in Vilshofen

⑰ Osterhofen

Road map F2. 🏔 11,600. 🚍
🚉 Altenmarkt. 🛈 Stadtplatz 13, (09932) 40 30. Ⓦ **osterhofen.de**

This small Bavarian town, whose history goes back almost six centuries, boasts a jewel of Baroque architecture, the **Asambasilika**.

The church was built in 1726 on the site of a medieval Premonstratensian church. Its appearance is the result of a collaboration between the architect Michael Fischer and the Asam brothers. While its exterior is somewhat austere, with the façade merging with a wing of the monastery, the decorative scheme of the interior is phenomenal.

The unusual shape of the single-nave interior is created by its oval side chapels and serpentine walls. The architecture, painting and stuccowork, fused into a single entity, are highly distinctive, both as an ensemble and as individual elements.

While the extensive ceiling frescoes by Cosmas Damian Asam create an illusion of extensive space, Egid Quirin Asam's stuccowork blurs the boundaries between reality and illusion. Absorbing the exquisite artistry and admiring the artists' skill can take some time *(see p72)*.

The Asambasilika made a profound impression on Pope John Paul II, who visited Osterhofen during his pilgrimage to Germany in 1980.

The Bavarian Forest

The area between the Danube, Regen and Cham and the Czech border is covered by one of the largest woodlands in Europe. Once Bavaria's most destitute region, it now draws tourists with its stunning scenery and prices that are lower than in its neighbouring cities. The region is renowned for its locally made glass and crystal, its hiking trails and skiing areas. The heart of the Bavarian Forest is the densely wooded National Park Reserve.

A historic Alpine house in the open-air museum at Finsterau

UPPER BAVARIA (EAST)

Lying between the rivers Inn and Salzach, this region
is very popular with tourists, who flock here for the breathtaking natural
scenery. The steep, snow-covered Alpine slopes, the lush green vegetation
of the valleys and the large lakes, such as Chiemsee and Königssee, all
have a magical atmosphere.

Alexander Humboldt, the famous geo-
grapher and explorer, named Berchtesgaden one of the most beautiful places
in the world, alongside Naples, Constan-
tinople and Salzburg. The region is
equally appreciated today. The Berchtesgaden National Park, which includes
Königssee and Watzmann, Germany's
second-highest peak of 2,713 m (8,900 ft),
covers an area of about 210 sq km
(80 sq miles) and was established in
the southeast of the region in 1978.

The region has more to offer than
breathtaking scenery. The Romans
discovered health springs here, and the
spa of Bad Reichenhall attracts visitors
from all over the country. The groundwater
contains up to 25 per cent salt, which
is extracted throughout the region.
Berchtesgaden has one of the oldest
working saltworks, in use since 1517.

Here visitors can see excellently preserved
tunnels and can cross a 100 m (328 ft)
underground lake on a raft.

Many previous rulers of Bavaria felt a
special attraction for this area, and Hitler's
"Eagle's Nest" residence was located on
Mt Kehlstein. A silver urn in a chapel in
Altötting contains the hearts of 21
Bavarian kings. The town also attracts
many pilgrims, who come to the church
with the figure of the Black Madonna,
which is famed for its reputed miracle-
working powers.

The region is dotted with fine
historic buildings. The little churches
of Maria Gern and St Bartholomä
possess a quaint charm. Burghausen
boasts the world's longest castle, and
one of the islands in Chiemsee was
chosen by Ludwig II for yet another
of his magnificent residences.

The Kapellplatz in Altötting in winter

◄ Picturesque view of the church in Ramsau

Exploring Upper Bavaria (East)

The town of Rosenheim on the River Inn could be regarded as the capital of this region. Although not well endowed with historic features, it is well worth a visit in late summer, when the local folk (beer) festival takes place. While it vies with Munich's Oktoberfest, it has a much more authentic, local atmosphere. There are historic towns on the river Inn, Wasserburg and Rott, the latter containing the grave of the Christian Democrat leader Franz Josef Strauß. The towns in the Salzach and Traun valleys are also worth exploring. The towns of Tittmoning and Laufen, with their captivating southern atmosphere, are very underrated.

Castle courtyard in Burghausen

Sights at a Glance

1. Altötting
2. Burghausen
3. Tittmoning
4. Laufen
5. Anger
6. Bad Reichenhall
7. Maria Gern
8. Berchtesgaden
9. Königssee
10. Ramsau
11. Ruhpolding
12. Reit im Winkl
13. Aschau
14. Herrenchiemsee
16. Stein an der Traun
17. Kloster Seeon
18. Amerang
19. Wasserburg am Inn
20. Rott am Inn
21. Bad Aibling
22. Neubeuern

Excursion

15. Around Chiemsee

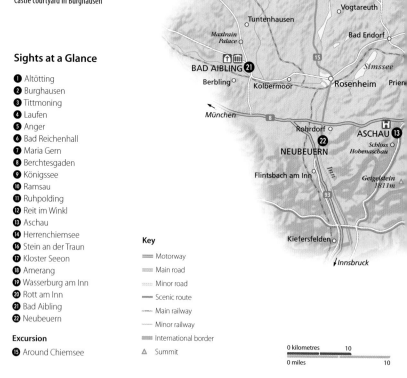

Key

- Motorway
- Main road
- Minor road
- Scenic route
- Main railway
- Minor railway
- International border
- △ Summit

0 kilometres   10

0 miles   10

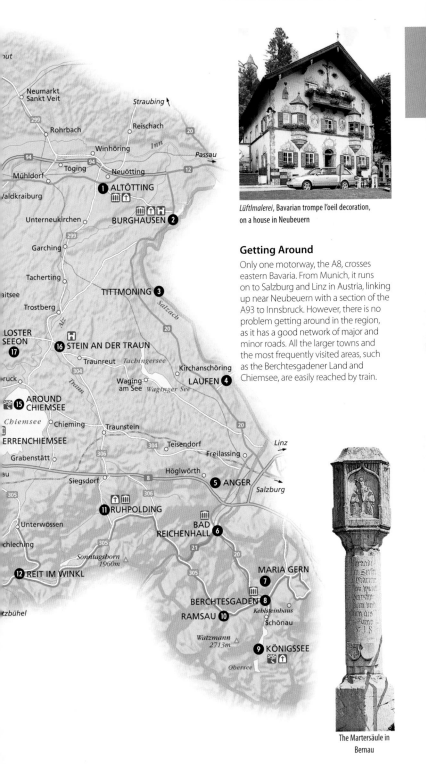

Lüftlmalerei, Bavarian trompe l'oeil decoration, on a house in Neubeuern

Getting Around

Only one motorway, the A8, crosses eastern Bavaria. From Munich, it runs on to Salzburg and Linz in Austria, linking up near Neubeuern with a section of the A93 to Innsbruck. However, there is no problem getting around in the region, as it has a good network of major and minor roads. All the larger towns and the most frequently visited areas, such as the Berchtesgadener Land and Chiemsee, are easily reached by train.

The Martersäule in Bernau

Burghausen Castle, the longest castle in Europe

❶ Altötting

Road map F4. 🚋 12,800. 🚌
ℹ️ Kapellplatz 2a, (08671) 50 62
19/38. 🌐 **altoetting.de**

This town, established in the 8th century, is one of the earliest Christian sites in Europe. It is also the earliest place of pilgrimage in Bavaria, and is called the Heart of Bavaria by some. Every year about half a million pilgrims come here to pay their respects to the Black Madonna. This early 13th-century statue is kept in the **Heilige Kapelle** (Holy Chapel) which stands in the centre of a large square. The chapel, with a Carolingian apse and a Gothic nave, is surrounded by an ambulatory whose walls are covered with votive images. Pilgrims holding crosses inch up to it on their knees. Pope John Paul II paid a visit to the shrine during his pilgrimage to Germany in 1980.

The treasury of the late Gothic **Stiftskirche** contains valuable votive offerings from the Holy Chapel. The most highly prized of these is the Goldenes Rössl (Golden Steed) of 1404, a masterpiece of French goldwork. The crypt contains the mortal remains of Johann Tilly, the renowned military leader in the Thirty Years' War.

Another feature of interest is the **Panorama** re-creating the view from the hill of Golgotha in Jerusalem. It is located in a building dating from 1902–03, and was made by Gebhard Fugel and Joseph Krieger.

🏛 Panorama
Gebhard–Fugel–Weg 10. **Tel** (08671) 69 34. **Open** Mar–Oct: 10am–5pm daily; Nov–Feb: 11am–2pm Sat & Sun. 🅿️ 🌐 **panorama-altoetting.de**

Environs
Two km (1.5 miles) north, on the River Inn, is **Neuötting**. Notable buildings here include the Gothic Nikolauskirche, designed by Hans von Burghausen, and the late Gothic Annakirche completed in 1515.

❷ Burghausen

Road map F4. 🚋 18,300. 🚌 ℹ️
Stadtplatz 99, (08677) 887 140/141.
🌐 **burghausen.de** 🎷 Jazz Festival (May); Historisches Burgfest (Jul).

Situated on the River Salzach, which forms the border with Austria, Burghausen is famous for having the longest **castle** in Europe. With its six court-yards, the castle stretches some 1,051 m (3,448 ft) along a ridge between the river and Wöhrsee. The castle was built in 1025 and rebuilt in 1490. The main castle (Hauptburg) contains several **museums**, including a local history and a photographic museum. In the rooms that are open to the public, German paintings and furniture are on display.

Angel in Burghausen's Schutzengelkirche

The Old Town, between the castle and the river, has an old-world atmosphere. The market square is surrounded by what are Burghausen's finest buildings: the Gothic **Jakobskirche**, with a Baroque tower, the **town hall**, the mid-16th-century **old Bavarian government building**, with a Renaissance courtyard, the **Schutzengelkirche** of 1731–46, and many historic houses.

On the north side of the square is the Jesuit **Josefskirche** of about 1629 and the **Marienbrunnen**, a mid-17th-century fountain.

Arcade on the the market square in Neuötting

❸ Tittmoning

Road map F4. 🚆 5,800. 🚌
🚉 Laufen, Burghausen. 🛈 Stadtplatz
1, (08683) 70 07 10. 🆆 **tittmoning.eu**

The entrance to this little town on the River Salzach is through a gate in the town walls. The market square is lined with colourful houses with bay windows and wood carvings. Among them is the tall **town hall**, its tower and façade dating from 1711–12. The hill above the town, the summit crowned by a 13th-century **castle**, gives a fine view of the surrounding countryside and the Alps. The **Maria Ponlach** pilgrimage chapel of 1617 is reached by a road round the castle that follows a ravine overlooking the River Ponlach.

Column of St Mary in Anger's main square

its huge roof and late 12th-century Romanesque tower, it dominates the town.
North of the church is the **Dechantshof**, the old archbishop's castle, which contains plaques from the church. Its staircase is decorated with the portraits of bishops. The four-winged **castle**, with an inner courtyard, was built in 1606–08 by Vincenzo Scamozzi.

❺ Anger

Road map F5. 🚆 4,300. 🚌 🚉
🛈 Dorfplatz 4, (08656) 98 89 22.
🆆 **anger.de**

Ludwig I deemed Anger the prettiest village in Bavaria. Much of its charm has been eroded by the arrival of a motorway and commercial development, but it still has a delightfully situated late Gothic **church**. The large square, which is lined with interesting houses, has a column with the statue of St Mary in the centre.

Environs
Two km (1.5 miles) to the north is **Höglwörth**, a tiny former Augustine abbey built in the 12th century on an island in a lake covered with water lilies.

❻ Bad Reichenhall

Road map F5. 🚆 17,400. 🚉
🛈 Wittelsbacherstr. 15, (08651) 60 60.
🆆 **bad-reichenhall.com**

The town has been known for its salt since Celtic and Roman times, and in the mid-19th century it became an important spa. Noteworthy buildings include the **St Zeno**

former Augustinian monastery dating from the first half of the 12th century. Although it was remodelled after the Gothic period, it retains its original Romanesque portal, which features two lions supporting the columns.
Gradierwerk, the inhalation house in the Kurpark built in 1909–10, gives an idea of how salt used to be produced by evaporation. In the **Alte Saline**, the old saltworks, which date from 1836–51, Ludwig I ordered a salt **museum** to be built. The exhibits include old salt-making equipment. The saltworks' marble enclosures date from 1524–36 and, together with an underground passage, were designed by the sculptor Erasmus Grasser.

🏛 **Alte Saline mit Salzmuseum**
An der Salinenstr. **Tel** (08651) 70 02
146. **Open** May–Oct: 10am–11:30am and 2–4pm daily; Nov–Apr: 2–4pm Tue–Fri and the first Sunday in the month. 🆆 **alte-saline.de**

The Gradierwerk in Bad Reichenhall's spa park

Iron bridge at Laufen, crossing over the border with Austria

❹ Laufen

Road map F4. 🚆 6,800. 🚉
🛈 Rathausplatz 1, (08682) 89 87 49.
🆆 **stadtlaufen.de**

Set on a bend in the River Salzach, this town has a southern, almost Italian feel. It was originally a Roman settlement, and flourished during the Middle Ages. Entry into the town is through two medieval **gates**. The streets are lined with arcaded houses with oriels and concave roofs typical of the region.
The 14th-century **parish church** is the oldest single-nave Gothic church in southern Germany. With

Maria Gern church seen against snowy Alpine peaks

❼ Maria Gern

Road map F5. 🚍 🚉 Berchtesgaden.
🛈 Berchtesgaden, Königseer Str. 2, (08652) 96 70.

This pilgrimage church is in a serene and picturesque setting among woodland pastures. Built in 1708–10, its pink pilasters on the exterior make a pleasing contrast with the white walls and the steep polygonal roofs harmonize with the Baroque onion dome of the tower.

The interior is decorated with stuccowork by Joseph Schmidt. The walls of the presbytery are hung with votive images spanning the 12th to the 20th centuries, and the altar has a beautiful wooden carving of the Madonna by Wolfgang Huber before which the faithful pray for forgiveness.

The **Ölbergkapelle** below the church dates from 1710.

❽ Berchtesgaden

Road map F5. 🚠 7,900. 🚍 🚉
🛈 Maximilianstraße 9, (08652) 65 65 050. 🌐 **berchtesgadener-land.com**

The area known as Berchtesgadener Land enjoys an excellent climate. The town is set in beautiful Alpine scenery on the River Ache at the foot of the Watzmann, which at 2,713 m (8,900 ft) is Germany's second highest peak.

The town is an ideal base for hikes throughout the region but with its old-world charm it also has plenty to offer. Here are houses with walls decorated with *Lüftlmalerei (see p216)*. One of them, the **Gasthof zum Hirschen**, an inn dating from about 1600, has paintings depicting monkeys parodying human vices. Another interesting building is the Gothic **Franziskanerkirche**, while a major attraction is the nearby saltworks – the **Salzbergwerk und Salzmuseum**. A little way from the town is the **Kehlsteinhaus**, also known as Hitler's Eagle's Nest *(see p205)*. A scenic excursion follows the **Roßfeld-Panoramastraße**, which winds its way along hairpin bends to a height of 1,600 m (5,249 ft).

The **Königliches Schloss**, formerly an Augustinian monastery and now owned by the Wittelsbach family, contains a museum with an interesting collection of furniture, paintings and Gothic woodcarving. The adjoining **church** was remodelled in the Gothic

style, although it retains its original Romanesque portal. The façade with its rose window and two towers were added in 1864–8. The Romanesque cloisters, unusual in southern Germany, date from the 12th century.

🏛 **Salzbergwerk und Salzmuseum**
Bergwerkstr. 83. **Tel** (08652) 60 020.
Open May–Oct: 9am–5pm daily; Nov–Apr: 11am–3pm daily.
🌐 **salzbergwerk.de**

🏛 **Königliches Schloss**
Schlossplatz 2. **Tel** (08652) 94 79 80.
Open 16 May–15 Oct: 10am–noon & 2– 4pm Sun–Fri; 16 Oct–15 May: 11am–2pm Mon–Fri. 🕐 11am & 2pm.
🌐 **schloss-berchtesgaden.de**

A jetty on Königssee

❾ Königssee

Road map F5. 🛈 Berchtesgaden, Maximilianstr. 9, (08652) 94 45 300
🌐 **nationalpark-berchtesgaden.de**

With its crystal-clear water and fjord-like setting between mountain ridges, Königssee is Bavaria's loveliest lake. The area also forms part of a national park.

The electric-powered boats that are used on the 8-km (5-mile) lake take visitors to the pilgrimage church of **St Bartholomä**, built in about 1700 and set on a peninsula below the eastern escarpment of the Watzmann. Nearby is a well-frequented inn. The boat trip offers views of awesome rock formations, enchanting little spots, waterfalls and echoing cliffs that throw back the sound of the boat's horn. The trip goes all the way to the northern end of Königssee, from where **Obersee** can be reached on foot.

The town of Berchtesgaden, nestling in an Alpine valley

For hotels and restaurants in this region see p268 and pp280–81

The main street in Reit im Winkl, a popular tourist resort

⑩ Ramsau

Road map F5. 🏔 1,700. 🚌
🚏 Berchtesgaden. 🛈 Tal 2, (08657)
98 89 20. 🆆 **ramsau.de**

This resort town, nestling amid
wooded mountain slopes, has
one of the most photographed
churches in the world – the
Pfarrkirche St Sebastian, dating
from 1512. Its picturesque
cemetery, which was laid out in
1658, contains tombstones
spanning the 17th to the 20th
centuries. The church is
situated above a stream, and
stands out wonderfully against
the magnificent backdrop of
the Reiteralpe.

⑪ Ruhpolding

Road map E5. 🏔 7,000. 🚌 🚉
🛈 Hauptstr. 60, (08663) 88 060.
🆆 **ruhpolding.de**

Ruhpolding attracts a high
volume of tourists. It is overlooked by the **Georgskirche**,
built in 1738–54 with highly
decorated altars and a pulpit
dating from the same period.
The right-hand altar features
a small Romanesque figure
of the Virgin Enthroned, with
large almond-shaped eyes,
dating from about 1200. Above
the church is the old **cemetery**,
which has a Baroque chapel
and tombstones dating from
the 18th and 19th centuries.
    The old Renaissance **hunting
lodge** houses the **Heimatmuseum**, which has a collection
of furniture, glass and jewellery
spanning the 17th to the 19th
centuries. Also on display in the

museum is a collection
of fossils and interesting
minerals that were found in
the surrounding mountains.
Among the displays at the
**Museum für Bäuerliche
und Sakrale Kunst**
(Museum of Folk and
Religious Art) is a fine
collection of church
ornaments, as well
as royal jewels
and crowns.

🏛 **Heimatmuseum**
Schlossstr. 2. **Tel** (08663)
41 230. **Open** 10am–noon
Tue–Fri. **Closed** Nov–Dec.

🏛 **Museum für Bäuerliche
und Sakrale Kunst**
Roman-Friesinger-Str. 1. **Tel** (08663)
5078. **Open** 9:30am–noon & 2–4pm
Tue–Sat, 9:30am–noon Sun.
Closed 25 Oct–25 Dec.

⑫ Reit im Winkl

Road map E5. 🏔 7,200. 🚌
🚏 Marquartstein. 🛈 Dorfstraße 38,
(08640) 80 027. 🆆 **reitimwinkl.de**

This small town, at an altitude
of almost 700 m (2,296 ft),
may not have any buildings
of historic interest, but it is
still a very popular tourist
resort. Picturesquely set in the
middle of the forest, with its
colourful storybook houses
and narrow streets, it is easy
to see why the place is so
appealing. Many people
come here, especially in winter,
as the area has the best snow
cover in the Bavarian Alps.
The town is also filled
with visitors in summer,
especially hikers using it
as a base for day trips
into the surrounding
area or even
into the whole
Berchtesgadener
Land. The road to
Ruhpolding, about
24 km (15 miles)
in length, is excep-
tionally scenic.
Forming part of
the Alpine Route, it
winds among lakes

The Madonna of
Ruhpolding

which, when seen from above,
resemble a necklace of green
beads strung on either side
of the road that traverses
spectacularly beautiful
mountain scenery.

Kehlsteinhaus – "The Eagle's Nest"

Set on the summit of Kehlstein, this stone building resembling a
mountain shelter is known as the Adlerhorst (Eagle's Nest). It was
given to Hitler by Martin Bormann on behalf of the Nazi Party in
1939 and became the Führer's
favourite residence. The building was attached to the summer residence built in 1933
and is situated on the slopes
of Obersalzberg. The approach
to Kehlsteinhaus is a masterpiece of engineering. First,
a road with stunning views
passes through five tunnels,
after which there is an elevator
whose shaft is cut into the
rock. The last stage of the trip
is a ride up in a high-speed
elevator, which is taken by
the thousands of tourists
who come here.

Hitler's famous "Eagle's Nest"

Road leading towards the Alps near Aschau

⓭ Aschau

Road map E5. ⛰ 5,500. 🚌 🚊
ℹ Kampenwandstr. 38. **Tel** (08052)
90 490. 🌐 **aschau.de**

In the centre of this small
town, set against fine
mountain backdrops, stands
a twin-towered **church**.
Originally built in the Gothic
style, it was rebuilt in the
Baroque period and in the
early 18th century was
decorated with stuccowork
and paintings of scenes
of the life of St Mary. Beside
the church is the small
Kreuzkapelle, built in the
mid-18th century, while
opposite, at Kirchplatz 1, is
an old **inn**, built in 1680 and
today named the Post Hotel.

Environs
From Aschau a road leads
south towards **Schloss
Hohenaschau**, which, set
on a height, is visible from
a distance. This mighty
12th-century fortress was
decorated in the Baroque style
in the 17th century,
although its medieval
walls still survive. The
reception hall on the
second floor was
decorated in 1682–4
with Baroque mouldings.
The grounds are also
worth exploring;
the castle is home to
a falconry and there
are regular birds of
prey demonstrations.

🏰 **Schloss Hohenaschau**
Tel (08052) 90 490. 🗝 only
guided tours: 1:30 & 3pm Tue,
Thu, Sun & hols; 10 & 11:30am
Wed & Fri (closed Sat). 🏞

⓮ Herrenchiemsee

Road map E4. 🚊 to Stock. ⛴
🌐 **herrenchiemsee.de**

Herreninsel, the largest island
in Chiemsee, has been settled
since prehistoric times. Thanks
to Ludwig II, it is among the
region's main tourist attractions.
The king aimed to build a huge
palace set in a vast park filled
with statues, fountains and a
canal along its axis. It was to be
the Versailles of Bavaria.

The **Schloss Herrenchiemsee**, based on Louis XIV's great
Palace of Versailles, was built
to satisfy Ludwig II's absolutist
leanings. Built in 1878–86, it
was to outdo all previous
royal palaces, but it was
never finished.

Ludwig II spent a mere nine
days in it, and at the time of his
death only 20 of the 70 rooms
that were planned for the three
wings were ready. They show
an astonishing lavishness and
splendour. Particularly spectacular
are the Große Spiegelgalerie
(Hall of Mirrors), and the

Fountain at Schloss Herrenchiemsee

Chambre de Parade. The
palace also houses a **museum**
dedicated to Ludwig II.

There are also the remains
of a church and an Augustinian
monastery on the island.
These are known collectively
as **Altes Schloss**.

🏛 Schloss Herrenchiemsee,
König-Ludwig II-Museum and
Altes Schloss
Tel (08051) 68870. 🗝 Apr–Oct:
9am–5pm daily; Nov–Mar:
9:40am–3:50pm daily. 🏞

The medieval castle of Höhlenburg, Stein
an der Traun

⓰ Stein an
der Traun

Road map E4. 🚌 🚊
ℹ Rathausplatz 3, Traunreut, (08669)
85 70. 🌐 **traunreut.de**

One of Upper Bavaria's
most distinctive buildings is
Höhlenburg, a castle set 50 m
(160 ft) above the River Traun.
It forms part of a system of
three castles. Torch in hand,
visitors pass through a series
of caves and tunnels. This is
said to be the home of the
fearful Heinz von Stein, a
legendary giant knight who
abducted girls. Casemates
lead between the medieval
upper castle, the lower
castle and the new castle,
which dates from the 15th
century and was rebuilt in
the Neo-Gothic style
in 1885–9.

🏰 **Höhlenburg**
Tel (08621) 25 01. 🗝 Apr–third Sun in
Oct: 2pm Tue–Sun; mid-Jul–mid-Sep:
2 & 4pm Tue–Sun. 🏞

⓫ Around Chiemsee

Chiemsee, also known as the Bavarian Sea, covers an area of 80 sq km (30 sq miles) and reaches a depth of 73 m (240 ft). Bavaria's largest lake, it is a favourite place for holiday-makers, and its shores are dotted with towns and holiday villages. The Alpine scenery, the watersports facilities and some fascinating buildings are the main attractions here.

⑥ Seebruck
This little town, whose history goes back to Roman times, is today a watersports centre with a large marina.

⑤ Frauenchiemsee
The Benedictine monastery on this island has a Romanesque church with a distinctive onion dome.

④ Herrenchiemsee
This is a favourite destination for visitors, who come to Ludwig II's grand unfinished palace.

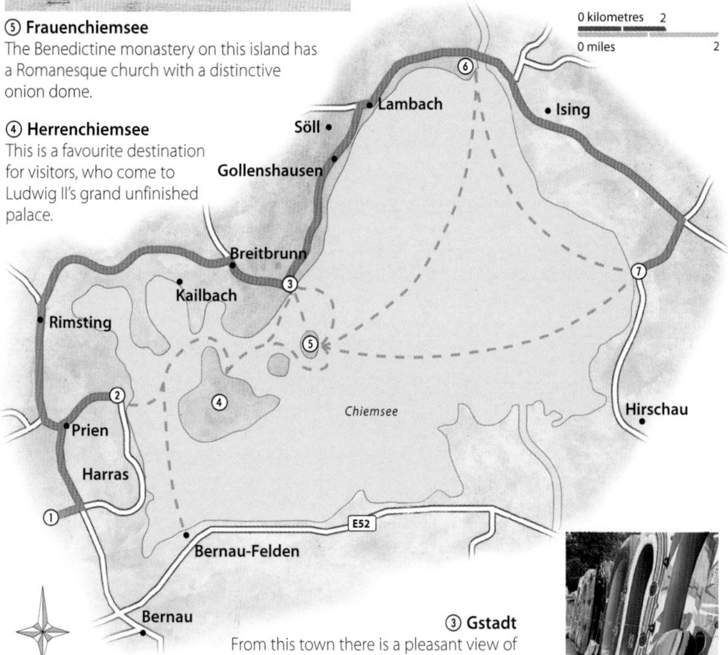

0 kilometres 2
0 miles 2

Lambach
Söll •
• Ising
Gollenshausen
Breitbrunn
Kailbach
③
Rimsting
⑤
② Chiemsee
Prien ④ Hirschau
Harras
① E52
Bernau-Felden
⑥
⑦

Bernau

③ Gstadt
From this town there is a pleasant view of Frauenchiemsee, which can be reached by boat from here. An interesting sight is the church "Peter und Paul", decorated in the Baroque style in about 1720.

① Urschalling
The 12th-century Jakobskirche has some fine mural paintings dating from the 13th and 14th centuries.

⑦ Chieming
Attractions here are the beach, with a 7-km (4-mile) long promenade and houses with *Lüftlmalerei (see p216)* and lavish floral displays.

② Stock
The Bockerl, a steam railway over 100 years old, provides a link between Stock and Prien. There are also boats to the lake's other islands and towns.

Tips for Drivers

Tour length: about 65 km (40 miles)
Stopping-off points: There are many cafés and restaurants in all the small towns round Chiemsee.

Key
▬ Suggested route
‎⁓ Other route
-- Ferry route

Kloster Seeon, the Benedictine monastery, set on a promontory on Klostersee

⓱ Kloster Seeon

Road map E4. 🚌 🚉 Bad Endorf
or Traunstein. 🛈 Kultur-und
Bildungszentrum des Bezirks
Oberbayern, Klosterweg 1, (08624)
89 70. 🌐 **kloster-seeon.de**

On the edge of Klostersee stands
Kloster Seeon, a monastery that
was taken over by Benedictine
monks. The original Romanesque
church was built in stages in
the 11th and 12th centuries.
Remodelled by Konrad Pürkhel,
it acquired its Gothic appearance
in 1425–33. The ceiling was
decorated by Salzburg painters
in 1579.

St Barbara's Chapel contains
the magnificent tomb of Aribo I
dating from about 1400 and
ascribed to the Salzburg sculptor
Hans Heider.

South of the church is a
cloistered courtyard of 1428–33,
which has Gothic tombstones.

⓲ Amerang

Road map E4. 🏔 3,700. 🚌 🚉
🛈 Wasserburger Straße 11, (08075)
91 97 31. 🌐 **amerang.de**

The Renaissance **palace** in this
small town was built by several
Italian architects, prominent
among whom were members
of the Scaligeri family of Verona.
Its large cloistered courtyard
is a venue for open-air concerts.
There is also a museum.

At the other end of the town
is the **Bauernhausmuseum**
(open-air museum) with farmhouses, a bakery, a mill and a
forge. The **EFA-Automobil-
Museum** (Museum of German
Automobile History) has 220
cars dating from 1886 to
the present.

🏛 **Schloss Amerang**
Open Easter–mid-Oct. **Tel** (08075) 91
920. 🕐 Fri–Sun & public hols.
🌐 **schlossamerang.de**

🏛 **Bauernhausmuseum**
Hopfgarten 2. **Tel** (08075) 91 50 90.
Open mid-Mar–Oct: 9am–6pm Tue–Sun.
🌐 **bhm-amerang.de**

🏛 **EFA-Automobil-Museum**
Wasserburger Str. 38. **Tel** (08075) 81 41.
Open Apr–Oct: Tue–Sun (daily Jul &
Aug). 🌐 **efaautomuseum.de**

Amerang's Renaissance palace, designed
by the Scaligeri family

⓳ Wasserburg am Inn

Road map E4. 🏔 12,900. 🚌 🚉
🛈 Marienplatz 2, (08071) 10 522.
🌐 **wasserburg.de**

Wasserburg is set on a
promontory on a bend
in the Inn, and is one
of the best-preserved
historic towns on the
river. The best view of
it is from the bridge
across the Inn, which
leads to a picturesque
Gothic **gate** which
in turn leads into
Bruckgasse. At
No. 25 in this lane
is the **Mauthaus**, the
ducal customs office, dating
from about 1400, with stepped
gables and three Renaissance
oriel windows, added in 1539.

The street leads to Marienplatz,
which is lined with houses.
Among them is the **Kernhaus**,
which once belonged to the
patrician Kern family. The façade
features decorative mouldings
by Johann Baptist Zimmermann.
Opposite stands the Gothic
town hall, which occupies two
buildings with stepped gables.
The **Frauenkirche** was built
in 1368 and is attached to
the watchtower.

The large **Jakobskirche** was
begun in the early 15th century
by Hans von Burghausen. The
castle, with its covered staircase,
can be reached from the church.
Remaining parts of the castle
include the residential wing,
which was converted into a
granary during the Renaissance,
and a 15th-century chapel. The
streets of the town are lined
with old houses with typical
gateways, courtyards, oriel
windows and arcades.

The Gothic façade of Wasserburg's town hall

⑳ Rott am Inn

Road map E4. 🗺 4,000. 🚌 🚲
ℹ Kaiserhof 3. **Tel** (08039) 90 680.
🌐 **rottinn.de**

The former Benedictine church of **Sts Marinus und Anianus** was rebuilt in 1759–63 to plans by Johann Michael Fischer, preserving the 12th-century Romanesque tower. The church has one of the finest Rococo interiors, decorated by the greatest artists of the time: the stuccoist Jakob Rauch, the fresco-painter Matthäus Günther and the sculptor Ignaz Günther. The church has undergone extensive restoration work and is open to the public.

Franz Josef Strauß, the former leader of Bavaria's ruling conservative party, is buried in the cemetery of the church, which is regularly visited by members of his CSU party.

The town square in Rott am Inn

㉑ Bad Aibling

Road map D4. 🗺 18,400. 🚌 🚲
ℹ Wilhelm-Leibl-Platz 3, (08061) 90 800. 🌐 **bad-aibling.de**

Bad Aibling is known for its mud baths, which were in use as far back as Roman times. However, it was only in the mid-19th century that it acquired its present status as a spa town.

There is much of architectural interest here. On a hill stands the church of **Mariä Himmelfahrt**, built in the late Gothic style but later remodelled in the Rococo style by Abraham Millauer to plans by Johann Michael Fischer. **Sebastianskirche** was built on the site of a 16th-century votive chapel after the plague epidemic of 1634, which

decimated the local population. After a series of fires that destroyed most of the town only a few houses survived. One is the 17th-century house at Kirchzeile 13 (today the **Hotel Ratskeller**), which has painted exterior walls and three oriel windows. The **Heimatmuseum** is also worth a visit.

🏛 Heimatmuseum
Wilhelm-Leibl-Platz.
Tel (08061) 46 14. **Open**
3–5pm Fri, 2–5pm Sun.

Environs
Some 6 km (4 miles) southwest of Bad Aibling is **Berbling**, with an authentic Bavarian village atmosphere. The charming Rococo church, the old houses, the barns, the maypole and the fields that stretch right up to the houses are quintessentially Bavarian. The painter Wilhelm Leibl once stayed here, while he was living in Bad Aibling from 1882 to 1889. The Renaissance **Maxlrain Palace**, with its palace brewery, lies on the other side of Bad Aibling, 4 km (2.5 miles) to the north. It was built in 1580–88 and has a steeply pitched roof and four onion-domed towers. At the neighbouring 18th-century inn, beer from the palace brewery is served.

㉒ Neubeuern

Road map E5. 🗺 4,400. 🚌
🚲 Raubling or Rohrdorf. ℹ
Marktplatz 4. **Tel** (08035) 21 65.
🌐 **kulturdorf-neubeuern.de**

This small town situated in the valley of the River Inn is held to be one of the prettiest in Bavaria, if not in the whole of Germany. It owes its present appearance to Gabriel von Seidl, who rebuilt the town and the medieval castle after two devastating fires in 1883 and 1893. Today it is often used by film-makers. With its **town gates**, **houses** and **church**, all of which are covered with trompe l'oeil paintings, it possesses everything that a director needs to re-create an old-style Bavarian town.

Oriel window in Neubeuern

Above the houses, decked with greenery and colourful window boxes, towers the **castle** with its tall keep, built in the local historical style in 1904–8. On fine days there is a good view of the Alps from the castle terraces.

Environs
Some 4 km (2.5 miles) to the east is **Samerberg**. From its peak there is a panoramic view of the town of Rosenheim, Simssee and the surrounding area. It is worth taking a round-about route via the delightful village of **Rohrdorf** to reach the summit.

The Renaissance Maxlrain Palace near Bad Aibling

UPPER BAVARIA (SOUTH)

With the Alps rising majestically over unspoiled forest and farmland, dotted with pretty villages and charming towns, southern Upper Bavaria looks like it has been lifted straight from the pages of a holiday brochure. Germany's highest mountain, the Zugspitze, overlooks a region ideal for sporting activities of all kinds, especially those involving snow. Away from the rock and ice, there is a world of traditional Bavarian life to explore, too.

The Werdenfelser Land, the southernmost region of the Bavarian Alps, stretches from Murnau to Garmisch-Partenkirchen. Its name comes from that of the now ruined Werden castle, which once defended the surrounding area. The backdrop of this fine sub-Alpine landscape is made up of the imposing Karwendel, Wetterstein and Ammergauer mountain ranges.

The small towns and villages of the region are the essence of Bavaria. The houses are covered with *Lüftlmalerei (see p216)*, and have wooden balconies that overflow with geraniums and other bright flowers.

From the high pastures you can sometimes hear the *Almschroa* (the traditional Alpine calls) and in the evenings you can join a yodelling concert. Bavarian folk costume *(see p33)* is widely worn whenever (which is often) local festivities can be deemed to be a special occasion.

Between the rivers Ammer and Lech, from Wessobrunn to near Steingaden, is the Pfaffenwinkel, or Clerics' Corner, which was named in jest in the 18th century due to the amount of abbeys, churches and chapels here. The finest church is Wieskirche, a popular stop on the Romantic Road tourist route.

The largest town in the region is Landsberg, whose historic buildings and inviting small streets, alleys and squares make it an interesting place to explore. The most famous town in the region is Garmisch-Partenkirchen, where the 1936 Winter Olympics and the 2011 Alpine World Ski Championships took place.

Traditional festivals and holidays are celebrated enthusiastically in the towns and villages. The best are the painted carts parade and the St Leonard's Day horseback pilgrimage to Mount Calvary in Bad Tölz.

Ancient and modern: satellite receivers outside a historic church in Raisting

◀ Alpine peaks forming a spectacular backdrop to Lake Lautersee, Mittenwald

Exploring Upper Bavaria (South)

This region is Munich's natural recreation ground. The journey south to Garmisch-Partenkirchen, the area's largest winter sports and hiking centre, takes less than an hour and a fast suburban train connects the Bavarian capital with Starnberger See and the Ammersee. These lakes, together with the Weßlinger See, Wörthsee and Pilsensee, make up the Fünfseenland (Land of Five Lakes), popular with city folk from Munich. Rafting expeditions down the Isar start at Wolfratshausen.

Sights at a Glance

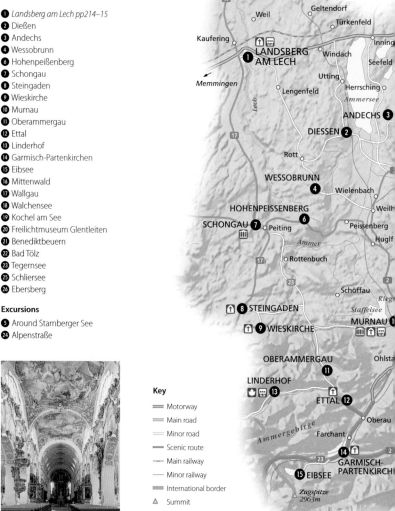

The ornate interior of the Welfenmünster church in Steingaden

Key

— Motorway
— Main road
⋯ Minor road
— Scenic route
⊷ Main railway
— Minor railway
▬ International border
△ Summit

For keys to symbols see back flap

Sculpture in the gardens of Ludwig II's palace at Linderhof

Getting Around

The southern region of Upper Bavaria is easily reached. The A8, A95 and A96 motorways from Munich lead to the region. The larger towns all have rail links, and those nearer Munich can be reached on the S-Bahn railway. The smaller towns, particularly those in the foothills of the Alps, are all served by convenient bus routes.

Public park on the shores of the Starnberger See

Forstinning

Haag

Anzing

Ebersberger Forst

Zorneding

EBERSBERG **26**

Grafing

München

München

Krailling

Grünwald

Höhenkirchen

Starnberg

Schäftlarn

Sauerlach

Berg

5 AROUND STARNBERGER SEE

Aying

Wolfratshausen

Geretsried

Bernried

Eurasburg

Königsdorf

Holzkirchen

Weyarn

Rosenheim

Seeshaupt

Miesbach

BAD TÖLZ **22**

Waakirchen

Penzberg

Gaissach

Hausham

21 BENEDIKTBEUERN

Bad Wiessee

23 TEGERNSEE

25 SCHLIERSEE

Rottach-Egern

FREILICHTMUSEUM

20 GLENTLEITEN

Lenggries

Mangfaligebirge

Bayrischzell

19 KOCHEL AM SEE

Klaffenbach

Kreuth

18

WALCHENSEE

A L P E N S T R A S S E

24

WALLGAU

Vorderriss

MITTENWALD

Isar

Isar

Isar

0 kilometres   5

0 miles   5

● Landsberg am Lech

Landsberg, which rises in terraces up the elevated banks of the River Lech, is well worth more than a brief visit. Enclosed by walls set with towers and pierced by gateways, it has largely retained its medieval character. The narrow streets, hidden alleys, market square and the steep-roofed houses make for a picturesque visit. Landsberg was also the place where Adolf Hitler was jailed after his abortive putsch, during which time he wrote *Mein Kampf*.

Gothic bas-relief on the church of Mariä Himmelfahrt

The lavishly decorated stuccowork façade of the Historisches Rathaus

Exploring Landsberg

With its many streets, alleyways and squares boasting fine architecture and historic houses, Landsberg is a lovely place to explore on foot. There are delightful little corners, such as the Hexenviertel, Seelberg and Blattergasse. The Hintere Salzgasse is a particularly striking alley with rows of mid-18th-century single-storey cottages with large, steeply pitched roofs.

🏛 Historisches Rathaus

Hauptplatz 152. **Tel** (08191) 12 82 68.
Open 8am–noon & 2–5pm Mon–Thu, 8am–12:30pm Fri

The Historisches Rathaus, or town hall, stands on the west side of the square. The façade and rooms on the second floor have fine mouldings executed by Dominikus Zimmermann in 1718–20. Outside the Rathaus is the Marienbrunnen, a fountain with a statue of the Madonna, dating from 1783.

🏛 Lechwehr

This weir was built in the 14th century at the point where the Mühlbach stream branches off from the River Lech. Over the centuries, the weir has been repeatedly washed away by floods and rebuilt. The cascades are scenically set against the backdrop of the Old Town.

🏛 Klosterkirche der Dominikanerinnen Hl. Dreifaltigkeit

Peter Dörfler Str. 🚻

The church, with its uniform Rococo decoration, was built in 1764–6. It stands in the same street as the Dominican convent, whose façade was painted with murals in about 1765. This entire group of buildings was the last work that Dominikus Zimmermann executed before his death.

The Bayertor, one of the finest town gates in Bavaria

🏛 Bayertor and Town Walls

Open May–Oct: 10am–noon, 2–5pm daily.

One of the best-known gateways in Bavaria is Landsberg's colourful Bayertor. Built in 1425, it has a 36-m (118-ft) high crenellated tower whose interior contains a stone sculpture of the Crucifixion and armorial cartouches.

The other surviving gates are the Mannerist Sandauertor, dating from 1625–30, the Bäckertor of about 1430, and the Färbertor, built in the later 15th century. The Sandauertor is crowned by the tall, circular Luginsland tower, which functioned as a watchtower during the Middle Ages.

Except for those on the west side, the medieval town walls have been preserved almost in their entirety. The earliest parts, built in the 13th century, can be seen on Vordere Mühlgasse and Hintere Salzgasse. The Schmalzturm, or Schöner Turm, dates from the 13th century. The most recent section of the walls was built in the early 15th century.

🏛 Heilig-Kreuz-Kirche and Neues Stadtmuseum

Von-Helfenstein-Gasse 426. Neues Stadtmuseum: **Tel** (08191) 12 83 60.
Open 2pm–5pm Tue–Fri, 10am–5pm Sat, Sun & public holidays. 🚻

The Heilig-Kreuz-Kirche was built in 1752–4 to a plan by Ignaz Merani, replacing the previous building of 1580. It was the first Jesuit church in southern Germany. Set high up on a slope overlooking the town, it has a flat façade flanked by belfries with Baroque roofs. The ceiling is decorated with two trompe l'oeil paintings by Thomas Scheffler, a pupil of the Asam brothers. The paintings create the striking illusion of the Holy Cross falling from above. Monastery buildings stand beside the church. Prominent among them are the former Jesuit college's Renaissance cloisters, dating from 1576–1609.

Opposite the church, a little further down the hill, is the former Jesuit college, built in 1688–92 in a refined but pleasingly simple style. Since 1989 the building has housed the local history museum.

The Neues Stadtmuseum and, in the background, Heilig-Kreuz-Kirche

⛪ Mariä Himmelfahrt

Georg-Hellmair-Platz.

The church, built in 1458–88 and retaining its Romanesque tower, was given its present Baroque appearance in about 1700. The windows of the presbytery have late Gothic stained glass, although this is unfortunately obscured by the high altar.

Also in the presbytery, in the Altar of the Rosary made by Dominikus Zimmermann in 1721, is a Gothic figure of the Madonna and Child, an outstanding work executed by Hans Multscher of Ulm in about 1440.

⛪ Johanniskirche

Vorderer Anger.

Built by Dominikus Zimmermann in 1750–52, this church has an oval plan, four semi-circular external corner niches and a separate circular presbytery. Zimmermann, working with Johann Luidl, was also responsible for the decoration of the interior, which features a magnificent high altar.

VISITORS' CHECKLIST

Practical Information
Road map C4. 🚗 28,700.
🛈 Hauptplatz 152, (08191)
12 82 46. email: info@landsberg.
de 🎭 Ruethenfest (Jul, every four years, the next will be in 2019).
🌐 **landsberg.de**

Transport
🚉 Bahnhof-Platz.
🚌 Bahnhof-Platz.

🏛 Mutterturm

Von-Kühlmann-Str. 2. Herkomer Museum: **Tel** (08191) 12 83 60.
Open May–Oct: 1–6pm Tue–Sun; Nov–Apr: noon–5pm Sat & Sun.

The Mother Tower, built in 1884–7 on the side of the river opposite the town, was the summer residence and studio of Hubert von Herkomer, the painter and dramatist, who died in 1914. Dedicated to his mother (hence the name), the house was built in the style of a Norman castle keep and stands 30 m (98 ft) high.

The museum in the tower has objects from the artist's studio; drawings, etchings and paintings.

Landsberg Town Centre

① Historisches Rathaus
② Lechwehr
③ Mutterturm
④ Klosterkirche der Dominikanerinnen Hl. Dreifaltigkeit
⑤ Bayertor and Town Walls
⑥ Heilig-Kreuz-Kirche and Neues Stadtmuseum
⑦ Mariä Himmelfahrt
⑧ Johanniskirche

For keys to symbols *see back flap*

Yacht jetty at Dießen on Ammersee

❷ Dießen

Road map C4. 🚶 10,300. 🚌 🚉
i Bahnhofstr. 12, (08807) 10 48.
w tourist-info-diessen.de

This small fishing town is located on Ammersee, Bavaria's third-largest lake. The area is very popular with people from nearby Munich. Although large numbers of tourists come here, their presence is not especially noticeable. It is pleasant to walk along the lakeside promenade, and especially to visit one of the homely restaurants and to sample Ammersee's speciality, the salmon-like *Renken*.

A few old houses survive here, including the oldest wooden **peasant cottage** in Upper Bavaria, dating from 1491. The most exquisite historic building is the early Rococo **Marienmünster**, a church built for the Augustinian monastery in 1732–9 to a design by Johann Michael Fischer. The fine ceiling paintings, executed by Johann Georg Bergmüller in 1736, depict the saints and blessed members of the von Andechs family. The side altars feature depictions of St Sebastian by the Venetian painter Giovanni Battista Tiepolo and of St Stefan by Battista Pittoni.

❸ Andechs

Road map C4. 🚶 3,500. 🚌
🚉 Herrsching. *i* Andechser Str. 16, (08152) 93 250.
w gemeinde-andechs.de

Andechs is home to one of the oldest **churches** in Germany. The main part of the building dates from 1420. The church was remodelled in the Baroque style in 1669–1751. The stuccowork and painting are the work of Johann Baptist Zimmermann. The church attracts some 200,000 pilgrims every year. Because of its situation almost 180 m (590 ft) above the level of Ammersee, together with the Rococo decoration of its late Gothic church, the Benedictine monastery draws large numbers of visitors.

Another reason for the monastery's popularity with visitors is the strong beer that is brewed here. It is served at the monastery's inn and on the terrace, from which there is a breathtaking view over the lake.

The Rococo interior of the church in Wessobrunn

❹ Wessobrunn

Road map C4. 🚶 2,200. 🚌 🚉
Weilheim. *i* Zöpfstr. 1, (08809) 31 300.
w wessobrunn.de

The exterior of the former Benedictine abbey here conceals a fine courtyard, lavish stuccowork in the **monastery** and Rococo decoration in the **church**, which was built in 1757–9. Of the original Romanesque buildings, all that remain are the defence tower and the Crucifix in the church. The stuccowork and Rococo painting in the cloisters and on the monastery staircase were executed by the workshop of Johann Schmuzer in 1680–96.

It was here in 814 that the *Wessobrunner Gebet* was written. This two-part poem describing the Creation is the oldest extant document in the German language. It is today preserved in the Bayerischen Staatsbibliothek in Munich (*see p69*).

Lüftlmalerei

Lüftlmalerei is the style of painting that is widely seen on houses in Upper Bavaria and the Allgäu, particularly in the Alpine and sub-Alpine areas. Dating from the 17th century, it was derived from Italian trompe l'oeil painting. A famous exponent of *Lüftlmalerei* was Franz Seraph Zwinck (1748–92), who lived in Oberammergau in a house called Zum Lüftl. It was probably after his house that this style of painting was named.

Lüftlmalerei in Berchtesgaden

❺ Around Starnberger See

It was in Starnberger See, near the town of Berg, that Ludwig II, much loved by the Bavarians, drowned in 1886. Like many of Munich's elite, he owned a summer palace on the lake. This scenic region has long enjoyed great popularity. The wealthy citizens of Munich build fine residences here, while those of more modest means come for weekend breaks.

① Starnberg

Linked to Munich by a railway since 1854, Starnberg boasts luxury villas and has a large marina.

⑨ Possenhofen

Royal visitors to this palace have included Elisabeth, future consort of Franz Joseph of Austria, and Sofia, Ludwig II's betrothed.

Fürstenfeldbruck ⬋ München

② Berg

The spot where Ludwig II met his death is marked by a Neo-Romanesque chapel built on the lakeshore in 1896–1900, and a wooden cross in the shallow water.

⑧ Feldafing From 1855 to 1863
Ludwig II stayed in a romantic palace on nearby Roseninsel with his cousin Elisabeth (known as Sisi), the future empress of Austria.

③ Assenhausen

In an extensive park stands Bismarck Tower, built in 1896–9 in honour of the German Chancellor.

⑦ Tutzing

A monumental horseshoe-shaped palace surrounded by a landscaped park is currently the home of an evangelical academy.

Weilheim

Starnberger See

⑥ Bernried

The popular Buchheim Museum (north of Bernried) houses a collection of Expressionist and folk art (www.buchheimmuseum.de).

Weilheim

④ Ammerland

The palace here, built in 1683–5, was presented by Ludwig I to the German poet and painter Franz Graf von Pocci in 1841.

Tips for Drivers

Tour length: about 46 km (28 miles).
Stopping-off points: There are many restaurants and cafés in every town on the route. Overnight accommodation is available, although it may be harder to obtain in summer.

Penzberg

⑤ Seeshaupt

This bustling resort, with a marina and elegant lakeside promenade, is very popular with watersports enthusiasts.

Key

0 kilometres 2
0 miles 2

▬▬ Suggested route
═══ Other road

➏ Hohen-peißenberg

Road map C5. 3,700. 🚍
🚆 Peißenberg or Peiting.
ℹ️ Blumenstr. 2, (08805) 12 90.
🆆 **hohenpeissenberg.de**

The mountain known as Hoher Peißenberg rises east of the town of Peißenberg. The summit, at a height of 988 m (3,241 ft) above sea level, is reached by a scenic winding road and offers an extensive panorama of Upper Bavaria, from Ammersee and Starnberger See to the Alps.

On the summit stands the **Gnadenkapelle**, built in the late Gothic period and remodelled in the Baroque style, the church of **Mariä Himmelfahrt**, built in 1616–19, and a former **chapterhouse** of 1619. The chapel contains a miracle-working image of the Madonna Enthroned dating from 1460–80 and brought here from Schongau in 1514.

➐ Schongau

Road map C5. 12,300. 🚍 🚆
ℹ️ Münzstr. 1–3, (08861) 21 41 81.
🆆 **schongau.de**

Schongau is picturesquely located on the river Lech and surrounded by idyllic fields and pastures. The town is enclosed by almost completely preserved **town walls** with wooden walkways and towers. They were built in the 14th century and later reinforced in the 17th century. The main street in Schongau is the wide Münzenstraße, which is lined with shops and restaurants.

One of the town's finest buildings is the church of **Mariä Himmelfahrt**, which was built by Dominikus Zimmermann in 1751–3 on the site of a Gothic church. Also of interest is the former **castle** of the Wittelsbachs, dating from the 15th century and refurbished in 1771–2, and the late Gothic **Ballenhaus**, whose ground floor with open-beamed ceiling houses the town hall.

The **Stadtmuseum Schongau**, a local history museum, is to be found in **Erasmuskirche**, a former hospital church, established in the 15th century and rebuilt in the 17th century.

Michaelskirche font, Altenstadt

🏛️ **Stadtmuseum Schongau**
Christophstr. 55. **Tel** (08861) 25 46 05. **Open** 2–5pm Wed, Sat, Sun & public hols.

Environs
Some 3 km (2 miles) northwest is **Altenstadt**, which boasts **Michaels-kirche**, the finest surviving monumental Romanesque basilica in Upper Bavaria. Dating from about 1200, it is surrounded by a wall. It is decorated with Gothic frescoes and contains the Great God of Altenstadt, a crucifix 3 m (10 ft) tall, and a carved Romanesque font.

Pavement café tables in the medieval town of Schongau

Romanesque cloisters of the abbey in Steingaden

➑ Steingaden

Road map C5. 2,700. 🚍
🚆 Peiting. ℹ️ Krankenhausstr. 1, (08862) 91 01 13. 🆆 **steingaden.de**

This town has a well-preserved Romanesque **Pfarrkirche St Johannes der Täufer**, built in the second half of the 12th century and partially rebuilt in the 15th century. The columned basilica has a triple apse and twin towers above the west front. The interior was decorated with Rococo mouldings and paintings in 1771–4.

In 1147, the Premonstratensians built an **abbey** here, of which the western cloisters, dating from the early 13th century, survive. The architect Dominikus Zimmermann was buried in the Romanesque chapel of St John in 1766.

➒ Wieskirche

Road map C5. 🚍 🚆 Füssen or Peiting. ℹ️ Krankenhausstr. 1, Steingaden, (08862) 91 01 13
🎵 Abendkonzerte, Festlicher Sommer in der Wies (May–Sep).
🆆 **wieskirche.de**

The attractive pilgrimage church of **Zum Gegeißelten Heiland**, nestling in the sub-Alpine scenery, is not only the most resplendent example of South German Rococo, but probably the finest Rococo church in the world. UNESCO listed it as a World Heritage Site in 1983.

In 1738, the figure of Christ in a small chapel in the fields southwest of the present church is said to have wept genuine tears, and soon afterwards pilgrims began to flock to the site of the miracle. In 1743–4, the Premonstratensian abbot of Steingaden commissioned Dominikus Zimmermann to design a church here.

Built in 1754 and decorated in 1765, the church represents the work of Dominikus and Johann Baptist Zimmermann at its peak. The nave is built to an oval plan and the ceiling is supported by eight pairs of columns. There is an elongated presbytery. The entire building displays an extraordinary fusion of painting, woodcarving and stuccowork and an almost mesmerising interplay of colour and light. The many windows, in fantastic and varied shapes, enliven the exterior and illuminate the interior. Not surprisingly, the church has been called the Lord God's Ballroom.

⑩ Murnau

Road map C5. 🏔 12,200. 🚌 🚉
ℹ️ Kohlgruber Str. 1, (08841) 61 410.
🌐 **murnau.de**

Murnau is situated on an elevation between two lakes, Staffelsee and Riegsee, north of the marsh known as the Murnauer Moos, on what was once the Roman road to Augsburg. During World War II

Rococo interior of the church in Wies, a World Heritage Site

an officers' prisoner-of-war camp existed here. Today Murnau is famous for its two breweries.

The **Nikolauskirche** is an interesting building. It was designed by Enrico Zucalli and was completed in 1734, after 17 years' work. The small Baroque **Maria-Hilf-Kirche** stands on Marktstraße, the main street, which commands a view of the Alps to the south.

There are numerous inns and guesthouses, a Neo-Gothic **town hall**, houses with oriel windows and decorative signboards, and narrow, winding alleys which give the town a unique charm. The **monument to Ludwig II**, on Kohlgruber Straße, was erected in 1894 and is the earliest monument to be dedicated to the king.

The finest building in Murnau is the Art Nouveau **Münterhaus**, where the artist Wassily Kandinsky lived from 1909

to 1914 with his student and lifetime companion Gabriele Münter. Today it houses a museum dedicated to the famous painter couple, along with works by other members of the Blaue Reiter group.

🏛 **Münterhaus**
Kottmüllerallee 6. **Tel** (08841) 62 88 80.
Open 2–5pm Tue–Sun.

Der Blaue Reiter

Cover of the first issue of
Der Blaue Reiter

Wassily Kandinsky and Franz Marc produced the first issue of *Der Blaue Reiter* in 1911. The journal is now considered one of the most significant manifestos of 20th-century art. The contributors were artists whose aim was to renew art, while retaining their stylistic individuality. They included Paul Klee, Alexej Jawlensky, August Macke and Gabriele Münter. The Blaue Reiter group marked the beginning of lyrical abstract painting.

A colourful flower stall on Untermarkt in Murnau

The Baroque basilica of the Benedictine abbey at Ettal, set in an Alpine valley

⓫ Oberammergau

Road map C5. 🏔 5,200. 🚌 🚉
ⓘ Eugen-Papst-Str. 9a, (08822) 922
740. 🅦 **oberammergau.de**
🎭 Passionsspiele (Easter, every ten
years, the next in 2020).

Oberammergau is one of the
best-known towns in Upper
Bavaria. Its renown rests on its
painted houses, and it is the
centre of the colourful style of
trompe l'oeil house-painting
known as *Lüftlmalerei*, which is
typical of the region *(see p216)*.
The town also has an
international reputation for
its Passion play, which has
been performed here at Easter
ever since 1633, when an
epidemic of the plague finally
passed. Originally an open-
air event, the play has been
performed in a purpose-built
theatre since 1930.
The spectacle, which last
for six hours, is performed by
1,400 amateur actors, all of
whom must be local people
or their family members. The
play attracts an audience from
all over the world.

⓬ Ettal

Road map C5. 🏔 800. 🚌 🚉
ⓘ Oberammergau. ⓘ Ammergauer
Str. 8, (08822) 92 36 34. 🅦 **ettal.de**

Set in a scenic Alpine valley,
this Benedictine **abbey** was
founded by Ludwig IV in 1330.
In 1710, when the church was
remodelled in the Baroque style
to plans by Enrico Zucalli, a
Gothic rotunda was added. The
two-storey façade that Zucalli
intended was not completed
until the early 20th century.
The impressive interior
decoration is in a pure
Rococo style, crowned
by the large dome
that is visible from afar.
The paintings were
executed in 1748–50 by
Johann Jakob Zeiller, and
the stuccowork, one of the
great achievements of
its time, is by Johann
Georg Üblher and
Franz Xaver Schmuzer.
The high altar has a 14th-century
marble statue of the Madonna
made in the workshop of
Giovanni Pisano. The church,

Vase in the Linderhof
park

which attracts many pilgrims,
is surrounded by various
monastic buildings.

⓭ Linderhof

Road map C5. 🚌 🚉 Ettal. Palace:
Tel (08822) 92 030. **Open** Apr–15
Oct: 9am–6pm daily; 16 Oct–Mar:
10am–4pm daily. 🎫 🅿 Park:
Open Apr–mid-Oct. 🅦 **linderhof.de**

Of all Ludwig II's many
fairy-tale residences, the
palace at Linderhof best
shows his great fondness
for France and his regard
for the Bourbons and
Louis XIV. The smallest
of Ludwig II's castles
and the one he
visited most often, it
was built by Georg von
Dollmann in 1870–86
and is surrounded by
an extensive park.
The extravagant
luxury of the
interior decoration
is based on French Baroque
style. Although it was intended
as a private residence, the
palace still has an ornate
royal audience chamber. The
other rooms in the palace,
including the Tapestry Room
and Hall of Mirrors, are no less
extravagantly decorated.
The palace is surrounded
by French-style formal gardens
and by Italianate terraced
gardens with cascades, which
in turn are surrounded by
landscaped grounds. There is
an artificial **grotto** dating from
1876–7 with a lake, a stage

The Hotel Alte Post in Oberammergau

and a throne with colourful lighting that brings to mind the Venus Grotto in Wagner's opera *Tannhäuser*. Ludwig II would take rides on the lake in a conch-shaped boat.

Another attraction of the park surrounding the palace is the **Moorish kiosk**, made by Karl von Dibitsch in 1850 and purchased by the king in 1876. Inside it is a lavish Peacock Throne. Just as resplendent is the **Moroccan House** of 1878–9, which was installed here in 1989.

Visitors admiring Ludwig II's palace at Linderhof

⑭ Garmisch-Partenkirchen

Road map C5. 🏔 26,800. 🚌 🚊 ℹ Richard-Strauss-Platz 2, (08821) 18 07 00. 🌐 gapa.de

Two villages, Garmisch and Partenkirchen, separated by the rivers Loisach and Partnach, were conjoined one year before the 1936 Winter Olympics. Thus came into being one of the best-known winter sports centres in Germany, with a convenient motorway link to Munich. The town is famous for its ski slopes and for hosting international skiing events.

Partenkirchen, the older of the two villages, has its roots in the Roman town of Partanum, while Garmisch is first mentioned in a document from the 9th century. Both parts of the town have many houses with characteristically painted façades, some old and others quite modern.

Skiing above Garmisch-Partenkirchen, popular with winter sports enthusiasts

The finest churches here include **St Anton**, in Partenkirchen, a pilgrimage church dating from the first half of the 18th century, with trompe l'oeil painting by Johann Holzer. There are also two **churches** in Garmisch dedicated to St Martin. One is medieval, with Gothic frescoes in the interior, and the other is Baroque, with stuccowork executed by Josef Schmuzer in 1730–33 and paintings by Matthäus Günther of 1733.

The **Olympic stadium** in the south part of Partenkirchen was built in 1934. As well as having ski-jumps, it is decorated with larger-than-life sculptures that are typical of Fascist art.

Environs
A road south of Partenkirchen leads to the scenic **Partnach river gorge** (Partnachklamm). Further along, an uphill walk of several hours leads to Ludwig II's hunting lodge in Schachen, just below the summit of Dreitorspitze. Built in 1870 in imitation of a Swiss chalet, the lodge has an ornate Oriental-style interior. The king celebrated his birthdays in the lodge, and also came here on hunting trips.

⑮ Eibsee

Road map C5. 🚌 🚊 Garmisch-Partenkirchen.

The greenish-blue waters of this lake, surrounded by wooded mountain slopes, lie 974 m (3,195 ft) above sea level. The scenic paths along its shores lead to secluded jetties for yachts and boats.

A regatta, with processions of yachts and great firework displays, takes place here every summer. Above the lake towers **Zugspitze**, which at 2,963 m (9,718 ft) is the highest peak in the German Alps. The summit can be reached by cablecar or a funicular train, which passes through many tunnels.

Eibsee, the lake at the foot of Zugspitze

Mittenwald, a town on a former trade route at the foot of the Alps

⑯ Mittenwald

Road map C5. 🚘 7,400. 🚌 🚈
ℹ️ Dammkarstr. 3, (08823) 33 981.
W alpenwelt-karwendel.de/mittenwald

Situated at the foot of the Karwendel mountain range, this small town stands on what was once the main trade route between Verona and Augsburg. Up until the Thirty Years' War, its wealth was founded on trade but from the 17th century its mainstay was craftsmanship, particularly violin-making.

The beginnings of the local violin-making trade can be traced back to the 17th century and Matthäus Klotz (1653–1743), a pupil of the famous Nicolo Amati. A violin school was founded in 1853, and in 1930 the **Geigenbaumuseum** (Museum of Violin-Making) was established in the house where Klotz was born.

St-Peter-und-Paul-Kirche was built in 1738–40 by Josef Schmuzer. The late Gothic presbytery survives, and the tower was completed in 1746. The *Lüftlmalerei* on the façade is an outstanding example of this type of decoration *(see p216)*. It is by Matthias Günther, who also executed the paintings inside the church. The monument to Matthäus Klotz that stands outside the church was designed by Ferdinand von Miller in 1890.

Mittenwald is now known as a tourist resort, and is popular with winter sports enthusiasts.

🏛️ **Geigenbaumuseum**
Ballenhausgasse 3. **Tel** (08823) 330.
Open 10am–5pm Tue–Sun (11am–4pm Jan, mid-Mar–mid-May & mid-Oct–Nov). W geigenbaumuseum-mittenwald.de

⑰ Wallgau

Road map C5. 🚘 1,400. 🚌
🚈 Mittenwald. ℹ️ Mittenwalderstr. 8, (08825) 92 50 50. W alpenwelt-karwendel.de

This delightful village has small wooden **cottages** built in the 17th and 18th centuries with *Lüftlmalerei (see p216)* by Franz Kainer dating from the 1770s. Most of the cottages have been thoroughly modernized and now function as hotels.

The town is popular with the smart Munich set, who come to play golf on the fine local courses. The **Gasthaus zur Post** is renowned as the place where Heinrich Heine stayed in 1828 on his journey to Italy.

One of the many fine golf courses around the town of Wallgau

⑱ Walchensee

Road map C5. 🚘 600. 🚌
🚈 Kochel am See. ℹ️ Ringstr.1, (08858) 411. W walchensee.de

This lake, which lies in an attractive green valley, is swept by strong winds, and is therefore very popular with windsurfers.

The small **church** near the lake was built in 1633 and refurbished in 1712–14.

Environs

In the nearby town of **Zwergern** stands the picturesque Margarethenkirche, which was built in the 14th century and remodelled in the Baroque style in 1670. Beside it stands a monastery known as the Klösterl. Built in 1686–9, it has striking white walls and a tall, steeply pitched roof.

Near **Urfeld**, hidden in the woods, stands a small bust of the great 19th-century German writer Johann Wolfgang von Goethe, who stayed in the town when he set off on his famous Italian travels in 1786.

Walchensee hydroelectric power station on the banks of Kochelsee

⑲ Kochel am See

Road map C5. 🚘 4,000. 🚌 🚈
ℹ️ Bahnhofstr. 23, (08851) 338.
W kochel.de

Kochel is a popular resort on Kochelsee. The local church, **Michaelskirche**, was built in 1688–90, probably by Kaspar Feichtmayr. The frescoes and stuccowork were added in about 1730.

For hotels and restaurants in this region see pp268–9 and pp281–2

Two famous figures are associated with Kochel. One is the blacksmith who became the hero of the Bavarian uprising against Austria in 1705 – a statue of him was erected in 1900. The other is the painter Franz Marc. The house in which he lived is now a museum of his paintings and the works of other artists of the group Der Blaue Reiter *(see p219)*.

🏛 **Franz Marc Museum**
Franz-Marc-Parc 8–10. **Tel** (08851) 924880. **Open** 10am–6pm Tue–Sun & public hols (until 5pm Nov–Mar). **Closed** 24 & 31 Dec. 📷 ✏
🌐 **franz-marc-museum.de**

Environs
On the banks of Kochelsee is **Walchensee hydro-electric power station**. It was built in 1918–24 to a design by Oskar von Miller, who aimed to electrify the Bavarian rail network and to supply electricity to the whole country. Walchensee power station is still one of the largest in Germany today.

⑳ Freilichtmuseum Glentleiten

Road map C5. 🚌 🚉 Kochel am See, Murnau. ℹ️ (08851) 18 50. **Open** 19 Mar–11 Nov: 9am–6pm Tue–Sun (Jun–Sep: also on Mon). 📷
🌐 **glentleiten.de**

The largest Freilichtmuseum (open-air museum) in Upper Bavaria opened near Großweil in 1976. It re-creates the atmosphere of a traditional Bavarian village, with cottages and workshops. The interiors show the way villagers lived. Fields and meadows are cultivated in the traditional way, with grazing cows, horses, sheep and goats.

The extensive cloisters of the monastery at Benediktbeuern

㉑ Benediktbeuern

Road map C5. 🏔 3,500. 🚌 🚉
ℹ️ Prälatenstr. 3, (08857) 248.
🌐 **benediktbeuern.de**

The holiday resort of Benediktbeuern, at the foot of the Benediktenwand mountains, is known for its former Benedictine **monastery**. Founded in 739 as part of the see established by St Boniface, it was one of the first missionary monasteries that he founded in Bavaria.

Work on the present late Baroque **church**, which stands on the site of a Romanesque church, began in 1682 under the direction of Kaspar Feichtmayr of Wessobrunn. The interior features some fine stucco-work strongly influenced by Italian art. The vaulting over the nave and the side chapels was painted by Hans Georg Asam, father of the renowned Asam brothers, in 1683–7. The monumental altar, built to resemble a triumphal arch, is made out of three different kinds of marble.

By the presbytery, which is fronted by towers, stands the two-storey **Anastasiakapelle**. It was built in 1750–53 by Johann Michael Fischer and has an oval floor plan. The decoration, by Johann Michael Feichtmayr and Johann Jakob Zeiller, is a masterpiece of Bavarian Rococo style.

Also worth visiting are the **monastery buildings**, now owned by Silesians. Dating from 1669–1732, they are arranged around two courtyards. The Alter Festsaal (Old Banqueting Hall), the Kurfürstensaal (Assembly Hall) and the former library, now a refectory, are particularly worth seeing.

Franz Marc 1880–1916

Blue Horse I, one of Marc's best-known paintings

The Munich-born painter Franz Marc began his artistic career under the influence of the Impressionists and of Wassily Kandinsky, with whom he set up the group Der Blaue Reiter *(see p219)*. Marc adopted Robert Delaunay's pure palette of Symbolist colours and the crystalline forms of the Italian Futurists. His paintings of humans and animals show them in harmony with their surroundings. Marc enjoyed painting from nature outdoors and was often visited in his home by followers of the movement. He was killed in 1916 at the Battle of Verdun at the age of 36.

Wooden figure of a fisherman in the lakeside resort of Kochel am See

⑫ Bad Tölz

Road map D5. ⚑ 18,500. ⚏
ℹ Max-Höfler-Platz. 1, (08 041) 78
670. ⚑ Leonhardifahrt (6 Nov).
W bad-toelz.de

Until quite recent times, the
inhabitants of Bad Tölz, on
the River Isar, made their living
through a combination of
trade, logging and making and
selling their famous painted
chests, cases and beds. The
rafting and brewery trades also
flourished here. When iodine-
rich springs were discovered
here in 1846, the village
became a health spa.

A painted cart used in the festival of St Leonhard

The character of the old
town has been well preserved
around **Marktstraße**, which
leads down to the Isar. Many
of the houses, dating from
the 17th to the 19th centuries,
have characteristic trompe
l'oeil wall paintings and striking
stuccowork, and distinctive
overhanging eaves.

The Baroque **church** on
Kalvarienberg, one of the most
famous in Bavaria, was begun
in 1726 and completed at the
end of the 19th century. It has
two elegant towers, and
particularly impressive is the
Holy Staircase inside the
church. At the festival
of St Leonhard, patron
saint of horses and
cattle, a procession
with old-fashioned
painted carts and
horses (Leonhardiritt)
ascends Kalvarienberg
and is then blessed.
A small fair and
dancing events are
part of the celebration.

⑬ Tegernsee

Road map D5. ⚑ 3,900. ⚏
⚏ Tegernsee. ℹ Hauptstr. 2, (08022)
92 73 860. **W tegernsee.de**

For the inhabitants of
Munich, Tegernsee, within
easy reach of the bustling
capital, is an upper-class
recreation ground.

The first settlement to be
founded in the valley was the
Benedictine **monastery** near
Tegernsee, established in the
8th century. The monastery
became an important centre
of culture, and in the 11th
century the Romanesque
stained-glass windows made
here were renowned.
Examples can be seen in
Augsburg cathedral. In 1823–4
Leo von Klenze converted the
monastery into a summer
residence for Maximilian I
Joseph. Von Klenze also
designed a new façade for
the monastery church, built
by Enrico Zucalli in the
Baroque style.

⑭ Alpenstraße

In 1927, plans were made for a panoramic road
that was to pass through the most beautiful parts
of the German Alps. The route alternates between
the High Alps and the foothills lying between
Bodensee and Königssee. It traverses the most
scenic areas, allowing travellers to admire Lower
Bavaria's stunning scenery. Particularly impressive
are the winding sections of the route, such as
those around Hindelang and Bayrischzell, which
offer breathtaking views.

② **Jochstraße**
The scenic road
that winds round
Hindelang, at
altitudes varying
as much as 300 m
(985 ft) along a 7
km- (4 mile-) long
route, offers views
of Ostrachtal.

Key

▬ Suggested route

⋯ Other road

▬ Scenic route

① **Immenstadt**
This picturesque little
town, which has
some fine historic
buildings, is situated
near the lake, Alpsee.

③ **Zugspitze**
At 2,962 m (9,718 ft), this peak is
the highest in Germany. It is
topped by a distinctive cross.

0 kilometres 20
0 miles 20

The town of Schliersee seen from the lake

figure of God the Father with Christ ascribed to Erasmus Grasser, and a Madonna ascribed to Jan Polack. The interesting **Heimatmuseum** (local history museum) is housed in an 18th-century hut.

㉕ Schliersee

Road map D5. 🔼 6,800. 🚍
ℹ Perfallstr. 4, (08026) 60 650.
🌐 schliersee.de

Situated east of Tegernsee and known as its "younger brother", Schliersee offers visitors much peace and quiet and makes for a popular escape in the summer. The houses on the northern lakeshore all have balconies laden with window boxes.

The local **church of St Sixtus** has frescoes and stuccowork executed by Johann Baptist Zimmermann in 1714. The church also has a distinctive

🏛 **Heimatmuseum**
Lautererstr. 6. **Tel** (08026) 43 97.
Open May–Oct: 2–5pm Tue–Sat.

㉖ Ebersberg

Road map D4. 🔼 12,000. 🚍
ℹ Marienplatz 1, (08092) 82 55 92.
🌐 ebersberg.de

This little town lies at the southern end of Germany's largest expanse of forest. Of the Augustinian monastery that was founded here in AD 934 all that remains is the **Sebastianskirche**, built in 1217–31 and remodelled in 1472–1504 in the Gothic style.

Notable among the tombs, which span the 14th to the 16th centuries, is that of the couple who founded the church. It features a model of the church made by Wolfgang Leb in 1501. On Marienplatz, along with Baroque and Neo-Classical houses, is the **monastery inn**, now the town hall.

Doorway of Sebastianskirche in Ebersberg, with gilded figures

④ Bayrischzell
In this famous health resort beneath the Wendelstein mountains, the first Alpine folklore association was founded, in 1883. Traditional Bavarian dress is still worn here today.

⑥ Berchtesgaden
This architecturally rich town, at the foot of Watzmann, is the hub of the tourist area known as Berchtesgadener Land.

⑤ Hintersee
The forest covering the foothills around this lake east of Ramsau – one of the many lakes in Berchtesgadener Land – is known as the Zauberwald (Magic Forest).

Tips for Drivers

Tour length: About 450 km (280 miles).
Stopping-off points: The route takes in Bavaria's best-known places, where restaurants and accommodation are plentiful.

Map labels: Munich, A8 E52, Regensburg, Chiemsee, Traunstein, Cham, A95 E533, 318, A8 E52, A8 E52, A1, Linz, Munich, 304, 20, Salzburg, Bad Tölz, 472, Bad Tölz, 472, 307, ④, 305, A10 E55, rnau, 307, 305, 533, Walchensee, 181, ⑥, Isar, ⑤, Königssee, Spittal, E533, sbruck

THE ALLGÄU

The Allgäu is the part of Swabian Bavaria lying between the Landsberg-Memmingen motorway and the Allgäu Alps. In the east it borders the Lech valley, and in the west Baden-Württemberg, into which it protrudes as far as Bodensee (Lake Constance). The Allgäu is one of the least industrialized regions of Bavaria. The region's main draws are its mountains and Ludwig II's most outrageous architectural creation, Schloss Neuschwanstein.

This verdant, hilly region, set against the backdrop of the sheer, craggy peaks of the Alps, attracts holidaymakers from Europe all year round. The gentle climate, the unspoiled scenery, the villages and towns with their historic buildings, and the excellent terrain for various sports makes this a suitable area for the developing tourist trade. The lush meadows and pastures are grazed by the characteristic brown Allgäu cows. The region's dairy produce is famous throughout the country and Germany's largest dairy processing plant is located in Kimratshofen, near Kempten.

Traditions and customs are still very much alive in the region. Local folk costumes, which vary from one district or village to another, are donned not exclusively for special occasions but are worn as everyday clothing. After World War II, the influx of migrants (many from Sudetenland) considerably altered the structure of the population. The former inhabitants of Gablonz (Jablonec), in the Czech Republic, settled near Kaufbeuren in Neugablonz, bringing with them their traditional trade of jewellery-making.

In the Allgäu Alps, world-class sports are practised. In Oberstdorf, which is famous for its huge ski-jump, there is also a figure-skating school for young men and women from all over the country. The Alpine rockfaces are suitable for both amateur and professional mountaineers, while the cliff-tops are ideal starting-places for colourful paragliders and hang gliders. Schloss Neuschwanstein, the most extravagant of Ludwig II's castles, attracts visitors from all over the world.

Rolling green countryside around Immenstadt

◀ The magnificent setting of Schloss Neuschwanstein

Exploring the Allgäu

The capital of the Allgäu is Kempten, a town with Roman origins. Memmingen also has many historic monuments, but these are not the region's main attraction. Tourists are drawn to the castles of Hohenschwangau and Neuschwanstein at the foot of the Alps, which are reached by the Romantische Straße (Romantic Road). Equally splendid are the Renaissance castles of the Fuggers in Babenhausen and Kirchheim, and Ottobeuren Abbey. The south of the Allgäu has breathtaking Alpine scenery, including the Breitach gorge and Sturmannshöhle, a cave with stalactites, near Oberstdorf. This town is renowned for the Four Ski Jumps Tournament.

The church in Wasserburg on Bodensee (Lake Constance)

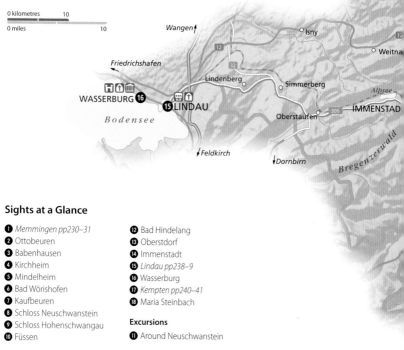

Sights at a Glance

Cows grazing in pastures at the foot of the Allgäu Alps

Getting Around

All the region's major towns have rail links, while the smaller towns are served by buses. The Allgäu can be reached by motorway A96. Lindau is the starting point of the Deutsche Alpenstraße, one of the finest scenic roads in Germany. Motorway A7 runs from north to south via Memmingen and Kempten. The Allgäu has convenient links with Munich and Stuttgart airports.

Key

- ▬▬ Motorway
- ▭▭ Main road
- ▭ ▭ Minor road
- ▬ Scenic route
- ▬▬ Major railway
- ▬ Minor railway
- ▬▬ International border
- ▬▬ Regional border

Schloss Hohenschwangau, in a stunning location

❶ Memmingen

Memmingen, a town known as the gateway to the Allgäu, was founded in the 12th century. It stands on the site of an Alemani settlement, on the course of an old Roman road. In 1438 Memmingen became a Free Imperial City, in 1522 it accepted the Reformation, and in 1803 it became part of Bavaria.

Memmingen has retained all the characteristics of a large trading centre. Various residential and artisans' districts have developed both within and outside the town walls. The wide streets often functioned as cargo-handling areas. The mainly timber-framed houses that line them have preserved their Gothic character.

The façade of the town hall, with decorative Rococo stuccowork

🏛 Rathaus

Marktplatz 1.
Originally built in 1488, the Gothic town hall was remodelled and enlarged in the 16th century. Its current appearance dates from 1589, the Rococo stucco-work was added later to the façade in 1765. This elegant Renaissance building has a projecting central axis with oriel windows on the lower storeys culminating in a polygonal tower, and the wings are flanked by side towers.

🏛 Steuerhaus

Marktplatz 16.
The former customs house was built in 1495 to an elongated rectangular plan. It opens on to Marktplatz with an arcade of 20 arches. The second floor and the shaped gables were added in 1708. The painting on the façade dates from 1906–09. The building currently houses various municipal offices.

🏛 Hermansbau

Zangmeisterstr. 8. Stadtmuseum und Heimatmuseum Freudenthal:
Tel (08331) 85 01 34. **Open** May–Oct: 10am–noon and 2–4pm Tue–Sat, 10am–4pm Sun & public holidays. 🅿

This late Baroque patrician palace with an arcaded courtyard was built in 1766 for Benedikt Freiherr von Herman. The façade is lavishly decorated with stuccowork, and the central section has a gable with an armorial cartouche.

🏛 Martinskirche

Zangmeisterstr. 13.
Tel (08331) 85 69 20.
The Protestant Martinskirche was built in the 15th century, replacing a Romanesque basilica. This late Gothic church has a quadrilateral tower with a later steeple.

The interior has notable wall paintings dating from the 15th and 16th centuries. The most interesting feature of the interior, however, is the presbytery stalls, made by craftsmen from Memmingen in 1501–07. The decorative carvings, with lifelike portraits of the founders, are among the most outstanding examples of late Gothic Swabian art.

The rich Gothic carvings on the stalls in Martinskirche

🏛 Westertor and Town Walls

The walls of the old town were completed before 1181. The outer walls were added in the 13th–15th centuries. In the 19th century they were partially demolished, but significant fragments with bastions and walkways have been preserved.

The most noteworthy gate is Westertor, which was rebuilt in 1648, and Kemptentor, built in 1383 and topped by a tall brick tower.

🏛 Antonierhaus

Martin-Luther-Platz 1. Strigel- und Antoniter-Museum: **Tel** (08331) 85 02 45. **Open** 10am–noon and 2pm–4pm Tue–Sat, 10am–4pm Sun & public holidays. 🅿

This former Antonine monastery and hospital, the oldest established by the order, was built in 1383. It stands on the site of an earlier castle.

The four-winged building has internal cloisters with external staircases. Pain-stakingly rebuilt, since 1996 they have housed a library as well as a café and cultural institutions.

Decorative armorial cartouche on the façade of the Steuerhaus

⌂ Fuggerbau

Schweizerberg 8.

The house of the Fugger family (see p256) was built in 1581–91 for Jakob Fugger. It is a monumental four-winged building with two square stairwells rising from the corners of the courtyards.

⌂ Frauenkirche

Frauenkirchplatz 4.

This three-nave basilica was originally a Romanesque building. It was enlarged at the end of the 14th century, and was remodelled in 1456. From 1565 to 1806 the church was shared by Catholics and Protestants.

The late Gothic paintings on the walls and ceiling were uncovered in 1893. Their state of preservation and wide thematic range make them among the most significant in southern Germany.

⌂ Siebendächerhaus

Gerberplatz 7.

The "House with Seven Roofs", built in 1601, was specially designed for drying hides.

Destroyed in April 1945 and painstakingly rebuilt, it is one of the town's most distinctive buildings.

Theater

Theaterplatz 2. **Tel** (08331) 94 59 16.

The building on what is now Theaterplatz was originally a monastery's barn. Built in 1680, it became an arsenal and then a theatre in 1803, when the Neo-Classical façade was added.

The distinctive Siebendächerhaus, the "House with Seven Roofs"

⌂ Kreuzherrenkirche

Hallhof 5. **Open** Apr–Oct: 2–5pm Tue–Fri & Sun; 10am–12:30pm, 2–5pm Sat.

This two-nave church with a tall onion-domed clock tower was built in 1480–84 in the Gothic style. In 1709 the interior was decorated with lavish Baroque stuccowork by Matthias Stiller and paintings in the style of Johann Baptist Zimmermann.

When the church was deconsecrated in 1803, the interior was horizontally divided to make two storeys. After World War II it was restored and has since served as a gallery and concert hall.

Memmingen Town Centre

① Rathaus
② Steuerhaus
③ Hermansbau
④ Martinskirche
⑤ Westertor and Town Walls
⑥ Antonierhaus
⑦ Fuggerbau
⑧ Frauenkirche
⑨ Siebendächerhaus
⑩ Theater
⑪ Kreuzherrenkirche

The lavishly decorated interior of the abbey church at Ottobeuren

❷ Ottobeuren

Road map B4. 🏔 8,000. 🚌 🚉
ℹ️ Marktplatz 14, (08332) 92 19 50.
🌐 ottobeuren.de

The Benedictine abbey in Ottobeuren, whose beginnings go back to the 8th century, is one of the finest Baroque monasteries in Germany. The **Church of St Theodore and St Alexander**, rebuilt and refurbished on numerous occasions, received its present appearance in 1748–66, when it was remodelled by Johann Michael Fischer.

Nestling in wooded slopes overlooking the River Günz, this fine monumental building is a breathtaking sight. The lavish interior, in a uniform Rococo style, features four domes, the largest of which is 25 m (82 ft) high. The decoration and furnishings are by various artists, including Johann Michael Feichtmayr and Johann Jakob and Franz Anton Zeiller.

The **abbey**, to the west of the church, is known as "the Escorial of Swabia". Built to plans by Christoph Vogt in 1711–31, it is an imposing quadrilateral edifice with four cloisters.

Ottobeuren Abbey has been in the hands of Benedictine monks since its foundation. Today the Library, the Abbot's Chapel, the Theatre Hall and the Knights' Hall are open to visitors.

The **Klostermuseum** contains sculpture dating from the 12th to the 18th centuries, the works of artists who worked in Ottobeuren, clocks and other artifacts.

The abbey's Kaisersaal is occupied by the **Staatsgalerie**, an interesting art gallery devoted to the works, mostly on religious themes, of Swabian Gothic painters. The gallery forms part of the Bayerische Staats-gemäldesammlungen.

🏛 **Klostermuseum Abtei Ottobeuren and Staatsgalerie**
Ottobeuren, Kaisersaal Abbey. **Tel** (08332) 79 80.
Open Palm Sunday–end-Oct: 10am–noon & 2–5pm daily; Nov–Mar: by request for tourist groups; Christmas Day–Epiphany (6 Jan): 10am–noon, 2–4pm daily. 🗐 🗐
🌐 abtei-ottobeuren.de

❸ Babenhausen

Road map B4. 🏔 5,500. 🚌 🚉
ℹ️ Marktplatz 1, (08333) 94 00 32.
🌐 vg-babenhausen.de

The most prominent landmarks in this town are the castle and the parish church.

The **castle**, which is mentioned as early as 1237, became the property of the von Rechberg family after 1378. It was probably they who were responsible for the steep-roofed two-storey edifice built here in the 15th century and incorporated into the castle. In 1539 the castle passed into the hands of the Fuggers *(see p257)*, who refurbished it in 1541, adding the west and south wings. In 1955 the **Fuggermuseum** was founded, with the family retaining owner-ship of the park surrounding the castle.

The **church**, which is connected to the castle, was rebuilt in the Baroque style in 1715–30. The interior contains Baroque altars and a pulpit, as well as the tombs of the Rechbergs and Fuggers.

🏛 **Fuggermuseum**
Tel (08333) 29 31. **Open** Apr–Nov: 10am–noon & 2–5pm Tue–Sat, 10am–noon & 1–6pm Sun. 🖼

The castle and church in Babenhausen

❹ Kirchheim

Road map B4. 🏔 2,600. 🚌 🚉
Mindelheim. ℹ️ Marktplatz 6, (08266)
86 080. 🌐 **kirchheim-schwaben.de**

The main attraction of this small
town is the Renaissance **castle**,
owned by the Fugger family
since the mid-16th century.
The famous Cedar Hall is
decorated with wood-
carvings on its ceiling
and door, and on its
window surrounds and
chimneypieces.

The altar of **St-Peter-
und-Paul-Kirche** features
a painting of the Holy
Family ascribed to
Domenichino and of the
Assumption ascribed
to Rubens. Also worth
seeing is the tomb of
Hans Fugger, who died
in 1598. Made of white
limestone, it was the work
of Alexander Colin.

Knight statue,
Kirchheim Castle

Part of the inlaid ceiling of the Cedar Hall
at Kirchheim Castle

❺ Mindelheim

Road map B4. 🏔 14,600. 🚌 🚉
ℹ️ Maximilianstr. 26, (08261) 99
15 20. 🌐 mindelheim.de 📷
Frundsbergfest (every three years
in Jun–Jul, the next in 2018).

During the 15th and 16th
centuries **Mindelburg**,
built by Heinrich der Löwe
in 1160, belonged to the
Frundsberg family, as did the
whole town. The castle was
rebuilt in the late 15th to early
16th centuries and again
in the late 19th century.

The town's two main
streets, Maximilianstraße and
Kornstraße, are lined with fine
town houses. The former Jesuit
Maria-Verkündigungs-Kirche,

built in 1625–6 and refurbished
in 1721, has fine stuccowork
and altars.

Stephanskirche, built in
the early 18th century and
rebuilt in the early 20th
century, contains the tomb
of Duke Ulrich von Teck
and his two brides. In
the former St Sylvester
is the **Schwäbisches
Turmuhrenmuseum**,
displaying belfry clocks.

🏛 Schwäbisches
Turmuhrenmuseum
Hungerbachgasse 9.
Tel (08261) 90 97 60.
Open 2–5pm Wed & the
last Sun in the month.

❻ Bad Wörishofen

Road map B4. 🏔 15,500. 🚌 🚉
ℹ️ Hauptstr. 16, (08247) 99 33 55/56.
🌐 bad-woerishofen.de

This spa resort owes its
existence to the priest Sebastian
Kneipp. Among the 19th-cen-
tury guest houses here are the
Sebastianeum at Kneippstraße
8 and the **Kneippianum** at
Alfred-Baumgartenstraße 6. The
Justinakirche and **Klosterkirche**
both have decoration by
Dominik and Johann Baptist
Zimmermann.

🏛 Sebastian-Kneipp-Museum
Klosterhof 1. **Tel** (08247) 39 56 13.
Open Feb–mid-Nov: 3–6pm Tue–
Sun; 26 Dec–6 Jan: 3–5pm Sun.

❼ Kaufbeuren

Road map D4. 🏔 41,800. 🚌
🚉 ℹ️ Kaiser-Max-Str. 3a, (08341)
437 850. 🌐 kaufbeuren-
tourismus.de 📷 Tänzelfest (Jul).

With steep, winding narrow
streets lined with colourful
houses, the hilltop town of
Kaufbeuren retains much of
its medieval character.

The old town still has its
fortifications, complete with
walls and defensive towers, one
of which is the Fünfknopfturm,
which was built in about 1420.
After World War II, Neugablonz,
a settlement for refugees from
Sudetenland, now part of the
Czech Republic, was built here.

The Gothic Fünfknopfturm, part of
Kaufbeuren's fortifications

Sebastian Kneipp (1821–1897)

Sebastian Kneipp, a parish priest from St Justina's
Church in Bad Wörishofen, introduced a
method of therapy involving five factors –
water, movement, herbal treatment, diet
and inner harmony – but above all cold
baths, showers and exercise. In 1903 a
monument to Duke Kneipp was erected
in the street bearing his name. Portraits
of the clergyman (painted in 1936) can
be seen on the ceiling of Justinakirche,
and the town's former Dominican monastery
contains a museum dedicated to him.
The local rose-gardens also grew a new
variety of rose, the Kneipp Rose.

The Kneipp Monument in Bad Wörishofen

Schloss Neuschwanstein seen against its woodland backdrop

❽ Schloss Neuschwanstein

Road map B5. **ℹ** Neuschwansteinstr. 20, Hohenschwangau, (08362) 93 08 30. **Open** Apr–15 Oct: 9am–6pm daily; 16 Oct–Mar: 10am–4 pm daily. **Closed** 1 Jan, 24, 25, 31 Dec. **🖼 ♿ 🌐 neuschwanstein.com**

Schloss Neuschwanstein, one of Ludwig II's most renowned castles, was built at enormous expense from 1868 to 1892. It received its present name after the king's death in 1886.

The monumental castle was built to plans by the theatre designer Christian Jank, who expressed the king's vision inspired by Wagner's operas *Lohengrin* and *Tannhäuser*. The interior decoration was executed by Julius Hoffmann in 1880.

The castle has a breathtaking situation on an outcrop of rock towering over a gorge in the River Pöllat. There is a particularly memorable view from Marienbrücke, which giddily spans the rushing waters in the ravine below.

❾ Schloss Hohenschwangau

Road map B5. **ℹ** Alpseestr. 12, (08362) 93 08 30. **🌐 hohenschwangau.de**

This 14th-century castle, which was destroyed during the Napoleonic Wars, was acquired by Maximilian II, the king of Bavaria, in 1832. The restoration and rebuilding work executed up to 1837

was primarily the work of Domenico Quaglio.

A bulky building, set with towers and painted yellow, it is situated over a lake against a picturesque backdrop of Alpine scenery.

🏰 Schloss Hohenschwangau
Open Apr–15 Oct: 8am–5:30pm daily; 16 Oct–Mar: 9am–3:30 pm daily. 🖼

Statue of the Madonna and Child in St Mang-Kirche at Füssen

❿ Füssen

Road map B5. **🚗** 15,300. **ℹ** Kaiser-Maximilian-Platz 1, (08362) 93 850. **🌐 fuessen.de**

The town's location in the foothills of the Alps, surrounded by lakes and overlooking the River Lech, together with its proximity to Schloss Neuschwanstein and Schloss Hohenschwangau, ensure that it is always full of tourists.

In Roman times Füssen stood on the road connecting northern Italy with Augsburg. In 1313 it passed into the hands of the bishops of Augsburg, who made it their summer residence.

The town's rapid growth was interrupted by the Thirty Years' War and a fire in 1713. After the secularization of the state and its incorporation into Bavaria in 1803, Füssen again enjoyed a period of prosperity, thanks to the interest that the Bavarian kings took in the region.

Füssen has many fine old buildings. The medieval **castle** has an arcaded façade decorated with trompe l'oeil paintings executed in 1499. Its halls now house the **Filialgalerie der Bayerischen Staatsgemäldesammlungen** (art gallery).

The **Benedictine monastery**, founded in the 9th century, houses the **Museum der Stadt Füssen**, a local history museum, where a collection of locally made lutes and violins is displayed. Beside it is **St Mang-Kirche**, built in 1720–21. The façade of **Heilig-Geist-Spitalkirche**, painted by Joseph Anton Walch in 1749, is also of note.

🏛 Museum der Stadt Füssen
Lechhalde 3. **Tel** (08362) 90 31 46. **Open** Apr–Oct: 11am–5pm Tue–Sun; Nov–Mar: 1–4pm Fri–Sun. 🖼

🏛 Filialgalerie der Bayerischen Staatsgemäldesammlungen
Magnusplatz 10. **Tel** (08362) 90 31 46. **Open** Apr–Oct: 11am–5pm Tue–Sun; Nov–Mar: 1–4pm Fri–Sun. 🖼

The painted façade of Heilig-Geist-Spitalkirche in Füssen

⓫ Around Neuschwanstein

This tour, probably the most scenic in the whole of Bavaria, takes about a day, as it inevitably involves queueing for entry at both the castles. They are reached from car parks at the foot of Schloss Hohenschwangau. An effortless way of reaching the giddy heights of Schloss Neuschwanstein is by horse-drawn chaise. Another memorable experience is a boat trip on Alpsee.

① Kolomanskirche
This small, distinctive Baroque church of 1673–82 stands in isolation at the foot of Schwangauer Berge.

② Tegelbergbahn
Recently discovered remains of Roman buildings can be seen from the lower station of this cable car, which runs to the summit of Tegelberg.

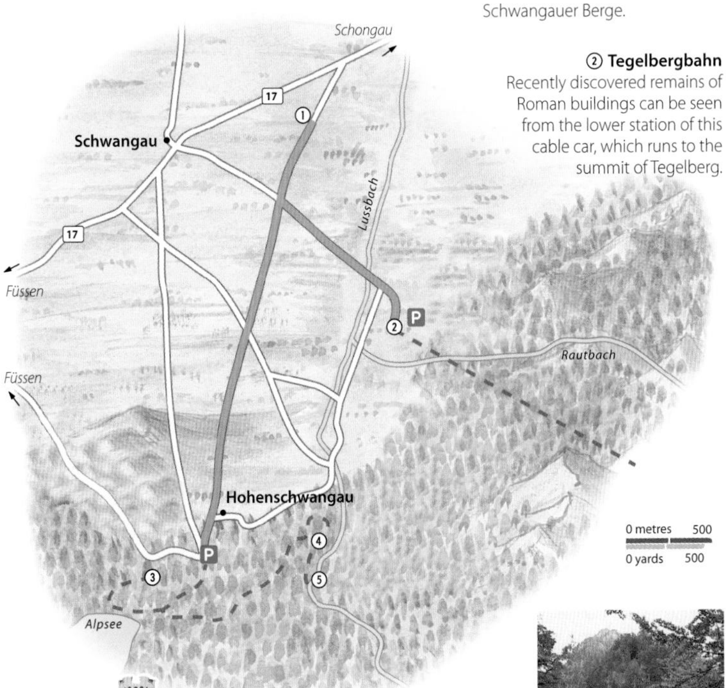

0 metres 500
0 yards 500

③ Schloss Hohenschwangau
Part of the richly furnished interior of this castle is open to visitors.

⑤ Marienbrücke
The cast-iron bridge that spans the Pöllat gorge is constantly occupied by people fascinated by staring 90 m (300 ft) down into the giddy depths.

④ Schloss Neuschwanstein
The white silhouette of Ludwig II's castle, set with numerous turrets, has an almost surreal appearance when it is seen against the woodland backdrop, which changes colour through the seasons.

Key

▬ Suggested route
▬▬ Suggested walk
⋯ Other road
▬▬ Railway line

Tips for Drivers
Tour length: about 15 km (9 miles).
Stopping-off points: Meals and refreshments are available near Schloss Hohenschwangau and Schloss Neuschwanstein.

For map symbols *see back flap*

The Oberstdorf ski jumps, where the Four Ski Jumps Tournament is held

⓬ Bad Hindelang

Road map B5. ⛰ 5,000. 🚍
🚉 Sonthofen. 🛈 Am Bauernmarkt 1,
(08324) 89 20. 🆆 **badhindelang.net**

This health resort is set in
beautiful woodland scenery
in the Ostrach river valley.
The town is best explored
by walking down
Marktstraße, starting
from the Neo-Gothic
church. The 17th-
century **bishop's
palace** opposite now
houses the town hall.
The beautifully
restored houses are
covered in colourful
flowers in summer.

Lüftlmalerei on a hotel
in Hindelang

Environs
About 1 km (0.6 mile)
south of Hindelang is the
spa resort of **Bad Oberdorf.
Hinterstein**, 6 km (4 miles)
further on, is popular with
mountaineers. The road to
Oberjoch, 6.5 km (4.5 miles)
northeast, known as the
Jochstraße, is the most
tortuous section of the
Deutsche Alpenstraße.

⓭ Oberstdorf

Road map B6. ⛰ 9,600. 🚍 🚉
🛈 Prinzregenten-Platz 1, (08322)
70 00. 🆆 **oberstdorf.de**

The best-known health resort
and holiday centre in the Allgäu,
Oberstdorf, situated in the Iller
river valley, is also renowned for
its **ski jumps** on the slope of
Schattenberg. One event in the
Four Ski Jumps Tournament is

held here every year. The best-
known ski jump in Oberstdorf
is in the Stillach valley. It was
the first large-scale ski jump
(Skiflugschanze) in the world,
and competitors can achieve
distances of more than 170 m
(550 ft). It was built in 1949–50
by the ski jumper and architect
Heini Klopfer. The town
itself, with its narrow
streets and old
houses, is extremely
attractive. The
Heimatmuseum
has exhibits relating
to local history, and
includes the world's
largest shoe.

🏛 **Heimatmuseum**
Oststr. 13. **Tel** (08322) 54
70. **Open** 10am–noon, 2–
5:30pm Tue–Sun & public hols. **Closed**
3 weeks in Apr & May; Nov–Christmas.
🆆 **heimatmuseum-oberstdorf.de**

Environs
The **Breitach river gorge**, 6 km
(4 miles) west of Oberstdorf, is
a major attraction. A vertiginous
track winds for 2 km (1.25 mile)
above the water that rushes
between sheer cliffs rising to
heights of 100 m (325 ft).

To walk the track, a waterproof
overgarment and sturdy hiking
boots are needed.
At the **Sturmannshöhle**
cave outside **Fischen**, some
200 steps lead to a large cavern
with impressive stalactites and
stalagmites. The cave's galleries
are connected by rushing
underground streams that can
be heard from the cave mouth.

⓮ Immenstadt

Road map B5. ⛰ 14,200. 🚍 🚉
🛈 Marienplatz 12, (08323) 99 88 77.
🆆 **immenstadt.de**
🎭 Klausentreiben (5–6 Dec).

Approaching Immenstadt from
the north provides a fine view of
lake Alpsee. The town has much
to offer to watersports enthusiasts and mountaineers and is
also home to many historic
buildings. **Nikolauskirche** has
been rebuilt several times since
the Middle Ages. In 1602–20 a
palace was built on the market
square. One of its apartments
has a stuccowork ceiling of
about 1720 with hunting scenes
and views of castles. The **town
hall** was built in 1649 and the
local history museum is in a
mill dating from 1451.

Environs
2 km (1.25 mile) north is **Bühl**,
where Stephanskirche contains
a chapel that was built as a
replica of the Holy Sepulchre
in Jerusalem. The nearby Maria
Loreto Chapel with the Cottage
of Our Lady of Loreto is made
up of the Baroque choir of
St Annakapelle.

⓯ Lindau

See pp238–9.

Sarcophagus in Nikolauskirche in Immenstadt

⓰ Wasserburg

Road map A5. 🏔 3,600. 🚌 🚉
ℹ Lindenplatz 1, (08382) 88 74 74.
🆆 **wasserburg-bodensee.de**

With a stunningly beautiful
location on the tip of a
promontory on Bodensee (Lake
Constance), Wasserburg is a
charming village of flower-filled
streets with views of the lake and
its backdrop of hills. Its location
makes it a popular place for
sailing and other watersports.

The village's history dates
from the 8th century, then in
the 10th century a **castle** was
built here to resist Hungarian
invaders. The castle was
modernized in the 13th century
and rebuilt after a fire in 1358. It
is a three-winged building with
an irregular plan. The east wing
is a vestige of the medieval
structure, while the south wing
dates from the 16th century and
the west wing from the 18th
century. It is now a hotel.

Georgskirche is equally
historic. It was founded in
the 8th century but was later
converted and together
with the cemetery wall was
incorporated into the town's
fortifications. Remnants of these
defences reach down to the
shores of the lake. The present
building is a late Gothic fortified
hall dating from the second
half of the 15th century.

The square tower, built
in 1396–1403, was given its
onion dome in 1656. The
church is connected to a
two-storey presbytery.

The **Malhaus** (1597), once a
residence of the Fuggers *(see
p256)*, now houses a **museum**
illustrating the culture of the
region and also the fishing
industry, formerly Wasserburg's
main source of livelihood.

🏛 Museum im Malhaus
Halbinselstr. 77. **Open** mid-Apr–
Oct: 10:30am–12:30pm Tue–Sun,
2:30–5pm Wed, Sat & Sun.
🆆 **museum-im-malhaus.de**

Georgskirche beside Bodensee (Lake
Constance) in Wasserburg

⓱ Kempten

See pp240–41.

⓲ Maria Steinbach

Road map A4. 🚌 🚉 Leutkirch.
ℹ Markt Legau, Marktplatz 1, (08330)
94 010. 🆆 **legau.de**

Maria Steinbach is famed for
its pilgrimage church, **Mariä
Schmerzen**, which is a masterpiece of Rococo architecture.
Situated on a hill in the idyllic
rolling landscape of the Iller river
valley, the church was built in

The Rococo church in Maria Steinbach

1746–54 on the site of earlier
Romanesque and Gothic shrines.
The building was inspired
by the works of Dominik
Zimmermann. The undulating
façades, with trompe l'oeil
painting, conceal a dazzling
interior. The outstanding
mouldings and painting by
Franz Georg Hermann, the
stuccowork of the altars, pulpit,
stalls, confessionals and organ
loft combine to produce a
unified whole.

The figure of the Grieving
Madonna, which since 1730
has been renowned for its
miracle-working powers, was
an object of pilgrimage in
southern Germany during
the 18th century.

The group of **presbytery
buildings** set around a courtyard
west of the church dates from
the mid-18th century. The
Wallfahrtsmuseum contains
a large collection of votive
gifts made to the Madonna
by pilgrims.

🏛 Wallfahrtsmuseum
Kirchhof 4. **Tel** (08394) 92 40.
Open by appointment.

Bodensee (Lake Constance) and the Alps seen from Wasserburg

⑮ Lindau

Lindau is one of the three municipalities on Bodensee (Lake Constance) that belong to Bavaria. The old part of the town, which stands on an island in the lake, is connected to the mainland by a railway and a road bridge. Founded as a fishing settlement in Roman times, Lindau was granted the status of a city in the 13th century. It still retains its medieval plan, which is based around three long parallel streets. Most of the island is a pedestrian zone.

Maximilianstraße, the main street in Lindau

🏛 Maximilianstraße

The town's main street, Maximilianstraße, is also its widest. Like the parallel streets of In der Grub and Ludwigstraße, it contains houses dating from the 15th to 19th centuries.

The small, compact houses with gables facing the street have windows that are often divided by columns, while the façades are broken up by oriels. The arcades and the old hoisting devices of the warehouses in the garrets bear witness to the town's character as a centre of trade.

🏛 Altes Rathaus

Bismarckplatz 4.
The old town hall, built in 1422–36, was remodelled several times during the 16th century, and again in 1724 and 1865. The programme of rebuilding that took place in 1885–7 was undertaken by Friedrich von Thiersch, who restored the stepped gable that had been removed in 1865 and re-constructed the exterior staircase. The façade was painted in bright colours by Joseph Widmann.

🏛 Neues Rathaus

Bismarckplatz 3.
The new town hall, built in 1706–17, was also remodelled by Friedrich von Thiersch in 1885. A two-storey building crowned by a tall shaped gable decorated with vases and obelisks, it now houses a cloth shop.

🏛 Haus zum Cavazzen

Marktplatz 6. Stadtmuseum: **Tel** (08382) 94 40 73. **Open** Easter– Aug: 10am–6pm daily; Sep–mid- Oct: 11am–5pm Tue–Fri, Sun, 2–5pm Sat. 🖾
This elegant patrician building is named after the de Cavazzo family, in whose ownership it was from 1540 to 1617.

The present Baroque house was built for the von Seutter family in 1729–30. It has a tall mansard roof and the façade is covered with paintings of herms, atlantes, sphinxes and garlands of fruit. The house now accommodates the **Stadtmuseum** (local history museum), which contains an interesting collection of artisans' tools.

🏛 Stephanskirche

Marktplatz 8. **Tel** (08382) 33 44.
Originally a Catholic church, it became a Protestant church in 1528. The original 12th-century Romanesque building was refurbished several times during the 14th, 15th and 16th centuries. Its present-day form – a three-nave, barrel-vaulted basilica – dates from 1781–3, when it was remodelled.

🏛 Münster "Unserer Lieben Frau"

Stiftsplatz 1. **Tel** (08382) 58 50.
The church originally belonged to the Benedictine monks who settled here in about 800. Vestiges of the pre-Romanesque church, which was built after 948, are preserved in the west wall. In about 1100 a Romanesque basilica with a transept and a west tower was built.

After the fire that devastated the town in 1728, the church was rebuilt to its Romanesque plan. The present airy Baroque church, lavishly decorated with mouldings and wall paintings, resulted from work carried out in 1748–55 under the direction of Johann Caspar Bagnato.

Baroque epitaph in the Haus zum Cavazzen

A lion and a lighthouse framing the harbour entrance against the Alps

VISITORS' CHECKLIST

Practical Information
Road map A5. ⛰ 24,500.
ℹ Alfred-Nobel-Platz 1,
(08382) 26 00 30.
🅦 lindau.de
🅦 lindau-tourismus.de

Transport
🚌 🚎 🚊 **Tel** (08382) 27 58 40.

🚢 The Harbour

The harbour that was built at the southern end of the island in 1811 was modernized in 1856. A marble Lion of Bavaria set on a pedestal 6 m (20 ft) high was added to the tip of the mole at the harbour entrance. A new lighthouse, 33 m (108 ft) high was built on the tip of the opposite mole. These two structures came to symbolize Lindau.

The promenade beside the harbour, where the former lighthouse, known as the **Mangturm**, stands, is popular with tourists. Built in about 1200, the old lighthouse has a projecting upper storey with a pointed steeple covered in 19th-century glazed tiles. It was originally part of the city's fortifications.

🏛 Peterskirche

Oberer Schrannenplatz 5/7.
This is one of the oldest churches in the entire Bodensee region. The presbytery and eastern section date from about 1180. The western part was added in the late 15th century. The five-storey tower that stands near the apse, and that was originally in the Romanesque style, was rebuilt in 1425. The interior walls are decorated with frescoes dating from the 13th to 16th centuries. They include works ascribed to Hans Holbein the Elder. Since 1928 the church has functioned as a memorial to war heroes.

Beside the church stands the **Diebsturm** (Thieves' Tower), a circular watchtower built in 1370–80, which was used in conjunction with the Pulverturm (Powder Tower), Ludwigsbastion and Maximilianschanze (Maximilian's Redoubt).

The Mangturm, formerly a lighthouse and watchtower

Lindau City Centre

① Maximilianstraße
② Altes Rathaus
③ Neues Rathaus
④ Haus zum Cavazzen
⑤ Stephanskirche
⑥ Münster zur Lieben Frau
⑦ Harbour
⑧ Peterskirche

WASSERBURG
Seebrücke
Stadtpark
CHELLES-ALLEE
AUF DEM WALL
OSKAR-GROLL-ALLEE
ZWANGIGERSTRASSE
AUF DER MAUER
STORCHEN-GASSE
HOSTAT-GASSE
PARADIESPLATZ
ALTER SCHULPLATZ
NEUGASSE
MARKT-PLATZ
⑤ Stephanskirche
ZEPPELINSTRASSE
IN DER GRUB
Haus zum ④ Cavazzen
KIRCHPLATZ
⑥ Münster zur Lieben Frau
SCHRANNEN-PLATZ
⑧ Peterskirche
BINDERGASSE
LINGGSTRASSE
STIFTS-PLATZ
FISCHERGASSE
Pulverturm
MAXIMILIANSTRASSE ①
② Altes Rathaus
Neues ③ Rathaus
LUDWIGSTRASSE
REICHS-PLATZ
BURGGASSE
BARFÜSSER-PLATZ
Hauptbahnhof
BAHNHOF-PLATZ
INSELGRABEN
SEEPROMENADE
Bodensee
BRETTER-MARKT
SCHÜTZINGER WEG
⑦ Harbour

| 0 metres | 100 |
| 0 yards | 100 |

For keys to symbols *see back flap*

⑰ Kempten

Originally a Roman town, Kempten was divided into a monastic and a secular district in the Middle Ages. The monastic district was centred around a Benedictine abbey, and in 1712 the monks were granted city rights. The secular district of Burghalde, which grew at the foot of the hill, was a Free City of the Empire from 1289 and accepted the Reformation in 1527. In 1802 the two districts were combined into a single entity and incorporated into Bavaria. Today Kempten is the Allgäu's thriving capital.

The late Gothic façade of St-Mang-Kirche, with its tall tower

Façade of the town hall, featuring Kempten's coats of arms

🏛 Rathaus

Rathausplatz.
The late Gothic town hall, built in 1474, has a stepped gable crowned by a small tower. The wooden ceilings of the interior date from about 1460 and originally came from the house of the weavers' guild. Before the town hall stands a copy of a Mannerist fountain of 1601.

🏛 Rathausplatz

The square on which the town hall stands is lined with patrician palaces and merchants' and guildsmens' houses, which were either remodelled or newly built in the Baroque and Neo-Classical periods. The three-storey Londonerhof at No. 2 has a Rococo façade lavishly covered with stuccowork and featuring a Neo-Baroque doorway of 1899. The Hotel Fürstenhof at No. 8 was built in about 1600. The Ponickauhaus at Nos. 10 and 12 was created in 1740 when two 16th-century houses were knocked together, the first floor being converted into a lavishly decorated Festsaal.

🏛 St-Mang-Kirche

St-Mang-Platz 6.
The original church dedicated to St Mang was built in 869. The present church dates from 1426–28, when it was built as the parish church of the Free Imperial City. In 1525 it became a Protestant church, and was remodelled as a three-nave basilica with a tall tower. It was last rebuilt in 1767–8, when the vaulting and late Rococo mouldings were added.

🏛 The Residence

Residenzplatz. Prunkräume der Residenz: **Tel** (0831) 25 62 51.
Open Jan–Mar (& Nov): 10am–4pm Sat; Apr–Sep: 9am–4pm Tue–Sun; Oct: 10am–4pm Tue–Sun. 🅿 🗎

In 1651–74 a group of 11th-century buildings, which were destroyed in 1632, was replaced by a new Baroque monastery. It was also a residence. The monastery consists of buildings grouped around two courtyards. The elegant apartments on the second floor, which were decorated in 1732–42, echo those of the Residenz in Munich (see pp78–81). The mouldings were executed by stuccoists from Wessobrunn, while the vaulting is by Franz Georg Hermann. The Throne Hall is one of the finest examples of Bavarian and Swabian Rococo interiors.

🏛 The Orangery

The garden once adjoined the Residence on its southern side. The orangery that was built here in 1780 now houses the municipal library.

🏛 Alpinmuseum and Alpenländische Galerie

Landwehrstr. 4. **Tel** (0831) 25 25 740.
Open 10am–4pm Tue–Sun.
Closed mid-Nov–1 Mar. 🅿

The Alpine Museum, in the Residence's former stables, is dedicated primarily to skiing and mountaineering, but also encompasses topography and the natural environment, and poetry and painting relating to the mountains. There is also a gallery of regional art.

One of the fine apartments in the Residence

🏛 St-Lorenz-Basilika

Landwehrstr. 3.

The church is a three-nave basilica with two pairs of domed side chapels and an octagonal presbytery that is also crowned by a dome. This arrangement created two separate areas: one for the faithful and one for the friars. The interior is breathtaking. The stuccowork in the nave, aisles and presbytery was executed by Giovanni Zuccalli in 1660–70, and the ceilings were painted by Andreas Asper. A comparatively modest twin-towered façade is fronted by a grand staircase. To the east of the presbytery stands the Residence.

🏛 Kornhaus

Großer Kornhausplatz 1. Allgäu-Museum: **Tel** (0831) 54 02 120. **Open** 10am–4pm Tue–Sun.

The prominent towers and dome of the St-Lorenz-Basilika

This former grain warehouse was built in 1700. Today it houses a museum dedicated to the history, culture and art of the town and the region.

🏛 Burghalde

Burgstr.

In 1488 a castle was built on a hill beside the River Iller, where

VISITORS' CHECKLIST

Practical Information
Road map B5. 🚊 66,000.
ℹ Rathausplatz 24, (0831) 96 09 550.
🎭 Allgäuer Festwoche (Aug).
🌐 kempten.de

Transport
🚌 🚉 Bahnhofplatz.

a Roman fort once stood. The castle was incorporated into the town's walls but was demolished in 1705. Part of the town walls, together with the northern tower and its wooden gatehouse of 1883 survive. Today, Burghalde is an open-air theatre with concerts and cinema. You can also walk round the walls.

🏛 Archäologischer Park Cambodunum

Cambodunumweg 3. **Tel** (0831) 79 731. **Open** Mar–Apr & Nov: 10am–4:30pm Tue–Sun; May–Oct: 10am–5pm Tue–Sun. **Closed** Dec–Feb.
🌐 apc-kempten.de

Kempten was once the Roman settlement of Cambodunum. Excavations have uncovered a forum, a basilica and baths. The most impressive building was the basilica, which was as large as the present St Lorenz-Basilika.

Remains of Roman baths in the settlement of Cambodunum

Kempten Town Centre

① Rathaus
② Rathausplatz
③ St-Mang-Kirche
④ Residence
⑤ Orangery
⑥ Alpinmuseum and Alpenländische Galerie
⑦ St-Lorenz-Basilika

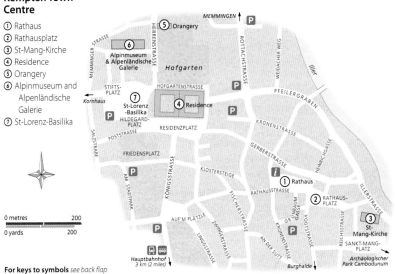

0 metres 200
0 yards 200

For keys to symbols *see back flap*

NORTHERN SWABIA

Northern Swabia constitutes that part of historical Swabia that now belongs to Bavaria, hence its name – Bayerisches Schwaben (Bavarian Swabia). In terms of its politics and its culture as well as its scenery, it is the most diverse region of southern Bavaria. Its main attractions for tourists are its historic towns, notably Augsburg, the great Ries Basin and its scenic river valleys.

Throughout the course of history, this region was divided into numerous ducal and monastic possessions and Imperial Cities (Reichsstädte). This served to promote the development of art, which can be seen in the region's castles and palaces and particularly in its churches and monasteries. From 1803 Swabia formed part of Bavaria, and was subjected to integration. However, in this transitional area between the German states of Bavaria and Baden-Württemberg, significant differences in attitude, language and customs survive to this day among Swabians.

The historical need for differentiation, self-definition and individuality has made Swabia a country of small towns each with their own character and history. This is particularly apparent during local festivals. The scenery is equally diverse and varied.

The north consists of the rolling wooded hills of the western Schwäbische Alb massif. Beside them lies the Nördlinger Ries. This area, renowned for its microclimate and its rich soil, has been inhabited since Palaeolithic times.

The Danube cuts through the northern part of Swabian Bavaria. The extensive moors of the Donauried (the Danube valley) bear witness to frequent river flooding in the past. Lying almost parallel from south to north are the great moraine valleys of the Iller, the Günz and the Lech.

Augsburg, almost in the centre of the region and founded in Roman times, was an early centre of the Reformation and of goldsmiths. West of Augsburg is the Westliche Wälder, a vast forest reserve whose unspoiled scenery makes it popular with hikers.

A flower shop in Augsburg, with its displays spilling onto the pavement

◄ The lush green landscape of Northern Swabia, viewed from Burgfelsen castle rock in Wallerstein

Exploring Northern Swabia

Northern Swabia's principal city is Augsburg. The third-largest city in Bavaria after Munich and Nuremberg, Augsburg demands several days' exploration, as it has much to offer of architectural interest. The city is also a useful starting point for various excursions. Within easy reach to the north are the Ries Basin, a huge crater nestling the town of Nördlingen, and the impressive Harburg Castle, as well as towns on the Danube such as Donauwörth, Dillingen and Günzburg. In the southwest are the castles belonging to the Fugger family. With their varied architecture and scenic settings, all of the region's towns have much to interest visitors.

Christ on a donkey, from the former Augustinian monastery at Wettenhausen

Sights at a Glance

Getting Around

Two motorways run through Swabia. The A8, running along an east–west axis, connects Munich and Stuttgart via Augsburg and Günzburg. The A7 runs in a north–south direction, following the course of the River Iller. Parallel to it is the Romantische Straße (Romantic Road), which passes through towns such as Nördlingen, Harburg, Donauwörth and Augsburg. The good road network makes the other towns of the region easily accessible by car or by bus. The larger cities also have rail links. Situated near to Munich, Augsburg has its own airport.

Gundelfingen
Heidenheim
Stuttgart
Ulm
Leipheim
Neu-Ulm
Nersingen
15 GÜNZBURG
Burg
WETTENHAUSEN 14
Pfaffenhofen
Ichenha
Senden
13 WEISSENHORN
Vöhringen
12 ROGGENBURG
Krumbach
Illertissen
Babenhausen
Mindelheim
Memmingen

Harburg Castle overlooking the Wörmitz river valley

For keys to symbols *see back flap*

Key

━━━ Motorway
━━━ Major road
┄┄┄ Minor road
╍╍╍ Main railway
─── Minor railway
━━━ Regional border

The Mannerist Stadtmetzg in Augsburg, designed by Elias Holl

Nürnberg ↗

emdingen

3 OETTINGEN 🏛🏛🏛

466

2 🏛🏛 WALLERSTEIN

R i e s

4 WEMDING

Nürnberg ↗

1 NÖRDLINGEN 🏛🏛

Monheim ○

Möttingen ○

25

2

Wörnitz

Schwäbische Alb

5 HARBURG 🏛🏛

6 KAISHEIM

7 LEITHEIM 🏛🏛

8 DONAUWÖRTH 🏛🏛🏛

Bissingen ○

Burgheim ○

Neuburg an der Donau →

kislingen

16

Tapfheim ○

Asbach-Bäumenheim ○

Rain ○

🏛🏛🏛 HÖCHSTÄDT **18**

Mertingen ○

16 🏛🏛🏛 LINGEN

Donau

Buttenwiesen ○

LAUINGEN 🏛🏛

Donauried

2

Lech

Pöttmes ○

Wertingen ○

Thierhaupten ○

Ingolstadt →

N a t u r p a r k

Langweid ○

Affing ○

Aichach ○

300

A u g s b u r g -

W e s t l i c h e

Gersthofen ○

10 🏛 SIELENBACH

W ä l d e r

8

Neusaß ○

heppach

10

Dinkelscherben ○

🏛🏛🏛 AUGSBURG **9** ✈

Stadtbergen ○

11 🏛🏛🏛 FRIEDBERG

8

München ↘

300

Kissing ○

Thannhausen ○

Königsbrunn ○

2

Mering ○

Bobingen ○

Kirchheim in Schwaben ○

17

Wertach

Lech

Schwabmünchen ○

Landsberg am Lech ↓

0 kilometres ——— 10

0 miles ——— 10

● Nördlingen

Nördlingen, encircled by defensive walls, is the "capital" of the Ries Basin and one of the most picturesque towns in Swabia. Several hours can be spent wandering along its streets and alleys, where the Gothic and the Renaissance periods have left their mark. In the 14th century the town almost doubled in size and was surrounded by walls. The streets that run from the five town gates merge on Marktplatz, at the heart of the town. A good time to visit is in July, when the Scharlachrennen, a horse race and parade dating back to the 15th century, is held.

Exploring Nördlingen

The most attractive aspect of Nördlingen is its houses, most of which are half-timbered, with colourful, cascading window boxes. Many of the houses are several storeys high, with attic store-rooms. In the Gerberviertel, the tanners' quarter, the houses on the River Eger are well preserved. Two of the town's most interesting houses are that at Paradiesstraße 4, dating from 1350 and the town's oldest half-timbered house, and the 1678 Wintersches Haus at Braugasse 2, the best-preserved private house in Nördlingen.

Bas-relief of a fool on the town hall

🏛 Rathaus

Marktplatz 1.

The town hall was built in the 13th century and rebuilt after 1500, acquiring its present form at the beginning of the 17th century. Its most noteworthy feature is the external stone stairway, built by Wolfgang Waldberger. Beside the doors beneath the stairway is a bas-relief depicting a fool, with the ironic inscription "*Nun sind unser zwey*" ("Now it is the two of us") addressing the reader. The wall of the grand Federal Room on the second floor has a painting of the heroic feats of the biblical Judith by Hans Schäufelein.

🏠 Georgskirche

Am Obstmarkt.

Georgskirche, built in 1427–1505, stands in the centre of the town. Like many other buildings in the region, it was built with suevite from the Ries Basin (*see p248*). The interior features finely carved late Gothic stalls and a pulpit, a sacrarium of 1522–5 and numerous epitaphs and tombs. The tower, 90 m (295 ft) high, known as the Daniel Tower, can be seen from far away. A flight of 331 stairs leads to the top. The effort of climbing them is rewarded by a panoramic view of the Ries Basin. For 300 years a night watchman has called from the top of the tower, sometimes every half hour. Today this occurs only between 10pm and midnight.

🏛 Tanzhaus

Marktplatz 15.

This Gothic half-timbered hall dating from 1442–4 was built for official dances and receptions. The ground floor contained bakers' shops, which is why the building was also known as the Brothaus (Bread House). On a console on the eastern façade stands a Gothic statue of 1513. Known as *The Last Knight*, it depicts Maximilian I as a knight in armour. Maximilian was a frequent visitor to Nördlingen, which he greatly admired.

The richly decorated Mannerist doorway of the Klösterle

🏠 Klösterle

Beim Klösterle 1.

The monastery church known as the Barfüßerkirche, built in 1422, was converted into a Renaissance-style grain ware-house by Wolfgang Waldberger in 1584–6. The southern façade has a fine doorway dating from 1586, crowned with the town's coat of arms and decorated with figures of tradesmen. Today the Klösterle houses a hotel.

🏛 Hohes Haus

Marktplatz 16.

This tall, nine-storey house, next to the Tanzhaus, is the oldest brick building in Nördlingen. It is mentioned as early as 1304 and was used as a warehouse.

Organ loft in the Gothic Georgskirche

⊞ Spital

Vordere Gerbergasse 1. Stadtmuseum: **Tel** (09081) 84 81 0. **Open** mid-Mar–4 Nov: 1:30–4:30pm Tue–Sun.
🌐 Eugene-Shoemaker-Platz 1. Rieskrater-Museum: **Tel** (09081) 84 710. **Open** Nov–Apr: 10am–noon, 1:30–4:30pm; May–Oct: 10am–4:30pm. 🌐

The town's former hospital complex is the largest in Germany. The buildings that form part of it have been converted into museums.

The **Stadtmuseum**, founded in 1960, has a collection of paintings on panel by late Gothic and Renaissance artists including Friedrich Herlin, Hans Schäufelein and Sebastian Daig, and a model of the Battle of Nördlingen of 1634 with 6,000 tin soldiers. The **Rieskrater-Museum** features among its exhibits Moon rocks donated by NASA.

⊞ Hallgebäude

Weinmarkt 1.
On the south side of the Wine Market stands a fine building of 1543 with four attic storeys. A corner has polygonal oriels, one of them decorated with the civic coat of arms. The building was once used for storing wine and salt, for currency offices and the town weights.

The domed Löpsinger Tor, one of Nördlingen's five town gates

🏛 Bayerisches Eisenbahnmuseum

Am Hohen Weg 6A. **Open** May–Sep: noon–4pm Tue–Sat, 10am–5pm Sun; Oct–Mar: noon–4pm Sat, 10am–5pm Sun. 🆆 bayerisches-eisenbahnmuseum.de

Just behind the railway station you'll find this large outdoor railway museum, which occasionally runs steam locomotives up the otherswise defunct line to Gunzenhausen.

⊞ Löpsinger Tor and Town Walls

Stadtmauermuseum: **Open** Apr–Oct: 10am–4:30pm Tue–Sun.

Construction of the walls encircling Nördlingen was begun in 1327. The walkway around the fortifications provides a variety of views over the town. The walls are pierced by five gates, 12 towers and a bastion.

All the gates except the Baldinger Tor have towers. They are the Reimlinger Tor, the oldest and largest gate, on the road from Augsburg; the Berger Tor; the Löpsinger Tor, which houses the **Stadtmauermuseum**, whose domed circular tower dates from 1593–4, and the taller and narrower Deininger Tor.

Nördlingen Town Centre

① Rathaus
② Georgskirche
③ Tanzhaus
④ Hohes Haus
⑤ Klösterle
⑥ Spital
⑦ Hallgebäude
⑧ Bayerisches Eisenbahnmuseum
⑨ Löpsinger Tor and Town Walls

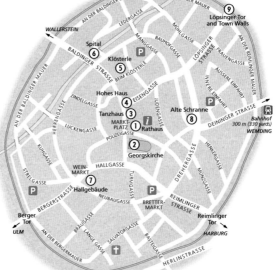

| 0 metres | 150 |
| 0 yards | 150 |

For keys to symbols *see back flap*

❷ Wallerstein

Road map B2. 🚉 3,400. 🚌 🚈
ℹ️ Weinstr. 19, (09081) 27 600.
🔳 **markt-wallerstein.de**

Wallerstein is a small town at the foot of a hill on which stands a castle that commands a fine view of the Ries Basin. On the hilltop are the remains of 12th-century fortifications, which were destroyed in 1648, as well as a restaurant and a ducal brewery. **Fürst Wallerstein Brauhaus** is a traditional brewery that has been brewing beer since 1598, using locally sourced Spalter hops.

Albanskirche was built in 1242 in the Gothic style. The **plague column** commemorates the Marseilles plague of 1722–25, has figures of saints and is crowned with figures of St Mary and the Holy Trinity.

Plague column in Wallerstein

🏭 **Fürst Wallerstein Brauhaus**
Berg 78. **Tel** (09081) 80 52 62 0.
🔲 guided tours only.

❸ Oettingen

Road map B2. 🚉 5,200. 🚌 🚈
ℹ️ Schlossstr. 36, (09082) 70 952.
🔳 **oettingen.de**

This town, with an oval outline, was surrounded by a wall in the late 13th century. The town gates on the south side – the **Unteres Tor** and the **Königsturm**, which was built in the 16th century – still stands.

Schlossstraße, the main street, is lined with half-timbered town houses built between the 15th and 18th centuries. The 15th-century Gothic **town hall** contains the local history museum.

Despite their elegance, the **town houses** pale in comparison to **Residenzschloss**, the resplendent Baroque residence of the Dukes of Oettingen-Spielberg, built in 1679–83. To the west the palace looks out over landscaped gardens, which are peopled with statues of dwarfs and a Hercules of 1678 based on the statue on the fountain in Augsburg by Adriaen de Vries. The palace, whose interior is decorated with stuccowork and mural paintings, is now the **Staatliches Museum für Völkerkunde**. Visitors can see the apartments and reception rooms and admire the collections of 18th-century pewter, porcelain and faience. The palace courtyard is surrounded by outbuildings and has a fountain dating from 1720–28 in the centre.

The **Jakobskirche** which stands nearby was remodelled in the Baroque style after 1680 and decorated with stuccowork by Matthias Schmuzer the Younger.

Inside is an interesting pulpit and baptismal font from the last quarter of the 17th century, and numerous tombstones as well as plaques from the 15th to 18th centuries.

❹ Wemding

Road map B2. 🚉 5,800. 🚌 🚈
ℹ️ Mangoldstr. 5, (09092) 96 90 35.
🔳 **wemding.info**

Set on the rim of the Ries Basin, this charming little town retains its medieval character. The main square, lined with Renaissance and Baroque houses with typically Bavarian decorated gables, has often been used as a location by filmmakers.

Prominent among these houses is the Renaissance **town hall** of 1551–2. On Wallfahrtstraße, near the gate tower, is a typical mid-16th-century house with a corner oriel, now the **Gasthaus zum Weißen Hahn** inn. The tower of **Emmeramskirche** dominates the skyline. The church dates from the 11th century, but its current Baroque form is the result of rebuilding carried out in the 17th century.

Renaissance tombstone in Jakobskirche, Oettingen

Ries Basin

This crater, 25 km (15 miles) across, was made when a meteorite hit the Earth 15 million years ago. The impact melted the rocks, creating suevite, or Swabian rock, which the local people used as a building material. NASA carried out scientific studies on the crater and used it for astronauts who were to be sent to the Moon. They later found rock identical to suevite on the Moon. A suevite moon rock donated by NASA can be seen in the Rieskrater-Museum (see p247).

Suevite on the edge of the Ries Basin

It is worth taking a walk along the **defensive walls**, built in the first half of the 14th century and particularly well preserved on the north side of the town.

On the road leading out towards Oettingen the small pilgrimage chapel of **Maria Brünnlein** can be seen in the distance. The interior is decorated with Rococo mouldings and frescoes by Johann Baptist Zimmermann.

The Baroque palace and palace chapel at Leitheim

One of the courtyards in Harburg Castle

❺ Harburg

Road map B2. 🚉 5,500. 🚌 🚊
ℹ️ Schlossstr. 1, (09080) 96 99 0.
🔲 stadt-harburg-schwaben.de

The large **castle** was built by the Hohenstaufens before 1150. It was later acquired by the counts of Oettingen, and since 1731 has been in the possession of the Oettingen-Wallerstein family. It is one of the oldest, largest and best-preserved castles in southern Germany.

Dramatically situated on a high rocky hill overlooking the Wörmitz river valley, Harburg castle dominates the entire area. In the 14th and 15th centuries it was surrounded by walls set with towers. It has an outer and an inner gate on the west side, with a picturesque gatehouse dating from 1703. Within the walls stands **Michaelskirche**, the castle church. At the bottom of the castle hill nestles the small

town of Harburg. It is worth a visit for a walk around the charming and diminutive market square and along the winding streets, which have picturesque old houses.

❻ Kaisheim

Road map C2. 🚉 3,800. 🚌 🚊
ℹ️ Münsterplatz 5, (09099) 96 600.
🔲 kaisheim.de

The extensive complex of the former Cistercian monastery consists of the 14th-century Gothic **Mariä Himmelfahrtskirche** as well as the monastery itself, which has two cloisters dating from 1716–21. The monastery was converted into a prison in the 19th century. The exquisite Kaisersaal (Imperial Hall), with ornate stuccowork, was completed in about 1720.

Notable features of the church include the Baroque organ loft of 1677, whose carvings are ascribed to Andreas Thamasch. In the nave is a sarcophagus of 1434 with a statue of the founder of the original Romanesque church, who died in 1142, showing him holding a model of the church in his hands.

Crest in the Kaisersaal, Kaisheim

❼ Leitheim

Road map C2. 🚌 🚊 Kaisheim.
ℹ️ Münsterplatz 5, Kaisheim, (09099) 96 600.

Set high on a bank of the Danube, **Schloss Leitheim and a chapel** were built in 1685 to designs by Wölfl as a summer residence for Cistercian monks from the monastery at Kaisheim. For centuries the monks tended vineyards on the sunny slopes around the residence. Indeed, Leitheim was one of the centres of wine-making in the Danube region, and the quality of the wine produced here rivalled that of the Rhine wines.

The chapel was decorated in the late 17th century by artists from Wessobrunn. In the mid-18th century an additional storey and a mansard roof were added to the palace. The stuccowork and painting in the state rooms on the second floor are among the finest examples of Bavarian-Swabian Rococo. After 1835 the palace passed into the hands of the Tucher von Simmeldorf family. The owners organize highly popular chamber concerts here.

🏰 **Schloss Leitheim**
Schlossstr. 1. **Tel** (09097) 10 16.
Open May–Sep: by prior arrangement only.
🔲 schloss-leitheim.de

❽ Donauwörth

Road map C2. 🔼 18,700. 🚍 🚉
ℹ️ Rathausgasse 1, (0906) 78 91 51.
🌐 **donauwoerth.de**
🎭 Schwäbischwerder Kindertag (first Sun in Jul), Reichsstraßenfest (Jul, every two years, the next in 2017), Donauwörther Kulturtage (Oct).

Donauwörth is one of the largest towns in Swabian Bavaria. It is located at the confluence of the Wörnitz and the Danube, and its development was shaped largely by its position at the point where major trade routes crossed the Danube.

Reichsstraße, the main street, is lined with colourful gabled houses and is one of the finest streets in southern Germany. It stretches from **Zu Unserer Lieben Frau**, the church built in 1444–67 and decorated with 15th- and 16th-century frescoes, to the **town hall**, remodelled in the Neo-Gothic style in 1854.

The west end of the town is dominated by a former Benedictine monastery, of which the **Kreuzkirche**, built by Josef Schmuzer in 1717–20, formed a part.

Romantische Straße

Information signpost at Schloss Neuschwanstein

The Romantic Road (www. romantischestrasse.de) follows the route of the Roman Via Claudia. Beginning in Franconian Würzburg, it passes through Nördlingen, Donauwörth, Augsburg, Landsberg, Schongau, Steingaden and Füssen, in southern Bavaria, and ends at Schloss Neuschwanstein, Ludwig II's famous castle. The best known and most frequented of the tourist routes in Germany, it is particularly popular with American and Japanese tourists. Directions are even given in Japanese.

The picturesque Reichsstraße in Donauwörth

Not to be missed is a walk along the **town walls**, which run parallel to an arm of the Wörnitz. The **Rieder Tor**, one of the two town gates, houses a museum dedicated to the town's history. Also worth visiting are the **Heimatmuseum** of local history and the **Käthe-Kruse-Puppen-Museum**, with a collection of dolls made by Käthe Kruse.

🏛️ **Käthe-Kruse-Puppen-Museum**
Pflegstr. 21a. **Tel** (0906) 78 91 70.
Open Apr and Oct: 2–5pm Tue–Sun; May–Sep: 11am–6pm Tue–Sun; Nov–Mar: 2–5pm Wed, Sat–Sun & public hols; 25 Dec–6 Jan: 2–5pm daily.

🏛️ **Heimatmuseum**
Insel Ried, Museumsplatz 2. **Tel** (0906) 78 91 70. **Open** May–Oct: 2pm–5pm Tue–Sun; Nov–Apr: 2pm–5pm Wed, Sat & Sun.

❾ Augsburg

See pp252–7.

❿ Sielenbach

Road map C3. 🔼 1,600. 🚍
🚉 Weißenhorn. ℹ️ Schwaigstr. 16, (08258) 91 40. 🌐 **sielenbach.de**

The pilgrimage church of **Unserer Lieben Frau im Birnbaum** (Mary in the Pear Tree) is located at the southern end of the town, which it dominates. It is an exceptional work of 17th-century Bavarian architecture. It was built in

1661–8 by Konstantin Bader to a design by Jakob von Kaltenthal, a Commander of the Teutonic Knights. It consists of five circular, semi-circular and oval rooms. In particular the towers and onion domes are unique, and are reminiscent of an Eastern church.

The interior, which is lit by large windows in the shape of upright ovals and decorated with stuccowork by Matthias Schmuzer the Younger, is far more unified.

The object of worship is a late Gothic Pietà dating from the early 16th century, to which miraculous powers are ascribed. It stands on the high altar in a pear tree. The tree and the name of the church commemorate the miraculous survival of the figure in 1632, during the Thirty Years' War when in the course of the Swedish invasion the figure survived thanks to its being hidden in a pear tree.

Unserer Lieben Frau im Birnbaum, an Eastern-style church in Sielenbach

⓫ Friedberg

Road map C3. 🔼 29,000. 🚍 🚉
ℹ️ Marienplatz 5, (0821) 60 02 612.
🌐 **friedberg.de** 🎭 Friedberger Zeit (every three years in Jul, the next in 2016).

During the Middle Ages this town was a fortress, its purpose being to protect the region from attacks by the inhabitants of Augsburg. In about 1490 defensive walls set with semi-circular towers were added.

The Baroque town hall in Friedberg's main square

The medieval **castle** in the north of the town was destroyed during the Thirty Years' War and rebuilt in 1559. It now houses a local history museum, the **Museum Wittelsbacher Schloss**.

The streets are lined with outstanding houses dating from the 17th and 18th centuries. In the centre of the main square stands the **town hall**, built in 1673 and decorated in the style of Elias Holl. **Jakobskirche**, which has an unusual design, was built in 1871 in imitation of the Romanesque cathedral of St Zeno in Verona.

The finest building in Friedberg is **Herrgottsruh**, a pilgrimage church located in the east of the town. In the Middle Ages it was built as a rotunda resembling the Church of the Holy Sepulchre in Jerusalem. Fragments of the building were uncovered beneath the presbytery of the present church.

The latter, built in 1731–51 by Johann Benedikt Ettl, has a tall tower and imposing domed rotunda. The paintings in the presbytery and the dome are by Cosmas Damian Asam, while those in the nave are by Matthäus Günther. The Rococo mouldings are

by Franz Xaver Feichtmayer and Johann Michael Feichtmayr. The silver antependium of the high altar was made by Johann Georg Herkomer of Augsburg. The altar in the south aisle contains a 15th-century group of figures of the Sorrowing Christ to which miraculous powers are ascribed. Votive images fill the aisles.

🏛 **Museum Wittelsbacher Schloss**
Schlossstr. 21. **Tel** (0821) 600 21 48.
Open reopens mid-2018 following renovation; check website for details.
🌐 **museum-friedberg.de**

⓬ Roggenburg

Road map B3. 🏘 2,700. 🚌 🚊
ℹ Vohringen. Prälatenhof 2. **Tel** (07300) 96 960. 🌐 **roggenburg.de**

The towers of the town's former Premonstratensian monastery can be seen from a distance and rightly suggest that this is an exceptional building. Despite its monumentality, the cavernous interior of **Mariä-Himmelfahrt-Kirche**, which was built in the late 18th century, produces an impression of levity, and it is light even though the windows, which are concealed behind the columns, cannot be seen. The organ loft is one of the finest in Germany. However, the real rarities here are the two reliquaries with

painted images of the bodies of St Severinus and St Laurentius, in fine costume of the period. The monastery, built from 1732 to 1766, houses local government offices, although parts are open to the public.

Painting from Oberes Tor, one of Weißenhorn's town gates

⓭ Weißenhorn

Road map A3. 🏘 13,300. 🚌 🚊
ℹ Memmingerstr. 59. **Tel** (07309) 840. 🌐 **weissenhorn.de**

Neat, quaint and tidy, Weißenhorn is a quintessential small Swabian town. Its historic character is preserved virtually intact. The main thoroughfare is the Hauptstraße, running from a large, irregular square where the church and palace stand, to the **Unteres Tor** (Lower Gate). The 15th-century **Oberes Tor** (Upper Gate), flanked by circular towers, opens on to the square. Adjoining the gate is the former **weighhouse**, dating from the 16th century, and the **Neues Rathaus**, built in the 18th century, which together form a harmonious group.

The **Altes Schloss**, dating from 1460–70, and **Neues Schloss**, built by the Fuggers (see p257) in the 16th century, are interconnected. The dominant building in the town is **Mariä-Himmelfahrt-Kirche**, built in 1864–71, one of the finest examples of the revivalist trend in Swabia's religious architecture.

Interior of the church in Roggenburg

❾ Street-by-Street: Augsburg

Bavaria's third-largest city, Augsburg has a population of just over a quarter of a million and is the main university town of Bavarian Swabia. Founded by the Emperor Augustus on the final stretch of the trans-Alpine Via Claudia, it was a bridgehead for Italian culture. It stands at the confluence of the rivers Lech and Wertach, and because of its system of canals it has been called the Venice of the North. Tourists are drawn by the city's history and magic. It is the city of the Protestant Confession of Augsburg and a centre of the goldsmith's art. It is also the birthplace of Bertolt Brecht, Rudolf Diesel and the ancestors of Mozart.

Period houses
on Steingasse were destroyed by World War II air raids in 1941, but were rebuilt in the 1960s.

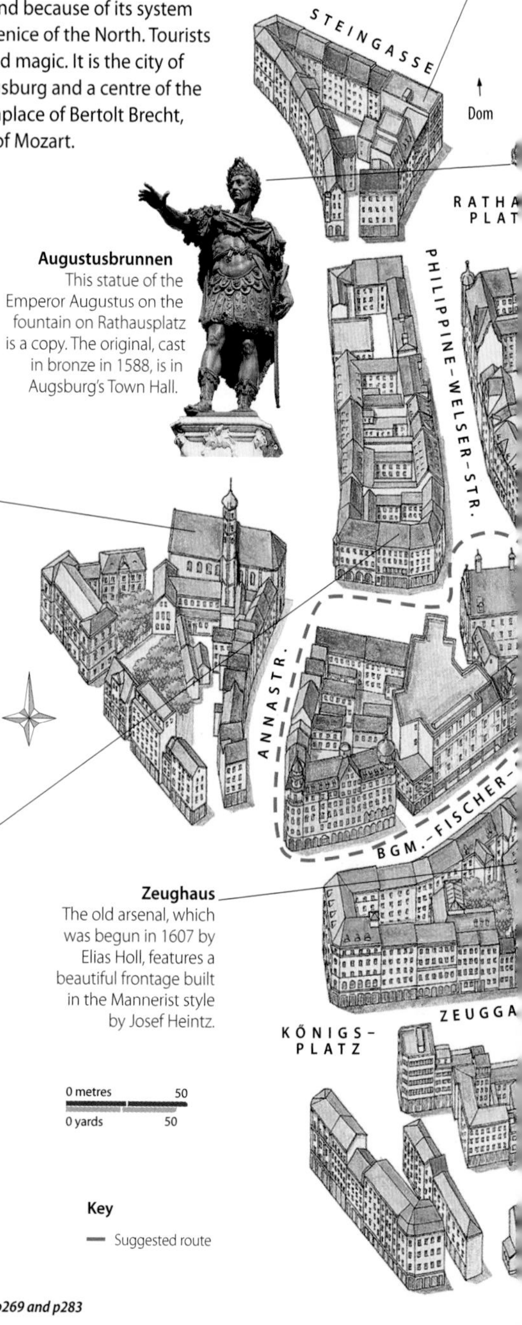

STEINGASSE

↑ Dom

RATHA PLAT

Augustusbrunnen
This statue of the Emperor Augustus on the fountain on Rathausplatz is a copy. The original, cast in bronze in 1588, is in Augsburg's Town Hall.

PHILIPPINE-WELSER-STR.

★ **Annakirche**
The chapel of the Fugger family (1509–12) is an architectural jewel. It is the earliest Renaissance building in Germany.

ANNASTR.

BGM.-FISCHER-

Zeughaus
The old arsenal, which was begun in 1607 by Elias Holl, features a beautiful frontage built in the Mannerist style by Josef Heintz.

ZEUGGA

KÖNIGS-PLATZ

0 metres   50
0 yards   50

★ **Maximilianmuseum**
The museum, currently being renovated, is located in two of the city's finest patrician palaces, built in 1543–6. Exhibits include artifacts by local goldsmiths.

Key

— Suggested route

The Perlachturm is a tower 70 m (230 ft) on the west front of Peterskirche. Its height was increased through the centuries, and in 1616 Elias Holl added the steeple.

★ Rathaus
Built in 1615–20 by Elias Holl, Augsburg's town hall is the finest secular Mannerist building in Europe. The famous Golden Hall is on the second floor.

Merkurbrunnen fountain has a sculpture cast by Wolfgang Neidhart in 1599 after a model by Adriaen de Vries. It is crowned by a statue of Mercury, god of trade.

Moritzkirche, a Gothic-Baroque church, was modernized several times over the centuries. Destroyed by bombing in 1944, it was rebuilt in 1946–51.

MAXIMILIANSTR.

MORITZ PLATZ

WINTERGASSE

KLEINES KATHARINENGÄSSCHEN

MAXIMILIANSTR.

Maximilianstraße
Augsburg's main street, with its two fountains, Mercury and Herkules, by Adriaen de Vries, is one of the finest in southern Germany.

↙ St-Ulrich-und-St-Afra-Kirche

Fuggerhäuser
The two adjacent palaces at Maximilianstraße 36 each have elegant, airy Renaissance courtyards.

Exploring Augsburg

Augsburg is known for its secular buildings. Although many of them were destroyed by air raids in 1944, they were rebuilt after World War II. The city's appearance was largely defined in the early 17th century by Elias Holl, the architect of many of the buildings here, most notably the Mannerist town hall. The surrounding countryside, with its forests and the Kuhsee, provides numerous options for weekend outings.

The entrance to the Baroque Fürstbischöfliche Residenz

The Gothic Dom Unserer Lieben Frau

🏛 Dom Unserer Lieben Frau
Frauentorstr. 1.
The cathedral, whose origins go back to the 9th century, retains the twin towers on the west front that were built in 1150, and two Romanesque crypts. It was remodelled in the Gothic style in the 14th and 15th centuries.

Among the cathedral's many notable features is the world's oldest Romanesque stained-glass window, dating from 1140 and depicting figures of the Prophets. Its 11th-century Romanesque bronze doors, with scenes from the Old Testament, are now on display in the Diocesan Museum.

🏛 Fürstbischöfliche Residenz
Fronhof 10.
The former bishop's residence was given its present appearance in 1743–52. Since 1817 it has housed the government offices of Bavarian Swabia.

It was in the ornate Festsaal in the west wing that the Emperor Karl V received the historic Confession of Augsburg in 1530. The Hofgarten

adjoining the residence contains a fountain and 8th-century gnomes.

🏛 Stadtmetzg
Metzgplatz 1.
This Mannerist building was built by Elias Holl in 1606–9 for the butchers' guild. A technological innovation of the time was routing one of the town's canals beneath the cellars of the Stadtmetzg so that they would be kept cool for the effective storage of perishable food.

🏛 Fountains
Augsburg is renowned for its beautiful fountains, of which there are more than 30. The most famous are the Mannerist Augustus, Mercury and Hercules fountains, made in the late 16th century to mark the city's 1,600th anniversary. The two latter, located on Maximilianstraße, were designed by Adriaen de

Vries (although they are copies, the originals now being in the Maximilianmuseum). Also noteworthy are the Neptunbrunnen of 1536, the Georgsbrunnen of 1565, and the Art Nouveau Goldschmiedebrunnen of 1913.

🏛 Schaezlerpalais
Maximilianstr. 46. **Tel** (0821) 32 44 102. **Open** 10am–5pm Tue–Sun. Staatsgalerie: **Open** 10am–5pm Tue–Sun. 🖼

The palace, the finest Rococo building in Augsburg, was built in 1765–70. The famous Festsaal features fine stucco-work, paintings, carvings, chandeliers and candelabras.

The palace's art galleries – the **Staatsgalerie** and the Deutsche Barockgalerie – contain works by such masters as Dürer, Hans Holbein the Elder, van Dyck and Tiepolo.

Town Hall

This, Europe's largest and finest Mannerist town hall, was built by Elias Holl in 1615–20. The building's showpiece is the Golden Hall. Its exquisite ornate ceiling is attached to the roof beams by means of 27 chains.

Destroyed during air raids in 1944, the town hall was meticulously restored, and the ceiling of the Golden Hall was reconstructed in 1985 to commemmorate the 2,000th anniversary of the foundation of the city in 15 BC.

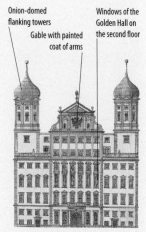

Onion-domed flanking towers

Gable with painted coat of arms

Windows of the Golden Hall on the second floor

⬆ Fuggerhäuser

Maximilianstr. 36/38.

These two neighbouring early 16th-century Renaissance palaces of the Fugger family were rebuilt after being destroyed in 1944. The splendour of the original buildings with their inner courtyards can be seen in the arcaded marble Damenhof. The palace was inhabited by the family of Jakob II der Reiche Fugger and his descendant Anton.

⬆ Zeughaus

Zeugplatz 6.

The arsenal, Elias Holl's first project and also one of his finest works, was built in 1607. The façade is decorated with a bronze sculpture by Hans Reichle depicting St Michael overcoming Satan.

⬆ Annakirche

Im Annahof 2.

The former Carmelite church of St Anne, now Protestant, was built in the 14th century, at the same time as the monastery. It was rebuilt in the 15th century and the tower, designed by Elias Holl, was added in 1607. In the mid-18th century the interior was remodelled in the Rococo style. It contains one of the earliest organ lofts in Europe, dating from 1512.

An exceptional example of Renaissance art is the burial chapel of the Fuggers (1509–12), with epitaphs by Albrecht Dürer, a sculpted *Lamentation* by Hans Daucher, and figures of putti on the balustrade.

⬆ Römisches Museum

Dominikanergasse 15. **Tel** (0821) 32 44 131. **Open** 10am–5pm Tue–Sun.

The Roman Museum is housed in the former Dominican monastery, built in 1513–15. The two-naved hall, which is divided by a row of columns, was rebuilt in the Baroque style in 1716–24. The ceiling, which dates from that time, is decorated with religious stuccowork and paintings. The museum has interesting exhibits from the Roman and as well as the early medieval periods, including a gilded horse's head that once formed part of a Roman equestrian statue.

⬆ St-Ulrich-und-St-Afra-Kirche

Ulrichplatz 23.

Putto in the burial chapel in Annakirche

This late Gothic triple-nave basilica is the most recent in a succession of churches built for the Benedictine monastery that has stood here since about 1000, but that was dissolved in the early 19th century. Work on the basilica began in 1474 and continued for almost 140 years. Although two towers were planned, only the northern one was built, in 1594. Rising a height of 93 m (305 ft) high, it is visible from a great distance.

Baroque grille, St-Ulrich-und-St-Afra-Kirche

Augsburger Puppenkiste

The celebrated Augsburg Puppet Shows take place in the central part of the Heilig-Geist-Spital, built in 1623–31 by Elias Holl. These outstanding shows are always played to a packed auditorium. It is not only the colourful marionettes themselves but the skilled artistry with which they are manipulated that inspires wonder. Such is their reputation that the shows are also broadcast on German television.

Scene from a puppet show

The Mannerist furnishings were added in 1604–8. The exquisitely designed and crafted altar, pulpit, organ loft and stalls harmonize well with the late Gothic architecture of the interior. The nave and aisles are separated by a delicate grille of 1712.

⬆ Rotes Tor and City Walls

The Rotes Tor (Red Gate) was built by Elias Holl in 1622, replacing the medieval gate. Leading in from the road that followed the old Roman Via Claudia, it was the main gate into the city. The Rotes Tor, together with the Wallanlage and the Heilig-Geist-Spital, are the finest group of buildings designed by Elias Holl.

Large sections of the city walls still stand to the north and east, as do the walls surrounding the Jakobervorstadt, with two bastions of about 1540, and the Gothic Jakobertor. There is a landing stage for canoes at the tower of the Oblatterwall bastion.

⬆ Synagogue

Halderstr. 6–8. Jüdisches Kulturmuseum: **Tel** (0821) 51 36 58. **Open** 9am–6pm Tue–Thu (to 8pm every 1st Wed of month), 9am–4pm Fri, 10am–5pm Sun.

Built in 1913–17, the synagogue is one of the finest to be built in Europe at the time. The exquisite interior is crowned by a tall dome decorated in the Byzantine style. The **Jüdisches Kulturmuseum** (Jewish Culture Museum) is laid out in one of the wings of the synagogue.

The Fuggerei of Augsburg

Among Augsburg's main tourist attractions is one of the world's oldest public housing projects. It was established by Jakob II Fugger, "the Rich", together with his brothers, for the people of Augsburg who had fallen on hard times. Built by Thomas Krebs in 1514–23, it was called the Fuggerei in honour of its founder. Situated east of Rathausplatz, in the Jakobervorstadt, this walled "town within a town" has retained its medieval atmosphere, and most of the houses are still occupied by the city's elderly. The Fuggerei is entered through gates that bear the original dedication, the date 1519 and the Fuggers' armorials.

VISITORS' CHECKLIST

Practical Information
The settlement is located east of Maximilianstr. **Open** Apr–Sep: 8am–8pm daily; Oct–Mar: 9am–6pm daily. No vehicular access. Fuggereimuseum: Mittlere Gasse 14. **Tel** (0821) 31 98 8114. **Open** as above.
W **fugger.de**

★ **Fuggereimuseum**
On view here is an apartment (bedroom and kitchen) furnished in the style of the period.

★ **Markuskirche**
The church was built in 1581 by Johannes Holl, father of the renowned Elias Holl. Destroyed in 1944, it was subsequently rebuilt.

0 metres 20
0 yards 20

Fountain
At the point where Herrengasse and Mittlere Gasse meet, forming a small square, stands a modest fountain. The focal point of the Fuggerei, it is also the favourite meeting place both of the local residents and of tourists.

Key

— Suggested route

Gardens at the rear of the houses in the Fuggerei

Exploring the Fuggerei

The estate originally comprised 53 buildings designed to house 106 families. Partly forming a continuous, symmetrical ensemble, they stand on an uneven plot of land and are surrounded by a wall with five gates.

The houses have modest façades and steep roofs with stepped gables. Each front door still has its bell-pull and iron handle, and the exterior walls still have sandstone plaques with the old house numbers inscribed on them.

The Fuggerei was badly damaged by the air raids of 1944. During the painstaking process of reconstruction, which was carried out in 1947–55 and was financed by the Fugger estate, 14 additional houses were built.

Today about 200 people live in the Fuggerei. All the houses have been modernized and have electricity, heating and other modern conveniences. The estate of the Fugger family decides who can live in the Fuggerei. Designated for needy people, this welfare housing project houses Catholics who must have lived in Augsburg for at least two years. Residents pay

a nominal annual rent equal to 1 Rhenish guilder (88 cents), in return for which they undertake to say three daily prayers for the founders. There is also supplement of €85 per month

Herrengasse, the main street in the Fuggerei

to finance communal services. An interesting feature of the Fuggerei is the fine late Gothic oriel of 1504–7 on the corner of the Seigniory House by the gate on Jakoberstraße. It was transferred from the bombed ruins of a house belonging to the Höchstetter family, contemporaries of the Fuggers. The **Seigniory House,** which was rebuilt after 1954, contains on its ground floor a Gothic chapel that was transferred here in 1962 from the ruined house of the Welsers.

Markuskirche, in Herrengasse, is decorated with a tall shaped gable and has an Angelus bell. It is furnished with items from various other churches. A *Crucifixion* by Jacopo Palma the Younger of about 1600 can be seen on the Mannerist high altar. Ulrich Fugger's epitaph, depicting the deceased wrapped in a shroud, was designed by Albrecht Dürer and made by Adolf Daucher in 1512–15.

The resident of the house at Mittlere Gasse 14 was Franz Mozart, great-grandfather of the composer Wolfgang Amadeus. He made himself unpopular with his clients by carrying out burials for the executioner, which was considered to be a disgraceful deed. As a result he lost business and became so impoverished that he had to move into the Fuggerei.

The Fuggers

The career of the Fuggers began in 1367, when Hans Fugger, a native of Graben, came to Augsburg. Jakob I (who died in 1459) founded the family of merchants and bankers that still exists today. His sons Ulrich, Georg and particularly Jakob II, "the Rich", acquired unheard-of wealth, ensuring a life of opulence for the entire family. Jakob II was banker to emperors, kings and popes. He funded the election of Karl V as German Emperor. He was also known as a patron of the arts, and thanks partly to him Renaissance art took root in Germany. He also founded social institutions. Once the owners of 100 villages, the Fuggers still own several castles in Bavaria.

Monument to Hans Jakob Fugger, Augsburg

Memorial plaque to Franz Mozart, one-time resident of the Fuggerei

The Imperial Hall of the former Augustine monastery in Wettenhausen

⓮ Wettenhausen

Road map B3. 🚌 🚉 Günzburg.
Abbey: Kammeltal, Dossenberger-
str. 46. **Tel** (08223) 40 040.

Standing like a fortress, the old Augustinian monastery in Wettenhausen dominates the surrounding landscape. **Mariä-Himmelfahrt-Kirche**, originally a Romanesque church, was rebuilt in the late Gothic style in the early 16th century and remodelled in the Baroque style in 1670. The frescoes, of about 1685, and the highly decorative altars and pulpit, dating from the same period, create a unified interior. The altar in the south chapel features a fine late Gothic Coronation of the Virgin carved in 1524.

Part of the **abbey**, including the Imperial Hall and the cloistered courtyard, are open to the public. The rooms in the cloister are visible through a decorative wrought-iron grille. One of them contains a figure of Christ seated on a donkey made in 1456, probably in the workshop of Hans Multscher of Ulm.

⓯ Günzburg

Road map B3. 🚗 19,700. 🚌 🚉
ℹ️ Schloßplatz 1, (08221) 200 444.
🌐 guenzburg.de

The origins of this sizeable town at the confluence of the rivers Günz and Danube go back to Roman times. Much of it has been pedestrianized, and it invites leisurely strolls through its attractive streets.

The main square, closed off by the 14th-century **Unteres Tor** (Lower Gate), is surrounded by Baroque houses with typically Swabian gables. These houses recall the days when the town was at its height. Notable is **Brentanohaus** at No. 8, built in 1747 with a tiled mansard roof and Rococo mouldings on its elegant façade.

Beside the old Franciscan monastery stands the **Frauenkirche**, built in 1736–41 by Dominikus Zimmermann. Substantial fragments of the town's 15th-century walls, defensive towers and gateways survive.

The attraction that draws most Germans and many tourists to this town is, however, **Legoland**, which is located a short distance to the south.

Houses in Münzgasse, one of Günzburg's most picturesque streets

⓰ Dillingen

Road map B3. 🚗 18,300. 🚌 🚉
ℹ️ Königstr. 37–38, (09071) 54 208, 54 209. 🌐 dillingen-donau.de

For centuries Dillingen, the spiritual capital of Swabia and a town dubbed the "Rome of Swabia", was the seat of the bishops of Augsburg and a major university town. The main street, Königstraße, lined with patrician town houses, defines the town's character. Königstraße leads into Kardinal von Waldburgstraße, on which the elongated Baroque façade of the **Jesuit University** rises. It was built in 1688–9 to a design by Michael Thumb and visitors can admire the Rococo Golden Hall within. The former **college** beside the university has a fine Baroque library, which occupies two floors and has furnishings carved by Johann Georg Bschorer. The highlight of the town is the formerly Jesuit **Mariä-Himmelfahrt-Kirche**, built in the early 17th century by Johann Alberthal. The early Baroque architecture of the building and its

Lion outside the castle in Dillingen

Rococo stuccowork, painting and furnishings combine to produce a splendid ensemble. The high altar still has its *Theatrum Sacrum*, where the tradition of performing Passion plays at Easter was recently revived.

The early Rococo **Franciscan monastery** and **church** were designed by Johann Georg Fischer. The stately 13th-century **castle**, which before the secularization of the state was the seat of the capital and of the bishops of Augsburg, has preserved its defensive character despite rebuilding on numerous occasions over the centuries. Fragments of the town walls, set with towers and pierced by the **Mitteltor** (Middle Gate), can still be seen today.

Roman ruins in Faimingen, a suburb of Lauingen

⑰ Lauingen

Road map B3. 🗺 10,800. 🚌 🚃
ℹ️ Herzog-Georg-Str. 17, (09072) 99 80. 🌐 **lauingen.de**

Set on a high bank overlooking the Danube, this town has largely preserved its medieval character. It has an oval outline and was once surrounded by walls, the surviving parts of which are a **gate** and two bastions.

The slender outlines of two tall towers that dominate the town can be seen from a distance. The more distinctive of the two is the former watch-tower that stands in the main square. Exceptionally tall and narrow, it was built in 1457–78 together with the adjacent arcades containing market stalls, and was extended in 1571. It is known as the **Schimmelturm** (Grey Mare Tower) because of the image of the horse near the bottom, which has been renewed and repainted several times.

The **town hall**, built in 1782 to a Neo-Classical design by Lorenz J Quaglio, was erected on the orders of the Elector Karl Theodor despite strong opposition from the townspeople.

Martinskirche, the parish church built in 1515, is one of the last Gothic hall-churches to have been built in southern Germany. Its triple-nave interior with web vaulting is unparalleled in height and the walls and ceilings are decorated with frescoes painted in 1521.

Among the many tombs and epitaphs is a fine cenotaph that is the symbolic tomb of Elisabeth, wife of the Palatine, who died in 1563. The tomb is surrounded by a wrought-iron grille and on it lies a white marble figure of the deceased supported by four lions. The tall free-standing **belfry** is, with the Schimmelturm, a defining feature of the town's skyline.

Environs
In the suburb of Faimingen, on the road to Günzburg, the remains of Roman buildings can be seen. The partially reconstructed **Temple of Apollo Grannus**, the Roman deity who also came to be worshipped by the Celts, bears witness to Lauingen's long history.

The Schimmelturm, the tallest tower in Lauingen

⑱ Höchstädt

Road map B3. 🗺 6,600. 🚌 🚃
ℹ️ Herzog Philipp-Ludwig-Str. 10, (09074) 44 12. 🌐 **hoechstaedt.de**

This little town on the banks of the Danube is flanked by its church and its castle. On the west side are the church and the town hall, on a square located between two streets that lead to the castle.

The late Gothic **Mariä-Himmelfahrt-Kirche**, which was completed in about 1520, is decorated with frescoes in the same style, painted in 1520–30 and also with Mannerist frescoes in a contrasting florid style dating from about 1600. The town's finest historic building is the turret-shaped Gothic sacristy, built in attractive sandstone in 1480–90. The Baroque altar was added in 1695.

The polygonal **chapel** beside the church was built in 1664. It features a deep niche containing a Pietà dating from the first quarter of the 18th century. Above the statue is a theatrical scene depicting Christ and the Apostles on the Mount of Olives. The scene, consisting of figures set against a painted background, was created by Johann Michael Fischer in 1760.

The **Heimatmuseum** has numerous collections of objects relating to local history, including a display of 9,000 tin soldiers re-creating the Battle of Höchstädt that took place in 1760.

On a hill overlooking the town stands the Renaissance **castle**, built in about 1589 to replace the medieval seat of Duke Philip Ludwig, the Palatine of Neuburg. Well restored, it is now used as the museum's headquarters. The castle complex has an almost square plan with a central courtyard, four circular corner towers and a chapel in the west wing. The main entrance is a doorway flanked by pairs of columns, with coats of arms in the tympanum and a barrel-vaulted archway with coffered ceiling.

🏛 **Heimatmuseum**
Marktplatz 7. **Tel** (09074) 44 12.
Open Apr–Oct: 2–5pm Sun; Nov–Mar: 2–4pm 1st Sun of month and by appointment.

The doorway of the castle in Höchstädt

TRAVELLERS' NEEDS

WHERE TO STAY

The Bavarian Alps are Germany's most popular tourist destination. The region offers a wide variety of hotels with different levels of service. Finding somewhere to stay, either in Munich itself or throughout the Bavarian Alps, is rarely a problem, whatever your requirements. As well as luxury hotels, which are often converted stately palaces or romantic castles, and international chains such as the Marriott, Hilton or Sheraton, travellers to the Bavarian Alps have a choice of many small hotels and guesthouses. However, accommodation of any sort in and around Munich for the Oktoberfest period must be booked well in advance; rooms can also be hard to find when trade fairs take place in the city, and during festivals and public holidays when tourist resorts become more crowded.

The Vier Jahreszeiten Kempinski hotel in Munich *(see p266)*

Finding Accommodation

In towns and cities hotels are usually in or near the historic centre or close to tourist attractions. When choosing somewhere to stay, try to ensure that it is not near a noisy street, a night-spot, or a church, as the ringing of church bells can awaken the deepest sleeper.

If you decide on a hotel in central Munich, you may need to enquire about parking. If you choose a hotel further from the centre, make sure that it is near public transport links. Most hotels, including luxury hotels, are on the periphery of the Old Town and in Schwabing. There are also hotels around Munich's main railway station, although these can be fairly basic. Hotels belonging to major groups such as the Marriott and Sheraton are located near main highways.

The Range of Hotels

Many hotels are marked with stars indicating their quality (and cost). Top-class hotels usually have their own high-quality restaurants, as well as swimming pool, gyms, saunas and laundry facilities. Those outside cities may also have tennis courts and golf links.

There is also a network of modern bed-and-breakfast hotels with far fewer ameni-ties. On motorways and major roads, you can find motels or *Rasthäuser*, which are basically restaurants with single-night accommodation.

In tourist towns a common type of accommodation is *Halbpension* (half-board lodgings), where a hot meal is offered in addition to breakfast, or *Vollpension* (lodging with full board).

All hotels and other types of accommodation are extremely clean. Toilet and bathroom facilities, even when shared, are of a high standard. Wi-Fi access comes almost as standard these days and is free in the vast majority of cases.

Hotel Prices

Hotel prices vary greatly. A single room can range from €35–80 in a tourist-class hotel to €150 in a top-class hotel, and over €500 in a luxury

One of the chic and trendy rooms at Flushing Meadows *(see p266)*

◀ Hotel Schiffmeister with the Alps in the background, Berchtesgaden

WHERE TO STAY | **263**

The old post office has been turned into a first-class hotel *(see p267)*

establishment. Prices in Munich are naturally higher than elsewhere, and highest during Oktoberfest.

At holiday and spa resorts a three-tier price system operates – high season, mid-season and low season. Prices at high season can be double those of low season. Many hotels offer reductions at weekends, especially those that cater for weekday business travellers. If you are planning a very long stay, you might be able to negotiate a discount at family-run guesthouses, especially at times of the year when business is slack. Otherwise prices tend to be fixed.

How to Book

These days most hotel accommodation is reserved online through popular booking websites, though you can still book direct by telephone or email. Travellers already in Bavaria can obtain useful brochures and lists of addresses from tourist offices. In some Alpine resorts, accommodation boards with a free telephone can usually be found at strategic locations.

On arrival guests are asked to complete a registration form and may be requested to show their passport. Full payment is made when

checking out and, especially in the case of small provincial hotels, it is always worth making sure in advance what means of payment are accepted. In health spas an additional charge known as a *Kurtaxe* is payable. In luxury hotels, tips are expected for additional services. Further down the hotel food chain tipping is rare.

Disabled Travellers

An increasing number of hotels and hostels cater for disabled travellers. Most have ramp access and a

Fantastic stairway at Hotel Stadt Rosenheim *(see p267)*

few rooms with bathrooms and toilets adapted for wheelchair users. Facilities are, however, most likely to be better in hotels of a higher standard than in budget hotels.

Handicapped-Reisen Deutschland (FMG Verlag www.behinderten-hostels.de) is a guide that lists hotels in Germany with facilities for disabled people. Information can also be obtained from BAGH and CBF *(see p261)*.

Travelling with Children

Travelling with children in the Bavarian Alps should not present any special problems. Most hotels will provide an additional bed or cot, often at no extra charge.

Many hotels have children's corners – play areas equipped with children's furniture as well as games and toys – and some have babysitting facilities. If a child is ill, the hotel's reception will call for a doctor or paediatrician.

A high chair for toddlers is standard equipment in many restaurants, while menus often include the option of smaller portions for children.

Tourist resorts offer special programmes of supervised activities for children.

Rooms in Private Houses

Viisitors should note that bed and breakfast accommodation is not widespread in cities. However, in popular tourist areas and most smaller towns, you will often come across houses with a sign that says *"Zimmer"* (rooms). The sign will be accompanied by another, saying either *"frei"* (vacancies) or *"belegt"* (no vacancies).

Prices for such rooms are relatively low – often as reasonable as €20 per person. Other benefits are a homely atmosphere and a lavish breakfast. Toilets and bath-rooms are usually shared, but rooms have washbasins and telephones.

The stunning Mandarin Oriental

Holiday Apartments

For visitors spending their holiday in one particular place, holiday apartments (Ferienwohnung) are the best and cheapest type of accommodation. They are available in all holiday resorts, with brochures at tourist information centres.

The size, standard and price of apartments vary. Most have a kitchen, TV, vacuum cleaner, iron, bookshelves, and cupboard with glasses and tablecloths.

Holiday apartments are found mainly in private houses and apartment blocks, and in some larger hotels. They are rented for at least a week. An additional charge for final cleaning (Endreinigung) is often levied.

Farm Stays

Staying on a farm (Bauernhof) is a popular and inexpensive way of spending a holiday. It is particularly suitable for families with children. Rooms in large farmhouses or separate apartments are provided, and range from modest to luxurious. Among other activities, guests have the opportunity to help with the daily farm work, and children can feed the animals. A popular attraction is the delicious food, particularly the fresh dairy produce.

Another type of getaway is a riding holiday. Guests stay on horse or pony farms (Reiterhöfe and Ponyhöfe), and go horse-riding or pony-trekking.

Hostels

Almost every sizeable Bavarian town has a youth hostel (Jugendherberge). These divide into four categories according to their location and standard. Many are relatively comfortable, although often the only available beds will be in a dormitory. Toilets and bathrooms are usually communal. Almost all youth hostels have dining rooms where breakfast and hot meals are served. Many hostels have their own sports facilities.

Bavarian youth hostels are open to anyone, though discounts are available for members and priority given to those under the age of 27. Many towns across Bavaria now have independent backpacker hostels with excellent, clean facilities.

Mountain Shelters

Mountain shelters offering food, rest and sometimes accommodation to skiers and hikers are found in many places in the Bavarian Alps. The German Alpine Association (Deutscher Alpenverein – DAV) alone has some 100 shelters. Members can use them at a discount and have priority in

Logo of the German Youth Hostel Association

booking. Along with individual rooms, the shelters have bunk beds in communal rooms.

Shelters are usually open during the summer months, from May or June to September or October. Shelters near skiing pistes and along the most popular hiking trails are also open in winter.

Campsites

Southern Bavaria's many campsites are usually in picturesque locations and ideal for peaceful holidays. Although they vary in size and standard, most have good toilet and washing facilities, and may also have a shop and café. Many also offer activity programmes. Most campsites are open April to October, although some are open year-round.

Gasthöfe

For travellers looking for unpretentious accommodation, roadside inns known as Gasthöfe, and found throughout Bavaria, are attractive and convenient. The sign "Gasthof" will probably be accompanied by another saying "Zimmer" (rooms). Prices are very affordable – usually between €30 and €50 for a double room. Drinking beer and eating simple homemade fare is one of the great pleasures of staying in a Gasthof.

A mountain shelter for hikers and skiers near Zugspitze

Spa Resorts

The bracing mountain air, and the many mineral springs and curative muds in the Bavarian Alps, have led to a large number of spa resorts. Most have the word *"Bad"* (bath) before the name of the town. In these resorts, a spa tax *(Kurtaxe)* is added to the room rate. This small additional charge allows for a reduction on the entry charge to many cultural and sporting facilities, and various kinds of therapy on offer.

Bavarian spas specialize mostly in respiratory and circulatory disorders and rheumatic ailments. Visitors to the spas have excellent rest and recuperation facilities at their disposal, with doctors and convalescence specialists to monitor their health.

Recommended Hotels

The hotel recommendations on the following pages have been allocated one of several categories. Pensions and Guesthouses

A well-kept *Gasthof*, one of the many roadside inns in Bavaria

cover smaller, family-run and usually less expensive places. Mid-range, Budget and Modern hotels are chain hotels or similar good-value standbys. Historic hotels are set in older buildings with a palpable sense of the past, whereas Boutique and Minimalist hotels offer stylish

accommodation, often with a modern feel. The final fifth category, Luxury, covers all the world-class places where you can spoil yourself. Places highlighted as DK Choice are especially recommended and guarantee a memorable night's stay.

DIRECTORY

Information on Accommodation & Reservations

Bayern Tourismus Marketing Gmbh
Arabellastr. 17, Munich.
Tel (089) 21 23 97 0.
W bayern.by

Tourismusamt München
Sendlinger Str. 1.
Tel (089) 23 39 65 00.
Neues Rathaus, Marienplatz.
Open 9:30am–7:30pm
Mon–Fri, 9am–4pm Sat,
10am–2pm Sun. Hauptbahnhof, Bahnhofplatz 2.
Open 9am–8pm Mon–Sat, 10am–6pm Sun.
W muenchen-tourist.de

Bed & Breakfast

Bed & Breakfast
Schulstr. 31, Munich.
Tel (089) 16 88 781.
W bed-breakfast-muc.de

City Mitwohnzentrale
Tel (089) 59 25 10.
W elodge.de

Farm Stays

AG Urlaub & Freizeit auf dem Lande
Lindhooper Str. 63 27283 Verden.
Tel (04231) 96650.
W bauernhofferien.de

Zentrale für den Landurlaub Landschriften–Verlag GmbH
Maarstr. 96, 53227 Bonn.
Tel (0228) 96 30 20.
W bauernhofurlaub.com

Youth Hostels

DJH München City
Wendl-Dietrich-Str. 20, Munich.
Tel (089) 20 24 44 90.

DJH München Park
Miesingstr. 4, Munich.
Tel (089) 78 57 67 70.

Haus International
Elisabethstr. 87, Munich.
Map 1 A1.
Tel (089) 12 00 60.
W haus-international.de

Landesverband Bayern des DJH
Mauerkircherstr. 5, Munich.
Tel (089) 92 20 980.
W bayern.jugendherberge.de

Mountain Shelters

DAV Summit Club
Am Perlacher Forst 186, 81545 Munich.
Tel (089) 64 24 00.
W dav-summit-club.de

Verband Deutscher Gebirgs- und Wandervereine
Wilhelmshöher Allee 157–159, 34121 Kassel.
Tel (0561) 93 87 30.
W wanderverband.de

Campsites

Deutscher Camping Club
Mandlstr. 28, Munich.
Map 2 F2.
Tel (089) 38 01 420.
W camping-club.de

Langwieder See
Eschenrieder Str. 119, Munich. **Tel** (089) 86 41 566.

München-Obermenzing
Lochhausener Str. 59.
Tel (089) 81 12 235.

Disabled Travellers

Bundesarbeits gemeinschaft Selbsthilfe (BAG)
Kirchfeldstr. 149, 40215 Düsseldorf
Tel (0211) 31 00 60.
W bag-selbsthilfe.de

Bundesverband 'Selbsthilfe' Körperbehinderter (BSK)
Altkrautheimerstr. 20, 74238 Krautheim.
Tel (06294) 428 10.
W bsk-ev.org

Club Behinderter und ihrer Freunde (CBF)
Pallaswiesenstr. 123a, 64293 Darmstadt
Tel (06151) 81 220.
W cbf-da.de

Where to Stay

Munich

Old Town (South)

Deutsche Eiche €
Boutique **Map** 3 C3
Reichenbachstraße 13, 80469
Tel *(089) 2311660*
🔳 deutsche-eiche.com
This stylish, gay-friendly hotel is popular with hip young guests. It's well located, and comes complete with a bar and sauna.

DK Choice

Motel One München Sendlinger Tor €
Modern **Map** 3 A3
Herzog-Wilhelm-Straße 28, 80331
Tel *(089) 51777250*
🔳 motel-one.com
This fantastic budget chain has taken off in Germany over the last decade. The rooms, with turquoise decor, have a certain minimalist elegance. There is a 24-hour lounge and café-bar as well.

Asam Hotel €€
Modern **Map** 3 A2
Josephspitalstraße 3, 80331
Tel *(089) 2309700*
🔳 hotel-asam.de
This comfortable hotel has a slightly 1990s ambience but rooms are bright, large and airy, staff friendly and the location good.

Concorde €€
Minimalist **Map** 4 D2
Herrnstraße 38–40, 80539
Tel *(089) 224515*
🔳 concorde-muenchen.de
Minimalism is the name of the game here, but not in a trendy design style. There's a friendly vibe, free Wi-Fi, parking nearby and early-starter breakfasts.

Hotel am Viktualienmarkt €€
Mid-range **Map** 3 B3
Utzschneiderstraße 14, 80469
Tel *(089) 2311090*
🔳 hotel-am-viktualienmarkt.de
Very reasonably priced for the super-central location. Expect comfortable rooms, a great breakfast buffet and a hearty welcome from the family owners.

Hotel Torbräu €€
Historic **Map** 3 C3
Tal 41, 80331
Tel *(089) 242340*
🔳 torbraeu.de
Housed in a historic building dating back to 1490, this hotel offers classically furnished rooms.

Louis Hotel €€
Modern **Map** 3 C3
Viktualienmarkt 6, 80331
Tel *(089) 41119080*
🔳 louis-hotel.com
Stay in style in lovely, airy rooms furnished with Italian fabrics, wooden floors and stone tiles. The restaurant gets good reviews.

Schlicker €€
Mid-range **Map** 3 C2
Tal 8, 80331
Tel *(089) 2428870*
🔳 hotel-schlicker.de
Family-owned, in a tiptop central location. Standard rooms are not huge, but bright and welcoming. Those at the back are quieter.

Cortiina €€
Boutique **Map** 3 C2
Ledererstraße 8, 80331
Tel *(089) 2422490*
🔳 designhotels.com
Super-cool, with urban designer style and a great cocktail bar – but pricy breakfasts and pay-for Wi-Fi.

The Flushing Meadows €€€
Luxury **Map** 3 B4
Fraunhoferstraße 32, 80469
Tel *(089) 55279170*
🔳 flushingmeadowshotel.com
Occupying the top two floors of an industrial building in a lively quarter near Viktualienmarkt, this hotel offers 16 luxurious, retro-styled rooms and a top-floor bar.

Old Town (North)

Bayerischer Hof €€€
Luxury **Map** 3 B2
Promenadeplatz 2–6, 80333
Tel *(089) 21200*
🔳 bayerischerhof.de
With five gourmet restaurants, six bars, a spa and a rooftop pool, this hotel is one of Munich's top addresses and regularly attracts world-famous celebrities.

Exterior of the Charles Hotel, on the edge of the Museums District

---

Price Guide
Prices are based on one night's stay in high season for a standard double room, inclusive of service charges and taxes.

€	under €100
€€	€100 to €200
€€€	over €200

Around the Isar

Admiral €€
Mid-range **Map** 3 C3/4
Kohlstraße 9, 80469
Tel *(089) 216350*
🔳 hotel-admiral.de
If you are looking for traditional antique style, classic rooms, a lush garden to relax in and bags of olde-worlde charm, the Admiral is the place to book.

Adria €€
Boutique **Map** 4 D1
Liebigstraße 8a, 80538
Tel *(089) 2421170*
🔳 adria-muenchen.de
Arty but practical decor and spacious bathrooms make a stay here comfortably pleasant. The breakfast buffet is a fine spread even by southern Germany's standards. Located on a quiet, residential street.

Domus €€
Modern **Map** 4 D1
St-Anna-Straße 31, 80538
Tel *(089) 2177730*
🔳 domus-hotel.de
The Domus has understatedly stylish but utterly modern rooms with balconies and 21st-century bathrooms. The in-house Italian restaurant is a well-respected nosh spot.

Hotel Ritzi €€
Boutique **Map** 4 F1/2
Maria-Theresia-Straße 2a, 81675
Tel *(089) 414240890*
🔳 hotel-ritzi.de
This beautiful hotel has retained many of its genuine Art Deco features, including in the bar and the (Italian-Asian fusion) restaurant. Rooms are individually themed with a mix of period furniture and artwork and knickknacks from around Asia.

H'Otello €€
Boutique **Map** 3 C3
Baaderstraße 1, 80469
Tel *(089) 45831200*
🔳 hotello.de
One of four in a German chain, the H'Otello goes heavy on the urban vibe with immaculately styled rooms in varying shade of grey. There's also a trendy bar.

Splendid-Dollmann €€
Historic **Map** 4 D3
Thierschstraße 49, 80538
Tel *(089) 238080*
W hotel-splendid-dollmann.de
This elegant 19th-century townhouse is a work of art. The delightful *fin-de-siècle* air extends from the communal spaces to the rooms with their reproduction antiques. The breakfast buffet is a generous affair.

Opera €€€
Guesthouse **Map** 4 D1
St-Anna-Straße 10, 80538
Tel *(089) 2104940*
W hotel-opera.de
Stay in this upmarket townhouse with a beautiful façade and courtyard and enjoy exquisitely understated rooms and attentive, personal service.

University District

Carolin €
Pension **Map** 2 E4
Kaulbachstraße 42, 80539
Tel *(089) 345757*
W pension-carolin.com
A family-run guesthouse with smart, modern rooms on the first floor of an apartment building. Free Wi-Fi.

Hauser €€
Modern **Map** 2 D4
Schellingstraße 11, 80799
Tel *(089) 2866750*
W hotel-hauser.de
This family affair located a textbook's throw from the university has slightly dated but well-maintained rooms as well as a spa, sauna and generous breakfast buffet.

Museums District

Leonardo Boutique €
Boutique **Map** 2 D5
Amalienstraße 25, 80333
Tel *(089) 287870*
W leonardo-hotels.com
One of many hotels in the Leonardo European chain, this incarnation boasts modern furnishings and classy rooms within a historic building.

Charles Hotel €€€
Luxury **Map** 5 A1
Sophienstraße 28, 80333
Tel *(089) 5445550*
W roccofortehotels.com
This top-class hotel has exquisitely decorated rooms, some with dreamy views of the neighbouring botanic gardens. The Sophia bar and restaurant is a very swish affair.

The elegant pastel facade of the Splendid-Dollman in Munich

Further Afield

Carat Hotel €
Modern **Map** 3 A3
Lindwurmstraße 13, 80337
Tel *(089) 230380*
W carat-hotel-muenchen.de
Enjoy the superb breakfast buffet at this centrally located hotel. A bar, parking and 24-hour reception are further pluses.

Hotel Laimer Hof €
Historic
Laimer Straße 40, 80639
Tel *(089) 1780380*
W laimerhof.de
Excellently located in a peaceful suburb near Nymphenburg Palace, this family-run place offers a warm welcome, 23 well-appointed rooms and free parking.

Hotel Seibel €
Mid-range
Theresienhöhe 9, 80339
Tel *(089) 5401420*
W seibel-hotels-munich.de
Located near the site of the Oktoberfest, this friendly guesthouse-hotel in a Jugendstil building offers pretty, light-filled rooms and lots of facilities.

Hotel Bavaria €€
Mid-range
Gollierstraße 9, 80339
Tel *(089) 94396954*
W hotel-bavaria.com
This long-established hotel in the Westend district has dramatically fitted-out guest rooms (some with modest balconies), big breakfast buffets and a flashy bar.

Hotel Stadt Rosenheim €€
Boutique
Orleansplatz 6a, 81667
Tel *(089) 4482424*
W hotel-stadt-rosenheim.de
Situated in the east of the city, rooms here are the height of minimalist design, equipped with orthopedic matresses, and all of them are different. There's also a full range of services available.

Upper Bavaria (North)

DACHAU: Fischer €
Mid-range **Map** D4
Bahnhofstraße 4, 85221
Tel *(08131) 612200*
W hotelfischer-dachau.de
This basic hotel has immaculate, modern rooms, a sturdy Bavarian restaurant, an ample buffet breakfast and a lively bar.

DK Choice

DACHAU: Zieglerbräu €
Guesthouse **Map** D4
Konrad-Adenauer-Straße 8, 85221
Tel *(08131) 454396*
W restaurant-hotel-dachau.de
This cheerful place in the old town has large, sleek rooms – including a romantic four-poster suite – and a fantastic Bavarian restaurant.

EICHSTÄTT: Adler Hotel €
Modern **Map** C2
Marktplatz 22, 85072
Tel *(08421) 6767*
W adler-eichstaett.de
The Baroque exterior gives way to contemporary, chic decor. Dining options include a Bavarian restaurant and an Italian cellar bar.

FREISING: Bayerischer Hof €
Mid-range **Map** D3
Untere Hauptstraße 3, 85354
Tel *(08161) 538300*
W bayerischerhof-freising.de
This traditional option offers 70 rooms and includes a bar, sauna and Asian restaurant.

INGOLSTADT: Hotel Ammerland Garni €€
Boutique **Map** D2
Hermann-Paul-Müller-Straße 15, 85055
Tel *(0841) 953450*
W hotel-ammerland.de
It's worth being outside the centre for the imaginatively designed rooms and communal spaces at this superbly run hotel.

For more information on types of hotels *see page 265*

Brightly coloured exterior of Neuwirt in Neuburg

NEUBURG: Neuwirt €
Mid-range Map C2
Färberstraße 88, 86633
Tel *(08431) 2078*
W neuwirt-neuburg.de
This typical Bavarian hotel has a jolly tavern and beer garden. The rooms are slightly dated but comfortable.

Lower Bavaria

DEGGENDORF: Parkhotel €
Modern Map F2
Färberstraße 88, 86633
Tel *(08431) 2078*
W nh-hotels.de
This trendy hotel belonging to a huge chain has large, airy rooms. There's also bike hire available and a steam room.

LANDSHUT: Romantik
Hotel Fürstenhof €€
Boutique Map E3
Stethaimerstraße 3, 84034
Tel *(0871) 92550*
W hotel-fuerstenhof-landshut.de
This family-run, three-star hotel has some gorgeous, timber-rich rooms, some with traditional Bavarian furniture. There's a pretty garden and sauna, and breakfast is a great setup for the day.

PASSAU: Hotel Schloss Ort €€
Mid-range Map G3
Ort 11, 94032
Tel *(0851) 34072*
W schlosshotel-passau.de
Pleasant boutique hotel with plenty of character located at the confluence of the Ilz and Danube rivers.

PASSAU: Hotel Weisser Hase €€
Historic Map G3
Heiliggeistgasse 1, 94032
Tel *(0851) 92110*
W weisser-hase.de
With its 16th-century charm, this hotel offers 108 standard but well-priced rooms in the heart of the old town.

DK Choice

PASSAU: Wilder Mann €€
Historic Map G3
Schrottgasse 2, 94032
Tel *(0851) 35071*
W wilder-mann.com
This hotel located in the shadows of Passau's town hall clock tower has attracted the likes of US astronaut Neil Armstrong and the Austrian empress Elizabeth II. The rooms sport antique furniture – one features Bavarian King Ludwig II's wedding bed.

STRAUBING: Römerhof Hotel €€
Mid-range Map E2
Ittlinger Straße 136, 94315
Tel *(09421) 99820*
W roemerhof-straubing.de
This three-star hotel is pretty standard fare but it does have a good regional restaurant.

Upper Bavaria (East)

ALTÖTTING: Zur Post €
Historic Map F4
Kapellplatz 2, 84503
Tel *(08671) 5040*
W www.zurpostaltoetting.de
Kings, archdukes and bishops have stayed in this wonderful Bavarian inn with its imaginative decor and much-praised restaurant.

DK Choice

BAD REICHENHALL:
Axelmannstein €€
Luxury Map F5
Salzburger Straße 2–6, 83435
Tel *(08651) 7770*
W wyndhamgrand badreichenhall.com
Pamper yourself in this Alpine spa hotel in a beautiful park setting, whose facilities include an array of massages and treatments, a putting green and tennis courts. There is also a lovely restaurant.

BERCHTESGADEN: Alpenhotel
Bergzauber €
Pension Map F5
Renothenweg 2, 83471
Tel *(08652) 5559*
W alpenhotel-bergzauber.de
Traditional Bavarian hotel with rooms that have balconies. Facilities include sauna and table tennis.

BERCHTESGADEN:
Vier Jahreszeiten €€
Mid-range Map F5
Maximilianstraße 20, 83471
Tel *(08652) 9520*
W hotel-vierjahreszeiten-berchtesgaden.de
Family-run hotel with Bavarian decor, Alpine views from many of the rooms, a pool and a sauna.

DK Choice

BERCHTESGADEN:
InterContinental
Berchtesgaden Resort €€€
Luxury Map F5
Hintereck 1, 83471
Tel *(08652) 97550*
W intercontinental.com
This exclusive five-star offers pristine views of the Bavarian Alps. It has posh bedrooms, a splendid spa, indoor and outdoor pools and gourmet restaurants that use a variety of local ingredients.

REIT IM WINKL: Unterwirt €€
Mid-range Map E5
Kirchplatz 2, 83242
Tel *(08640) 8010*
W unterwirt.de
A typical Alpine chalet-style hotel with wellness facilities, traditional furniture and a games room.

WASSERBURG AM INN:
Paulanerstuben €
Guesthouse Map E4
Marienplatz 9, 83512
Tel *(08071) 3903*
W paulanerstuben-wasserburg.de
This 16th-century house has simple, contemporary rooms that sit above a great old tavern.

Upper Bavaria (South)

BAD TÖLZ: Posthotel
Kolberbräu €
Guesthouse Map D5
Marktstraße 29, 83646
Tel *(08041) 76880*
W kolberbraeu.de
Head to Bad Tölz's pedestrian zone for the comfortable rooms and regional cooking at this no-nonsense Alpine tavern.

Key to Price Guide *see page 266*

DK Choice

GARMISCH-PARTENKIRCHEN: Gasthof Fraundorfer €
Guesthouse **Map** C5
Ludwigstraße 24, 82467
Tel *(08821) 9270*
w gasthof-fraundorfer.de
A guesthouse that celebrates
Bavarian culture. Murals decorate
the house, the rooms have
regional themes, and there is
nightly Bavarian dancing and
yodelling in the restaurant and bar.

GARMISCH-PARTENKIRCHEN: Hotel Edelweiss €
Guesthouse **Map** C5
Martinswinkelstraße 15–17, 82467
Tel *(08821) 2454*
w hoteledelweiss.de
True Alpine styling, chunky timber
furniture and a mountain welcome
can be found at this romantic
guesthouse with a country vibe.

KOCHEL AM SEE: Grauer Bär €
Pension **Map** C5
Mittenwalder Straße 82–86, 82431
Tel *(08851) 92500*
w grauer-baer.de
This family-run, lakeside guest-
house boasts pleasant rooms
and excellent wellness facilities.
The restaurant offers
wonderful views.

LANDSBERG AM LECH: Goggl Garni €
Historic **Map** C4
Hubert von Herkomer Str. 19/20, 86899
Tel *(08191) 3240*
w hotel-goggl.de
Rooms in this 1667 house have
traditional handpainted furniture.
The restaurant is wood-panelled.

OBERAMMERGAU: Hotel Maximilian €€
Guesthouse **Map** C5
Ettaler Straße 5, 82487
Tel *(08822) 948740*
w maximilian-oberammergau.de
One of the best places to sleep in
town: the gorgeous boutique
rooms are a treat and there's a
wellness spa and beer garden too.

The Allgäu

DK Choice

FÜSSEN: Hotel Hirsch €€
Modern **Map** B5
Kaiser-Maximilian-Platz 7, 87629
Tel *(08362) 93980*
w hotelfuessen.de
Enjoy live music in the beer
garden, or soak up the Alpine
view from the terrace. The rooms
are individually furnished with
historical themes, and the restaurant serves top-notch local food.

KEMPTEN: Bayerischer Hof €€
Boutique **Map** B5
Füssener Straße 96, 87437
Tel *(0831) 57180*
w bayerischerhof-kempten.de
Riverside hotel with a variety of
themed rooms, plus sauna,
solarium and pub-restaurant.

LINDAU: Spiegel-Garni €
Pension **Map** A5
In der Grub 1, 88131
Tel *(08382) 94930*
w hotel-spiegel-garni.de
Located right in the heart of
town, rooms here range from
simple to extravagantly Alpine.

LINDAU: Reutemann €€
Modern **Map** A5
Ludwigstraße 23, 88131
Tel *(08382) 9150*
w reutemann-lindau.de
An extraordinary harbour-side
location and a list of services as
long as an Alpine horn, including
a great restaurant, a wellness area
and swimming pools.

LINDAU: Bayerischer Hof €€€
Luxury **Map** A5
Bahnhofplatz 2, 88131
Tel *(08382) 9150*
w bayerischerhof-lindau.de
A Neo-Classical styled building in
a prime lakefront location. The
spacious rooms are furnished in
soft pastels for a bright, airy feel.

OBERSTDORF: Saschas Kachelofen €
Pension **Map** B6
Kirchstraße 3, 87561
Tel *(08322) 97750*
w saschas-kachelofen.de
This traditional inn has simple
but attractive rooms above a
rustic restaurant. Immaculately
maintained.

Northern Swabia

AUGSBURG: Dom Hotel €€
Modern **Map** C3
Frauentorstraße 8, 86152
Tel *(0821) 343930*
w domhotel-augsburg.de
Located in the serene cathedral
district, this solid Bavarian hotel
boasts wellness facilities. Rooms
have a free minibar and the
owners are mines of information.

AUGSBURG: Steigenberger Drei Mohren €€
Boutique **Map** C3
Maximilianstraße 40, 86150
Tel *(0821) 50360*
w steigenberger.com
Located in the thick of the action
in Augsburg city centre, offering
a higher standard of business
class rooms with stylish furnishings
and ultra-modern bathrooms.

DONAUWÖRTH: Posthotel Traube €
Modern **Map** C2
Kapellstraße 16, 86609
Tel *(0906) 706440*
w posthoteltraube.de
Basic but well-kept hotel in the
centre of town with a simple
restaurant and low prices.

NEU-ULM: Golden Tulip €€
Modern **Map** A3
Silcherstraße 40, 89231
Tel *(0731) 80110*
w goldentulip-parkhotel-neu-ulm.
com
Park hotel on the bank of the
Danube river, with great views
of the historic Ulm town centre and
the Gothic Ulm Minster.

DK Choice

NÖRDLINGEN: Klösterle €
Historic **Map** B2
Beim Klösterle 1, 86720
Tel *(09081) 87080*
w nh-hotels.de
Housed in a venerable Franciscan
monastery with a gabled roof, this
hotel has stunning, angular
rooms. Facilities include a sauna,
gym and bike rentals. The
breakfast buffet is also exemplary.

Spacious room with fantastic Alpine views at Hotel Hirsch, Füssen

For more information on types of hotels *see page 265*

WHERE TO EAT AND DRINK

Although the food normally served in the Bavarian Alps is rather basic traditional fare, it is always tasty and satisfying. Grilled knuckle of pork, sausage, dumplings and the ubiquitous litre beer mugs are enjoyed everywhere from village inns to renowned Munich pubs. Consumed against a background of conversation, laughter and singing, they are part of a much larger culinary experience. The beer garden (Biergarten), in particular, is one of Bavaria's trademarks. The best-known, often attached to breweries, are popular gathering places for both locals and tourists. However, those looking for more sophistication will find variety in most towns and holiday resorts, with Italian, Turkish, Greek and European-Asian fusion restaurants the most popular.

Dallmayr restaurant and coffee house, Munich Old Town (see p277)

Types of Restaurants

The variety of restaurants found in the Bavarian Alps reflects the fact that the region is orientated towards tourism. Genuine Bavarian meals are served primarily in Gasthaus-type establishments. In central Munich and in tourist resorts, restaurants tend towards the kitsch, and the quality can be poor. It is better to eat in an inn frequented by locals, where prices are lower and where dishes, although served with less ceremony, usually taste much better. Be prepared for a little local colour: local inns can be noisy with over-indulgent drinkers.

A good bet is usually the Ratskeller, a pub in the cellar of the town hall, serving regional specialities. There are also traditional wine bars (Weinstuben), which serve good, if pricier, food.

Other options for good regional food and local beer are Bierstuben and Bierkeller: pubs usually belonging to a local brewery. They are often noisy, and seating is on long benches where you soon fall into conversation with other diners and drinkers.

Attractive features of Bavarian beer-drinking rituals are the gigantic beer tents (Bierzelte) put up during local holidays, as well as the charming little beer gardens (Biergärten), where customers order their drinks from the bar. You can even bring your own food to some of them.

There are also Italian pizzerias, Greek tavernas, steak houses, and Chinese, Turkish and Balkan restaurants as well as fast-food outlets and snack bars. At the other end of the scale, particularly in Munich, there are elegant, discerning restaurants with elevated standards of service, decor and cuisine, with high prices to match.

Smoking is banned in all public places, including restaurants, bars and clubs.

What and When to Eat

Breakfast is usually hearty, with various types of bread accompanied by cheese, sausages and marmalade. On Sunday a brunch buffet is served in many places until 2pm. During the lunch period (noon to 2pm) most establishments serve excellent salads or bowls of filling soup, while many restaurants offer a

A sunny beer garden near the Viktualienmarkt, Munich

Stylish Davvero Restaurant in the Charles Hotel, Munich

fixed-price menu. Restaurants start to fill up in the evenings between 6 and 7pm, although dinner is often eaten after 8pm.

Opening Hours

Cafeterias and fast-food chains open at 9am, but most other establishments open at noon and usually close after the lunchtime period until about 6pm. Many restaurants close on one day of the week, known as a *Ruhetag*. Beer gardens in towns usually close at 11pm. Many restaurants stay open right up until midnight or 1am.

Menu

Most restaurants post their menu with its prices at the door, with daily or seasonal additions attached on a separate sheet. Desserts and soft and alcoholic drinks are usually listed on a separate menu. In many restaurants the menu is written in German and English, and sometimes in other languages including French, Russian and Chinese. In cafés and less expensive restaurants, the menu may be handwritten; staff may be able to help with translation.

Reservations

Reservations are essential at the best restaurants and advisable in most medium-standard restaurants on a Friday or Saturday night or on public holidays. Without a reservation, you may be asked to wait for a table to become available or to return later.

Many inns and restaurants in Bavaria have a *Stammtisch*, a table set aside for regular local people and groups at certain times on certain days.

Prices and Tips

Prices charged in Bavarian restaurants are diverse, those in Munich's top restaurants being the highest. A meal consisting of roast meat with dumplings and salad served in a country inn can cost considerably less.

The cost of a main course in an inn or restaurant ranges from €7–13 in the cheapest places to €14–20 in superior establishments. The average cost of a three-course meal including salad and beer is about €28. This includes tax and service, but it is customary to leave a small tip. If paying by card, this can be added to the bill.

Vegetarian Food

Vegetarian food is now a common choice in Germany.

The number of vegetarian restaurants has increased, and snack bars offering vegetarian meals are popular. More inns and restaurants all over Germany now include meat-free meals on their main menus, while vegetarian pizzas are a standard item in Italian restaurants.

Disabled Visitors

Many inns and restaurants sadly lack wheelchair access. Doorways are often too narrow and tables too closely placed, and adapted toilets absent. Be sure to enquire what the situation is when making a reservation.

Recommended Restaurants

The recommended restaurants on the following pages have been chosen to provide a taste of the cuisines of the region. As a result places serving good quality German and regional cuisine have been favoured. Where possible, alternatives have also been suggested – which will likely prove particularly useful to vegetarians or those wanting lighter fare.

In all cases we have picked restaurants where the quality of the food or the experience marks them out somehow. Places recommended for DK Choice are our top recommendations, chosen for offering something special or simply for being the best of their type.

The main room of the Munich Ratskeller

The Flavours of Munich and Bavaria

Bavarian cooking has a reputation for huge portions of hearty food, best enjoyed along with a beer. Sausages of all kinds, superb pork and beef, regional fish, and freshly baked breads and cakes are the standard fare for locals and visitors alike. But many restaurants now also prepare local and other German dishes with a lighter touch – indeed, Munich once spearheaded German *nouvelle cuisine*. While the city has lost its gourmet crown to the likes of Hamburg, Düsseldorf, and Berlin, the general standard of cooking in the Bavarian capital is still superb.

Harzer Roller and Emmentaler cheeses

Giant pretzels, best eaten warm and soft from the oven

Hearty Bavarian Cooking

Bavarian cooking developed in the countryside, where hard-working farmers needed high-carbohydrate food made using local, fresh produce – homemade bread, noodles and dumplings along with things like home-reared meat, farm-produced cheeses, and river fish such as trout. In Munich,

during its centuries as the seat of the Wittelsbach dynasty, these country influences were refined into a solidly bourgeois cuisine. To this day, the hearty, no-nonsense dishes of Bavaria are what the world considers to be German cuisine. *Weißwürste* (white veal sausages with a beer pretzel) are enjoyed in the morning, often with a beer. Dinner might be soup with liver

dumplings, roast pork, *Sauerkraut* and a pile of potato dumplings or noodles. Local produce is still held in high regard. Delicatessens abound in Munich, and markets are found throughout the region. Pride of place goes to the Viktualienmarkt, in the historic heart of town *(see p68)*, where you can shop for, sample and eat authentic Bavarian cooking at the many food stalls.

Mehrkornsemmel (mixed grain roll)

Laugensemmel (salty sourdough rolls)

Berliner Landbrot (mild rye bread)

Grau-oder Mischbrot (wholewheat)

Semmel (milk-dough roll)

Selection of typical German loaves and bread rolls

Bavarian Dishes and Specialities

Bavarian cooking is a great blend of filling dishes and tasty snacks or *Brotzeit* ("bread time") between main meals. A typical *Brotzeit* consists of any cold meat, such as smoked bacon or sausage, slices of roast pork or liver sausage, freshly sliced *Radi* (radish) and some cheese, preferably Obatzda, a creamy Camembert mousse. Main courses focus on pork, with the famous Schweinshaxe and Schweinsbraten (with beer gravy) leading the field. The Schweinshaxe in particular is a must-have in

Pork salamis

Munich. Both are eaten mostly with potato dumplings – the famous Bavarian *Knödel* – or with *Semmelknödeln* – wheat-flour dumplings. None of these dishes would be complete without a nice, cold beer.

Leberknödelsuppe is a rich, clear beef broth in which little liver dumplings are lightly poached.

Fresh vegetables on display at Munich's historic Viktualienmarkt

Munich's Gourmet Revolution

It may seem strange that a city of hearty and hefty cooking instigated a trend for low-fat gourmet German cuisine. At the forefront was chef Eckart Witzigmann who, inspired by French *nouvelle cuisine*, began to reinvent Bavarian and German dishes using unusual combinations of exquisite ingredients. Witzigmann's legendary Munich-based Aubergine was the first German restaurant to gain three Michelin stars. Munich's top restaurants still retain a reputation for innovative cooking. Certain chic venues have also attracted the *bussi-bussi* (air-kissing) crowd with Italian, Asian and Fusion cuisine, served in a stylish setting.

Bavarian Beer

Of the more than 1,250 breweries in Germany, many of the largest and most famous are in Munich, among them Löwenbräu, Augustiner, Paulaner and Hofbräu. Beer is still brewed in strict accordance

Beer served in a traditional Munich *Biergarten* (beer garden)

to the "Reinheitsgebot", a Bavarian decree of 1516 ordering that only malted barley, hops and water should be used. Today there many different kinds of beer available, from dark, strong Bock beer to lighter beers such as the famous Weizen or *Weißbier* (white beer).

Most beers on tap in Munich are served in a *Halbe*, a half-litre mug. In beer gardens and at Oktoberfest, they may be served in a *Maß*, a special 1 litre (2 pint) glass mug.

The exuberant annual highlight of Munich's proud beer culture is the famous Oktoberfest *(see p33)*.

WEIßWÜRSTE

There is no other dish from Bavaria as classic as a pair of Weißwürste. These delicious veal sausages are steamed and served hot with sweet, grainy mustard and a *Brezen* (beer pretzel). Traditionally, they should be eaten in the morning, as a second breakfast or a snack before lunch, but never at other times of the day; hence the old Munich saying that "the sausage should not hear the clocks sound noon". But even if it's early, a beer is the right accompaniment for Weißwürste. Some locals don't eat the sausages with a knife and fork, but simply suck out the meat from the Weißwürste's thin skin, an art called *Auszuzeln* in Munich.

Tafelspitz (poached beef brisket with vegetables), is usually served with red cabbage and horseradish.

Schweinshaxe, or roast pork knuckle, is a Bavarian classic. It is eaten with potato dumplings and krautsalat.

Rohrnudeln is a Bavarian yeasted dumpling cake that is soaked in a delicious vanilla-caramel sauce.

Beer in Bavaria

Bavaria is famous the world over for its excellent beer, which is exported to over 140 countries. As part of their cultural tradition, Bavarians scrupulously observe the *Reinheitsgebot*, a law of 1516 according to which the only ingredients brewers may use are barley, hops and water. The Bavarians even made accession to the Weimar Republic in 1919 conditional on the acknowledgment of this law. The Starkbieranstich, at the beginning of Lent, is the high point of Bavaria's brewing tradition.

The Oktoberfest – a folk festival that is cheerfully celebrated by the Bavarians

Logo of one of Bavaria's best-known breweries

The famous Löwenbräu beer

A beer mat

Bavarian Breweries

In 1040 the monks of Weihenstephan monastery, which is now on the outskirts of modern Freising, were granted a licence to brew beer by the city's bishop. The brewery, which still produces beer to this day, is the oldest in the world. Today, almost every small town in Bavaria has a brewery and the cities usually have several. Many Bavarian breweries have centuries of tradition behind them. The best-known are the main Munich breweries – Löwenbräu, Hofbräu, Paulanerbräu, Augustinerbräu, Spatenbräu and Hacker-Pschorrbräu.

The smaller breweries that are found throughout the region usually have their own inns *(Wirtschaften)* or pubs with beer gardens. Many of them are the object of special "pilgrimages" made both by Bavarians and by tourists. The most highly esteemed of these inns include the Klosterbrauerei Andechs, the Weltenburg and Irsee breweries, which continue the time-honoured tradition of monastic brewing, and Schlossbrauerei Kaltenberg, which belongs to Duke Luitpold of Bavaria. The long-standing debate over who brews the best beer will, quite obviously, never be resolved.

Traditional Dark and Light Beers

Until the 19th century, the only beer drunk in Bavaria was the sweeter dark beer *(Dunkel)*. Some breweries continue to specialize in *Dunkel* today; the best known of these are the Weltenburg monastery brewery (which makes Barock Dunkel) and the Schlossbrauerei Kaltenberg (König Ludwig Dunkel).

In the 20th century dark beer was replaced by lighter lager-type beer *(Helles)*, which is clear, a little more potent and with a less bitter taste. *Naturtrüb*, an unfiltered beer with an excellent taste, is slightly cloudy because of its yeast content.

Good beer is served cold and should have a thick head that does not settle quickly. It is served in a litre (2-pint) mug *(eine Maß)*, as a half litre (1 pint) *(eine Halbe)* and more rarely as a quarter litre (half a pint) *(ein Kleines)*. It tastes best when served from the barrel (as *Fassbier)*. Beer served from a keg under pressure is sacrilege to a Bavarian. On hot days, people may drink *Radler*, which is *Helles* mixed with lemonade.

Berchtesgaden lager

König Ludwig dark beer

Paulanerbräu lager

Märzenbier

Before the invention of refrigeration systems, beer was brewed in winter, when the heat would not disrupt the fermentation process. The last brewing was in March and the beer had a higher alcohol content, which helped to prevent it going off. If the brewers' stocks lasted until autumn, before the new season's beer was brewed the cellars were opened and a beer festival was held. The brewing of *Märzenbier* (March beer) continues to this day, even though modern technology has rendered the process obsolete.

At the big autumn beer festivals millions of litres of this strong-tasting light-brown beer are consumed. Beer brewed by the major Munich brewers specially for the Oktoberfest is called *Oktoberfestbier* or *Wiesnbier*. In the autumn it is on offer in many pubs and is sold bottled in shops.

The most widely used type of beer mug

Oktoberfestbier from the Paulanerbräu

Bock and Doppelbock

This famous beer gets its name from the town of Einbeck in Lower Saxony. The word "Einbeck" was transmuted by the Bavarian brogue into "Oanbock", which was abbreviated to "Bock". *Bockbier* was first brewed by the court brewery *(Hofbräu)*, founded in 1589. The Pauline monks were later renowned for making this type of beer. A more potent variety called *Doppelbock* was produced under the name Salvator. This beer, which the monks used to help them through the rigours of Lent, was brewed to celebrate 19 March, the feast day of St Joseph, the order's patron saint. To this day Josefitag marks the beginning of Munich's *Starkbierfest* (strong beer festival), which takes place in the Paulaner brewery's pub. Salvator inaugurated the production of several other *Doppelbock* beers. The beer is an amber colour and has a strong, slightly bitter taste and a 7 per cent alcohol content.

Salvator
Doppelbock

Pretzels – a perfect snack to enjoy with beer

Weißbier (Weizenbier)

This type of beer is very popular in southern Germany, particularly in summer as it is a refreshing drink. During the brewing process, twice the amount of malted wheat is added to the malted barley, which is why it is known as *Weizenbier* or *Weißbier* (wheat beer).

Weizenbier has a 5 per cent alcohol content and is a *Vollbier* (full beer). To enhance the flavour it is often drunk with a sliver of lemon. There are many kinds of wheat beer: the light and dark *Weizen-Bockbier* and the yeasty *Hefeweizen* beer. The frothy *Weizen* is slowly poured into a glass which broadens at the top. Mixed with lemonade, it is called *Russ*.

Franziskaner Hefe-Weißbier

Paulanerbräu wheat beer

Chinesischer Turm, a popular beer garden *(see p284)*

Where To Drink

Beer, the Bavarian national drink, is also called "liquid nourishment". It is drunk anywhere and everywhere throughout the region – from the most exclusive restaurants down to the smallest food stalls. However, beer is best enjoyed in beer gardens or at the inns of breweries.

Almost every town in Bavaria holds a folk festival at least once a year that involves a lot of beer-drinking.

Where to Eat and Drink

Munich

Old Town (South)

Augustinerbräu €
Regional Map 3 A2
Neuhauser Straße 27, 80331
Tel *(089) 23183257*
Very good beer, historical rooms
and a courtyard beer garden –
right in the pedestrian zone.

Bratwurstherzl €
Regional Map 3 C3
Dreifaltigkeitsplatz 1, 80331
Tel *(089) 295113* **Closed** *Sun*
Traditional tavern that serves
marvellous Bratwurst sausages,
especially those from Nürnberg.

Fraunhofer €
Regional Map 3 B4
Fraunhoferstraße 9, 80469
Tel *(089) 266460*
Pleasant inn with historic interiors
serving Bavarian cuisine, including
meat and vegetarian options.
There is a theatre in the backyard.

**Nürnberger Bratwurst Glöckl
am Dom** €
Regional Map 3 B2
Frauenplatz 9, 80331
Tel *(089) 2919450*
This traditional eatery specializes
in Nürnberg sausages. Try the
hearty noodle soups and
delicious ox filet.

Prinz Myshkin €
Vegetarian Map 3 B2
Hackenstraße 2, 80331
Tel *(089) 265596*
This arty restaurant is great for a
break from the otherwise meaty
Bavarian fare.

Ratskeller €
Regional Map 3 B/C2
Marienplatz 8, 80331
Tel *(089) 2199890*

Charming townhall cellar where
top-quality food is served.
Popular among tourists.

Riva Tal €
Italian Map 3 C3
Tal 44, 80331
Tel *(089) 220240*
Pizzeria and espresso bar with
cheerful service and an
appetizing variety of dishes.

Der Pschorr €
Regional Map 3 B3
Viktualienmarkt 15, 80331
Tel *(089) 442383940*
This tavern in the Schrannenhalle
(market hall) offers beer from the
Pschorr brewery and local fare.

Sushi Sano €
Japanese Map 3 A2
Josephspitalstraße 4, 80331
Tel *(089) 267490*
Authentic noodle dishes and
delicious sushi. Available in
takeaway boxes for picnickers.

Tegernseer Tal €
Regional Map 3 C2
Tal 8, 80331
Tel *(089) 222626*
This very central, light-filled beer
hall serves traditional fish and
meat dishes and the excellent
Alpine Tegernseer beer.

Weisses Bräuhaus €
Regional Map 3 C2
Tal 7, 80331
Tel *(089) 2901380*
Popular beer hall, whose liver
dumplings with *Sauerkraut* are
absolutely divine.

Café Glockenspiel €€
International Map 3 B2
Marienplatz 28, 80331
Tel *(089) 264256*
This café-cum-restaurant has a
lovely terrace with expansive views.

Price Guide

Prices are based on a three-course meal
per person, with a half-bottle of house
wine, including tax and service.

€ under €40
€€ €40 to €80
€€€ over €80

Try the seafood glass noodles, or
the salmon on saffron spinach.

Fisch Poseidon €€
Seafood Map 3 C3
Westenriederstraße 13, 80331
Tel *(089) 299296* **Closed** *Sun*
This eatery, with its convenient
self-service counter, serves
phenomenal Bouillabaisse and
superb seafood spaghetti.

Hofer – der Stadtwirt €€
Regional Map 3 C2
Burgstraße 5, 80331
Tel *(089) 24210444* **Closed** *Sun*
This restaurant in a historic
townhouse serves superbly
prepared Bavarian and Austrian
cuisine under Gothic vaults.

Weinhaus Neuner €€€
International Map 3 A2
Herzogspitalstraße 8, 80331
Tel *(089) 2603954* **Closed** *Sun*
Munich's oldest wine tavern
serves food strongly influenced
by the Mediterranean. Don't miss
the roasted vegetables and the
biting Bavarian mustard sauces.

Old Town (North)

Pfälzer Residenz Weinstube €
Regional Map 3 C1
Residenzstraße 1, 80333
Tel *(089) 225628*
This restaurant is set in a large
hall and several rooms in the
Baroque wing of the Residenz. It
specialises in the best Palatinate
dishes and wines.

Tavernetta €
Italian Map 4 D2
Hildegardstraße 9, 80539
Tel *(089) 21269424* **Closed** *Sun*
Fantastic food, with tasty
antipasti such as the courgette
and wild mushroom carpaccio.
Complete the meal with a
mean tiramisu.

Zum Franziskaner €
Regional Map 3 C1
Residenzstraße 9, 80333
Tel *(089) 2318120*
Venerable brewery and
restaurant that serves superb
meatloaf and a fine selection
of beer. Famous for its white
sausages, a local speciality.

Traditional dining room at Zum Franziskaner

Magnificent dining room overlooking the opera house at Spatenhaus an der Oper

Garden Restaurant €€
International **Map** 3 B2
Promenadeplatz 2–6, 80333
Tel *(089) 2120993*
Fine dining in this roof-garden restaurant at the luxury hotel, Bayerischer Hof. Mediterranean and South German dishes.

Kulisse €€
International **Map** 4 D2
Maximilianstraße 26, 80539
Tel *(089) 294728*
This Kammerspiele theatre restaurant offers a wide choice of Asian and Bavarian dishes.

Pageou €€
French **Map** 3 B1
Kardinal-Faulhaber-Straße 10, 80333
Tel *(089) 24231310* **Closed** *Sun*
Michelin-starred TV chef Ali Güngörmüş serves exquisite cuisine prepared with basic but excellent ingredients.

Refettorio €€
Italian **Map** 4 D1
Marstallplatz 3, 80539
Tel *(089) 22801680*
At this colourful Italian restaurant near the theatres and opera there's outdoor dining in summer.

> ### DK Choice
>
> **Spatenhaus an der Oper** €€
> Regional **Map** 3 C3
> *Residenzstraße 12, 80333*
> **Tel** *(089) 2907060*
> A bastion of Bavarian food. The lower floor is less formal with heartier food, while the more opulent upper floor offers opera house views.

Le Stollberg €€
French **Map** 4 D2
Stollbergstraße 2, 80539
Tel *(089) 24243450* **Closed** *Sun*
Bright and airy restaurant, serving delicious French-Bavarian cuisine. The menu is seafood focussed.

Tambosi €€
International **Map** 3 C1
Odeonsplatz 18, 80539
Tel *(089) 298322*
At Munich's oldest continously operating café (since 1775), guests sit at tables on the sidewalk or in the lively beer garden.

Austernkeller €€€
French **Map** 4 D2
Stollbergstraße 11, 80539
Tel *(089) 298787*
Long-established seafood eatery with expertise in cooking oysters. The dishes are inspired by what's best in the market.

Bar München €€€
International **Map** 4 D2
Maximilianstraße 36, 80539
Tel *(089) 229090*
This contemporary eatery offers good seafood, cocktails and a frequently changing menu.

Dallmayr €€€
International **Map** 3 C2
Dienerstraße 14, 80331
Tel *(089) 2135 100* **Closed** *Mon & Sun*
A Munich institution, famous for its coffee-house and patisserie, Dallmayr is attached to an elegant restaurant. Don't miss the zucchini ratatouille with lobster.

Friendly waiting staff display some of the offerings at Augustinerbräu

Matsuhisa Munich €€€
International **Map** 3 C2
Neuturmstraße 1, 80331
Tel *(089) 290980*
The restaurant of the Mandarin Oriental hotel offers fine dining with a Japanese touch, with prices to match.

Restaurant Pfistermühle €€€
International **Map** 3 C3
Pfisterstraße 4, 80331
Tel *(089) 23703865* **Closed** *Sun*
Small regionally-inspired menu that often changes. The dishes are served under 16th-century arches. Reservations are essential.

Trader Vic's €€€
Polynesian **Map** 3 B1
Promenadeplatz 2–6, 80333
Tel *(089) 2120995*
Celebrities including Michael Jackson and Tina Turner have eaten at this Munich hotspot. Creative food and cocktails are served in a great atmosphere.

Around the Isar

Crêperie Bernard et Bernard €
French **Map** 4 E3
Innere Wiener Straße 1, 81667
Tel *(089) 4801173*
A wide range of crêpes and galettes are on offer at this long-standing venue in Haidhausen.

Königsquelle €
Regional **Map** 3 C3
Baaderplatz 2, 80469
Tel *(089) 220071*
The whiskey bar here is a big draw for many, but the schnitzels are also highly-recommended. Friendly ambience.

> ### DK Choice
>
> **Wirtshaus in der Au** €
> Regional **Map** 4 D4
> *Lilienstraße 51, 81669*
> **Tel** *(089) 4481400*
> This lovely old Bavarian inn is a master in experimental dumplings – spinach and beetroot anyone? Come late September, it runs a dumpling restaurant – the Münchner Knödelei – on the Oktoberfest grounds. It also hosts cookery courses, and has published a dumpling cookbook.

Café Dukatz €€
Mediterranean **Map** 3 B1
St-Anna-Straße 11, 80538
Tel *(089) 23032444*
This splendid café serves delicious French tarts, cakes, cookies and fine coffee. A choice of savoury options is also available.

For more information on types of restaurants *see page 271*

Lavish interiors of the well-reviewed Königshof

Gandl €€
International **Map** 4 D1
St-Anna-Straße 1, 80538
Tel *(089) 29162525*
Part of the Opera Hotel *(see p267)*, Gandl serves Italian food during the day and French dishes at night.

Goa €€
Indian **Map** 4 D2
Thierschstraße 8, 80538
Tel *(089) 21111789*
This popular eatery offers a variety of chicken and lamb curries, kormas and koftas.

Nero €€
Italian **Map** 3 C3
Rumfordstraße 34, 80469
Tel *(089) 21019060*
Hip pizzeria with incredible thin-crust creations, as well as fresh antipasti, pasta and steaks.

Käfer-Schänke €€€
International **Map** 4 F1
Prinzregentenstraße 73, 81675
Tel *(089) 4168247* **Closed** *Sun*
This is an eminent gourmet destination for politicians and business high-flyers. The intimate dining room has a contemporary decor with a feel of traditional Bavaria.

University District

Alter Simpl €
Regional **Map** 2 D4
Türkenstraße 57, 80799
Tel *(089) 2723083*
This traditional Bavarian pub with dark wood panelling, a former Bohemian venue, has been an institution in the Maxvorstadt since 1903. It serves inexpensive hearty dishes, such as *Schweinbraten* (roast pork with gravy) or *Jägerschnitzel* (veal or pork cutlet in breadcrumbs).

Atzinger €
Regional **Map** 2 D4
Schellingstraße 9, 80799
Tel *(089) 282880*
This student tavern has been refurbished, but still exudes old-fashioned charm. The menu features well-prepared, affordable dishes.

Bei Mario €
Italian **Map** 2 D4
Adalbertstraße 15, 80799
Tel *(089) 2800460*
The oldest pizzeria in town, opened in 1966 by Mario Gargiulo from Sorrento – "the man who brought the pizza to Munich". The menu also includes pasta options.

Café Puck €
International **Map** 2 D5
Türkenstraße 33, 80799
Tel *(089) 2802280*
This well-established eatery in Maxvorstadt offers breakfast (to 7pm), lunch and dinner. Book ahead for weekend evenings.

Reitschule €€
Mediterranean **Map** 2 F4
Königinstrae 34, 80802
Tel *(089) 3888760*
Long-standing, chic bistro, named after its views of a riding school. Serves a small selection of daily specials.

Museums District

Rilano No. 6 €€
International **Map** 3 A1
Ottostraße 6, 80333
Tel *(089) 5491300* **Closed** *Sun*
Well-crafted gourmet food and expert wine pairings. The restaurant is housed in a Renaissance building.

Schmock €€
Jewish/Middle Eastern **Map** 1 B5
Augustenstraße 52, 80333
Tel *(089) 52350535*
Diners at Schmock (the Yiddish word for "clumsy fellow") enjoy kosher food and wines in an elegant, minimalist restaurant. The daily changing menu features Israeli and Arab specialities.

Königshof €€€
Gourmet **Map** 3 A2
Karlsplatz 25, 80335
Tel *(089) 551360* **Closed** *Sun*
Elegant 19th-century parlour ambience. The seasonal dishes are created by a Michelin-starred chef.

Further Afield

Augustiner Bräustuben €
Regional
Landsberger Straße 19, 80339
Tel *(089) 507047*
This jovial beer hall serves great dumplings with duck, pork knuckle or mushroom sauce, on benches.

Bella Italia €
Italian **Map** 4 F4
Weißenburger Straße 2 / Rosenheimer Platz, 81667
Tel *(089) 486179*
No-frills, good-value Italian fare – pasta, pizza, meat and seafood dishes – served in a friendly atmosphere.

Heimat Food €
German
Schwanthalerstraße 149, 80339
Tel *(089) 52033180*
At this restaurant with a beer hall and garden, star chef Karl Ederer serves excellent German dishes prepared with the best regional, seasonal products.

Leonrod €
Middle Eastern
Leonrodstraße 45, 80636
Tel *(089) 1235661*
Share a large mezze platter for a taste of different items, or try the Sunday brunch buffet, at this outstanding Lebanese joint.

Acetaia €€
Italian
Nymphenburger Straße 215, 80639
Tel *(089) 13929077*
This discreet yet stylish restaurant offers a menu based entirely around balsamic vinegar. Great soup and ravioli.

Marais Soir €€
French **Map** 4 E4
Schwanthalerstraße 131, 80339
Tel *(089) 62838663* **Closed** *Sun*
An excellent restaurant that crosses Mediterranean and French haute cuisines, which can be enjoyed with wines from a short list of European classics.

Ruffini €€
Eco-café
Orffstraße 22–24, 80637
Tel *(089) 161160* **Closed** *Mon*
Café and patisserie serving regional Italian fare since 1978. The menu is chalked up on a blackboard and changes daily. Brunch is popular, as is enjoying a glass of beer or wine on the upstairs terrace in summer.

Acquarello €€€
International
Mühlbaurstraße 36, 81677
Tel *(089) 4704848*
Savour Michelin-starred Italian food with fresh ingredients at this kitsch restaurant. Think fig-and-foie gras tortellini, or lettuce soup with buffalo mozzarella foam.

Smart, striking decor at Tantris, a Munich institution for over 30 years

Tantris €€€
Gourmet
Johann-Fichte-Straße 7, 80805
Tel *(089) 3619590* **Closed** *Mon & Sun*
Tantris has been offering delicious and contemporary food since the 1970s. The restaurant boasts two Michelin stars. Booking essential.

Upper Bavaria (North)

DACHAU: Altes Schulhaus €
International **Map** D4
Pfarrstraße 13, 85221
Tel *(08131) 2797360*
This venue in the heart of the old town offers good fare and cultural events like theatre and live music.

EICHSTÄTT: Tartufo €
Italian **Map** C2
Marktplatz 22, 85072
Tel *(08421) 7070360* **Closed** *Mon*
Widely thought to be the best Italian restaurant in town, Tartufo serves excellent pizza, pasta, meat and seafood dishes.

DK Choice

EICHSTÄTT: Domherrnhof €€
German **Map** C2
Domplatz 5, 85072
Tel *(08421) 6126* **Closed** *Mon*
High-class Bavarian cooking with local, seasonal products – asparagus in spring, berries in summer, venison and mushrooms in autumn and seafood in winter. Try Ochsenbackerl in Burgundy sauce, braised vegetables and stuffed pasta. Vegetarian meals too.

ERDING: Gaststätte Kreuzeder €
Regional **Map** D3
Münchener Straße 56, 85435
Tel *(08122) 5377*
Traditional inn with quick, helpful service. Portions are large, and the dumplings are to die for.

FREISING: Zur alten Schießstätte €
Regional **Map** D3
Dr-von-Daller-Straße 1–3, 85356
Tel *(08161) 532441*
This restaurant has a 16th-century vaulted beer cellar and garden. Part of the Dorint hotel, it serves top-notch food.

HAINDLFING (NEAR FREISING):
Gasthaus Landbrecht €€
Regional **Map** D3
Freisinger Straße 1, 85354
Tel *(08167) 8926* **Closed** *Mon & Tue*
Regional gourmet specials and seasonal dishes are served here. The classic tiled stoves add to the rustic ambience.

Ruffini café and patisserie with its roof terrace illuminated at night

INGOLSTADT: Taj Mahal €
Indian **Map** D2
Beckerstraße 11, 85049
Tel *(0841) 9814618*
Deliciously prepared north Indian food. The restaurant is known for its bargain lunch buffets.

INGOLSTADT: Daniel €€
German **Map** D2
Roseneckstraße 1, 85049
Tel *(0841) 35272* **Closed** *Mon*
For unbeatably good traditional food, visit this cult pub and brewery.

INGOLSTADT: Hummel €€
International **Map** D2
Feldkirchener Straße 69, 85055
Tel *(0841) 954530* **Closed** *Sun*
A friendly restaurant with a contemporary decor. Lovely potato soup and smoked trout.

INGOLSTADT: Restaurant
im Stadttheater €€
International **Map** D2
Schloßlände 1, 85049
Tel *(0841) 935150* **Closed** *Mon*
Impressive city views and a seasonal menu, which includes an array of interesting dishes.

NEUBURG AN DER DONAU:
Elisenlounge €
International **Map** C2
Elisenplatz 16, 86633
Tel *(08431) 6497099*
Fancy cocktails and a good range of simple dishes and delicious steaks. Elisenlounge is a fun place to unwind in the evenings.

NEUBURG AN DER DONAU:
Zum Klosterbräu €€
Regional **Map** C2
Kirchplatz 1, 86633
Tel *(08431) 67750*
Perfect Sunday roasts. The restaurant offers a choice of dining rooms for a more intimate feel.

For more information on types of restaurants *see page 271*

Lower Bavaria

DEGGENDORF: Gasthof Höttl €
Regional   **Map** F2
Luitpoldplatz 22, 94469
Tel *(0991) 3719960*
Höttl boasts an authentic regional menu in a rustic inn with an idyllic beer garden. The atmosphere is warm and cosy.

GRAFENAU: Säumerhof €€
Regional   **Map** G2
Steinberg 32, 94481
Tel *(08552) 408990*   **Closed** *Mon*
Pleasant restaurant that is part of a country hotel. The menu includes hearty local specialities made with ingredients from nearby farms, rivers and forests.

LANDSHUT: Restaurant Augustiner an der St Martinskirche €
Bavarian   **Map** E3
Kirchgasse 251, 84028
Tel *(0871) 4305624*
This is the perfect place to enjoy a down-to-earth Bavarian meal. All the classics are on the menu, and the beer is one of the most popular in the whole of Bavaria.

LANDSHUT: Restaurant Stegfellner €€
Bavarian   **Map** E3
Altstadt 71, 84028
Tel *(0871) 28015*
A family-run restaurant serving regional and seasonal cuisine with a fresh new take on classics. The restaurant is supplied by its own butcher's shop, delicatessen and fine wine cellar.

DK Choice

LANDSHUT: Schloss Schönbrunn €€
Regional   **Map** E3
Schönbrunn 1, 84036
Tel *(0871) 95220*
This magnificent 17th-century Bavarian castle is a must-visit. Specialities include grilled fish, crunchy pork knuckle, roast chicken and spare ribs.

PASSAU: Café Diwan €
Regional   **Map** G3
Nibelungenplatz 1, 94032
Tel *(0851) 4903280*
Take the lift to the top floor of this modern block to enjoy amazing views of Passau as you munch a well-crafted light lunch.

PASSAU: Heilig Geist €
Regional   **Map** G3
Heiliggeistgasse 4, 94032
Tel *(0851) 2607*   **Closed** *Wed*
This rustic winebar specializes in Bavarian food. Good local fish, pork and beef.

PASSAU: Kreuzweis €€
International   **Map** G3
Pfaffengasse 7, 94032
Tel *(0851) 20939075*
Off a narrow Old Town street, this tavern offers a variety of fish and meat. The eel and bison are superb.

PASSAU: Pizzeria Gallo Nero €€
Italian   **Map** G3
Schmiedgasse 5, 94032
Tel *(0851) 36315*   **Closed** *Tue*
Good pizzas and pastas, but also amazing grilled fish. The mussels in white wine are delicious. Cosy decor and friendly service.

STRAUBING: Seethaler €
German   **Map** E2
Theresienplatz 9, 94315
Tel *(09421) 93950*   **Closed** *Sun*
The Seethaler is a traditional inn that dates back to 1462. It serves excellent regional food, beer and wine.

STRAUBING: Unterm Rain €
Regional   **Map** E2
Unterm Rain 15, 94315
Tel *(09421) 22772*
Cheerful, modest restaurant and beer garden. Generous portions of pan-German specialities such as *Schnitzel* and sausages feature.

STRAUBING: Bella Vista €€
Italian   **Map** E2
Krankenhausgasse 19, 94315
Tel *(09421) 89154*   **Closed** *Mon & Sun*
Wonderful food and outstanding wines since 1996. The Sicilian swordfish is the house special.

Upper Bavaria (East)

ALTÖTTING: Graminger Weissbräu €
Regional   **Map** F4
Graming 79, 84503
Tel *(08671) 96140*   **Closed** *Thu*
This old brewery has a lovely beer garden in the shade of chestnut trees. Delightful Bavarian cooking.

ASCHAU IM CHIEMGAU: Residenz Heinz Winkler €€€
Gourmet   **Map** E5
Kirchplatz 13, 83229
Tel *(08052) 17990*
Splendid Baroque restaurant Heinz Winkler is named after the chef who took over in 1989. It has since become a fabulous gourmet pilgrimage destination. Booking is advised.

BAD REICHENHALL: St Aegidi-Keller €€
Italian   **Map** F5
Poststaße 20, 83435
Tel *(08651) 65333*
This 12th-century wine cellar and restaurant is replete with Gothic, wooden furniture.

BERCHTESGADEN: Gasthof Neuhaus €
Regional   **Map** F5
Marktplatz 1, 83471
Tel *(08652) 9799280*
Hearty traditional Bavarian fare and delectable cool beers in a centrally located Gasthof that has been in operation since 1576.

Beautiful outdoor seating with mountain views at Heinz Winkler, Aschau Im Chiemgau

Key to Price Guide *see page 276*

Elegant seating at Herrenhaus, popular for its classic Bavarian dishes

DK Choice

BERCHTESGADEN:
Restaurant 3'60° €€€
International Map F5
Hintereck 1, 83471
Tel *(08652) 97550*
As the name suggests, this
restaurant offers spectacular
views of the mountains. Part
of the InterContinental Resort
Berchtesgaden, Restaurant 3'60°
has a gorgeous open kitchen
where local ingredients come
together to form exquisite
dishes. The menu includes a
range of rich, meaty dishes, but
there are several excellent
healthy options as well. One of
the finest eateries among the
resort dining options.

BURGHAUSEN: Chillis €
International Map F4
Marktler Straße 5, 84489
Tel *(08677) 877550*
Chillis offers a broad selection
of dishes: Asian, Indian, steaks,
fresh fish, baked potatoes and
much more. Bargain lunches are
also available.

BURGHAUSEN:
Bayerische Alm €€
Regional Map F4
Robert-Koch-Straße 211, 84489
Tel *(08677) 9820*
Appetizing varieties of duck,
lamb, venison and trout can be
found at Bayerische Alm. Dine to
stunning Alpine and castle views.

CHIEMSEE:
Westernacher €€
Regional Map E4
Seestrasse 115, 83209
Tel *(08051) 4722*
This lakeside restaurant has an
eclectic menu, ranging from

traditional Bavarian to vegan wok
dishes. There's also a fabulous
beer garden in summer.

SEEON: Rauchhaus €€
Regional Map E4
Altenmarkter Straße 6, 83370
Tel *(08624) 829922* **Closed** *Tue*
Opened in 1679, this
atmospheric place, with its
aged interior, serves high-end
Bavarian food. Must try dishes
include the steak, ox, and
zander.

TITTMONING: Florianistube €
Regional Map F4
Stadtplatz 44, 84529
Tel *(08683) 1032* **Closed** *Thu*
Modest country restaurant
with a range of local dishes.
Cheerful, relaxed service and
great value meals.

WAGING AM SEE:
Strandkurhaus €
Regional Map F4
Am See 1, 83329
Tel *(08681) 47900* **Closed** *Mon & Tue*
This charming lakeside
restaurant has a traditional
Bavarian decor. It offers a menu
of fish and local specialities.
Strandkurhaus only uses organic
ingredients in the dishes.

WASSERBURG AM INN:
Herrenhaus €€
Regional Map E4
Herrengasse 17, 83512
Tel *(08071) 5971170* **Closed** *Mon
& Sun*
Herrenhaus, an exciting venture
run by four young restaurateurs,
offers a daily Bavarian seasonal
menu including some great
French specials. The fresh pike
in mushroom sauce and the
salmon in Riesling are
remarkably good.

Upper Bavaria
(South)

ANDECHS:
Klostergasthof Andechs €
German Map C4
Bergstraße 9, 82346
Tel *(08152) 93090*
A local monastery provides the
ingredients at this traditional
restaurant, where there are
beautiful valley views and
fantastic beer. Note that it only
accepts cash.

BAD TÖLZ:
Altes Fährhaus €€
Regional Map D5
An der Isarlust 1, 83646
Tel *(08041) 6030* **Closed** *Mon–Wed*
Located in a picturesque
setting, this old ferry house
sits on the banks of the River
Isar. The menu includes dishes
made using fresh local fish and
game. Don't miss the venison in
sloe gin.

BAYRISCHZELL:
Restaurant Seeberg €€€
International Map D5
Osterhofen 1, 83735
Tel *(08023) 906533*
Michelin-starred Restaurant
Seeberg offers gorgeous Alpine
views and serves international
gourmet dishes with a hint
of the Bavarian.

GARMISCH-PARTENKIRCHEN:
Colosseo €€
Italian Map C5
Klammstraße 7, 82467
Tel *(08821) 52809*
The well-sized pizzas and
delicious pasta choices ensure
that this Italian place is always
busy. It is located right above
a supermarket.

For more information on types of restaurants *see page 271*

Tasteful and colourful interiors of Restaurant Vaun, Garmisch-Partenkirchen

GARMISCH-PARTENKIRCHEN:
Restaurant Vaun   €€
German   **Map** C5
Zugspitzstraße 2, 82647
Tel *(08821) 7308187*   **Closed** *Sun*
Try the delicious lime and
sweet potato soup, or the
smoked cod with radish.
Evening reservations are
recommended.

DK Choice

GARMISCH-PARTENKIRCHEN:
Caspar B   €€€
International   **Map** C5
Burgstraße 97, 82467
Tel *(08821) 7020*
This charming restaurant is
part of the Grand Hotel
Sonnenbichl, a venerable Art
Nouveau hotel. It has an
inventive regional menu that
allows guests to choose from
delicious renditions of
Bavarian favourites.

GARMISCH-PARTENKIRCHEN:
Best Western Hotel   €
International   **Map** C5
Mühlstraße 22, 82467
Tel *(08821) 7040*
Magnificent Alpine vistas and
assorted dishes. A less formal bar
serves rustic Bavarian specials.

GARMISCH-PARTENKIRCHEN:
Reindl's   €€
French   **Map** C5
Bahnhofstraße 15, 82467
Tel *(08821) 943870*
The gourmet options at this
elegant restaurant include
marinated wild salmon, veal
kidneys, rack of lamb and venison.
Fantastic wine list too.

MITTENWALD:
Das Marktrestaurant   €€
German   **Map** C5
Dekan-Karl-Platz 21, 82481
Tel *(08823) 9269595*   **Closed** *Mon*
Chef Andreas Hillejahn offers
traditional German cooking
prepared with regional products
and a modern touch.

OBERAMMERGAU:
Zauberstub'n   €
German   **Map** C5
Ettaler Straße 58, 82487
Tel *(08822) 4683*   **Closed** *Tue*
Traditional food and a magic show
makes Zauberstub'n a must-visit
when travelling with kids.

OBERAMMERGAU: Böld   €€
Regional   **Map** C5
König-Ludwig-Straße 10, 82487
Tel *(08822) 9120*
This restaurant is in a classic
chalet-style hotel with a rustic
decor. Regional recipes.

TEGERNSEE: Lieberhof   €
Regional   **Map** D5
Neureuthstraße 52, 83684
Tel *(08022) 4163*
Lieberhof is a chalet-style
restaurant with several Alpine
dining rooms. It serves hearty
Bavarian food.

The Allgäu

FÜSSEN: Michelangelo   €
Italian   **Map** B5
Reichenstraße 33, 87629
Tel *(08362) 924924*   **Closed** *Mon*
Find giant pizzas and home-
made pasta in this bright
restaurant. Lovely terrace.

DK Choice

FÜSSEN: Hotel
Luitpoldpark   €€
Gourmet   **Map** B5
Bahnhofstraße 1–3, 87629
Tel *(08362) 9040*
Relish the many dining
options at this magnificent
hotel: from classic Bavarian
to Mexican and international
cuisines. There is also a lovely
Viennese-style café.

FÜSSEN-HOPFEN AM SEE:
Hotel am Hopfensee   €
Regional   **Map** B5
Uferstraße 10, 87629
Tel *(08362) 50570*
The fish from the Hopfen lake is a
speciality here. Stunning views of
the Alps.

KEMPTEN: Peterhof   €
Italian   **Map** B5
Salzstraße 1, 87435
Tel *(0831) 52440*
This contemporary Italian
restaurant in the Peterhof Hotel
serves all the local favourites.

DK Choice

KEMPTEN:
Rendez-vous à Quiberon   €€
French   **Map** B5
Rathausstraße 2, 87435
Tel *(0831) 5208116*   **Closed** *Sun*
& Mon
One of the best French
restaurants in Bavaria, this
eatery is well-priced and
serves light bites. Don't miss
the smoked salmon and radish
galette (a type of crêpe) –
the perfect summer meal.

LINDAU: Alte Post €€
German Map A5
Fischergasse 3, 88131
Tel *(08382) 93460*
This inn serves schnitzels,
boiled beef and home-made
Maultaschen. The cobbled terrace
is a gorgeous summer venue.

**LINDAU: Hotel Engel – Bier-
und Weinstube** €€
Regional Map A5
Schafgasse 4, 88131
Tel *(08382) 5240*
Very cosy with excellent regional
specialities – from *Käsespätzle*
(pasta and cheese) to *Felchen*
(white fish) from Lake Constance.

LINDAU: Zum Sünfzen €€
Regional Map A5
Maximilianstraße 1, 88131
Tel *(08382) 5865*
Charming 14th-century place.
Fresh Bodensee fish is the
speciality, and the venison
is also excellent. The outdoor
seating is great for people
watching.

LINDAU: Villino €€€
Regional Map A5
Mittenbuch 6, 88131
Tel *(08382) 93450*
This is an exquisite family-run
hotel and restaurant with an
idyllic garden and terrace. The
gourmet dishes have their roots
in Asia and Italy.

MEMMINGEN: Da Enzo €
Italian Map B4
Rennweg 14, 87700
Tel *(08331) 2585*
Da Enzo is a modest Italian
eatery that offers a few Balkan
dishes as well. Friendly service
and good prices.

Typical Japanese seating area at Kon-Ya
Sushi, Neu-Ulm

**OBERSTDORF:
Restaurant Café Allgäu** €
Regional Map B6
Pfarrstraße 10, 87561
Tel *(08322) 809657* **Closed** *Mon*
Typical Bavarian food and
hospitality. The *Schnitzel* with
seasoned spinach and cheese
is wonderful.

OBERSTDORF: Exquisit €€
Regional Map B6
Lorettostraße 20, 87561
Tel *(08322) 96330*
Country-style restaurant with a
range of choices from gourmet
to low-calorie. Splendid lawns
and views.

Northern Swabia

AUGSBURG: Drei Königinnen €
Regional Map C3
Meister-Veits-Gäßchen 32, 86152
Tel *(0821) 158405*
Highly recommended for its
bustling beer garden. Good variety
of *Spätzle* and pasta dishes.

AUGSBURG: Berghof €€
Regional Map C3
Bergstraße 12, 86199
Tel *(0821) 9984322*
Simple German food, such as
grilled chicken with roasted
potatoes, cooked to perfection.

DK Choice

AUGSBURG: Manyo €€
Japanese Map C3
Schertlinstaße 12a, 86159
Tel *(0821) 571119* **Closed** *Tue*
Thanks to eateries like this,
Japanese food is now an
integral part of the urban
gastronomic landscape. Much
showmanship accompanies the
teppanyaki while it is being
prepared at your table. The food
is first-class and this lovely place
is deservedly popular.

AUGSBURG: Ratskeller €€
Regional Map C3
Rathausplatz 2, 86150
Tel *(0821) 31988238*
This vaulted cellar restaurant
serves hearty Bavarian dishes,
and there's live jazz music on
Monday nights.

AUGSBURG: August €€€
International Map C3
Johannes-Haag-Straße 14, 86152
Tel *(0821) 35279* **Closed** *Sun–Tue*
This two Michelin-starred establish-
ment offers seasonal cooking with
an emphasis on light flavours. The
preparation is atypical of Bavaria.

AUGSBURG: Die Ecke €€€
Regional Map C3
Elias-Holl-Platz 2, 86150
Tel *(0821) 510600*
Die Ecke is a sophisticated
Swabian-Bavarian restaurant
which specialises in catfish.
Choices here include catfish
baked with horseradish, and
rice with Riesling sauce.
Impeccable service.

**AUGSBURG: Magnolia
Restaurant im Glaspalast** €€€
International Map C3
Beim Glaspalast 1, 86153
Tel *(0821) 3199999*
Part of a wave of creative gourmet
places in Germany, Magnolia
Restaurant im Glaspalast is a
strong Michelin contender.

DILLINGEN: Storchennest €€
Regional Map B3
Demleitnerstraße 6, 89407
Tel *(09071) 4569* **Closed** *Mon & Tue*
The dining room at Storchennest
centres around an attractive tiled
stove. There are daily specials, a
six-course menu and great wines
on offer here.

FRIEDBERG: Jedermanns €
International Map C3
Aichacher Straße 7, 86316
Tel *(0821) 2678596* **Closed** *Mon*
Jedermanns offers a good choice
of international dishes with a
Mediterranean touch. The focus
is on meat, but vegetarian
options are available too.

NEU-ULM: Kon-Ya Sushi €€
Japanese Map A3
Ludwigstraße 11, 89231
Tel *(0731) 4061511*
With its Japanese minimalist
decor and light dishes, Kon-Ya
Sushi is a real delight. The sushi
is creative and delicious.

NEU-ULM: Landhof Meinl €€
Regional Map A3
Marbacher Straße 4, 89233
Tel *(0731) 70520* **Closed** *Mon–Sat
lunch*
Landhof Meinl is a pleasant
restaurant that serves Swabian
food, fresh fish and chicken
salads. Traditional rustic decor
meets modern elegance.

**NÖRDLINGEN:
Meyers Keller** €€€
International Map B2
Marienhöhe 8, 86720
Tel *(09081) 4493* **Closed** *Mon & Tue*
An elegant restaurant, where
quality ingredients are used to
produce creativite dishes. A
choice of interesting seasonal
specials are on offer, with seating
at lovely garden tables.

For more information on types of restaurants *see page 271*

Pubs, Cafés and Bars in Munich

Munich abounds with bars, cafés, clubs and, of course, hugely popular pubs and beer gardens. There is something for every taste. Places where people go to drink coffee or beer, to have a snack or simply to socialize informally are mostly concentrated in the city centre and in Schwabing. Even in the more outlying districts an abundance of pleasant cafés and bars can be found. Many food shops also set aside a corner for eaters and drinkers.

Pubs and Beer Gardens

The features most typical of Munich, and seen everywhere in the city, are spacious pubs often fronted by gardens shaded by chestnut or linden trees. These pubs serve beer from the local breweries as well as generous helpings of good Bavarian food. Waitresses dressed in the traditional *Dirndl* wind their way among the tables and sometimes there is an oompah band playing a repertoire of folk melodies.

Munich's most famous pub is the **Hofbräuhaus**, which today is filled with more American and Japanese tourists than local drinkers. Seated on wooden benches at large tables arranged in spacious rooms, raucous crowds of drinkers enjoy their favourite tipple as they sing along with and sway in time to the Bavarian music.

Almost equally renowned is the **Augustiner Gaststätte**, which also has a restaurant. The interior is decorated in late 19th-century style, and has a very pleasant courtyard surrounded by arcades, which induce the desire to linger for as long as possible.

Munich's next most famous pubs are the **Löwenbräukeller** and the **Donisl**. In the latter, with its old-style furnishings, authentic Bavarian folk music is also played. The city's finest beer garden is the **Chinesischer Turm** in the Englischer Garten, where there are a total of 6,000 seats for its international clientele and stalls offering traditional beer garden food.

Many beer gardens allow drinkers to bring their own food.

Beer is best served straight from the barrel. A popular type of beer is *Helles*, a light lager beer. Also widely drunk is *Radler*, beer to which lemonade is added (see p274).

Cafés, Bars and Bistros

A great variety of different establishments come under the name of "café". They include traditional coffee shops, where people go for *Kaffee und Kuchen* (coffee and cake), the coffee helping to wash down a large pastry or slice of cake. Two such coffee shops are the old-world **Café Kreutzkamm**, which moved here from Dresden after World War II (it is known for its chocolates, **Dresdner Stollen** and pyramidal cakes), and the **Café Luitpold**, which tempts with its equally excellent cakes and chocolates.

A real oasis of peace – a commodity highly valued by the citizens of Munich – is the **Café am Beethovenplatz**. Time passes more slowly here, and the gentle classical music seems to make the coffee smell and taste better than elsewhere. The atmosphere of the **Kaffeehaus Altschwabing** takes you back to the turn of the 19th and 20th centuries. Thomas Mann and other writers once enjoyed the strong coffee that is served here.

Another type of café is a place offering hot and cold food and a range of soft and alcoholic drinks. The atmosphere is more like that of a bar or bistro. These bar-type cafés are the centre of the social life of Munich. They range from somewhere to

go to grab a sandwich or drop in for a coffee or beer, to pretentious places where high society meets. There are also gay and lesbian bars, such as **Café Glück** and **Café Nil**, and bars for businessmen, as well as bars for connoisseurs of wine or whisky and for pool players.

Many bars serve large and delicious breakfasts and lunches. Others specialize in ice cream. Many, including the **Roxy**, are open until late at night.

A feature once unique to Munich was Kunstpark Ost, an extensive leisure park near the Eastern Station. Some of its famous clubs, discos (such as the hugely popular Babylon) restaurants and bars (such as the much-frequented Bongo Bar) still exist or have moved to the Optimol Area.

Takeaways (Takeouts)

Numerous booths and stalls selling takeaway food are to be seen in the streets of Munich, particularly in the main shopping areas of the Old Town and Schwabing, as well as in pedestrian subways and at railway stations.

The traditional takeaways are those of the well-known international fast-food chains. There are also many takeaway pizza, sausage, baguette and kebab houses. The **Nordsee** restaurant offers delicious freshly made sandwiches with herring, fried fish or crab salad, and the **Wienerwald** restaurants sell chicken cooked in every possible way.

There are also takeaway stands in almost all butcher's shops, where pre-packaged lunch dishes in aluminium trays are sold. The food sold in Munich's most renowned delicatessens, the **Dallmayr** and **Käfer**, is excellent, although the prices can seem a little high (see p287). A good alternative is the hot food stalls to be found in **Viktualienmarkt** (see p68).

ll

285

DIRECTORY

Pubs

Andechser am Dom
Weinstr. 7A. **Map** 3 B2, 6
D3. **Tel** 24 29 29 20.

Augustinerbräu
Neuhauser Str. 27. **Map** 3
A2, 5 B3. **Tel** 23 18 32 57.

Augustiner-Keller
Arnulfstr. 52. **Tel** 59 43 93.

Chinesischer Turm
Englischer Garten 3.
Map 2 F4. **Tel** 38 38 730.

Donisl
Weinstr. 1.
Map 3 B2, 6 D3.
Tel 22 01 84.

Franziskaner-Garten
Friedenspromenade 45.
Tel 43 00 996.

Hofbräuhaus
Am Platzl 9. **Map** 3 C2, 6
E3. **Tel** 29 01 36 100.

Hofbräukeller
Innere Wiener Straße 19.
Tel 45 99 250.

Kaisergarten
Kaiserstr. 34.
Tel 34 02 02 03.

Löwenbräukeller
Nymphenburger Str. 2.
Tel 54 72 66 90.

Paulaner Bräuhaus
Kapuzinerplatz 5.
Tel 54 46 110.

**Seehaus im
Englischen Garten**
Kleinhesselohe 3.
Tel 38 16 130.

Tassilogarten
Auerfeldstr. 18.
Tel 44 80 022.

Wintergarten
Elisabethplatz 4b. **Map** 2
D3. **Tel** 27 37 31 34.

Zum Flaucher
Isarauen 8.
Tel 72 32 677.

Cafés and Bars

Atzinger
Schellingstr. 9. **Map** 2 D4.
Tel 28 28 80.

Bar Centrale
Ledererstr. 23. **Map** 3 C2.
Tel 22 37 62.

Le Bouchon
Thierschstr. 65. **Tel** 23 70
83 55. **Map** 4 E2.

Café Altschwabing
Schellingstr. 56.
Map 1 C4. **Tel** 27 31 022.

**Café am
Beethovenplatz**
Goethestr. 51.
Tel 54 40 43 48.

Café Glück
Palmstr. 4. **Map** 3 A5.
Tel 20 11 673.

Café Glyptothek
Königsplatz 3. **Map** 1 B5.
Tel 28 80 83 80.

Café Kreutzkamm
Maffeistr. 4. **Map** 3 B2.
Tel 99 35 570.

Café Luitpold
Brienner Str. 11.
Map 6 D1. **Tel** 24 28 750.

Café Nil
Han-Sachs-Straße 2.
Map 3 B4. **Tel** 23 88 95 95.

Café Puck
Türkenstr. 33. **Map** 2 D4.
Tel 28 02 280.

Café Reitschule
Königinstr. 34.
Tel 38 88 760.

Café Rischart
Marienplatz 18. **Map** 3 B2,
6 D3. **Tel** 23 17 00 320.

Café Wienerplatz
Innere Wienerstr. 48.
Map 4 E3. **Tel** 44 89 494.

Cyclo Restaurant Bar
Theresienstr. 70. **Map** 1
C5. **Tel** 28 80 83 90.

ELLA im Lenbachhaus
Luisenstr. 33.
Map 1 B5.
Tel 700 88 177.

Jazzbar Vogler
Rumfordstr. 17. **Map** 3 C3,
6 D5. **Tel** 29 46 62.

Kaffee Giesing
Tegernseer Landstr. 96.
Tel 62 00 03 57.

Kao Kao
Tulbeckstr. 9. **Tel** 50 54 00.

Königsquelle
Baaderplatz 2.
Map 3 C3, 6 E5.
Tel 22 00 71.

Mauz
Leopoldstr. 20.
Map 2 E3.
Tel 38 32 99 47.

Niederlassung
Buttermelcherstr. 6
Map 3 C3, 6 D5.
Tel 32 60 03 07.

Pacific Times
Baaderstr. 28. **Map** 3 C3,
6 E5. **Tel** 20 23 94 70.

Pusser's
Falkenturmstr. 9.
Tel 22 05 00.

Roxy
Leopoldstr. 48.
Map 2 E3.
Tel 34 92 92.

Sarfati
Kazmairstr. 28.
Tel 45 23 78 67.

Schumann's
Odeonsplatz 6.
Map 4 D2, 6 F3.
Tel 22 90 60.

**Spatenhaus an
der Oper**
Residenzstr. 12.
Map 3 C2, 6 D2.
Tel 29 07 060.

**Stadtcafé im
Stadtmuseum**
St-Jakobs-Platz 1.
Map 3 B2, 5 C4.
Tel 26 69 49.

Tambosi
Odeonsplatz 18.
Map 3 C1, 6 D1.
Tel 29 83 22.

Tresznjewski
Theresienstr. 72.
Map 1 C5. **Tel** 28 23 49.

**Westend Café
and Restaurant**
Anglerstraße 32.
Tel 50 83 41.

Wiener's Kaffeebar
Neuturmstr. 2.
Map 3 C2. **Tel** 29 25 69.

Takeaways

Der Kleine Chinese
Tal 28. **Map** 3 C2, 6 D3.
Tel 29 16 35 36.

Nordsee
Viktualienmarkt 10.
Map 3 B3.
Leopolstr. 82.
Map 2 E3.

Thai Magie
Blumenstr. 1.
Map 3 B3, 5 B5.

Wienerwald
Leonrodstraße 91.
Tel 20 20 94 71.

SHOPS AND MARKETS

Retailers in the Bavarian Alps, who cater both to the tourist trade and to the more affluent Bavarians, offer for sale virtually everything from the finest luxury goods to local arts and crafts. A particularly ubiquitous Bavarian speciality is sports, hiking and mountaineering equipment, which is displayed for sale in many outlets. There is also a large market for anything in traditional Bavarian style, from beer steins to *Lederhosen* to fine glass and porcelain. An enjoyable way of spending a few hours is to stroll among the stalls in the spa towns selling locally made items. In complete contrast, Munich, one of the most sophisticated European cities, has some very exclusive shops.

A lavish display of cheese and wine at one of Munich's elegant delicatessens

Where to Shop

Shops ranging from department stores to boutiques to souvenir shops can be found in Munich. All larger towns in the Bavarian Alps have a shopping district, usually pedestrianized.

Also popular are the out-of-town superstores, which attract large numbers of shoppers because of their competitive prices and ease of parking for drivers.

Shopping in Munich

Munich's main shopping district is the pedestrianized area of the Old Town around Neuhauser Straße, Kaufingerstraße and the Marienplatz area, where stores and shops of major European retailers are located. This whole area probably has the largest daily turnover in the whole of Germany, and one of the best stores is Ludwig Beck am Rathauseck on Marienplatz.

Around Theatinerstraße, Maximilianstraße and Brienner Straße are exclusive clothes shops such as Versace, Gucci, Escada and Donna Karan, whose prices are out of the reach of most tourists. In the famous Schwabing district, particularly in the area between Amalienstraße, Schellingstraße and Türkenstraße, exclusive boutiques and tasteful second-hand shops can be found, as well as many bookshops (selling both new and second-hand books) and a selection of antique shops.

Opening Hours

Shops are legally permitted to open from 6am to 8pm from Monday to Saturday. In practice, most food shops open between 7am and 9am (bakeries opening the earliest), and close at 8pm. Other shops, including supermarkets, are usually open from 9am to 8pm.

Small shops, particularly in more out-of-the-way places, often close for lunch then stay open until 6pm. At railway stations in large towns it is possible to buy food and beverages until 11pm, even on Sunday. Petrol (gas) stations that also sell food and drink are often open until late at night; some open 24 hours.

Paying

Cash is still king in Germany, though most shops take credit and debit cards, with Visa and MasterCard the most widely accepted plastic. The exceptions might be small boutiques and second-hand shops. Avoid paying small amounts with foreign cards as they can attract some hefty charges.

The showroom of a shop specializing in Nymphenburg porcelain

The Hugendubel bookshop on Karlsplatz sells books on art, architecture and design

Food and Drink

As elsewhere in Europe, food shops have largely been taken over by retail chains. The exceptions are small butcher's shops, bakeries and confectioners. Fruit and vegetables are still sold in markets, with the most famous being the Viktualienmarkt *(see p68)*. There are fine delicatessens to be found in **Dallmayr** and **Käfer**.

Gifts and Souvenirs

It is virtually impossible to leave the Bavarian Alps without a souvenir beer mug or a decorative bottle of beer. Particularly suitable as presents are bottles of the local spirits and drinks pres-ented in stoneware bottles, often bearing the portrait of the legendary king Ludwig II.

Tourist resorts are full of souvenir shops. Besides the folksy kitsch there is some good-quality woodcarving, pottery, painted glass and porcelain. Stylized Bavarian costume and accessories made of natural materials are ubiquitous. Conforming to the latest fashion, they are often quite attractive. The best place in Munich for gifts of this type are the **Trach-ten Angermaier** and **Lodenfrey**.

Specialist Shops

Munich boasts several specialist shops of renown. **SportScheck**

is an outstanding sports shop. The best bookshops include **Geobuch**, which specializes in maps and guidebooks, **Hugendubel** and **L. Werner**, which sell books on art, architecture and design. **Hieber Lindberg** specializes in musical instruments and literature. Lovers of fine antique furniture and paintings should visit the famous antique shop **Bernheimer Fine Old Masters**. Or for something more unique, visit the department "store of the senses", **Ludwig Beck**, a luxury emporium on Marienplatz with seven floors devoted to fashion, beauty and lifestyle.

A shop in Augsburg selling pottery and basketware

What to Buy in the Bavarian Alps

Besides a vast range of German and European goods, the visitor to the Bavarian Alps can also purchase local products that make perfect gifts and souvenirs. They are usually inspired by folk traditions, and their artistic merit varies greatly. The sheer quantity of gift-shop kitsch is quite overwhelming, particularly items related to beer-drinking ceremonies and devotional art. However, it is also perfectly possible to find good-quality, tasteful and authentic examples of the arts and crafts of the Bavarian Alps.

Porcelain
Dolls dressed in Bavarian costume make good presents for collectors.

Folk Art

Many shops selling folk art can be found in the Bavarian Alps. As well as wood carvings, for which Oberammergau is particularly renowned, good-quality paintings and antique items of often striking simplicity are available.

Copy of a Baroque statue

S HUBERTUS

Painting on Glass
Painting on glass is a widespread craft in the region, with the main centre being Murnau. Subjects are usually images of saints or religious scenes depicted in a naïve style.

A 19th-century votive painting

Flat tin figure painted in enamels

Glass and Ceramics

Workshops in the Bavarian Forest region are famous for their glassware (Waldglas). They produce both classic functional items, as well as modern art glass in a range of novel shapes and colours. Folk ceramics include painted pottery and stoneware that characteristically has the colour of grey granite. One of the most prominent centres of ceramic production is Dießen.

Stoneware snuff box

Plate with the Bavarian coat of arms

Bavarian Waldglas

Nymphenburg Porcelain
Usually of a high artistic quality and relatively expensive, hand-painted figurines like this are produced by the famous Nymphenburg porcelain factory.

Regional Costume

Bavarian folk costume is attractive and practical in its modern-day form. Usually made of high-quality wool, linen or leather, it gives protection from cold or heat. Recommended for children are the famous Bavarian Lederhosen, which are practically dirt-proof but also machine washable should the need arise.

A soft woollen *Janker*

The famous Bavarian *Lederhosen*

A decorated leather belt

Leather Goods

Bavaria is renowned for its high-quality leather goods. The material is surprisingly soft, and the items often have a crude but deliberate old-worldliness about them.

Knitted woollen socks

Decorated hunter's bag

Leather shoes in Bavarian folk style

Silver necklace with colourful pendants

Embroidered tasselled shawl

Drinking Accessories

Among the articles most widely produced by the souvenir industry are beer mugs of all descriptions, ranging from simple stoneware vessels to highly colourful mugs decorated with paintings or reliefs and fitted with pewter lids. They are characteristic of Bavaria and make good gifts.

A finely decorated beer bottle

Collectors' Items

Both beer-related artifacts as well as antique beer mugs and lids are valued items that are bought and sold by international antiques collectors.

Beer mug with the coat of arms of Bavaria

Antique beer mug lids

OUTDOOR ACTIVITIES AND SPECIALIST HOLIDAYS

Munich and Bavaria offer an amazing variety of sporting and leisure activities. Throughout the year active holiday makers head to the region's hills, forests, mountains, rivers and lakes. Various national organisations can provide details on a particular sport and have regional contacts. Cycling, running and Nordic walking rank highest among the area's most popular sports, while snow sports in the easily accessible Alps keep visitors active during the winter months. During the summer this nation of outdoor lovers flock to the lakes and rivers to swim and sail.

Hiking amongst the spectacular scenery of the Mittenwald Alps

Walking and Hiking

Walking and hiking is a popular activity for both young and old. Numerous paths are well preserved and marked along rivers, through forests and up mountains. Every town has its own rambling or hiking club. The foothills of the Alps provide some easy terrain for gentle hikes but the higher you go the more demanding it becomes. Family-friendly trails on higher terrain involve taking a cable car up the mountain. Lenggries near Bad Tölz (see p224) is good for family trails and the **Deutscher Wanderverband** (German hiking Club) and **Deutscher Volkssportverband** (German Sports Federation) can provide further details. For information on guided walking tours contact the local tourist office in each area, or the **Verband Deutscher Gebirgs/und Wandervereine** (German Mountaineering and Hiking Club) who will direct you to smaller regional clubs. The

Kneipp-Verein München or **DAV Summit Club** also have regional clubs who organize hikes and tours.

Cycling

Because cycling is such a popular sport the cycling paths here are excellent. Bikes can be hired in towns and cities throughout the region and there are plenty of bike stands available. Munich is Germany's most bike-friendly city with some 700 km (435 miles) of cycle paths. Cycling is one of the best ways to take in the beautiful scenery between Lake Constance and Bad Tölz, and to see the towns and villages of Dachau, Passau, Wasserburg and Bayerischzell. Contact the **Allgemeiner Deutscher Fahrrad Club** (German Cycling Federation) in Munich for details and tips before planning a trip. They provide tour plans, maps, route suggestions and tips for all over Bavaria. They also give advice on the latest regulations for transporting bikes on trains, which is possible with prior booking and a nominal fee.

Watersports

If you are in this part of Germany in the warmer months, you simply have to take a dip in one of the lakes or rivers. The water is very clean, safe and totally refreshing. The Strandbad, indicating the beach area, is visible in every lakeside town and denotes free public bathing. Excellent sailing conditions can be found on Starnberger See, Ammersee, Chiemsee and Bodensee, and the area near Lindau is famous for its yacht building wharves and sailing clubs. Contact the **Deutscher Segler-Verband** (German Sailing Club) for information on locations, regulations and possibilities of sailing or hiring a boat. To hire or sail a yacht, you will need a current licence showing your sailing abilities and competence. Sailing on Bodensee requires a special Bodensee license. Canoeing is also popular on the Bavarian

Cyclists touring the beautiful Bavarian countryside

rivers, especially on the Altmühl between Gunzenhausen and Kelheim or at Loisach near Garmisch, where the World Wild Water Championships have been held. For further details contact the **Deutscher Kanu-Verband** (German Canoe Federation) or the **Bayerischer Kanu-Verband** (Bavarian Club).

Canoeing on the popular Altmühl River in Bavaria

Skiing in one of the many resorts in the Bavarian Alps

Skiing and Mountain Sports

Garmisch-Partenkirchen (see p221) is Germany's best ski area, others include Reit im Winkl (see p205). There are plenty of hotels and ski hire companies in these areas and the relevant tourist office can provide further details as well as maps of ski lifts and runs. Skiing is also possible at other Alpine peaks in Lenggries or near Berchtesgaden. Langlauf (cross-country skiing) can be pursued on many well-kept routes, marked clearly in towns at the foothills of the Alps. Other enquiries can be directed to the **Deutscher Skiverband** (German Ski Association) who can give tips and suggestions for planned visits or tours. **Sporthaus Schuster** or **SportScheck**, two large sports department stores in Munich centre, have travel offices that organise skiing trips and can advise on the hiring of equipment and on ski packages available.

Climbing is also big in the mountainous areas of Bavaria. Whichever level you are you can find your match here,

especially in the Allgäu. If you want to hire a guide to accompany you contact the **Verband Deutscher Berg-und Skiführer** (Association of German Mountain and Ski Guides). Climbing walls such as **High-East Kletterhalle** in Munich offer an indoor alternative, or a chance to practice. Further information regarding climbing, or rock formations for example, can be obtained from the German Alpine Association, **Deutscher Alpenverein** (DAV).

Golf and Tennis

Both golf and tennis are popular sports and a number of towns in Bavaria have excellent clubs, golf courses and tennis courts. To be allowed on a golf course, you will need to prove proficiency and pre-book, so plan well ahead. Contact the **Deutscher Golf Verband** for information on courses and rules. Many Bavarian golf enthusiasts head out to the course at Wallgau (see p222) where the conditions are good and the scenery beautiful. Tegernsee and the Bayerischer Wald have a few golf-oriented hotels with special packages.

The **Deutscher Tennis Bund** has information on local tennis clubs and the procedure for booking a court. Some hotels are geared towards tennis, such as the Tannenhof in Allgäu, the Espacio in Garmisch or the Ödhof Sporthotel in the Bayerischer Wald.

National Parks

The **Bayerischer Wald** is Germany's oldest National Park (see p191). Lying in the area behind Grafenau, it has a wealth of unusual wildlife, forests and rivers. Tours operate within the protected area of the park, but the surrounding forest area has camping sites and hiking routes where you will find people mountain biking and Nordic walking. An all-round outdoor fitness sport that involves walking at a brisk pace with the support of sticks, Nordic walking has increased in popularity over the past decade. For further details contact the **Nordic Walking Association**.

Summer is a good time to visit the park when you can see more of the wildlife and fauna indigenous to the woods and waterways. Be sure to stick to the marked paths and to observe the safety and conservation regulations.

Nordic walking in a peaceful park in Lower Bavaria

Camping and Caravanning

Large numbers of Germans head south in the summer months from June to August to the sites at lakesides, forests and riversides throughout Bavaria. The Germans love the great outdoors and for this nation of campers, sites are plentiful and well organised. The majority of families who camp are in caravans, while tents are favoured by the younger generation and foreign tourists. Pitching a tent is highly regulated and allowed only at official camping grounds. The majority of camp sites are privately owned, friendly and offer plenty of extras. Washing facilities are always available, and some sites have shops, a bar and restaurants. Well established and more expensive sites tend to offer group activities, especially for children, and electricity. Campfires are popular and sites have designated areas for them. For details and advice on camping and caravanning, contact the **Deutscher Camping Club** and also **ADAC – Camping Welt**, which offers discounted camping for card holders.

Historic and Scenic Routes

Travelling along the Alpenstraße, the German Alpine Road, is a great way to experience the best of the scenery in the Bavarian Alps. The road was built in 1927 and connects Lake Constance with Berchtesgaden.

Family fun at one of Germany's well-equipped camp sites

The fairy-tale Linderhof Palace, one of many of Ludwig II's residences

At its highest point the road reaches 1,735m (5,690 ft) and is ranked among the world's best scenic routes. Travel between Lindau, Füssen, Oberammergau, Garmisch, Kochel, Chiemsee, Tegernsee, Bad Reichenhall and on to Berchtesgaden. On route take in Linderhof Palace and Neuschwanstein Castle, the Zugspitze mountain in Garmisch and the salt mines at Berchtesgaden. For more information visit www.alpenstrasse.de.

The Romantische Straße, Romantic Road, also runs through Bavaria between Würzburg and Füssen, with old medieval town centres, churches and the rivers Lech and Danube on route. The Alpine foothills form part of the scenery, as does the Ammersee lake, moors and the Allgäu mountains. There is plenty to enjoy from thermal baths, to tobbogan runs, nature conservation areas and hiking paths. Visit www.romantischestrasse.de for further details.

Steingaden is the point where these two routes intersect and has a health resort as well as a famous pilgrimage and ecclesiastical treasures.

Specialist Holidays

For the best information on German language courses in Bavaria, contact the **Goethe Institut** in London or Munich. The institute runs its own courses for various lengths of time and from beginner to advanced levels. It can also recommend reasonably priced accommodation. There are many other language schools in Munich, which can be found online. Augsburg for example has a small but good language school.

Cooking holidays are increasing in popularity and Bavaria has a few to offer. The holidays give you the opportunity to learn the basics of gourmet cuisine from masterchefs in their own restaurants. Students stay in the hotel itself and partake in cookery lessons on site. Two great places to visit in Bavaria are Heinz Winkler's Residenz hotel and restaurant at Aschau near Chiemsee (see p280) and André Greul's Fürstenhof in Landshut.

Although Bavaria is famous for its beer rather than its wines, cookery courses also teach you about great German wines. The stretch of Lake Constance behind Lindau produces several varieties of white wine. The best way to experience the country's offerings is to visit a wine festival, held in many towns towards the end of the summer. For more information visit **Deutsches Weininstitut**.

Another popular holiday activity is horse-riding and a weekend of riding can be arranged with one of several private equestrian centres. The **Deutsche Reiterliche Vereinigung** can provide information on centres throughout the region.

Spa Vacations

"Wellness" is a term cropping up in many hotels in the countryside. This denotes a spa area for health and wellbeing. It is now possible to take a weekend, or longer stay, to enjoy a variety of spa treatments including water therapy, swimming, steam rooms, massages, exercise routines and walks in the healthy, fresh air. **Deutscher Heilbäderverband**, the German association of spas, has information on hotel spas and packages throughout the region. Towns with the word "Bad" preceding the name signifies a spa town. Here you are guaranteed a longstanding tradition of health regimes, rest and relaxation as well as thermal baths. The **Therme Erding** is a paradise of thermal baths, just outside Munich. It is Europe's largest thermal bath complex, accommodating 4,000 visitors each day for both day and lodging packages.

DIRECTORY

General Sporting Information

Deutscher Olympischer Sportbund
Otto-Fleck-Schneise 12, 60528, Frankfurt am Main.
Tel 069 67000. **w** dosb.de

Walking and Hiking

DAV Summit Club
Am Perlacher Forst 186, 81545, München.
Tel 089 642400.
w dav-summit-club.de

Deutscher Volks-sportverband
Fabrikstraße 8, 84053, Altötting. **Tel** 08671 96310.
w dvv-wandern.de

Deutscher Wanderverband
Wilhelmshöher Allee 157–159, 34121, Kassel.
Tel 0561 938730.
w wanderverband.de

Kneipp-Verein München
Prinz-Ludwig-Straße 6, 80333, München. **Tel** 089 283780. **w** kneipp verein-muenchen.de

Cycling

Allgemeiner Deutscher Fahrrad Club (ADFC)
Platenstraße 4.
Tel 089 773429.
w adfc-muenchen.de

Watersports

Bayerischer Kanu-Verband
Georg-Brauchle-Ring 93, 80992, München.
Tel 089 15702418.
w kanu-bayern.de

Deutscher Kanu-Verband
Bertaallee 8, 47055, Duisburg.
Tel 0203 997590.
w kanu.de

Deutscher Segler-Verband
Gründgensstr. 18, 22309, Hamburg. **Tel** 040 6320090. **w** dsv.org

Skiing and Mountain Sports

Deutscher Alpenverein (DAV)
Von Kahr Straße 2–4, 80997, München.
Tel 089 140030.
w alpenverein.de

Deutscher Skiverband
Am Erwin-Himmelseherplatz, Hubertusstraße 1, 82152, Planegg. **Tel** 089 857900.
w ski-online.de

High-East Kletterhalle
Sonnenallee 2, 85551, Kirchheim/Heimstetten.
Tel 089 92794796.
w high-east.de

Sporthaus Schuster
w sport-schuster.de

SportScheck
w sportscheck.com

Verband Deutscher Berg-und Skiführer (VDBS)
Fraunhoferstraße 4, 82377, Penzberg. **Tel** 08856 9360913.
w bergfuehrer-verband.de

Golf and Tennis

Deutscher Golf Verband
Kreuzberger Ring 64, 65189, Wiesbaden.
Tel 0611 990200.
w golf.de/dgv

Deutscher Tennis Bund
Hallerstraße 89, 20149, Hamburg. **Tel** 040 411780.
w dtb-tennis.de

National Parks

Naturpark Bayerischer Wald
Infozentrum 3, 94227, Zwiesel.
Tel 09922 802480.
w naturpark-bayer-wald.de

Nordic Walking Association
w nordicportal.net

Camping and Caravanning

ADAC – Camping Welt
Hansastraße 19, Munich.
Tel 089 76760.
w adac.de/camping

Deutscher Camping Club
Mandlstraße 28, 80802, München.
Tel 089 3801420.
w camping-club.de

Specialist Holidays

Goethe-Institut
Dachauer Straße 122, 80637, München.
Tel 089 159210.
w goethe.de
(UK) 50 Princes Gate, Exhibition Road, London, SW7 2PH.
Tel 020 7596 4000.

Deutsche Reiterliche Vereinigung
Freiherr von Langen-Straße 13, 48231, Warendorf.
Tel 02581 63620.
w pferd-aktuell.de

Deutsches Weininstitut
Gutenbergplatz 3–5, 55116, Mainz.
Tel 06131 28290.
w deutscheweine.de

Spa Vacations

Deutscher Heilbäderverband
Charlottenstraße 13, 10969, Berlin.
Tel 030 2463 6920.
w deutscher-heilbaederverband.de

Therme Erding
Thermenallee 1, 85435, Erding.
Tel 08122 5500.
w therme-erding.de

SURVIVAL
GUIDE

PRACTICAL INFORMATION

Famous for breathtaking scenery and historic monuments, the Bavarian Alps are the most popular destination for visitors to Germany. Like Munich, the regional capital, the mountains are well equipped to receive tourists. Hotels and catering facilities, as well as excellent road, rail and urban transport, make travelling in the area a pleasure. The Bavarians are generally friendly and hospitable, although communication may be difficult in smaller towns and villages unless you speak German. This, however, is not a problem in cosmopolitan Munich.

When to Go

Bavaria is a year-round destination, but the weather is finest from June to September. Prices tend to be lower in spring (March to May) and early autumn (October), and the crowds smaller. Ski resorts operate from late November to sometime in March, depending on the snow. The Bavarian calendar is packed with cultural and sporting events, religious celebrations and festivals (see pp34–5). Entertainment listings can be found in the local press, including free newspapers.

Travel Safety

Visitors can get up-to-date travel safety information from the Foreign and Commonwealth Office in the UK, the State Department in the US and the Department of Foreign Affairs and Trade in Australia.

Visas and Passports

Controls at the borders with Austria and the Czech Republic are practically non-existent, but sporadic passport checks have been imposed.

Citizens of the EU, the US, Canada, Australia and New Zealand do not require a visa if their stay does not exceed three months. Visitors from India and South Africa will need a visa. While citizens of most EU countries do not require a passport to enter Germany, a national ID card with photograph is necessary. Visa requirements may change so check details before you travel.

Customs

German regulations prohibit the import of firearms, drugs, animals and exotic plants that are under special protection.

Customs limits for travellers from outside the EU are 200 cigarettes, or 250g (9oz) of tobacco or 50 cigars, one litre of spirits or two litres of wine. Items for personal use, provided they are not in quantities intended for trade, are not subject to customs duty.

CityTourCard

Tourist Information

Tourist information bureaux are generally found in town centres, main squares and near railway stations. In Munich, the best source of information is **Tourismusamt München**, with big offices in the main train station and on Marienplatz, and an excellent website. In small towns, the town hall (Rathaus) or civic centre (Gemeindever Waltung) does the job; in spa resorts try the Resort Administration Kurverwaltung. Tourist offices provide free town maps and brochures on local attractions, and can also assist in finding accommodation.

Admission Prices

Many museums and historic monuments offer reductions on admission prices; ask at tourist offices or hotel reception desks.

A good discount option is the CityTour-Card, valid for one or three days for one person or for groups of up to five people (prices range from €11.90 to €72.90). The card offers reduced entry (of up to 50 per cent) to more than 60 attractions including museums, theatres and sight-seeing tours, plus free use of public transport throughout the city. The card is sold at all suburban railway stations, underground stations, tram and bus stations, and selected hotels – look for the CityTourCard logo.

The Bavarian Palaces Department offers a 14-day pass for €22 that gives entry to over 40 of Bavaria's royal palaces, including the Munich Residenz and all the castles except Hohenschwangau. The pass can be bought at any palace ticket desk or ordered online at www.schloesser.bayern.de before travel (allow time for posting).

Tourists in the formal gardens at Schloss Nymphenburg in Munich

◄ Cattle-drive celebration on Konigssee lake, Berchtesgadener Land, Upper Bavaria

Opening Hours

Most museums are open from 10am to 5pm or 6pm, Tuesday to Sunday. Bavarian state-run museums, exhibition halls and castles are usually free on Sundays. In Munich, major museums such as the three Pinakothekes and the Bayerisches Nationalmuseum charge just €1 on Sundays. Churches are generally open to visitors from 8am until evening worship, but visitors should note that sightseeing is frowned upon during services.

Large department stores are generally open from 9am or 9:30am to 8pm, Monday to Saturday. Large supermarkets operate from 8am to 8 pm or 9pm, Monday to Saturday. Smaller retailers tend to keep shorter hours, opening from 10am to 6pm or 7pm.

Etiquette and Smoking

Bavarians tend to dress conservatively. For business or social events such as the opera or theatre, and to get into Munich's upmarket nightclubs, smart dress is recommended.

A firm handshake is the standard greeting among both men and women, but also be prepared for a hug or kiss on the cheek. On the telephone, start by giving your last name both when calling and picking up. In smaller shops, it is good form to greet the owner with *"Grüß Gott"* and bid *"Auf Wiedersehen"* when you leave.

Try to be on time for both formal and informal occasions; arriving late is considered impolite. At large parties, things may be more relaxed.

In Bavaria, smoking is prohibited in all public buildings as well as restaurants, bars, cafés and beer tents. Individuals can be fined if they flout the law. In supermarkets and bars, the minimum age is 16 for purchasing cigarettes and alcohol (beer and wine), and 18 for stronger drinks such as whiskey and spirits.

Public Conveniences

In Bavaria's larger towns and cities, public conveniences can be found without too much difficulty and are usually clean. Look for the familiar male and female silhouettes, or the letter D *(Damen)* for Ladies and H *(Herren)* for Gentlemen. Department stores are equipped with restrooms, although a small payment of €0.20 to €0.50 should be given to the on-site attendant. Toilets are also provided in restaurants and cafés, but if you are not a customer you should ask permission to use the facilities. Other options in town include shopping centres, public institutions and hotels, and coin-operated, self-cleaning cubicles. On the road, seek out car parks and petrol (gas) stations.

Taxes and Tipping

Most goods sold in Germany are subject to 19 per cent value-added tax *(Mehrwertsteuer)*. Books, foodstuffs, artworks and concert tickets are taxed at 7 per cent VAT. Visitors from countries outside the EU are entitled to a tax refund on the price of any non-edible goods. Shops with the Tax Free sign will issue a certificate or Tax-Free cheque when the value of the items purchased exceeds a specified total, which is usually around €50. You will need to show your passport before a certificate or cheque can be issued. When going through Customs on leaving Germany, the certificate must be stamped. Visitors may be asked to show the goods, which must be in their original packaging, unopened and unused. The tax is either refunded at the border or mailed to you.

By law, sales tax and a service charge are included in restaurant bills. However, it is customary to add a small tip

Tax-free shopping

of 5 to 10 per cent if you are happy with the service. Give the tip directly to your waiter, rather than leaving it on the table, and state the total amount including the tip. If you do not expect change back, say *"es stimmt so"*. For taxi drivers, add 5 percent or round up to the nearest euro on small transactions. Porters are usually given €1 per bag.

Tourist enjoying the sights in bustling Marienplatz

Travellers with Special Needs

Almost all modern public buildings have ramps and other access facilities for disabled visitors, and designated parking spaces are common. Seats on public transport near doors are to be vacated on demand for mobility-impaired, pregnant or senior travellers.

For the sight-impaired, pavements are equipped with a grooved guidance system, and speakers at pedestrian crossings beep at a higher frequency when it is safe to cross. Train timetables are published in Braille.

The Munich tourist office has a useful guide, in print or for download, with details on public transport, hotels and restaurants with facilities for disabled visitors. Munich's Association for the Disabled (**Sozialverband VDK**) offers a series of guides, but only in German.

Travelling with Children

Munich has plenty to charm younger visitors – a large zoo and aquarium, playgrounds and sprawling parks, child-friendly museums and even a regular circus. Bavaria-Filmstadt is as much a theme park as a working film studio (see p147). Cycling the city on safe, dedicated paths is always an adventure (see pp312–13). A wide range of discounts are available for children so be sure to ask about them.

Public attitudes towards children are fairly tolerant, but parents are expected to keep their children in line. A few hotels have a no-children policy, so check before you book. Many restaurants have high chairs and children's menus. Hotels should have a list of babysitters on hand. Facilities for changing nappies are generally limited to department stores, major museums and train stations. Breast-feeding in public is accepted if done discreetly.

When driving children must be restrained in suitable car seats, which car rental firms will provide for a small fee.

Children enjoying the Olympiapark in Munich

Senior Travellers

Older travellers (usually from age 65) are entitled to many discounts on public transport, admission to museums and other attractions. Proof of age is sometimes needed at ticket counters, and a passport or ID card is sufficient.

Munich's public transport system offers monthly passes to travellers aged 60 and older (check the website for current prices). Another great deal is the *BahnCard 50* from German rail service **Deutsche Bahn**, giving 50 per cent off of tickets and available to seniors at half-price.

Diversity flags flying in the New Town Hall, Munich

Gay and Lesbian Travellers

While homosexuality is legal in Germany, Bavaria's gay (Schwule) and lesbian (Lesben) community keeps a low profile. The exception is Munich, where the scene is vibrant. The city's Christopher Street Day celebrations in July are nearly as lively as those in Berlin and Cologne. Nuremberg and Regensburg have modest communities of their own. Even in more conservative rural areas attitudes are changing, and openly gay couples should have no problems.

Travelling on a Budget

While Bavaria is not a bargain destination, travellers under 18 years, and in some cases under 20, can benefit from many reductions to tourist attractions, exhibitions and cultural events – just ask about discounts at the ticket counter. Holders of an International Student Identity Card (ISIC) are entitled to reductions at many cultural institutions.

The growing ranks of youth hostel-hotels offer a surprisingly high level of comfort and facilities for a bargain price (see p264). Europe-wide train passes InterRail (for EU citizens only) and Eurail (for non-EU) offer significant savings for a month's travel, while the German national *BahnCard* gives reductions of 25 or 50 per cent for a full year (see p308). Lift services from a carpool company like **Citynetz Mitfahrzentrale** are a good-value travel option.

Time

Germany is on Central European Time (GMT plus one hour). Clocks move forward one hour on the last Sunday in March and back on the last Sunday in October.

Electricity

The electrical system in Germany provides 230-volt, 50 Hz AC. Electric plugs are of the two-pin European type. UK 230-volt appliances can be plugged into German sockets with an adaptor. US 110-volt appliances will have to be used with a transformer. All hotels in Germany have 230-volt sockets for razors and hair-dryers. Certain appliances run on both 110-volt and 230-volt current.

Responsible Tourism

In Germany, Bavaria has long been at the forefront of green travel and environmental trends. Recycling of rubbish is highly organized and most households have access to bins for sorting packaging, paper and glass. Larger communal recycling banks for various colours of glass bottles and jars, paper and card, and tin cans are dotted around town centres. Packages marked with the green triangle (Grüner Punkt) are recyclable.

Logo of Deutscher Alpenverein, a provider of tourist information

In larger towns there are organic (bio) supermarkets and farmers' markets, and organic produce features on many restaurant menus.

Eco-friendly tours are readily available; leading operators include **Viabono** and **Forum Anders Reisen**, who promote responsible travel to protected nature areas. Package tours feature outdoor activities, organic meals and spa treatments with a view to minimizing their environmental impact. Accommodation often includes like-minded hotels, guesthouses, B&Bs and holiday rentals. Hike-and-sleep holidays can be booked through **Deutscher Alpenverein**, where overnight stops range from sparse mountain huts to plush lodges.

Since 2003, certified EU eco-hotels must meet strict standards for the use of renewable energy, lower energy and water consumption, and waste reduction. Bavaria's regional tourist offices (see p296) carry an up-to-date list.

DIRECTORY

Tourist Information

Bayern Tourismus Marketing Gmbh
Arabellastraße 17,
Munich. **Tel** (089) 21 23
970. W **bayern.by**

Neues Rathaus
Marienplatz, Munich.
Tel (089) 233 965 00.
W **muenchen.de**

Tourismusamt München
Sendlinger Str. 1, Munich.
Map 3 B2, 6 D3.
Tel (089) 23 39 65 00.
W **muenchen.de**

Tourismusverband Allgäu/Bayerisch Schwaben
Schießgrabenstr. 14,
Augsburg. **Tel** (0821) 45
04 010. W **allgaeu.info**
W **bayerisch-schwaben.de**

Tourismus Oberbayern München
Balanstr. 57, Munich.
Tel (089) 90 77 82 70.
W **oberbayern.de**

Tourismusverband Ostbayern
Im Gewerbepark D 02/
D 04, Regensburg.
Tel (0941) 58 53 90.
W **ostbayern-tourismus.de**
(in German)

Tourist Information Hauptbahnhof
Bahnhofplatz 2, Munich.
Tel (089) 23 39 65 00.
W **muenchen.de**

Travel Safety

Australia Department of Foreign Affairs and Trade
W **dfat.gov.au**
W **smartraveller.gov.au**

UK Foreign and Commonwealth Office
W **gov.uk/foreign-travel-advice**

US Department of State
W **travel.state.gov**

Travellers with Special Needs

Club Behinderter und ihrer Freunde
Johann-Fichte-Str. 12,
Munich.
Tel (089) 35 68 808.
W **cbf-muenchen.de**

Vdk Bayern
Schellingstr. 31, Munich.
Map 2 D4.
Tel (089) 211 170.
W **vdk.de/bayern**

Travelling with Children

Bavaria Tourism
Arabellastraße 17,
Munich. **Tel** (089) 21 23
970. W **bavaria.by**

Senior Travellers

Deutsche Bahn
Tel 0180 6 99 66 33.
W **bahn.de**

Skan-Club 60 plus
(Travel club for senior travellers)
Gehrenkamp 1,Isenbüttel.
Tel (0800) 12 31 919.
W **seniorenreisen.de**
(in German)

Gay and Lesbian Travellers

International Gay & Lesbian Travel Association
1201 NE 26th St, Fort
Lauderdale, USA.
Tel (01) 954 630 1637.
W **iglta.org**

Travelling on a Budget

Euraide, Hauptbahnhof
Bahnhofplatz 2, Munich.
Tel (089) 59 38 89.
W **euraide.de**

mitfahren.de
Rossertstr. 8, Frankfurt
am Main.
Tel (069) 38 09 77 796.
W **mitfahren.de**

Railway Passes
W **bahn.de/bahncard**
W **interrail.net**
W **eurail.com**

Responsible Tourism

Deutscher Alpenverein
W **alpenverein.de**
(in German)

Forum Anders Reisen
Wippertstr. 2, Freiburg.
Tel (0761) 40 12 69 90.
W **forumanders reisen.de**

Viabono
Hauptstr. 230, Rösrath
Tel (02205) 91 98 350.
W **viabono.de**

Embassies

Australia
Wallstr. 76–79,
10179 Berlin.
Tel (030) 880 08 80.

Canada
Embassy
Leipziger Platz 17,
10117 Berlin.
Tel (030) 20 31 20.

Consulate
Tal 29, Munich.
Tel (089) 21 99 570.

New Zealand
Friedrichstr. 60,
10117 Berlin.
Tel (030) 20 62 10.

Republic of Ireland
Jägerstr. 51, 10117 Berlin.
Tel (030) 22 07 20.

South Africa
Embassy
Tiergartenstr. 18,
10785 Berlin.
Tel (030) 22 07 30.

Consulate
Sendlinger Tor Platz
5, Munich.
Tel (089) 23 11 630

United Kingdom
Embassy
Wilhelmstr. 70,
10117 Berlin.
Tel (030) 20 45 70.

Consulate
Möhlstraße 5, Munich.
Tel (089) 21 10 90.

USA
Embassy
Pariser Platz 2,
10117 Berlin.
Tel (030) 83 050.

Consulate
Königinstr. 5, 80539
Munich.
Map 2 E5.
Tel (089) 28 880.

Security and Health

Like the rest of Germany, Munich and the Bavarian Alps benefit from a rigorous public safety policy, and are exceptionally safe for travellers. The police presence is discreet yet the state has one of the lowest crime rates in the country, a tribute to Bavaria's buoyant economy and a deep respect for law and order amongst its fairly conservative constituents. Stations and trains are patrolled by officers of the Border Police (Bundesgrenzschutz). Munich is safer than other large German cities, although, as in all large urban areas, you have to watch for pickpockets. Tourists who experience crime of any kind should go to the police for help.

Police

German federal police (Bundespolizei) wear blue uniforms and drive blue-and-white vehicles. For municipal and state police in Bavaria the primary colour is currently green, but a switch to blue is partly carried out. Traffic police (Verkehrspolizei) take care of safety on the streets, roads and motorways, and are distinguished by their white caps. Parking inspectors in navy-blue uniforms are responsible for catching motorists who have parked illegally or who have failed to pay the correct parking fee. Criminal investigation officers (Kriminalpolizei) are usually dressed in plain clothes, but will produce their identification and insignia as necessary.

What to Be Aware of

Although theft is not a major problem in Munich, special care should be taken in crowded trains and U-Bahn and S-Bahn stations, in and around the central railway station and around large beer-halls, all of them places where pickpockets operate. Keep your wits about you at Oktoberfest, a gold mine for light-fingered thieves. At any time of year, the station is not somewhere to linger, as it is frequented by drug addicts and a few harmless albeit annoying drunks and tramps.

Tourists should take basic safety precautions, such as not carrying large sums of money and keeping cameras safe. Most hotels have secure lockers or safes to store documents and valuable items. For owners of expensive cars, the extra cost of a guarded car park is worth the peace of mind. Never leave valuables in view in a parked car, and it is wise to lock or remove your car radio and sat-nav.

It is advisable to take out comprehensive insurance cover before travelling. Victims of theft should immediately report the crime to the police, who will issue a certificate enabling you to make an insurance claim.

In an Emergency

For assistance in an emergency, dial 112 (toll-free) for any emergency service (police, ambulance and fire brigade), 110 can also be called for the police only. The fire brigade can also be notified by operating special alarms. You will be asked to provide your name, the reason for the call and your location. Once you have explained what has happened, the relevant emergency vehicle should arrive quickly. You may be asked to visit a police station to file a report on the incident. Bring a passport or ID card for any possible paperwork.

Lost and Stolen Property

If property has been lost, it is worth asking at the local police station or lost property office (**Städtisches Fundbüro**). Lost property offices in smaller towns and spa resorts are generally located within the town hall or spa administration building.

For items lost on trains in Munich, contact the **Deutsche Bahn Fundbüro** there. For things that go missing on city rail, buses or trams, contact the **MVG Fundstelle**. The regional transport network, **Regionalverkehr Oberbayern**, deals with lost property found on buses. The central post office has a lost property office for any items left in its branches.

Ambulance

Fire engine

Police van

Pharmacies dispense both medicines and simple medical advice

Hospitals and Pharmacies

Germany has some of the world's best healthcare services. When called, ambulances arrive promptly. People able to reach a hospital by themselves should enter by the entrance marked *Notaufnahme* (Accident and Emergency). Less serious cases can be dealt with in the many private clinics or simple medical advice can also be obtained in a pharmacy *(Apotheke)*. Most pharmacies are open until 6pm, some until 8pm. Every district is assigned one all-night pharmacy, the location of which changes according to schedule. You will find the address of the nearest all-night pharmacy posted on the door of each pharmacy.

Travel and Health Insurance

All EU citizens can receive medical and dental treatment in Germany at a reduced rate. Currently, British visitors should obtain a European Health Insurance Card (EHIC) before travelling – the form is available from Post Offices – and seek a refund on their return home. It is still a good idea to take out some form of health insurance, and visitors from other countries should do the same.

Pharmacy logo

If your plans include hiking, skiing or other sporting activities, make sure that the policy covers the costs of rescue services. Insurance against loss of luggage and holiday cancellation is also advisable.

Safety in the Mountains

One of the greatest attractions of the Bavarian Alps is the scope that they offer for hiking, skiing and snow-boarding. However, personal safety depends on awareness and preparation. Hikers can easily be misled by fine weather. For hiking in the mountains, it is essential to take proper hiking-boots, a rucksack with warm clothes and something to eat and drink. Be sure to carry a detailed map, a first-aid kit and a form of identity. A mobile phone has become a vital asset because rescue teams can sometimes use GPS signals to locate them. Reception is variable in remote areas.

Hikers should plan their route in advance, match its level of difficulty with their own physical condition, and keep to marked routes. Skiers and snowboarders should beware of avalanches, and never go off-piste or use closed runs. For more difficult routes, it is advisable to hire a guide or consult the local **Deutscher Alpenverein** office or tourist information bureau.

In an emergency, summon help by repeating a sound or light signal six times a minute, with one-minute breaks. Respond to a call for help with a signal three times a minute.

DIRECTORY

Emergency Services

Ambulance
Tel 112.

Duty Doctor and Pharmacy Information
Tel 116/117.

Emergency Dentist
Tel (089) 72 40 10.
W notdienst-zahn.de

Fire Brigade
Tel 112.

Police
Tel 110/112.

Lost Property

Deutsche Bahn Fundbüro
Hauptbahnhof, Munich.
Tel (089) 13 08 66 64.
Open 7am–8pm Mon–Fri,
8am–6pm Sat–Sun.

MVG Fundstelle
Elsenheimerstr. 61,
Munich.
Tel 0800 3 44 22 66 00.
Open 7:30am–noon Mon,
Wed & Fri, 8:30am–noon
& 2–6pm Tue & Thu.

Regionalverkehr Oberbayern (RVO)
Hirtenstr. 24, Munich.
Tel (089) 55 16 40.

Open 8am–4pm Mon–
Thu, 8am–2:30pm Fri.
W rvo-bus.de

Städtisches Fundbüro
Oetztaler Str. 17, Munich.
Tel (089) 23 39 60 45.
Open 7:30am–noon Mon,
Wed & Fri, 8:30am–noon
& 2–6pm Tue, 8:30am–
3pm Thu.

Hospitals and Pharmacies

Bavarian Pharmacists Association
W lak-bayern.
notdienst-portal.de
(all-night online branch
locator, in German)

Städtisches Klinikum München
Englschalkinger Str.
77, Munich.
Tel (089) 92 700.
W klinikum-
muenchen.de

Mountain Safety

Deutscher Alpenverein (DAV)
Von-Kahr-Str. 2–4, Munich
Tel (089) 14 00 30.
W alpenverein.de

Banks and Currency

Although there is no limit to the amount of currency that can be taken in or out of Germany, for large amounts of cash a statement of import (or export) may be required by the customs department. Credit cards are widely accepted in large shops and restaurants. You will be expected to pay for small purchases in cash, although a European bank debit card will often be accepted. Foreign currency can be exchanged in larger banks, at exchange bureaux and at currency exchange machines. Preloaded currency cards are a useful alternative to carrying cash.

Banks and Bureaux de Change

Banks in Germany are open from at least 9am to 4pm Monday to Thursday, and until 2pm on Friday. Branches in urban centres tend to stay open until 6pm one or two days a week. Currency can be changed at branches of major banks and bureaux de change *(Wechselstuben)* located throughout Munich and in larger towns in the Bavarian Alps. Generally, a flat fee of €3 is charged for amounts under €100, or one per cent with a minimum charge of €5 for amounts above €100. Some of the most competitive rates are offered by **Reisebank**, which has branches in large train stations. Another reliable option is the **American Express** foreign exchange service.

Commissions for credit card withdrawals are usually more expensive. Currency can also be exchanged at automatic exchange machines.

A typical *Geldautomat* or automatic cash machine (ATM)

ATMs

The cheapest and fastest way to obtain cash is by using a withdrawal card at a *Geldautomat*, or ATM. Cards with a Cirrus, Delta, Maestro, Plus or Star logo can be used to withdraw cash and pay for goods and services all over the country. Machines are usually located in bank lobbies, in all large shopping centres and in many post office branches.

Debit and Credit Cards

Credit cards are accepted in most hotels and restaurants, all department stores and many shops. Smaller shops, restaurants, bars and cafés may not accept them. European bank debit cards equipped with the EC logo or international payment networks such as Maestro are happily accepted. A minimum transaction of €5 in supermarkets and grocery stores and €15–20 in restaurants is expected. When using a debit card, you will be asked either to provide a four-digit PIN code or a signature.

DIRECTORY

Banks in Munich

American Express
Werneckstraße 19. **Map** 2 F2.
Tel (089) 38 88 740.
W americanexpress.com

Bayerische Landesbank
Brienner Str. 18. **Map** 3 B1.
Tel (089) 21 71 01.
W bayernlb.de

Commerzbank
Leopoldstr. 230. **Map** 2 F1.
Tel (089) 35 640.
W commerzbank.de

Deutsche Bank
Promenadeplatz 15.
Map 3 B2, 5 C2. **Tel** (089) 23 900.
W deutschebank.de

HypoVereinsbank
Kardinal-Faulhaber-Str. 4. **Map** 3
B1, B2, 5 C2. **Tel** (089) 37 80.
W hypovereinsbank.de

Reisebank
Hauptbahnhof. **Tel** (089) 54 50 60
97. Franz Josef Strauß Airport.
Tel (089) 97 01 721.
W reisebank.de

Sparda-Bank
Oskar-von-Miller-Ring 35.
Map 2 5D. **Tel** (089) 55 14 24 00.
W spardabank.de

Stadtsparkasse München
Sparkassenstr. 2.
Map 3 C2, 6 D3. **Tel** (089) 52 16
71 01 91. W sskm.de

Wiring Money

W moneygram.com
W westernunion.com

Main branch of Stadtsparkasse München, in Munich

Wiring Money

If you have funds wired from home, you can expect commissions as high as 12 per cent. **Moneygram** and **Western Union** can arrange an instant cash transfer to virtually any large bank and post office in Bavaria.

Currency

The euro (€) is the common currency of the European Union. It went into general circulation on 1 January 2002, initially for 12 participating countries. Germany was one of those 12 countries, with the original currency phased out the same year.

Euro notes are identical throughout the Eurozone, each bearing designs of fictional architectural structures. Notes and coins are exchangeable in each of the participating euro countries.

Euro Bank Notes

Euro bank notes have seven denominations. The €5 note (grey in colour) is the smallest, followed by the €10 note (pink), €20 note (blue), €50 note (orange), €100 note (green), €200 note (yellow) and €500 note (purple). All notes show the stars of the European Union.

5 euros

10 euros

20 euros

50 euros

100 euros

200 euros

500 euros

2 euros

1 euro

50 cents

20 cents

10 cents

Coins

The euro has eight coin denominations: €1 and €2; 50 cents, 20 cents, 10 cents, 5 cents, 2 cents and 1 cent. The €2 and €1 coins are both silver and gold in colour. The 50-, 20- and 10-cent coins are gold. The 5-, 2- and 1-cent coins are bronze.

5 cents

2 cents

1 cent

Communications and Media

The postal and telecommunications services in Germany are very efficient. Although it may be necessary to queue for a while in the post office, letters and postcards are usually delivered within the country in 24 hours. Telephone boxes can still be found on street corners and in train stations, but in dwindling numbers as users rely on mobile phones. Wireless Internet is a common feature in hotels, cafés and some public areas. Mail boxes (yellow with a postal horn logo) are found everywhere, even in the most out-of-the-way corners of the Bavarian Alps.

A typical public telephone booth
in Munich

International and Local Telephone Calls

Germany's public telephone network is fast and efficient. Public telephones run by national provider Deutsche Telekom are located in U-Bahn and S-Bahn stations, post offices, restaurants and cafés, and on some street corners. Phone boxes (booths) are magenta and grey in colour, although you may still find some older ones in yellow.

The number of payphones taking either cards *(Telefonkarten)* or sometimes coins is constantly shrinking. Telephone cards (costing €5 to €25) can be bought at post offices and most newsagents. Public telephones operated by credit card can be found in busy areas.

Avoid making calls on the phone in your hotel room, as this can be much more costly than using a payphone.

Mobile Phones

Visitors rely primarily on mobile phone services. The most popular providers are T-Mobile and Vodafone. If you have a SIM card from an EU country, roaming rates were virtually abolished in 2017, meaning you can use your phone abroad as you would at home. Your handset will need to be compatible with the GSM network used in much of Europe. Visitors from North America need to take a tri-band handset. Be sure to take a plug adapter for your phone charger.

Buying a local SIM card with a German telephone number and a chip can give you access to local rates. Your handset will need to be unlocked to accept a different SIM card. The phone manufacturer should do this for you if requested. Alternatively, many small electronics shops can unlock your phone on the spot for a small fee.

Another option is to purchase an inexpensive phone from a German electronics warehouse such as **Saturn** or **MediaMarkt**. Companies like **Telestial** or **Planet Omni** sell mobile phone packages from around €30 including airtime.

Internet and Wi-Fi

Most hotels now offer Internet access, either from dedicated terminals in the lobby or via wireless Internet (WLAN or Wi-Fi). Many bars, cafés and some public places are equipped for wireless surfing, although you may need to buy a drink or time on the local network to use the service.

For owners of smartphones, there are numerous free Wi-Fi apps to guide you to the next hotspot. Internet cafés, though now rare, charge around €1 to €2 per half-hour. Some surviving access points include **Internetcafé München** in the basement of the Hauptbahnhof and **Coffee Fellows** at Leopoldstraße and Schützenstraße.

Postal Services

Post offices are run by **Deutsche Post** which has a bright yellow logo. In large towns post offices are usually open from 8am to 6pm on weekdays and from 8am until noon on Saturdays. At airports and in large railway stations, branches are open longer hours and open on Sundays.

Stamps *(Briefmarken)* for letters and postcards can be bought at post offices and from vending machines. Some newsstands and souvenir shops also sell stamps.

Mailboxes usually have two slots – for local post and for all other destinations. Collections times are also displayed. Delivery services are quick, with letters to German destinations usually arriving the following day and within three or four days to most of Europe. Letters sent to North America, Australia or Asia take about a week.

Useful Telephone Numbers

- National directory enquiries in English: 11 837.
- International directory enquiries: 11 834.
- To make an international call: dial 00, wait for the dialling tone, then dial country code, area code + number, omitting the first 0.
- Country codes: UK 44; Eire 353; Canada and USA 1; Australia 61; South Africa 27; New Zealand 64.
- Country and area code for Munich: 49 89.

Deutsche Post also operates an international courier and parcel service, **DHL**. You can send packages from all postal outlets or arrange a pick-up from your address. Prices are competitive and delivery can be tracked online.

Slot for local letters   Collection times   Slot for long-distance mail

The most typical style of mail-box seen in Germany

Newspapers and Magazines

International newspapers such as the *International Herald Tribune, The Guardian, Le Monde, El País, Neue Zürcher Zeitung* and *Corriere della Sera* are available at kiosks on the day they are published, while others appear a little later. *The Economist, Newsweek* and *Time* are also found on newsstands at major train stations.

The serious German press is led by the centre-right newspaper **Frankfurter Allgemeine Zeitung**, the centre-left **Süddeutsche Zeitung** and the more conservative **Die Welt**. The weekly newspaper **Die Zeit** covers intellectual and literary topics. Published in Munich, the **Süddeutsche Zeitung** is issued with a large local supplement. Weekly magazines **Focus** and the legendary **Der Spiegel** set the standard for investigative journalism. All these publications have online editions.

Also widely read in Munich is the sensationalist **Bild**, as well as the regional tabloids **Abendzeitung** and **tz**. In the evenings, papers are sold by vendors doing the rounds in bars and restaurants.

The magazines **Prinz**, the free **InMünchen**, and **Munich Found** in English carry good entertainment listings, as does **The Local** online. Throughout the Bavarian Alps you will find local magazines such as *Allgäu* and *Journal Kempten*.

A newspaper kiosk in Munich

Television and Radio

The main public television networks ARD and ZDF, and regional channel BR, face stiff competition from a host of cable and satellite broadcasters. These include the sophisticated cultural and news channel Arte (a French-German joint venture), plus popular entertainment options on RTL, ProSieben, SAT.1 and VOX.

German radio offers a familiar mix of mainstream pop, chat, classics and oldies. Bavarian radio stations are Antenne Bayern (101.3 FM), with modern music and news and Bayerischer Rundfunk (91.3, 88.4 and 97.3 FM), with music and local news. Traffic news (with reports of delays on motorways) is broad-cast mainly on Bayern 3 (97.3 FM).

DIRECTORY

Mobile Phones

MediaMarkt
w mediamarkt.de

Saturn
Neuhauser Str. 39.
Map 3 A2.
Tel (089) 23 6870.

Telestial
w telestial.com

Internet Access

Coffee Fellows
Leopoldstraße 70.
Map 2 E23.
Tel (089) 38 89 84 70.
Schützenstraße 14.
Tel (089) 59 94 68 18.
w coffee-fellows.de

Postal Services

Deutsche Post
Tel 0228 43 33 111.
w deutschepost.de

DHL
Tel (0180) 63 45 30 01
(national delivery),
(0180) 60 03 321
(international delivery).
w dhl.com

Post Office Branches
Alter Hof 6–7.
Map 3 C2, 6 D2. **Open**
9am–6:30pm Mon–Fri,
9:30am–12:30pm Sat.

Bahnhofplatz 1
Open 8am–7pm Mon–Fri,
9am–3pm Sat.

Franz Josef Strauß
Airport (3rd floor)
Open 7:30am–9pm
Mon–Fri, 10am–5pm Sat
& Sun.

Newspapers and Magazines

Abendzeitung
w abendzeitung-
muenchen.de

Bild
w bild.de

Der Spiegel
w spiegel.de

Die Welt
w welt.de

Die Zeit
w zeit.de

Focus
w focus.de

**Frankfurter
Allgemeine Zeitung**
w faz.net

InMünchen
w in-muenchen.de

Munich Found
w munichfound.de

Prinz
w prinz.de

Süddeutsche Zeitung
w sueddeutsche.de

The Local
w thelocal.de

tz
w tz.de

TRAVEL INFORMATION

Thanks to Bavaria's excellent road and rail network, and to Munich's large, modern international airport, reaching the Bavarian Alps is easy from anywhere in Europe. Buses are comfortable and efficient and are particularly useful in rural areas not served by rail. In Munich, public transport is a swift and convenient way of moving around the city. The Bavarian Alps are also a gateway on the route into Italy, and roads heading south can be congested at peak holiday times.

Green Travel

Bavaria is a long-time leader in environmental trends. The state prides itself on the high quality of its air and water in its pristine lakes and rivers. The famous Bavarian car manufacturer, BMW, has been developing zero-emission, hydrogen-powered cars.

The state's excellent train and bus networks mean you can easily plan holidays without a car, reducing your carbon footprint. Only in remoter Alpine regions will you need your own car, as bus services can be infrequent there.

The train is the cleanest, most viable alternative to carbon-heavy air and road travel. The national railways run by **Deutsche Bahn** (DB) are modern and efficient and many trains run on electric power. DB also offers special CO_2-neutral trips to nature reserves near Berchtesgaden and in the Allgäu.

In Munich, there are park-and-ride options from the suburbs, which is not only a green scheme, but also solves the problem of parking in the city centre. Other great ways to go green are through cycle hire and walking and bicycle tours; perfect for exploring the city (see pp312–13). Bicycles are allowed on the U-Bahn and there are especially designated spaces for bicycles on trains and the S-Bahn.

Arriving by Air

Munich's **Franz Josef Strauß International Airport** is Germany's second-busiest airport after Frankfurt am Main. Main airlines with links between the UK and Bavaria include **British Airways** and **Lufthansa**, Germany's national airline. Both operate regular flights from London direct to Munich. Low cost air-lines **EasyJet** and **BMI Regional** also offer regular flights from several airports in the UK.

For domestic flights, **German Wings** and Air Berlin run services to Munich from many German destinations. However, it is worth noting that unless you are coming from Berlin in northern Germany, flights are hardly faster than the train once you take into account time for waiting and travel to the airport.

Direct flights to Germany are available from major US cities, including New York (JFK),

Airplanes outside the control tower at Munich airport

Washington DC, Boston, Chicago, San Francisco and Los Angeles. Most arrive at Munich or Frankfurt. Airlines from North America with regular services to Munich include **Air Canada**, **Delta Air Lines**, and **United Airlines**. Many connections to Munich are routed through the large international hub of Frankfurt am Main.

On international flights, visitors from countries outside the European Union will be given a landing card to fill out before arrival. It should be presented with a passport to the border guards. For customs regulations, see p296.

Air Fares

Scheduled air fares can vary considerably, with possible reductions for children, students, people under the age of 26, senior travellers, and groups. The cheapest fares tend to be offered by the low-cost airlines, and you can make big savings by booking early, travelling mid-week (Tuesday

Inside Terminal 1 at Munich's Franz Josef Strauß International Airport

to Thursday), or by staying over a Saturday. Apart from the popular Christmas period, some of the cheapest fares are available from November to March, coinciding with the best Alpine skiing conditions.

Big international websites such as **Expedia**, **Skyscanner** or **Budgetair**, and German sites such as **billigflieger.de** enable users to personalize searches of many or all flights to a destination and to find good prices. Also check the airlines' own websites for deals.

There's no need to worry about any kind of departure tax as this is always included in the price of a ticket.

Munich Airport

Many airlines such as British Airways and Lufthansa have self-service check-in stations to speed boarding. Passengers waiting for their flights have a wide variety of shops, bars, fast-food outlets and restaurants to choose from. Travellers wishing to shop can buy Bavarian delicacies, as well as clothes, toys and souvenirs. Terminal 1 has dozens of retail and restaurant outlets, including a pharmacy, a hairdresser and a post office, as well as bookshops and newsagents. The larger Terminal 2 offers even more.

For travellers needing to stay near the airport there are several hotels nearby.

Arriving by bus or train, two ways of getting to Munich airport

Getting to the City Centre

Franz Josef Strauß International Airport is 28 km (17 miles) outside Munich, but you can reach the city centre by public transport in about 45 minutes. The motorway can take longer, especially during the rush hour.

The quickest and most reliable way of getting to and from the airport is by the S-Bahn – lines S1 and S8 run from about 4am to 1am (with a service every 20 minutes after 5am). Travellers taking the S1 to the airport should board one of the rear carriages marked "*Flughafen*" (airport), as the train's front carriages are uncoupled at Neufahrn and continue to Freising.

The station for commuter rail service **MVV** is situated beneath the airport, and all directions are clearly signposted. Before boarding, buy a ticket at the automated ticket machines with cash, EC debit cards or credit cards. The fare between Munich and the airport costs €11.20 but a *Streifenkarte (see p311)* for €13.50 works out slightly cheaper, as you need to stamp only eight of the 10 sections to get to the city centre, leaving two for another trip. Children aged 6–14 pay €1.40 for a single ticket or must stamp one section of a *Streifenkarte*. A group ticket *(Gruppen-Tageskarte)* costs €22.30 for up to five people.

Taxi fares between Munich and the airport are high – around €50–60. An **Airport-Bus** runs between Munich's Central Station and the airport every 20 minutes: the fare is €10.50 for adults and €5.50 for children. The first bus leaves Central Station at 5:15am and the last at 7:55pm. There are also bus links to other towns and cities in Bavaria.

DIRECTORY

Airlines

Air Canada
Tel (069) 27 11 51 11.
W aircanada.com

BMI Regional (UK)
Tel (069) 770 673 016.
W bmiregional.com

British Airways
Tel (01805) 26 65 22.
W britishairways.com

Delta Air Lines
Tel (01806) 80 58 72.
W delta.com

EasyJet
Tel 01806 060 606.
W easyJet.com

GermanWings
Tel (01806) 32 03 20.
W germanwings.de

Lufthansa
Tel (069) 86 79 97 99.
W lufthansa.com

Qantas
Tel (069) 29 95 71 421.
W qantas.com.au

United Airlines
Tel (069) 60 50 21 02.
W united.com

Transport

Deutsche Bahn
Tel 0810 6 99 66 33.
W bahn.de

Franz Josef Strauß Airport
Tel (089) 97 500.
W munich-airport.de

Lufthansa Airport Bus
Tel (089) 32 30 40.
W airportbus-muenchen.de

MVV

Tel (089) 41 42 43 44.
W mvv-muenchen.de

Flight Websites

W billigflieger.de

W budgetair.co.uk

W expedia.com

W skyscanner.net

Hauptbahnhof, Munich's central railway station

Arriving by Train

Bavaria has a vast railway network. Trains are frequent and delays are a rarity. You can buy tickets and plan your journey on the website of **Deutsche Bahn**, the national railway service. Munich has direct connections with most major European cities. The most popular route is to travel to Brussels by Eurostar and pick up an onward connection to Germany from there. Ferry connections still operate from the UK, but cheap flights have all but eclipsed them.

German Rail

Deutsche Bahn's trains have a reputation for being swift, comfortable and efficient. Services are generally on-time but trains are sometimes crowded, especially during the peak holiday season. The fastest trains, the high-speed InterCity Express (ICE), have air-conditioning and airline-style seats, a bistro and restaurant, Wi-Fi, and newspapers and earphones on sale. Somewhat slower and less costly are the InterCity (IC) trains and EuroCity (EC), on which a small supplement is payable regardless of the distance travelled. The network also runs short-distance links between towns: Regional-Express (RE), Regionalbahn (RB) and suburban S-Bahn trains.

Munich's busy main station, Hauptbahnhof, serves 300,000 passengers daily. It is a 20-minute walk from Marienplatz or a short ride by U-Bahn, S-Bahn or bus.

Train Tickets

Train tickets can be bought at railway stations, from ticket machines and the ticket office, or online. You can buy them in advance and reserve seats. Tickets cost the same from the machines and at the counter, but it is wise to allow 10–15 minutes extra time (staff are on hand to help at the complicated vending machines). Tickets bought for high-speed ICE trains are valid only for a specific journey, meaning you will need to exchange tickets if you need a later connection. Tickets for IC journeys are valid for a month. Short journeys up to 100 km (62 miles) are valid only on the day of purchase.

Train fares in Germany are expensive. However, a wide range of discounts is available. One way to travel more cheaply is to buy a *BahnCard*, which gives a 25 or 50 per cent discount, costing €62 and €255 respectively per year. The InterRail pass, available to all EU citizens, and the Eurail pass for non-EU citizens, are both valid for a month's train travel.

In Bavaria, the *Bayern-Ticket* offers good value. A one-day ticket for one person costs €25 from machines and €27 from counters. Each additonal

passenger (up to four persons) costs an additional €6. These tickets are valid only on RE, RB and S-Bahn trains and most regional public buses and time restrictions apply. The *Schönes Wochenende-Ticket* (up to €56 for up to five people) can be used only on RE, RB, IRE and S-Bahn trains, but is valid all day and most of the night on either a Saturday or a Sunday. Both tickets also give free travel on urban transport in Munich.

Arriving by Coach

Munich and other cities in the Bavarian Alps can be reached by coach (long-distance bus). Coaches from Vienna, Zurich or Bozen (Bolzano) terminate at Munich's central bus terminal at Hackerbrücke. Routes from the UK are operated by **Eurolines**, while **Flixbus** runs services across Germany and beyond. **Busabout** is a hop-on, hop-off network offering passes of varied duration to 33 destina-tions in Europe, including Munich.

Travelling by Bus

Almost all Bavarian towns and villages are connected by a local bus network, particularly in places where there is no railway station. Bus timetables are designed to suit commuters, so that the service is frequent at peak hours and sparse at weekends and on public holidays.

Most towns have a *Zentraler Omnibus Bahnhof* (ZOB) close to the train station. It is here that most bus services originate and where tickets can be purchased, and service timetables and other information can be obtained.

Stops are frequent in rural areas, sometimes by request in the middle of nowhere.

Comfortable, long-distance, double-decker coach

A timetable is posted at every stop, and the driver sells tickets on board.

Boat Trips

Bavaria's many rivers and lakes make boat trips a great attraction. The most scenic of these trips are on the region's largest lakes – Starnberger See, Ammersee, Tegernsee, Chiemsee and Königssee – and on rivers such as the Danube.

To the north of Munich, kayaking and canoeing are popular activites in the Altmühl Naturpark *(see p187)*. On the Königssee, you can take an electric-powered boat to the picturesque church of St Bartholomä, which is framed on all sides by vertiginous Alpine slopes *(see p204)*.

On the smaller lakes you can hire boats with or without a captain. Rafting is popular on the River Salzach near Burghausen *(see p202)*, and on the River Isar from Wolfratshausen to Thalkirchen, a southern district of Munich. **Flößerei Josef Seitner** offers trips on traditional wooden rafts. Tours are 5–7 hours long, depending on the water level.

Longer cruises are available on the Danube from Passau to Vienna, and can be combined with a tour of the historic sights along the Danube valley.

DIRECTORY

Train Travel

Deutsche Bahn
Information and reservations
Tel 01806 99 66 33.
W bahn.de

Arriving by Coach

Busabout
Tel 08450 267 514 (UK).
W busabout.com

Eurolines
Hackerbrücke 4.
Tel (089) 88 98 95 13.
W eurolines.com

Flixbus
W flixbus.com

Boat Trips

Flößerei Josef Seitner
Lindenweg 1, 82515 Wolfratshausen.
Tel (08171) 78 518.
W flossfahrt.de

Boats moored at the jetty at Stock am Chiemsee

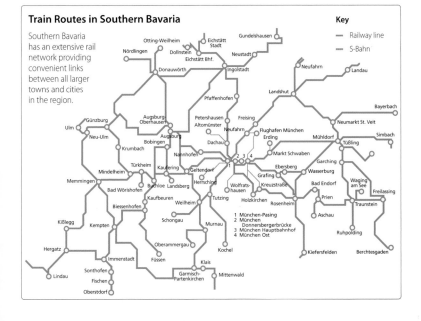

Train Routes in Southern Bavaria

Southern Bavaria has an extensive rail network providing convenient links between all larger towns and cities in the region.

Key
— Railway line
— S-Bahn

Munich's Buses, Trams, U-Bahn and S-Bahn

Astonishing in its detail, coordination and efficiency, Munich's public transport will get you where you want to go quickly. As well as eight underground (U-Bahn) lines, the city has an extensive network of bus and tram routes. The environs are connected to the core by fast suburban (S-Bahn) trains, mostly overground lines which link into the city centre and ongoing transport. In short, the whole of greater Munich is blanketed by public transport, making the car superfluous for many travellers. All four networks are part of Munich's municipal transport services, MVV and MVG, so with one ticket you can switch effortlessly from bus or tram to the local Bahn.

Travelling by Bus

With over 60 bus routes, Munich is easily visited without a car. For tourists in particular, buses and trams (see below) are an attractive alternative to the U-Bahn and S-Bahn networks, and go to places the railway lines do not. They are also less crowded and allow passengers to see the city as they travel.

Buses run generally at 10-minute intervals during the day and every 20 minutes in late evening. Five lines (10 at weekends) of Night Buses (Nachtbusse) run hourly between 12:30am or 1am and 4:30am or 5am, to make up for the reduced U-Bahn and S-Bahn services.

Each bus stop has a route map giving details of timetables and connections. Tickets can be purchased at vending machines at stops, as well as on the buses. To buy a ticket, press a button to select your fare, insert coins or notes into the slot, and retrieve your ticket with any change. When boarding, you must validate the ticket by inserting it into a franking machine located just inside the doors. Stops are either announced by a recorded voice (or the driver) or displayed on a screen. If in doubt, ask fellow passengers or the driver.

Typical bus stop, Munich

Travelling by Tram

Munich is well-served by 11 tram services, which merge seamlessly into the bus, U-Bahn and S-Bahn networks. Trams run generally at 10-minute intervals during the day and every 20 minutes in late evening. Tickets can be purchased from the onboard machine – the driver (in his separate compartment) won't sell tickets. Many trams stop at raised platforms for mobility-impaired passengers.

Travelling by U-Bahn and S-Bahn

Munich's underground rail network – the U-Bahn – first opened in 1971 and is constantly being expanded. The S-Bahn, the fast suburban train network, coincides in some places with the U-Bahn, which emerges above ground outside the city centre. All, except one – S20, S-Bahn lines run through the centre of the Old Town, linking the Hauptbahnhof (main station) to Karlsplatz and a main tourist hub at Marienplatz.

The fare system on the U-Bahn and S-Bahn is the same as on Munich's buses and trams. You can buy tickets at vending machines or counters in most stations. Before boarding the train, be sure to frank your ticket in a time-stamping machine, which is often located at the top of the stairs leading down to the platform.

Tickets for events such as concerts or football matches often include the price of the fare to the venue on the U-Bahn or S-Bahn. This is stated on the ticket for the event.

U-Bahn and S-Bahn trains are frequent and reliable, although they are likely to become quite crowded during the morning and evening rush hours. Before boarding an S-Bahn train, check the destination given on the electronic information boards. On the U-Bahn, trains travelling in opposite directions come in on either side of the platform, so boarding the wrong train can easily happen. Check the direction (Richtung) panel as well as the destination to ensure that you board the correct train.

A Munich bus, serving one of many routes in the city

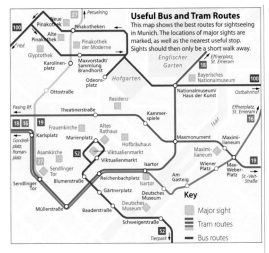

Useful Bus and Tram Routes
This map shows the best routes for sightseeing in Munich. The locations of major sights are marked, as well as the nearest useful stop. Sights should then only be a short walk away.

Key
- ▬ Major sight
- ▬ Tram routes
- ▬ Bus routes

Nearly all U-Bahn and S-Bahn stations are fitted with special ramps, lifts or travelators to assist mobility-impaired passengers.

Many U-Bahn and S-Bahn stations are decorated with local motifs. For example, the U-Bahn station at Königsplatz reflects exhibits displayed in the museums on the square.

One of the MVG trams that serves the 11 lines in Munich

Tickets

Munich and its environs are divided into four zones, each indicated on maps by a different colour. For tourists, Zone 1 (white zone) is the most important because it covers the city centre. Single tickets cost €2.80 for travel within one Zone, €5.60 for two Zones,

€8.40 for three Zones and €11.20 for four Zones. If you intend to make several journeys, it is cheaper to buy a *Streifenkarte* (strip card), which costs €13.50. The card is divided into ten sections; you will need two sections for each zone you enter. The ticket should be folded at the appropriate place and inserted into the franking machine. The last stamp made cancels all previous ones.

For short journeys of up to four bus and tram stops, or two U-Bahn and S-Bahn stops, you can buy a *Kurzstrecke* ticket costing €1.40. Alternatively, you can frank just one section of a *Streifenkarte*. If you forget to validate your ticket, you could be fined €60 for fare-jumping by roving plain-clothed officers.

For tourists, one of the most useful tickets is the one-day *Tageskarte*, or the three-day *3-Tageskarte*. Valid only for Zone Innenraum, or the city centre, they are available for a single person *(Single)* or for groups of up to five people *(Gruppe)*. Two children aged 6–14 count as one person. A *Tageskarte* costs €6.60, while a *3-Tageskarte* costs €16.50. These tickets are available at all ticket vending machines. Once stamped they are valid until 6am the next day.

For visitors staying in Munich for a longer period, a weekly, monthly or even annual *IsarCard* may be the best option.

This card allows unlimited travel on public transport. Single tickets for travellers aged 6–14 cost €1.30, or one strip.

Business travellers participating in trade fairs and conferences should check to see if they are eligible for a MVV Congress Ticket, which allows travel within a selected area. Many events often include the price of public transport in the ticket, such as those held at the Staatstheater am Gärtnerplatz *(see p146)*.

If you are confused about which ticket to buy, ask staff or use the MVV's online ticket navigator, which works out the cheapest fare and highlights possible price reductions. In addition, the online journey planner of the MVV and the **MVG**, its inner-city sister organization, will guide you to your destination with a timetable and the most appropriate mix of public transport.

One of the trains in Munich's suburban transport network

Getting around Munich on Foot, Bicycle, Taxi and Car

Most of Munich's tourist attractions and historic monuments are located in the city centre and distances between them are not far, making it easy to enjoy many sights on foot. Numerous cafés, squares and parks provide ample opportunity to relax in pleasant surroundings. Due to traffic congestion and a perennial shortage of parking, driving in Munich is less inviting. By contrast, cycling is very popular and bicycles are widely available for hire.

A typical Munich street sign

Around Munich on Foot

Exploring Munich on foot is a rewarding experience. Much of the Old Town has been closed to traffic, and only in the main shopping streets do you have to struggle through crowds.

Most of the tourist attractions in the Old Town are within less than 20 minutes' walk of each other. Further afield, strolling through the city's outlying districts can be a pleasant experience in itself.

Drivers are courteous to pedestrians, especially when it comes to stopping at pedestrian crossings. Almost no-one crosses against the light even if the road is clear, in part to set an example for children. Keep an eye out for the many cyclists, who can pose a hazard to tourists who unwittingly stray into the cycle lanes.

Locating a particular address in Munich is straightforward. Street names are posted at junctions and buildings are clearly numbered, with odd and even numbers on opposite sides of the street.

Munich's many parks make walking in the city a delight. To escape the urban bustle, seek out the Englischer Garten or the green spaces of Maximiliansanlagen on the river bank, or take a trip to Nymphenburg Park or the Botanical Gardens. In summer, paths along the Isar River lead you through lush greenery to beaches filled with sun-worshippers. A cold brew in a beer garden is an excellent reward.

For an overview of the city, the steeples of the Frauenkirche *(see pp64–5)* and Peterskirche *(see p66)* provide views over the Old Town, Marienplatz and Viktualien-markt. From its 190 m (623 ft) high observational platform, the Olympic Tower *(see p139)* affords breathtaking vistas as far as the Alps, and has a fine restaurant.

Pedestrian zone

Guided Tours

Munich has a wide variety of guided walking and cycle tours, usually with hired bikes provided. You may be able to just show up and join a scheduled tour, but it is advisable to reserve ahead. Some of the best trips are given by **Radius Tours**, located within a bike-rental shop in the Hauptbahnhof. Daily themed tours (in English) last around 2 hours and cover the major historical sights, Third Reich and Bavarian beer. Excursion tours take in Neuschwanstein Castle *(see p234)* and Dachau Concentration Camp *(see p175)*.

Other reliable operators include **Mike's Bike Tours**, which conduct a popular beerhall-and-gardens tour, and **Spurwechsel**, focusing on cultural and historic tours for groups by advance booking.

Tours in open-topped, double-decker buses run by **Münchner Stadtrundfahrten** require less energy.

For a more personalized experience, **Taxi Guide München** offers themed tours of the city's main sights in several languages, famous palaces, Olympiapark *(see pp138–9)* and places as far afield as Salzburg. Prices range from €80 for a 1-hour tour for up to eight passengers to €480 for a full day's outing.

By Bicycle

Munich is tailor-made for cyclists. The city centre is largely flat and easy to navigate, with cycle lanes marked on pavements (sidewalks) and on the edges of roads. Bicycle stands are situated throughout the city, including large facilities at railway and S-Bahn stations. Bicycles should always be locked to an immovable object.

Bicycles can be taken on the U-Bahn and S-Bahn in the last carriage marked with a cycle logo, except at rush hour from

Cycling – a quick and popular way of getting around Munich

6am to 9am and 4pm to 6pm. In addition to a regular passenger ticket, you will need to buy a one-day *Farrad-Tageskarte* for €3.

You can find bicycle hire points *(Fahrradverleih)* in the city centre, at MVV stations and major tourist spots. In addition, **DB Call-a-Bike** bikes are scattered throughout the city for immediate use. Look for a blinking green light, which means the silver-and-red bike is ready to be activated. Provide a credit card number by phone and you will receive a code to unlock the bike. After a modest sign-up fee, rates are €0.08 per minute and €15 per day. After use, lock the bike to a fixed object and call the bike return number. Bikes can also be hired from **Aktiv-Rad**.

Tourist offices provide cycle maps of Munich with routes of the best cycling tours. MVV's guide entitled *Radeln mit dem MVV* (Cycling with MVV), shows 52 scenic cycle routes around the city. You can order it online before you arrive.

By Taxi

As elsewhere in Germany, taxis in Munich are large cream-coloured cars with a "TAXI" sign on the roof; this is illuminated when the taxi is available. Taxis can be hailed on the street, booked by telephone or picked up at a taxi rank. If the rank is empty, a cab can be called from the telephone at the rank. The standard starting fare is €3.70, plus a per-kilometre fee of €1.90. A tip of 5–10 per cent is customary – or just round up the bill. A leisurely alternative is the pedicab rickshaw. The covered three-wheelers of **Riksha-Mobil** depart from Marienplatz with fares starting at €3. A 20-minute trip for two people to the Chinesischer Turm, English Garden, will cost around €17.

A taxi in Munich, identifiable by its cream colour and "Taxi" sign

Driving in Munich

Munich is the hub of a motorway network radiating in many directions. To the south are motorways A8 to Salzburg and A95 to Garmisch-Partenkirchen, to the southwest is motorway A96 to Lindau, to the west is motorway A8 to Stuttgart, to the north motorway A9 to Nuremberg, and to the east motorway A95 to Passau.

There is a ring road (Autobahnring) around the city, although this is often congested. Munich also has two smaller ring roads, the Mittlerer Ring and the Altstadtring, which relieve some congestion but are also often full of traffic. Only vehicles with low-emissions are allowed to drive in the central green zone. Be sure to buy an environmental badge (Umweltplakette) before entering the city centre or you could be fined. Motorway signs direct drivers to automobile testing centres where badges cost €8 to €12, or you can buy one online from the **Environmental Badge Climate Company**.

One of the biggest challenges is finding a parking space. Although there are many multi-storey car parks (Parkhäuser), they are expensive and often full. ("Frei" indicates that spaces are available.) Most on-street parking must be paid for, either by inserting coins into a meter or by buying a pay-and-display ticket. Another issue is the time limit, 1 hour often being the maximum in the centre. Parking attendants issue fines when cars are illegally parked or parking is unpaid.

Parking sign

Travelling by Car

By far the swiftest and most comfortable way to tour Bavaria is by *Autobahn*, or national motorway. Secondary roads are usually of excellent quality too. However, during the holiday season, roads in the Bavarian Alps swell with motorists from northern Europe travelling to Austria and Italy. To avoid a tiresome *Stau* (traffic jam), check the holiday calendar in advance or avoid the motorways altogether. Although slower, travelling off the main motorways gives you a more intimate view of the countryside.

One of the many picturesque roads with a view of the Alps

Getting to the Bavarian Alps

Visiting the area by car is quite easy. However, in the summer months and over public holidays, considerable queues can build up at border crossings into Germany, especially from the Czech Republic. During Oktoberfest (*see p33*), routes to and from Italy through Switzerland are also congested. At other times, drivers can expect few delays or border formalities.

Non-EU citizens do not need to declare goods for customs on arrival, but limits do apply to the amount of duty-free goods that can be brought into the country (*see p296*).

What to Take

Drivers must carry a valid driving licence, their vehicle's registration document and their insurance policy. Before leaving home, check with your insurer whether you are covered in Germany. If you plan on driving in the city entre and your vehicle is a low-emission vehicle,

you must obtain an environmental badge (*Umweltplakette*). You can pre-order a badge through the **Environmental Badge Climate Company** or buy one from automobile testing centres TÜV or Dekra in Bavaria. These are signposted on motorways.

Cars must bear a sticker or plate indicating country of origin. A first-aid kit, a fluorescent yellow or orange safety jacket and a red warning triangle, for use in case of breakdown, are also required.

Roads and Motorways

National motorways (*Autobahnen*) in Germany are toll-free and have petrol stations and facilities with toilets, restaurants and motels spaced at regular intervals. An *Autobahn* is indicated by the letter "A" followed by a number. Some motorway signs also have the letter "E" and a number, indicating that the road crosses the German border. A *Bundesstraße* (main road) is indicated by the letter "B" and a number.

Car Rental

Major international car rental companies such as **Hertz** and **Avis** have offices in the Bavarian Alps, particularly near railway stations and at airports. They are rivalled by Munich-based **Sixt** and up-and-coming firms such as **Buchbinder**.

Rates for car rental vary greatly so shop around before booking. Be sure to look at combined tickets offered by airlines and travel agencies. These include car rental and often turn out cheaper than booking each separately.

For holidaymakers another option is to rent a camper van (*Wohnmobile*), which outside the holiday season can be rented for the price of a mid-sized car, but offers a great deal more freedom.

Parking

Towns and cities in the Bavarian Alps are crowded during normal business hours, making parking a problem. Weekends are more relaxed, and parking tends to be free from midday Saturday. As elsewhere in Germany, parking attendants will issue a ticket even if you are only a few minutes over the limit.

Roadside Assistance

Germany's system of roadside assistance is superb. On motorways, emergency telephones (*Notrufsäulen*) are situated at intervals of 1 km (0.6 miles). The main port of call is **ADAC** (Allgemeiner Deutscher Automobil-Club), the German motoring association. If you break down, call from any roadside telephone and help will arrive quickly. ADAC repairmen will tow the stricken vehicle to a garage, but be prepared to pay extra if you are not an ADAC member. In the event of a road accident, the police, ambulance, fire brigade and air ambulance (helicopter) will attend as necessary.

Motorway telephone

An Aral petrol (gas) station, one of the most widely seen in Bavaria

Petrol Stations

On motorways, petrol and diesel stations are most often located at junctions or at *Rasthöfe* – rest areas. Their facilities include car parks, restaurants, bars, shops and toilets with showers.

The price of fuel by the main providers (Shell, BP, Aral and DEA) is fairly uniform. Petrol stations in shopping centres are often a cheaper option, and Jet is always cheap.

Many petrol stations stay open late at night or even 24 hours, and also sell food, refreshments, newspapers and motor oil. In rural areas, petrol stations are few and far between, so it is always a good idea to fill up when you do see one.

Rules of the Road

Speed limits in Germany are 50 km/h (30 mph) in built-up areas and 100 km/h (62 mph) elsewhere. They are clearly marked when you enter the speed zone. Although Germany's famous *Autobahnen* were designed without speed limits, many sections actually have them. Limits of 100–130 km/h (62–80 mph) apply in curvy or built-up areas, and may be slower along construction sites.

When travelling with a caravan or camping trailer, the basic limit is 80 km/h (50 mph) and on motorways 100 km/h (62 mph). Speed traps are frequent and fines stiff. The maximum blood limit for alcohol is 0.5 per cent.

Signs to the motorway

Seat belts must be worn at all times, with children under 12 in the back seats and infants secured in child seats. For drivers, mobile phones can be used only with hands-free sets.

Scenic Routes

An hour's drive southeast of Munich, some jaw-dropping Alpine scenery beckons. From the A8 near Bernau, exit onto the E52 to explore the *Deutsche Alpenstraße*, a 322-km (200-mile) scenic route dating from the 1930s. Stops include an 11th-century castle at Marquartstein, where Richard Strauss composed *Salome;* Reit im Winkl, a mecca for skiers with Tyrolean-style houses; and Ruhpolding, home to a Madonna carved in around 1230. The route meanders through forests and pastureland into a vast national park around Berchtesgaden *(see p204)*. Here, the church at Ramsau enjoys a setting framed by snow-capped Alps (route: 90 km/56 miles total).

Bavaria's crystalline lakes are legendary. About 30 km (19 miles) southwest of Munich, Starnberger See *(see p217)* is rimmed with upmarket villas and restaurants serving freshly-caught char *(Saibling)*. From the motorway E533, take the Starnberg exit and the St2063 down the western shore. Continue on the St2063 until you rejoin the motorway, and drive 15 km (9 miles) south to the Zell exit, where the St2062

travels through peaceful farmland towards beautiful Kochelsee. At Kochel am See *(see p223)*, turn right on the B11. Here the road is at its most scenic, climbing higher through a dense forest of firs, beech and spruce. Gradually you descend towards the pristine blue Walchensee *(see p222)*, where the Nazis were said to have deposited gold – but none was ever found. Today the lake is better known for its windsurfing championships (route: 70 km/43 miles total).

DIRECTORY

Emergency Numbers

Ambulance
Tel 112.

Fire Brigade
Tel 112.

Police
Tel 110 & 112.

What to Take

Environmental Badge Climate Company
Tel (030) 39 88 72 140.
W green-zones.eu

Roadside Assistance

ACE (Auto Club Europa)
Tel 0711 530 33 66 77; 0711 530 34 35 36 (24 hour emergency call).
W ace-online.de

ADAC
Tel 0180 22 22 222.
W adac.de

Car Rental

Avis
Tel (0180) 217702.
W avis.com

Buchbinder
Tel (089) 9789 18820.
W buchbinder.de

Europcar
Tel 040 520 188 000.
W europcar.de

Hertz
Tel 01806 333 535.
W hertz.de

Sixt
Tel 01806 25 25 25.
W sixt.com

General Index

Acknowledgments

Dorling Kindersley would like to thank the many people whose help and assistance contributed to the preparation of this book.

Additional Photography
Horst Höfler, Claire Jones, Katarzyna and Sergiusz Michalscy, Tomasz Myśluk, Werner Nikolai, Ian O'Leary, Gregor M. Schmid, Oda Sternberg, Paweł Wójcik

Additonal Contributor
Susi Cheshire, Jeremy Gray

Publishing Managers
Kate Poole, Helen Townsend

DTP Designers
Jason Little, Conrad Van Dyk

Production
Sarah Dodd

Consultant
Gerhard Bruschke

Fact Checker
Barbara Sobeck

Proofreader
Stewart Wild

Indexer
Hilary Bird

Director of Publishing
Gillian Allan

Revisions and Relaunch Team
Louise Abbott, Emma Anacootee, Hansa Babra, Sonal Bhatt, Subhadeep Biswas, Arwen Burnett, Jo Cowen, Marc di Duca, Vidushi Duggal, Alice Fewery, Harald Graetz, Marcus Hardy, Rupanki Kaushik, Juliet Kenny, Sumita Khatwani, Shikha Kulkarni, Leena Lane, Delphine Lawrance, Jude Ledger, Dieter Löffler, Carly Madden, Sam Merrell, Kate Molan, Casper Morris, Marianne Petrou, Dave Pugh, Sands Publishing Solutions, Azeem Siddiqui, Neil Simpson, Beverly Smart, Sadie Smith, Rachel Symons, Roseen Teare, Stuti Tiwari, Karen Villabona.

Picture Research Assistant
Rachel Barber

Special Assistance
The publisher would also like to thank the following for their assistance on the guide:

Anette Alwast, Ingrid Baudrexl-Czuraj, Prof. Dr Adrianowi von Buttlarowi, Tamarze and Jackowi Draberom, Daniel Fink (Pinakothek der Moderne), Erica Gingerich at Munich Airport, Iris and Wolf-gangowi Hermannom, Barbarze Januszkiewicz, Irenie Hiemeyer, Aleksandrze Markiewicz German Book Information Centre, Goethe-Institut in Warsaw, Ulliemu Nerdingerowi, Wilhelminie and Wernerowi Nikolai, Dr Elisabeth Pfaud, Margarete Roeck, Dr Thomasowi Weidnerowi and Kartographie Huber (Gerhild Kemper-Wildtraut), Käthe-Kruse-Puppen-Museum in Donauwörth, Kultur- und Fremdenverkehrsamt der Stadt Landsberg am Lech (Ulla Kurz), Kur- und Ferienland Garmisch-Partenkirchen, Kurverwaltung Schwangau, Meteorologisches Institut der Universität München (Heinz Lösslein), Presse -und Öffentlich-keitsarbeit der Stadt Pfaffenhofen an der Ilm Sr. (Elisabeth Benen), Rieskrater-Museum in Nördlingen (Dr Michael Schieber, Monika Spörl), Stadt Donauwörth (Bernhard Kunz, Gudrun Reißer), Steigenberger Drei Mohren (Robert Strohe), Theresienthaler Kristallglasmanufaktur GmbH (Ralph A.W. Wenzel), Tourismus Straubing (Bettina Schauer), Tourist Info Kochel am See (Sabine Rauscher), Touristinformation Stadt Freising (Barabara Sibinger), Verkehrsverband Laufen, Verkehrsverein Lindau (Hans Stübner), Wittelsbacher Ausgleichsfonds, Inventarverwaltung (Andreas von Majewski, Sibille Herz).

Photography Permissions
The publisher would also like to thank all the people and institutions who allowed photographs belonging to them to be reproduced, as well as granting permission to use photographs from their archives: AB PhotoDesign in Kellberg (Dionys Asenkerschbaumer), Alois Dallmayr in Munich (Patricia Massmann), Alpines Museum in Munich (Ulrike Gehrig), Amt für Tourismus Straubing (Frau Baumhof), Archäologische Staatssammlung in Munich (Dr Dorothea van Endert) Artothek (Jürgen Hinrichs), Augsburger Puppenkiste, Bavaria Filmstadt in Munich, Bayerische Staatsgemäldesammlungen (Prof. Dr Christian Lenz, Christina Schwill, D. Cornelia Syre), Bayerische Verwaltung der Staatlichen Schlösser, Gärten und Seen (Eva Gerum, Michael Teichmann), Bayerisches Nationalmuseum in Munich (Dr Nina Gockerell, Dr Sgoff) Benediktinerabtei Ottobeuren, Bildvorlagen Römerschatz – Gäubodenmuseum in Straubing (Dr Prammer), Bischöfliches Ordinariat Augsburg (Monsignore Josef Heigl), Bischöfliches Ordinariat Passau (Franz Sr. Gabriel) BMW Group Mobile Tradition and.V. (Nikola von Ondarza), Britstock-Ifa in London, Café Luitpold in Munich (Carmen Brenner), Deutsche Bahn (Hans-Joachim Kirsche), Deutsche Press Agentur (Tanja Teichmann), Deutsches Museum in Munich (Marlene Schwarz), Diözesanbauamt Eichstätt (Dr Claudia Grund), Erzbischöfliches Ordinariat München (Dr Norbert Jocher, Dr Hans Ramisch, Hans Rohrmann, Gabriele Skornia), Flash Press Media (Sylwia Wilgocka), Flughafen München GmbH (Wilhelm Hennies, Fr. Kiener), Foto-Production in Gilching (Gregor M. Schmid), Fremdenverkehrsamt in Altötting, Fremdenverkehrsamt in Mühldorf (Peter-Alexander Berger), Haus der Bayerischen Geschichte Bildarchiv in Augsburg (Dr Rudolf Wildmoser), Haus der Kunst in Munich (Claus Vogel), Heimatmuseum der Stadt Bad Tölz, Hilton München Park (Katharina Rösel), Hotel Königshof in Munich (Frieder Lempp), Hotel Residenz Passau (Dieter Austen), Hunsingers Pacific in Munich (M. Hunsinger), Institut für Kunst Geschichte TU in Brunswick 40br, 41c, 41br, 41bl, 43c, 48c, 49c, 53cl, Jura-Museum in Eichstätt (Jutta Streit), Alter Simpl Café in Munich, Kristall Museum Riedenburg, Kurdirektion des Berchtesgadener Landes (Vroni Aigner, Birgit Tica), Landeshauptstadt München, Referat für Arbeit und Wirtschaft Fremdenverkehrsamt (Stefan Böttcher), Leopold restaurant in Munich, Marionettenbühne in Munich, Mineralogische Staatssammlung in Munich (Dr G Simon), Münchner Stadtmuseum (Dr Götz), Museum "Reich der Kristalle" in Munich, Neue Messe München GmbH (Julia Spiegelhalder), Nürnberger Bratwurst Glöckl am Dom in Munich (Nadja Beck), Paläontologisches Museum in Munich (Dr H. Mayr), Parkhotel in Donauwörth (Eugen Schuler), Passauer Glasmuseum (Birgitte Holles), Ratskeller München (Renate Werner), SiemensForum in Munich (Dr Marie Schlund), Shop with devotional figures C. Huber in Augsburg, Staatliche Antikensammlungen und Glyptothek (Dr Martin Schulz, Vincent Brickmann), Staatliche Sammlung Ägyptischer Kunst in Munich, Stadt Kempten (Elli Cascio, Marlene Köhler), Stadtarchiv München (Dr Graf), Stadtbildstelle Augsburg, Städtische Galerie im Lenbachhaus in Munich (Daniela Müller), Stadtmuseum in Munich, Ursulinenkloster Straubing (Sr. Judith Reis, Oberin), Verkehrsamt der Stadt Nördlingen (Katja Jaumann), Villa Stuck in Munich, ZEFA (Ewa Kozłowska).

Picture Credits
a=above; b=below/bottom; c=centre; f=far; l=left; r=right; t=top.

The following works of art have been reproduced with the permission of the copyright holders:
Cover of *Der Blaue Reiter* (1912) © ADAGP, Paris and Dacs, London, 2011: 219cr
View of Munich Suburbia (1908) © ADAGP, Paris and Dacs, London, 2011: 109cl
Still Life with Geraniums (1910) artwork and photograph © Succession H Matisse/DACS, 2015: 120ca
A1 Pix Stefan Herbke 291br
Alamy Images Aflo Co. Ltd 204bl; Agencia Fotograficzna Caro / Riedmiller 51tl; Albaimages/Ronald Weir 15br; Arco Images 273tl; avatra images 301tl; Bildarchiv Monheim GmbH / Florian Monheim 137crb; BL Images Ltd 145cr; Danita Delimont 139c, David Sanger Photography 272cla; Elvele Images Ltd 11tl; F1online digitale Bildagentur GmbH / Schwind 161tl; FAN travelstock/Jürgen

Wackenhut 291tr; Foto28cla; Fotosonline/Klaus-Peter Wolf 291cla; imagebroker 14bc, 34br, 140tl, 224cl; imagebroker/Manfred Bail 145tl; imageBROKER / Sarah Peters 114; imagebroker/Martin Siepmann 13tr; Andre Jenny 144cr; Kunsthistorisches Museum, Vienna/ Maximilian I (1519) by Albrecht Dürer / Ian G Dagnall 44cla; Yadid Levy 144bl; LOOK Die Bildagentur der Fotografen GmbH/Jan Greune 290br; nagelestock.com 292tr; Sean Pavone 5cr; Christoph Weiser 273c; travelstock44 132; VPC Animals Photo 141bc; Westend61/Franz Faltermaier 290cla; Craig Yates 210.
Allianz Arena Munchen Stadion GmbH Wiki Commens: Patrick Huebgen 53b, 147tl. Alpines Museum (Munich) 93bc, 95c. Amt für Kultur und Tourismus (Neuburg) Leander Hopf 172b; Amt für Tourismus Straubing 35cra. Archäologische Staatssammlung (Munich) 40b, 111c Artothek 31tr, 56tr, 123tl, 129tr; W. Bahnmüller 47c, 47bl; Bayer & Mitko 123bl, 128tr; Joachim Blauel 46tr, 47tc, 47tr, 47cl, 47bl, 117cr, 122ca, 122cb, 123cra, 123cla, 124br, 125cl, 125br, 126ca, 127crb, 127bl, 128tr, 128cla, 129cl, 129br; Blauel & Gnamm 47bl, 123cra, 120cb, 122tr, 122cl, 123br, 124tr, 124c, 125tc, 127ca, 127tc, 127cr; Sophie-R. Gnamm 96tl; Toni Ott 46bl, 46br. Augsburger Puppenkiste 255tr. Augustiner, Munich 227bc.
Bayerische Staatsgemäldesammlungen (Munich) 119tc; Neue Pinakothek Munich 126clb. Bayerische Staatsoper Wilfried Hösl 146bl. Bayerisches Nationalmuseum (Munich) 57cra, 112tr, 112cla, 112clb, 112bl, 113tl, 113ca, 113crb, 113bc. Bier- und Oktoberfestmuseum 68c. Bildvorlagen Römerschatz-Gäubodenmuseum (Straubing) 39br, 188tl. Bischöfliches Ordinariat Passau 27c, 30tr, 45cl, 192cla, 192br, 197tr. BMW Group Mobile Tradition & V. (Munich) 23tr, 138tr.
The Charles Hotel, Rocco Forte Hotels 266bc, 271tl. City of Munich – Fire Department 300crb. City Tour Card 296c. Corbis Walter Geiersperger 158-9; Zefa/Guenter Rossenbach 13br; Zefa/Herbert Spichtinger 146cr. CSD München Michaela Handrek-Rehle 298ca. Dallmayr 270ca. DCC Europa-Preisträger 292bl. Deutsche Bahn (Berlin) Mann 308tl. Deutsche Presse Agentur (DPA) 23bl, 25tl, 32bl, 37cra, 37bc, 53bra, 274tr. Deutscher Alpenverein (Munich) 298br. Deutsches Historisches Museum (Berlin) 43b, 52c, 53bl. Deutsches Museum (Munich) 12, 98t, 98ca, 98cb, 98b, 99t, 99ca, 99cb, 99b,100tr, 100c, 100b, 101t, 101c, 101b, 174br. DK Verlag Stefanie Franz 95tl, 96br; Jörg Theilacker 140bc. Dreamstime.com: Coralimages2020 130tl; Sergey Dzyuba 66tl; Luisa Vallon Fumi 178, 286cla; Gary718 54-5; Vichaya Kiatying-Angsulee 2-3; Kyrien 23c; Manfredxy 12tr; Markus Gann 10bl; Meinzahn 218bl; Mikhail Markovskiy 58; PeJo29 208t; Plotnikov 35br; Renedreuse 4crb; Sonyakamoz 221tr; Cellai Stefano 33tr; Superbo 74; Dariusz Szwangruber 228cl; Camille Tsang 79tl; Zwawol 213br. Erzbischöfliches Ordinariat München 64clb, 65tl, 65cr, 65bl, 65bc, 65bl, 67tc.
Flash Press Media 52bl. Flughafen München GmbH 306cr, 306bl, 307tr. Fremdenverkehrsamt (Altötting) 24tl, 34cra, 199b. Fremdenverkehrsamt (Mühldorf) 32c.
Gasteig München: 97tl. Getty Images Bloomberg / Guido Krzikowski 287tl; DEA/G. DAGLI ORTI 8-9; DeAgostini 50cl, 51cra; Peter von Felbert/ LOOK 294-5; John MacDougall/AFP 300cr; Hans-Peter Merten/The Image Bank 198, 226.; Portrait of Emperor Karl VII By Adam Friedrich Oeser / Imagno 136br.
Robert Harding Picture Library: 14tr. Haus der Bayerischen Geschichte Bildarchiv 49tr, 52t. Haus der Kunst (Munich) 111t. Restaurant Herrenhaus: 281t. Horst Höfler 264br; Hotel Hirsch Füssen: 269bl. Hotel Königshof (Munich) 263tl, 278t.

Hotel Flushing Meadows 262br. Hotel Stadt Rosenheim Nadine Ingold 263bc. Hunsingers Pacific (Munich) 270cra.
The International Design Museum Munich George Meister 121br. iStockphoto.com: frederikloewer 108tl; graemenicholson 20; Juergen Sack 33bl; titoslack 90.
Jüdisches Zentrum Munich 69t Jura-Museum (Eichstätt) 168b. Kon-Ya Sushi: 283bl; Kristall Museum Riedenburg 187cr. Kurdirektion des Berchtesgadener Landes 52crb, 205bc. Landeshauptstadt München, Referat für Arbeit und Wirtschaft Fremdenverkehrsamt: Bjarne Geiges 275bl; Robert Hetz 53tl. Mandarin Oriental, Munich: 264tl.
Katarzyna and Sergiusz Michalscy 21t, 225clb, 248bl. Münchner Stadtmuseum 30cl, 30bl, 69br; Dorothee Jordens-Meintker 38, 48b.
Munich Police 300br. Munich Tourist Office Bernd Roemmelt 297cr. MVG Münchner Verkehrsgesellschaft (Munich) 311tr, Christian Bullinger 310b, 311bl
Neue Messe München GmbH Loske 143tr. Neuwirt: 268tl. Paläontologisches Museum (Munich) 116tr.
Passauer Glasmuseum 195c. Pinakothek der Moderne Proust's Armchair, 1978, Alessandro Mendini 120bc; 120ca, 121cra. Ratskeller München 271br. Residenz Heinz Winkler: 280bl. Ruffini (Munich) 279tr
Photo Scala, Florence 126tr
Sea Life München 147cr. Gregor M. Schmid half-title. SiemensForum (Munich): Bernd Müller 85cra. Sofitel Hotel (Munich) 263tl, 267tr. Spatenhaus (Munich) 277tl. Staatliche Antikensammlungen und Glyptothek (Munich) 56cla, 118cr. Staatliche Sammlung Ägyptischer Kunst (Munich) 81cl. Stadt Kempten 241tc, 241bl. Stadtarchiv München 106b. Städtische Galerie im Lenbachhaus (Munich) 109cl, 109crb, 116cla, 219cr, 223cr. Superstock: Imperial Palace (Kaiserpfalz), Goslar, Germany / Friedrich Barbarossa at a battle against Islamic army / age fotostock / M&G Therin-Weise 42tl; imageBROKER / Helmut Meyer zur Cape 169clb; Manfred Bail/imagebro/imagebroker. net 162; imagebroker.net 242, 260-1; Martin Siepmann/image/ imagebroker.net 102. Oda Sternberg 88br.
Tantris Restaurant: 279bl. Tomasz MyЁÉluk 230tr, 230cl, 231c. Restaurant Vaun: 282t. Villa Stuck (Munich) 19cr
Paweł Wójcik 24tl, 27b, 27bl, 33c, 35c, 49bl, 53br, 61clb, 66cr, 72tl, 72tr, 76br, 77tl, 82b, 84c, 84b, 86tl, 87c, 88tl, 89c, 104t, 105t, 107c, 116cb, 118tl, 142tl, 186tr, 209cra, 209br, 230br, 237tr, 237c, 240tr, 240cla, 240br, 264c, 288tr, 288cla, 288clb, 288cra, 288crb, 288cb, 288bl, 288cb, 289tl, 289tc, 289tr, 289cl, 289c, 289cra, 289crb, 289cr, 289bl, 289bc, 289bca, 289bc, 297b, 310clb, 315cb, 315tl, 315bl, 315b.
Wiki Commons Jorge Royan 2–3.

Front Endpaper: Alamy Stock Photos: imageBROKER / Sarah Peters Rbl. Dreamstime.com: Luisa Vallon Fumi Rtr; Mikhail Markovskiy Rbc; Superbo Lbr. Getty Images: Hans-Peter Merten/The Image Bank Rtl, Lcl. iStockphoto.com: titoslack Rcr. Superstock: Manfred Bail/ imagebro/imagebroker.net Ltr; imagebroker.net Ltl; Martin Siepmann/image/imagebroker.net Rc.

Cover images: Front & Spine: Alamy Stock Photo: Henk Meijer. Back cover: Dreamstime.com: Rosshelen
Map Cover – Alamy Stock Photo: Henk Meijer.
All other images © Dorling Kindersley.
For further information see: www.dkimages.com

Special Editions of DK Travel Guides

DK Travel Guides can be purchased in bulk quantities at discounted prices for use in promotions or as premiums. We are also able to offer special editions and personalized jackets, corporate imprints, and excerpts from all of our books, tailored specifically to meet your own needs.

To find out more, please contact:
in the US **specialsales@dk.com**
in the UK **travelguides@uk.dk.com**
in Canada **specialmarkets@dk.com**
in Australia **penguincorporatesales@
penguinrandomhouse.com.au**

Phrase Book

In an Emergency

Where is the telephone?	**Wo ist das Telefon?**	*voh ist duss tel-e-fone?*
Help!	**Hilfe!**	*hilf-uh*
Please call a doctor	**Bitte rufen Sie einen Arzt**	*bitt-uh roof'n zee ine-en artst*
Please call the police	**Bitte rufen Sie die Polizei**	*bitt-uh roof'n zee dee poli-tsy*
Please call the fire brigade	**Bitte rufen Sie die Feuerwehr**	*bitt-uh roof'n zee dee foyer-vayr*
Stop!	**Halt!**	*hult*

Communication Essentials

Yes	**Ja**	*yah*
No	**Nein**	*nine*
Please	**Bitte**	*bitt-uh*
Thank you	**Danke**	*dunk-uh*
Excuse me	**Verzeihung**	*fair-tsy-hoong*
Hello (good day)	**Guten Tag**	*goot-en tahk*
Hello	**Grüß Gott**	*grooss got*
Goodbye	**Auf Wiedersehen**	*owf-veed-er-zay-ern*
Good evening	**Guten Abend**	*goot'n ahb'nt*
Good night	**Gute Nacht**	*goot-uh nukht*
Until tomorrow	**Bis morgen**	*biss morg'n*
See you	**Tschüss**	*chooss*
See you	**Servus**	*sayr voos*
What is that?	**Was ist das?**	*voss ist duss*
Why?	**Warum?**	*var-room*
Where?	**Wo?**	*voh*
When?	**Wann?**	*vunn*
today	**heute**	*hoyt-uh*
tomorrow	**morgen**	*morg'n*
month	**Monat**	*mohn-aht*
night	**Nacht**	*nukht*
afternoon	**Nachmittag**	*nahkh-mit-tahk*
morning	**Morgen**	*morg'n*
year	**Jahr**	*yar*
there	**dort**	*dort*
here	**hier**	*hear*
week	**Woche**	*vokh-uh*
yesterday	**gestern**	*gest'n*
evening	**Abend**	*ahb'nt*

Useful Phrases

How are you? (informal)	**Wie geht's?**	*vee gayts*
Fine, thanks	**Danke, es geht mir gut**	*dunk-uh, es gayt meer goot*
Until later	**Bis später**	*biss shpay-ter*
Where is/are?	**Wo ist/sind…?**	*voh ist/sind*
How far is it to…?	**Wie weit ist es…?**	*vee vite ist ess*
Do you speak English?	**Sprechen Sie Englisch?**	*shpresh'n zee eng-glish*
I don't understand	**Ich verstehe nicht**	*ish fair-shtay-uh nisht*
Could you speak more slowly?	**Könnten Sie langsamer sprechen?**	*kurnt-en zee lung-zam-er shpresh'n*

Useful Words

large	**groß**	*grohss*
small	**klein**	*kline*
hot	**heiß**	*hyce*
cold	**kalt**	*kult*
good	**gut**	*goot*
bad	**böse/schlecht**	*burss-uh/shlesht*
open	**geöffnet**	*g'urff-nett*
closed	**geschlossen**	*g'shloss'n*
left	**links**	*links*
right	**rechts**	*reshts*
straight ahead	**geradeaus**	*g'rah-der-owss*

Making a Telephone Call

I would like to make a phone call	**Ich möchte telefonieren**	*ish mer-shtuh tel-e-fon-eer'n*
I'll try again later	**Ich versuche es später noch einmal**	*ish fair-zookh-uh es shpay-ter nokh ine-mull*
Can I leave a message?	**Kann ich eine Nachricht hinterlassen?**	*kan ish ine-uh nakh-risht hint-er-lahss-en*
answer phone	**Anrufbeantworter**	*an-roof-be-ahnt-vort-er*
telephone card	**Telefonkarte**	*tel-e-fohn-kart-uh*
receiver	**Hörer**	*hur-er*
mobile	**Handy**	*han-dee*
engaged (busy)	**besetzt**	*b'zetst*
wrong number	**falsche Verbindung**	*falsh-uh fair-bin-doong*

Sightseeing

entrance ticket	**Eintrittskarte**	*ine-tritz-kart-uh*
cemetery	**Friedhof**	*freed-hofe*
train station	**Bahnhof**	*barn-hofe*
gallery	**Galerie**	*gall-er-ree*
information	**Auskunft**	*owss-koonft*
church	**Kirche**	*keersh-uh*
garden	**Garten**	*gart'n*
palace/castle	**Palast/Schloss**	*pallast/shloss*
place (square)	**Platz**	*plats*
bus stop	**Haltestelle**	*hal-te-shtel-uh*
free admission	**Eintritt frei**	*ine-tritt fry*

Shopping

Do you have/ Is there…?	**Gibt es…?**	*geept ess*
How much does it cost?	**Was kostet das?**	*voss kost't duss?*
When do you open/ close?	**Wann öffnen Sie? schließen Sie?**	*vunn off'n zee shlees'n zee*
this	**das**	*duss*
expensive	**teuer**	*toy-er*
cheap	**preiswert**	*price-vurt*
size	**Größe**	*gruhs-uh*
number	**Nummer**	*noom-er*
colour	**Farbe**	*farb-uh*
brown	**braun**	*brown*
black	**schwarz**	*shvarts*
red	**rot**	*roht*
blue	**blau**	*blau*
green	**grün**	*groon*
yellow	**gelb**	*gelp*

Types of Shop

chemist (pharmacy)	**Apotheke**	*appo-tay-kuh*
bank	**Bank**	*bunk*
market	**Markt**	*markt*
travel agency	**Reisebüro**	*rye-zer-boo-roe*
department store	**Warenhaus**	*vahr'n-hows*
chemist's, drugstore	**Drogerie**	*droog-er-ree*
hairdresser	**Friseur**	*freezz-er*
newspaper kiosk	**Zeitungskiosk**	*tsytoongs-kee-osk*
bookshop	**Buchhandlung**	*bookh-hant-loong*
bakery	**Bäckerei**	*beck-er-eye*
butcher	**Metzgerei**	*mets-ger-eye*
post office	**Post**	*posst*
shop/store	**Geschäft/Laden**	*gush-eft/lard'n*
film processing shop	**Photogeschäft**	*fo-to-gush-eft*
clothes shop	**Kleiderladen, Boutique**	*klyder-lard'n boo-teek-uh*

Staying in a Hotel

Do you have any vacancies?	**Haben Sie noch Zimmer frei?**	*harb'n zee nokh tsimm-er-fry*
with twin beds?	**mit zwei Betten?**	*mitt tsvy bett'n*
with a double bed?	**mit einem Doppelbett?**	*mitt ine'm dopp'l-bet*
with a bath?	**mit Bad?**	*mitt bart*
with a shower?	**mit Dusche?**	*mitt doosh-uh*

I have a	Ich habe eine	ish **harb**-uh ine-uh
reservation	Reservierung	rez-er-**veer**-oong
key	Schlüssel	shlooss'l
porter	Pförtner	**pfert**-ner

Eating Out

Do you have a	Haben Sie einen	harb'n zee
table for…?	Tisch für…?	tish foor
I would like to	Ich möchte eine	ish **mer**-shtuh ine-
reserve a table	Reservierung	uh rezer-**veer**-
	machen	oong makh'n
I'm a vegetarian	Ich bin Vegetarier	ish bin vegg-er-**tah**-
		ree-er
Waiter!	Herr Ober!	hair **oh**-bare!
The bill (check),	Die Rechnung,	dee **resh**-noong
please	bitte	bitt-uh
breakfast	Frühstück	**froo**-shtock
lunch	Mittagessen	**mit**-targ-ess'n
dinner	Abendessen	**arb**'nt-ess'n
bottle	Flasche	**flush**-uh
dish of the day	Tagesgericht	**tahg**-es-gur-isht
main dish	Hauptgericht	**howpt**-gur-isht
dessert	Nachtisch	**nahkh**-tish
cup	Tasse	**tass**-uh
wine list	Weinkarte	vine-kart-uh
glass	Glas	glars
spoon	Löffel	**lerff**'l
fork	Gabel	**gahb**'l
teaspoon	Teelöffel	tay-lerff'l
knife	Messer	**mess**-er
starter	Vorspeise	**for**-shpize-uh
(appetizer)		
the bill	Rechnung	**resh**-noong
tip	Trinkgeld	**trink**-gelt
plate	Teller	**tell**-er

Menu Decoder

Apfel	upf'l	apple
Apfelsine	upf'l-seen-uh	orange
Aprikose	upri-kawz-uh	apricot
Artischocke	arti-shokh-uh-	artichoke
Aubergine	or-ber-jeen-uh	aubergine
		(eggplant)
Banane	bar-narn-uh	banana
Beefsteak	beef-stayk	steak
Bier	beer	beer
Bohnensuppe	burn-en-zoop-uh	bean soup
Bratkartoffeln	brat-kar-toff'ln	fried potatoes
Bratwurst	brat-voorst	fried sausage
Brezel	bret-sell	pretzel
Brot	brot	bread
Brühe	bruh-uh	broth
Butter	boot-ter	butter
Champignon	shum-pin-yong	mushroom
Currywurst	kha-ree-voorst	sausage with
		curry sauce
Ei	eye	egg
Eis	ice	ice/ ice cream
Ente	ent-uh	duck
Erdbeeren	ayrt-beer'n	strawberries
Fisch	fish	fish
Fleisch	flaysh	meat
Forelle	for-ell-uh	trout
Gans	ganns	goose
gebraten	g'braat'n	fried
gegrillt	g'grilt	grilled
gekocht	g'kokht	boiled
geräuchert	g'rowk-ert	smoked

Geflügel	g'floog'l	poultry
Gemüse	g'mooz-uh	vegetables
Gulasch	goo-lush	goulash
Hähnchen (Hendl)	haynsh'n	chicken
Hering	hair-ing	herring
Himbeeren	him-beer'n	raspberries
Kaffee	kaf-fay	coffee
Kalbfleisch	kalp-flysh	veal
Kaninchen	ka-neensh'n	rabbit
Karotte	car-ott-uh	carrot
Kartoffelpüree	kar-toff'l-poor-ay	mashed potatoes
Käse	kayz-uh	cheese
Knoblauch	k'nob-lowkh	garlic
Knödel	k'nerd'l	dumpling
Kuchen	kookh'n	cake
Lachs	lahkhs	salmon
Leber	lay-ber	liver
Marmelade	marmer-lard-uh	marmalade, jam
Milch	milsh	milk
Mineralwasser	minn-er-arl-vuss-er	mineral water
Nuss	nooss	nut
Öl	erl	oil
Olive	o-leev-uh	olive
Pfeffer	pfeff-er	pepper
Pfirsich	pfir-zish	peach
Pflaume	pflow-me	plum
Pommes frites	pomm-fritt	chips/ French
		fries
Rindfleisch	rint-flysh	beef
Rührei	rhoo-er-eye	scrambled eggs
Saft	zuft	juice
Salat	zal-aat	salad
Salz	zults	salt
Sauerkirschen	zow-er-keersh'n	cherries
Sauerkraut	zow-er-krowt	sauerkraut
Sekt	zekt	sparkling wine
Senf	zenf	mustard
scharf	sharf	spicy
Schlagsahne	shlahgg-zarn-uh	whipped cream
Schnitzel	shnitz'l	veal or pork cutlet
Schweinefleisch	shvine-flysh	pork
Semmel	tsem-mel	bread roll
Spargel	shparg'l	asparagus
Spiegelei	shpeeg'l-eye	fried egg
Spinat	shpin-art	spinach
Tee	tay	tea
Tomate	tom-art-uh	tomato
Wassermelone	vuss-er-me-lohn-uh	watermelon
Wein	vine	wine
Weintrauben	vine-trowb'n	grapes
Wiener Würstchen	veen-er voorst-sh'n	frankfurter
Zitrone	tsi-trohn-uh	lemon
Zucker	tsook-er	sugar
Zwiebel	tsveeb'l	onion

Numbers

0	null	nool
1	eins	eye'ns
2	zwei	tsvy
3	drei	dry
4	vier	feer
5	fünf	foonf
6	sechs	zex
7	sieben	zeeb'n
8	acht	uhkht
9	neun	noyn
10	zehn	tsayn
11	elf	elf
12	zwölf	tserlf
13	dreizehn	dry-tsayn
14	vierzehn	feer-tsayn
15	fünfzehn	foonf-tsayn
16	sechzehn	zex-tsayn
17	siebzehn	zeep-tsayn
18	achtzehn	uhkht-tsayn
19	neunzehn	noyn-tsayn
20	zwanzig	tsvunn-tsig

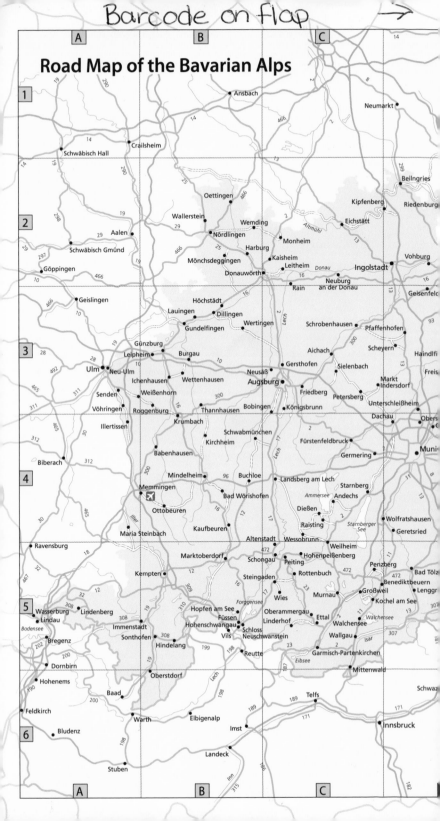

Barcode on flap →

Road Map of the Bavarian Alps